Building and Surveying Series

(continued overleaf)

List continued from previous page

Building and Surveying Series
Series Standing Order
ISBN 0–333–71692–2 hardcover
ISBN 0–333–69333–7 paperback
(outside North America only)

You can receive future titles in this series as they are published by placing a
standing order. Please contact your bookseller or, in the case of difficulty, write
to us at the address below with your name and address, the title of the series
and the ISBN quoted above.

Customer Services Department, Macmillan Distribution Ltd
Houndmills, Basingstoke, Hampshire RG21 6XS, England

Principles of Property Investment and Pricing

Second Edition

W. D. Fraser

BSc, MSc, PhD, FRICS
Professor and Head of Department of Land Economics
University of Paisley

First edition 1984
Reprinted five times
Second edition 1993

Published by PALGRAVE MACMILLAN
Houndmills, Basingstoke, Hampshire RG21 6XS and
175 Fifth Avenue, New York, N. Y. 10010
Companies and representatives throughout the world

PALGRAVE MACMILLAN is the global academic imprint of the Palgrave
Macmillan division of St. Martin's Press, LLC and of Palgrave Macmillan Ltd.
Macmillan® is a registered trademark in the United States, United Kingdom
and other countries. Palgrave is a registered trademark in the European
Union and other countries.

ISBN 0–333–60162–9

This book is printed on paper suitable for recycling and
made from fully managed and sustained forest sources.

A catalogue record for this book is available from the British Library.

Transferred to digital printing 2002

Printed and bound in Great Britain by
Antony Rowe Ltd, Chippenham and Eastbourne

Contents

x   *Contents*

Glossary of Terms Used

Note: Some of the following terms cannot be accurately defined by a brief summary only; in these cases, a fuller description is given in the text.

All risks yield The yield used to capitalise rent when valuing property by the Years Purchase method, being the rental income yield on rack-rented or fixed-income freeholds and the equivalent yield on reversionary freeholds.

Annuity An annual income received for life, or for some shorter period.

Bear A speculator who acts on an expectation of falling share prices, or anyone who expects investment prices to fall.

Bear market A market in which investment prices are falling.

Beta (β) A measure of a share's market risk; its volatility to the market as a whole.

Blue chips The equity shares of large reliable companies.

Bond Interest-bearing debt stock. Also an investment unit backing a unit-linked life assurance policy.

Bull A speculator who acts on the expectation of rising share prices, or anyone who expects investment prices to rise.

Bull market A market in which investment prices are rising.

CAPM Capital asset pricing model.

CBI Confederation of British Industry; an organisation of company employers.

CCC Competition and credit control agreement.

CGT Capital gains tax – a tax levied when investment gains are realised.

Collateral Assets which are pledged as security for a loan.

Convertible A stock which gives the holder an option to convert into another stock, usually equity shares.

Corporation tax A tax charged on company profits in the UK.

Cost push inflation Inflation caused primarily by rising factor costs.

Coupon The nominal rate of interest paid on a fixed-interest stock.

Covenant The terms of a lease contract which help to determine the quality of a property investment.

Cover The amount of assets or income available to pay the capital or income due to an investor.

DCF   Discounted cash flow.

Debenture   A corporate fixed-interest bond.

Demand pull inflation   Inflation caused primarily by excessive demand for goods and services.

Discount rate   The rate of return which reduces the sum of an investment's future income flow to its present value or price.

Dividend   The income periodically received by investors in shares.

Dividend yield   The annual dividend per share, grossed up for tax and expressed as a decimal (or percentage) of the share's price.

DIY   Do-it-yourself (home improvements).

DLT   Development land tax – a UK tax on the development value of land; discontinued.

Earnings   The net profits of a company available for distribution to ordinary shareholders.

EC   European Community.

EEC   European Economic Community.

Efficient market   A market in which prices fully reflect information affecting the worth of investments.

EMT   Efficient market theory.

Equated yield   The IRR – or total return per annum – from a property investment.

Equity shares   Ordinary shares issued by companies.

Equivalent yield   The total annual return (IRR) to be received from a reversionary investment over the period to reversion, assuming no change in the property's rental value or market yield.

Freehold   The highest form of land tenure under the Crown in England.

FRI   A lease under which the lessee is responsible for all repairs and insurance.

GDP   Gross domestic product.

Gearing   Financial leverage. The relationship of debt and possibly other fixed liabilities to total capital employed (but see Chapter 2 for distinction between capital and income gearing).

Gilts   Gilt-edged securities. Bonds issued by the British government.

Gross fund   An institution exempt from tax, e.g., pension funds and charitable trusts.

Ground rent   A rent paid under a lease of urban land, i.e. excluding buildings.

Head rent   The rent paid by a head tenant to his landlord.

Head tenant   The tenant under the head lease granted by the freeholder.

Income yield   An investment's annual income, expressed as a decimal (or percentage) of the investment's current market price.

Index-linked gilts   Government bonds on which the interest payments and redemption value are linked to the Retail Price Index (RPI).

Investment dollar premium   The percentage by which investment currency exceeded the spot price of foreign currency when the exchange control regulations were in force.

IRR   Internal rate of return – a true measure of total investment return. The discount rate at which an investment's NPV is zero.

Lessee   A tenant under a lease.

Lessor   A person who grants a lease, a landlord.

LIBOR   London inter-bank offered rate.

Liquid assets   Assets which can be quickly converted into cash.

LOB   Location of Offices Bureau.

M3   A statistical measure of money supply which includes notes and coins, and bank current accounts and deposit accounts.

Market risk   Risk that results from trends in market prices and which cannot be avoided by diversification.

Market yield   The rental yield of a property if let at its rental value. The all-risks yield.

MLR   Minimum lending rate.

Money market   The market in short-term deposits.

Moratorium   An agreed postponement of the payment of interest or repayment of debt capital.

Mortgage   A loan secured on property.

Mortgagee   The party which lends money by mortgage.

Mortgagor   The party which borrows money by mortgaging his property.

MPT   Modern portfolio theory.

Normal profit   A minimum profit sufficient to induce a firm to undertake business activity.

NPV   Net present value – the discounted value of future cash inflows, *less* present and discounted costs.

ODP   Office development permit.

OPEC   Organisation of Petroleum Exporting Countries.

Opportunity cost of capital   The expected return available from investments comparable with the one under consideration. A return foregone by making an investment.

Outgoings   Recurrent annual expenses faced by a property investor, e.g., on repairs, insurance and management.

Par value   The nominal value of a stock.

PEP   Personal equity plan. A scheme enabling private investors in Britain to avoid taxation on a limited portfolio of shares.

Peppercorn rent   A very small or negligible rent.

PE ratio   The ratio of price to earnings per share.

Perfect market   A market satisfying the notional concepts of perfect competition.

Prelet   A property for which a lease is arranged before the development is completed.

Profit rent   The difference between the net rent received by a head tenant and the head rent paid to his landlord.

Property bond   An investment unit based on property, the performance of which determines the benefits paid out under a unit-linked life assurance scheme.

PSBR   Public sector borrowing requirement – the capital which the government must borrow in order to finance the budget deficit.

Rack rent   A property's rental value.

Rates   A tax charged annually on the occupier of property in the UK, and based on the property's rental value.

Real return   Return after adjusting for inflation.

Redemption yield   The IRR to be received from a dated bond if held to maturity.

Rental value   The annual rent that would tend to be paid for the right to occupy a property if offered to let on the open market.

Rental yield   The yield on property, as distinct from the dividend yield on shares and the interest yield on bonds.

Retained earnings   Equity earnings which are not distributed as dividends to shareholders.

Reversion   The date at which the rent received by a property investor is reviewed, normally to rental value.

Reversionary property   An investment in which the current rent received is significantly different from rental value and in which a rent review is due within a reasonable time.

RICS   Royal Institution of Chartered Surveyors.

Rights issues   An issue of new shares offered for sale to existing shareholders.

RPI   Retail price index.

Sale and leaseback   The sale of a freehold or long-leasehold investment, on condition that the vendor becomes the tenant.

Scrip issue   Bonus issue – an issue of new shares to existing shareholders at nil cost.

Sensitivity analysis   The analysis of the impact on the profitability of a development project of changes in the cost of determinant variables.

Sinking fund   A fund established to accumulate to the sum necessary at a future date to repay debt or replace loss suffered by depreciation, especially to replace the value of a leasehold investment at the termination of a lease.

Specific risk   Risk that can be avoided by diversification.

Sub-rent   The rent paid by a sub-tenant to a head tenant.

Sub-tenant   The lessee under a sub-lease granted by a head tenant.

Systematic risk   Another name for market risk.

Target IRR   The expected total return required by investors from an investment.

Treasury bill   A short-term non-interest-bearing security issued by the government.

UBR   Uniform business rate. A tax charged annually on the occupier of business property in England and Wales.

Uplift   The capital gain deriving purely from the passage of time to reversion.

USM   Unlisted Securities Market.

Years purchase   The multiple by which the capital value of a property investment exceeds the net rent, which on a rack-rented property is the reciprocal of the rental income yield.

Yield to reversion   An alternative name for the equivalent yield.

Preface

Aims of the book

The essential purpose of this book is to explain the determination of the value of business property and its performance as an investment. It is a book about the economics of the commercial property investment market placed in the context of the local, regional, national and international economies. It identifies relevant principles and concepts of economics, finance and investment, and uses them to explain property pricing and the operation of the property market. Although arguments are explained and developed in a practical market context, the book concentrates on principles and underlying forces determining value rather than on providing a comprehensive description of the market. The emphasis is on the immutable rather than the current, and on answering the question why? rather than what?

The book explains how property values are determined by the market, not how values are assessed by the valuer, though it contains many implications for valuation practice. It explains the operation of the price mechanism in the property market, but makes few judgements on the market's efficiency or about the justification for planning or government intervention. The book provides no solution to the problems of the urban economy, nor does it set out to explain patterns of urban land use, though incidentally containing much of relevance to these subjects.

The book is written primarily as a student textbook, and is intended to bridge the gap between 'pure' economics and property market studies such as valuation, development, investment and management. It is particularly appropriate for degree courses in estate management and land economics which lead to membership of the Royal Institution of Chartered Surveyors. However, it is also intended for experienced property practitioners, and will provide students and practitioners of architecture and town planning with a detailed insight into the operation of the property market. The analysis is also relevant to urban economists and to investment analysts specialising in the property sector.

While fulfilling the needs of students and practitioners, the book also extends the boundaries of existing property market theory. In many subject disciplines these functions might conflict, but the theory of property market behaviour is relatively underdeveloped, and there is scope for presenting advanced material alongside the elementary without confusing the reader.

Although it is assumed that the reader has some elementary knowledge of economics, algebra and discounted cash flow (DCF), the principal theories and concepts are explained from first principles. Mathematics and complex graphics have been restricted to the minimum as, too frequently, they tend to obscure the argument rather than enlighten the reader. However, some passages may not be easy for those studying the subject for the first time, and when difficulty is encountered it is frequently best to read on and return later to the troublesome section. The reader should be prepared to read certain passages two or three times. The book follows a logical sequence and is intended to be read sequentially, however, most chapters and Parts should be comprehensible if read independently.

Second edition

The sequence and structure of the first edition have been retained, and the number of chapters and most of their titles are the same. However, the text has been reappraised, updated and amended to improve clarity and readability. Development of the theory of the determination of yields and rental values has necessitated the rewriting of certain chapters in Parts II and III, 'bullet point' summaries have been extended to all Parts, and the last chapter is new.

The new edition has been written near the bottom of perhaps the worst-ever property market slump in Britain. With a cyclical market, it is inevitable that fluctuating interest rates and yields can quickly outdate examples and illustrations. So, rather than adopting the unprecedently high yields current at the time of writing, examples have been based on yields in more stable times.

The first edition evolved from my lectures and tutorials to the BSc in Land Economics students at Paisley College over 1972–83, and this second edition owes much to the stimulus gained from subsequent teaching at City University and the University of Paisley. I apologise for any errors or passages which are confusing or turgid, and invite criticism from the reader.

Acknowledgements

In preparing this second edition, I have received help from a large number of people, including those firms which have allowed me to include their data. I would particularly like to thank Professor Russell Schiller, Kiran Patel and Rohina Grewal of Hillier Parker, Rupert Nabarro and Vida Godson of IPD, Siobhan Pandya and Jim Ward of Savills, Ian Kissane of Richard Ellis, Graham Whyte and Bob Thompson of King Sturge & Co., Peter Evans of DTZ Debenham Thorpe, Andrew Roberts of Datastream, Graham Wood of the W.M. Company, Lucinda Fisher of Ryden, Miles Larby of Finlayson Hughes, Mark Brown of UBS Phillips & Drew, Andrew Errington of Reading University, Ian Laird of Ian Laird & Associates, Alan Philipp of AP Information Services Ltd, Nigel Phillips, Stephen Connolly, Craig McNish, Henry Kennedy-Skipton, Nigel Mehdi and Jon Chandler. I am also indebted to Colin Jones, Cliff Legge, Eleanor Naismith, May Allan, Sandy Wilson, Mark Robertson, Craig Watkins, Allison Orr and my other colleagues at the University of Paisley. My thanks are also due to Lorna Muat and Alena Turner who typed the script.

The author and publishers would like to acknowledge Hamish Hamilton for short extracts from Oliver Marriott, *The Property Boom*, 1969, © Oliver Marriott; and the London Business School's 'Risk Measurement Service' for use of data (potential subscribers should contact: The Finance Database Manager, Institute of Finance, London Business School, Sussex Place, Regents Park, London NW1 4SA). Every effort has been made to contact all the copyright holders but if any have been inadvertently overlooked the publishers will be pleased to make the necessary arrangements at the earliest opportunity.

1 Introduction

Property in the economy

Theodore Roosevelt is reputed to have said that 'buying real estate is not only the best way, the quickest way and the safest way, but the only way to become wealthy'. Certainly land and property seem the very epitome of financial security. The value of property is much more stable than shares whose prices are subject to the regular antics of the stock market, and it has proved more enduring than government bonds, some of which have lost more than 98% of their real value in the post-war period. Arguably, property is the most secure of all marketable investments. Yet within the last twenty years the hub of the UK property market in central London has lurched into two monumental booms and crashes. Both cycles have featured deregulation of the financial markets, enormous surges in bank lending to property, relaxation of planning controls, unsustainable economic activity, escalation of interest rates, a plunge into recession, widespread company failures and the downfall of the two prime ministers responsible.

The experience is not unique to Britain. Like London, the property markets of New York and Tokyo have also recently experienced boom/bust cycles. It is not just a coincidence that these cycles have occurred simultaneously, nor that they have been located in the three main financial centres of the world. Rather, it is proof that in capitalist economies, property markets (like stock markets) are innately prone to cyclical fluctuation, and with the globalisation of the financial system, trends in the world's major economies tend to be synchronised.

Property values can be influenced by events which may seem remote and irrelevant. The 1974 property crash was precipitated by the outbreak of the Arab–Israeli war, and the recent property cycle had its origins in such diverse events as the abolition of exchange controls, the micro-electronic revolution, the third world debt crisis and deregulation of the stock market. Thus the cycle was founded upon political decisions, technological change and economic events, none of which has any obvious link with the property market. Property values are affected by such events because property is an integral part of the nation's economy, and anything which has implications for the economy will have implications for property.

What, then, is the relationship of property to the national economy, and how could the recent property cycle have originated from such remote and diverse events as the four listed above? This question is addressed throughout the book, but we can make a start here by identifying two of property's functions. Business property, e.g., shops, offices, factories and farms, is both a factor of production and an investment, and its value reflects both functions.

1

The capital value of a let property is some multiple of (perhaps ten or even twenty times) the annual rent paid by the tenant. The rent is determined by the property's value for business purposes and the multiple (years purchase) reflects the value of that rent to the investor.

The level of rents is determined in the *letting sector* of the property market by demand from tenants to occupy property, and capital prices of let property are determined by demand from investors in the *investment sector*. The level of rents and capital prices are also determined by the supply of properties produced in the *development sector* of the market. Thus we have three principal market sectors, but we also have an infinite number of sub-sectors according to a property's use-type, location, size, quality, etc. The UK property market is merely the amalgam of an infinite number of sub-markets, e.g., the prime office-investment market in the City of London, or the secondary shop-letting market in central Manchester. Both of these could be further sub-divided according to precise location, building size and quality. Rental and capital values are fixed by the forces of demand and supply in each sub-market, these forces being determined by local economic conditions which, in turn, are influenced by the regional, national and international economies.

We will now tentatively explain the relationship between the recent property cycle and the four events listed above. First, by changing the internal design and structure of office buildings best suited to the widespread use of computers, the micro-electronic revolution hastened the obsolescence of existing offices and created a need for modern buildings, thereby promoting a huge increase in office redevelopment. Second, the value of modern offices and the development boom was reinforced by the impact of deregulation of the stock market (Big Bang), which resulted in an increase in both the unit size and amount of floorspace demanded by firms in the financial services industry in the City of London. Third, the third world debt crisis in the early 1980s forced international banks to seek new outlets for their lending, which resulted in an enormous increase in lending to the property industry.

The fourth cause of the recent property cycle listed above was the abolition of exchange controls. This meant that money could flow freely in and out of Britain (and most other major world economies), thereby exacerbating the problems of monetary control. Together with the deregulation of building societies and banks, this led to a huge rise in borrowing by UK households, an unsustainable economic boom and a parallel boom in property values as the floorspace needs of businesses expanded. The abolition of exchange controls was also a factor leading to a decline in property investment by life assurance and pension funds in favour of overseas investments, so that property companies' development projects had to be financed by banks, and could not be sold on completion. This left many property companies inadequately financed, inherently unstable and highly vulnerable to bankruptcy when the economy sank into recession and property values started to tumble. The effect of forced sales and lack of investment demand has resulted in the *real* value of property arguably falling to its lowest level in living memory.

Thus, the four events crucially affected the letting, investment and development sectors of the London office market, leading to a huge fluctuation in value. But does that matter? The answer must be yes, because the property market and the economy are *interdependent*. It is not just a matter of the property market being affected by the economy, but the health of the property market affects the economy and the wealth of the nation.

First, the property market provides the accommodation in which business activity takes place, and the cost and quality of that accommodation will affect the efficiency and profitability of business. Second, commercial property as an investment is a medium by which all sections of the population hold wealth, principally through life assurance and pension funds. The total value of property investments in the UK probably approaches £100 billion, compared with some £400 billion of UK equity shares and £150 billion worth of British government bonds. Additionally, property held purely for business purposes may be worth a further £135 billion.[1] Third, property is the collateral on which a large proportion of corporate borrowing is secured. Borrowing is important for the creation of wealth, and a healthy economy needs a strong banking and financial system. However, by 'uncovering' much corporate debt, the slump in property values in 1974 caused the failure of many banks and threatened the foundations of the UK financial system, whose collapse would have had incalculable consequences for the economy as a whole. The property market and the national economy are intimately interdependent.

Structure of the book

The principal objectives of this book are to explain the nature and characteristics of property investments, the determination of property values and its investment performance. As property values are determined in the investment, letting and development sectors of the market, each of these sectors requires a separate analysis. However, before we can analyse property as an investment, it is important to identify relevant principles and concepts of investment pricing. Thus Part I consists of a study of stock market investments because, (a) these share many of the same characteristics as property investments, and (b) with the stock market being much more 'perfect' than the property market, reliable evidence of prices and yields is available and fundamental principles can readily be identified.

A study of stocks and shares is also important because they are the principal alternative investments to property for the investing institutions which dominate the UK investment market. Trends in property investment cannot be fully understood without an appreciation of the relative merits of these alternatives. Part I provides an understanding of the wider investment market of which the property market is a part, it explains the interrelationship between the investment market and trends in the national economy, and provides a historical perspective.

In Part II the characteristics of property investments and the property market are investigated, the principles of investment pricing identified in Part I are related to property, and a simple model of property pricing is developed. In Part III, the letting sector of the property market is investigated and the determination of rental values explained. In Part IV the determination of site values and development activity is analysed and methods of development finance explained. In Part V the functions and activities of property investors are analysed and the investment value of property explained.

The property pricing theory is developed largely on the assumption that the market is free from government interference, so this assumption is dropped in Part VI, and the impact of public sector intervention is examined. Finally, in Part VII, the theory of property pricing is synthesised by examining the interrelationship of the property market and the UK economy during three of property's most turbulent periods since 1945.

Price and value

Except where the term 'value' is used to indicate the worth of an investment to an individual investor, the terms 'price' and 'value' as used in the book are deemed to be market determined and are interchangeable.

The word 'price' is normally used when referring to stock market securities, whereas 'value' is traditionally used in the case of property. Price is the sum of money paid over when a good is sold, whereas value is an estimate of the price that would be paid if a sale had taken place. It is usual to talk about the changing price of stock market securities because there are usually millions of identical stocks issued by any one company and, as sales take place daily, there is constant evidence of prices paid. But each property is unique and tends to be sold infrequently, and it is impossible to be precise about the price that it would achieve if sold on the market. It is therefore, traditional to talk about property values, being estimates of prices which would be obtained if the properties were sold. Nevertheless, the terms are interchangeable, and it is common to talk about house prices rather than house values.

1 Principles of Investment and Asset Pricing

2 Debt and Equity – Risks and Returns

By way of introduction to the identity and characteristics of the principal investments we shall employ one or two examples, first in the context of housing then in business finance.

Housing finance

Example 2.1

Assume that an investor with £100 000 to invest has the following three alternatives:

(A) To deposit the money in a building society.
(B) To purchase a house for £100 000.
(C) To purchase a house for £400 000, using his £100 000 plus £300 000 borrowed from a building society.

Taking account of changing house prices and interest receipts or payments, but ignoring the value of the occupation benefit in (b) and (c), which of these three investments is likely to prove the most profitable in the future?

The answer depends, of course, on the level of interest rates and the movement of house prices, both of which can vary substantially under changing economic conditions. However, to predict the future we must examine the past, and we can gain a good insight into past experience by investigating the five-year period 1975–80. Over this period prices in general doubled (as measured by the Retail Price Index – RPI) and average house prices also doubled. With the building society interest rate for deposits averaging, say 7.5% per annum (net) and the mortgage rate 7.75% per annum (net of tax relief at the standard rate), the crude returns from the three alternatives can be calculated as follows. (Note that the figures in the calculation below are one-tenth of those in the question above in order to make them more consistent with the level of house prices in the 1970s.)

Investment A

	(£)
Value of investment in 1975	10 000
Compound interest at 7.5% p.a over 5 years	4 356
Value of investment in 1980 (assuming income reinvested)	14 356

But as the purchasing power of money halved over the period

	(£)
Real value of investment in 1980 (1975 prices)	7 178
So, total return in money (nominal) terms	43.6%
Total return in real (inflation adjusted) terms	−28.2%

Investment B

	(£)
Value of house in 1975	10 000
Value of house in 1980	20 000
Real value of investment in 1980 (1975 prices)	10 000
Total return in money terms	100%
Total return in real terms	0%

As house prices rose at the same rate as prices in general, the rise in the money value of the investment was exactly offset by the fall in the purchasing power of money.

Investment C

	(£)	(£)	(£)
Value of house in 1975		40 000	
Mortgage debt		30 000	
Net value of investment (1975)			10 000
Value of house in 1980		80 000	
Original mortgage debt	30 000		
Compound interest at 7.75% p.a	13 572		
Mortgage debt (1980)		43 572	
Net value of investment (1980)			36 428
Real value of investment (1980) (at 1975 prices)			18 214
Total return in money terms			264.3%
Total return in real terms			82.1%

Note: In the cause of simplicity, and in order to obtain comparability with investment *A*, it has been assumed that instead of regular interest payments, the borrower in *C* was provided with 'roll up' facilities, i.e. his debt was allowed to accumulate at the mortgage interest rate (compounded over the five years).

The profitability of the three investments has proved dramatically different. In a relatively brief period one investment lost over a quarter of its real value, the second exactly maintained its real value, and the third gained over 80% in real terms. If we had ascribed some value to the occupation benefit received from the two house investments *B* and *C*, then the relative unprofitability of *A* would have been even more pronounced.

Essentially it was inflation which caused this outcome, by:

(a) reducing the real value of debt and savings, and
(b) raising the monetary value of houses.

Inflation is simply the phenomenon of generally rising prices of goods and services, and conversely the fall in the purchasing power of money. So *A* performed badly because the investment was in money, *B* maintained its real value because the investment was in a durable asset whose money value rose with inflation, but *C* was even more successful because it gained from both (a) and (b) – the rise in the money value of the house and the fall in the real value of borrowed money. It was unprofitable to invest in money during these conditions, but profitable to borrow it.

However, inflation alone is not enough to explain the relative profitability of the three investments. We must also consider the level of interest rates. If the interest rate offered to the investor in *A* and paid by the borrower in *C* had exceeded the annual rate of inflation, then the relative profitability of *A* and *C* would have been reversed, despite the rise in the money value of the house and the fall in the real value of money. So the outcome derives from a combination of inflation and relatively low interest rates, or simply the phenomenon of negative real *interest rates*, i.e. interest rates below the rate of inflation. If a depositor is receiving an interest rate of 7.5% over a year during which prices rise by 20%, then his return is approximately −12.5%. He gains 7.5%, but loses 20%. His real return is negative. The real cost of borrowing under such conditions is also negative.

Until 1981, negative real interest rates predominated in the UK economy in the post-war period, especially after taking account of taxation of interest received by investors or taxation relief on interest payments made by borrowers. This phenomenon resulted in a massive transfer of wealth from savers to borrowers, particularly in the 1970s. The large real gains made by house buyers were made at the expense of the depositors who provided the mortgage capital.

Clearly, the depositor suffered a raw deal in these circumstances. One might have expected that the level of cash deposits would have declined as savers switched to spending on durable goods whose value could be expected to rise with inflation. To some extent they did, but (apart from the benefits of security and liquidity) the reason why many savers continued to deposit their money at negative real returns is probably because they were largely unaware of their losses; they suffered from 'money illusion'. Wealth is normally measured in money terms, and they saw their money wealth accumulating. Whilst they must have been aware of inflation, they did not appreciate the extent of its impact.

The above example has illustrated the main way – in fact, for many people the only way – to the accumulation of significant personal wealth in the post-war period in the UK. A realisation of the profitability of not just house ownership *per se*, but of maximising building society mortgage borrowing, has caused people to regard a house as an investment, rather than simply a place to live. However, housing's success as an investment has derived not only from its qualities as an inflation 'hedge' and the phenomenon of negative real interest rates, but from a number of other relatively unique characteristics which single it out from most other investments. House ownership avoids the payment of rent, no capital gains tax (CGT) is payable on the rise in value, mortgage interest payments attract income tax relief, and values have normally been stable on a rising trend.

These beneficial conditions have already been somewhat eroded by restrictions on the tax relief receivable on mortgage interest payments, but the fundamental change affecting the future profitability of borrowing for house purchase has been the decline in inflation and the transformation from negative to positive real interest rates.

In addressing the question in Example 2.1, we shall again assume that the growth of house prices exactly matches inflation, but at a rate totalling 25% over a five-year period in the future (about 4.5% p.a.). In estimating the relative returns to investments A and C we will also assume a building society deposit rate of 7% (net) and an average borrowing rate of 10%.

Clearly in this scenario of positive real interest rates the relative profitability of A and C is dramatically reversed. While the return from B again equals the rate of inflation, A now provides a positive return in both money and real terms but C proves to be highly unprofitable. Although C still benefits from the rise in the money value of the house and the fall in the real value of debt, the fact that the interest rate exceeds the growth of the house price means a substantial loss of wealth to the owner.

The example opposite illustrates the potential losses to those who borrow for house purchase. The fact that interest on debt is normally paid out of the borrower's income rather than being rolled up, as shown in the example, in no way invalidates the illustration. On the other hand, the example contains a number of simplicities. Most importantly, by ignoring the occupation benefit of house ownership it would be quite wrong to conclude that borrowing for house purchase is unjustifiable. The alternative to paying interest on debt may be to pay rent as a tenant.

Investment C

	(£)	(£)	(£)
Value of house, Year 0		400 000	
Mortgage debt		300 000	
Net value of investment, Year 0			100 000
Value of house, Year 5		500 000	
Mortgage debt	300 000		
Compound interest at 10% p.a.	183 153		
Mortgage debt, Year 5		483 153	
Net value of investment, Year 5			16 847
Less 25% loss of purchasing power			4 212
Real value of investment, Year 5 (Year 0 prices)			12 635
Total return in money terms			−83.2%
Total return in real terms			−87.4%

Another simplification is to assume that house prices are tied closely to inflation. In fact, house prices have a closer relationship with average wages than inflation, and are influenced by trends over the economic cycle. House prices grew dramatically in the boom of the late 1980s (despite positive real interest rates) but fell back in the recession of 1990–2. Thus good timing of buy and sell decisions can result in good returns.

The principal purpose of Example 2.1 has been to show the relative gains and losses from borrowing to buy property in times of negative and positive real interest rates. On the assumption that real interest rates are likely to remain positive in the foreseeable future, it is probable that borrowing for house purchase will incur a substantial real cost to the owner. This contrasts with the 1960s and 1970s, when it was profitable for a house buyer to raise the maximum debt which could be serviced out of his income in order to buy the most expensive house he could afford.

The principal conclusions so far are as follows:

- In times of negative real interest rates, ironically the best way to save may be to *borrow* money in order to purchase a durable asset such as property, whose value tends to rise in line with inflation.
- But in times of positive real interest rates, such an exercise is likely to prove unprofitable.
- Successful investment is choosing the best of a number of alternatives, although none of these might leave the investor better off in real terms.
- Because returns and wealth are measured in money terms, there is a tendency in times of inflation to suffer from 'money illusion'. Although henceforth in this book returns are measured in money terms, it is essential not to lose sight of *real value* (purchasing power) changes.

Risk and volatility

The reader was asked previously to consider which of the three investments — A, B or C — would be likely to prove the most profitable, now he should ask himself in which of these investments is the £100 000 at greatest risk? In A the capital and income is guaranteed by the building society, and could be lost only if the society was unable to meet its commitments. Building societies rarely go bankrupt, and the main uncertainty involved in this investment derives from the variability in the interest rate paid by the society.

In B, the capital is invested in the house, and thus the risk to the capital depends on the volatility of house prices (ignoring insurable risks such as fire and structural failure). Taking a medium- or long-term view, house prices have proved remarkably stable (on a rising trend). But in the short term house prices have occasionally fallen significantly, and if the owner was forced to sell a house during a market slump — say, as a result of a change in job — then he could well suffer loss. Investment B is therefore a less secure medium for the £100 000 than A.

The relatively low element of risk in B is dramatically magnified in investment C. If house prices fall by 10%, the investor in B will lose 10%, i.e. £10 000, but the investor in C will lose £40 000, 40% of his capital. The house buyer must eventually repay his mortgage debt in full, so the full loss of a fall in the house price from £400 000 to £360 000 must be suffered by the owner. If the house in C falls in value by 25% or more, the owner has lost all his £100 000 of capital. Conversely, if house prices rise by 25% the investor in C will double his net worth from £100 000 to £200 000, while investor B's capital will rise by just 25%.

This brief analysis of the risk and returns to the three investments has shown that their characteristics are very dissimilar. In fact, we really have three categories of investment, which we shall call 'interest bearing', 'equity' and 'geared equity', corresponding to investments A, B and C. The term 'interest bearing' is self explanatory; 'equity' is an investment which gains the residual profits (or suffers the losses) of an enterprise. 'Geared equity' indicates that the investment is subject to a prior charge — normally, as in Example 2.1, borrowed capital.

We shall now complete our analysis of this example with a word or two about 'gearing' and its significance. The 'capital-gearing ratio' refers to the proportions of debt and equity capital employed in some venture. Debt capital is borrowed capital, and equity capital is capital belonging to the owner of the equity interest, the house buyer in C. We shall define the capital-gearing ratio as the proportion, debt capital:total capital employed. So in C the ratio is 75%. Investment B is ungeared — all capital is equity capital.

A brief glance back to our original calculations (1970s context) will indicate the significance of the gearing ratio to risk and returns. If instead of borrowing £30 000 to buy a £40 000 house, our investor in C had borrowed £90 000 to buy a £100 000 house (90% gearing), his gains would have almost doubled, but his risk would also have increased. A mere 10% fall in the value of the house would have wiped out all his equity capital and put the debt capital at risk. Conversely, if he had borrowed £10 000 to buy a £20 000 house, the capital gain and risk would have been much less, and if ungeared (as in *B*), the gains and risk are lower still.

- The risk and capital gain potential of an equity investment depend on its level of capital gearing.

It should now be appreciated that investments are not physical but intangible 'claims' or 'interests' over a medium which itself may be physical, such as the house in Example 2.1. The house in C is not strictly *the* investment; there are two investment interests over the house – the interest of the owner and the interest of the building society whose loan is secured by mortgage deed on that house.

Example 2.1 was introduced to illustrate certain concepts and principles of investment – a full discussion about the housing market and home ownership has not been attempted as it is beyond the scope of this book. The example has now outlived its usefulness, having illustrated returns only in broad capital change terms. Example 2.2 will now look at investment in cash flow terms.

Business finance

Example 2.2

Let us examine the case of (the fictitious) Fred Daly, who some time ago decided to set up in business as a newsagent. He had £50 000 of his own capital available but as he required a total of £100 000 to fit out his shop, buy in stock, etc. he borrowed a further £50 000 from a bank at a variable interest rate of 15%. At commencement of business, he was thus employing £50 000 of equity capital and £50 000 of debt capital, thereby having a capital-gearing ratio of 50%.

In his first year of trading, Daly made profits of £20 000 – being the difference between income from sales and all costs including rent, rates, wages, heating, lighting and his own salary, but excluding interest on his bank loan. After deduction of interest payments (and taxation, ignored here for simplicity) the residual is 'equity earnings' (see Table 2.1). Whereas interest is the return to debt capital, equity earnings is the return to equity capital. As Mr Daly is the sole owner of the equity, the £12 500 belongs to him, being the reward for his enterprise and for putting his capital at risk. He could withdraw the money from the business for his personal use, or alternatively use it to improve his stock or equipment, or to repay part of his debt.

In Year 2, trading profits rose by 50% to £30 000, and with bank interest stable at 15%, equity earnings increased by 80%. Major problems, however, arose in Year 3. The bank increased its interest rate to 20%, Mr Daly was forced to pay his staff higher wages, various strikes by print unions disrupted publication of a number of his most lucrative journals, and a general fall in demand reduced his turnover. At £10 000, trading profits were just sufficient to cover the increased interest charges, resulting in nil equity earnings.

Table 2.1   Fred Daly, newsagent – trading record (£)

	Year		
	1	2	3
Trading profit	20 000	30 000	10 000
Interest on debt	7 500	7 500	10 000
Equity earnings	12 500	22 500	NIL

This crude and simplistic example serves to illustrate the relative risk (and potential return) to debt and equity:

- The return to debt capital (interest), being a contractual obligation which must be paid before any return can accrue to equity capital holders, is relatively *stable and secure*.
- Conversely, because equity earnings is a residual profit after all business expenses and other legitimate claims have been met, the return to equity capital is relatively *volatile and risky*.

As illustrated by the figures for Year 2 in Table 2.1, the growth potential of equity earnings in a geared business is considerable but, as illustrated by the Year 3 figures, these earnings are highly volatile and risky. This risk derives both from (a) falling trading profits and (b) rising interest rates. So by raising debt on a long-term fixed interest basis rather than the variable interest basis of a bank loan, the risk to equity earnings would be reduced.

Volatility of equity earnings is common to all businesses and depends on many factors, particularly the type of business transacted. But whatever is the inherent volatility of a particular business, earnings volatility will be increased according to the level of the firm's income gearing.

Impact of gearing on the volatility of returns

Gearing (termed 'leverage' in the USA) in one form or another is an ever-present force in investment, finance and property, and it is essential to an understanding of market pricing that its presence should be recognised and

Table 2.2   Income gearing

		Year						
		1	2	3	4	5	6	7
(a)	Variable cash flow	100	110	121	133	120	108	97
	Fixed deduction	20	20	20	20	20	20	20
	Residual cash flow	80	90	101	113	100	88	77
	Growth % of residual		+ 12.5	+ 12.2	+ 12.0	− 11.8	− 12.0	− 12.3
(b)	Variable cash flow	100	110	121	133	120	108	97
	Fixed deduction	50	50	50	50	50	50	50
	Residual cash flow	50	60	71	83	70	58	47
	Growth % of residual		+ 20.0	+ 18.3	+ 17.0	− 16.0	− 17.2	− 18.6

its significance appreciated. The concept of income gearing is illustrated in Table 2.2 where a fixed amount per annum is deducted from a variable income flow to leave a residual cash flow which must vary by a greater amount than the original income. In sections (a) and (b) of Table 2.2, the original income flow grows at 10% per annum until Year 4, after which it declines at the same rate. But the volatility of the residual is greater in (b) than in (a) because the fixed deduction is a higher proportion of the income flow – i.e. its 'income-gearing ratio' is higher. The income gearing ratio is normally defined as the proportion that the deduction bears to the variable income. In Year 1, it is 20% in (a) and 50% in (b).

● If a fixed sum is deducted from a variable cash flow, the residual cash flow must vary by a greater amount, and this extra variability is proportional to the *income-gearing ratio.*

Note that the income-gearing ratio varies from year to year, and that if an income continues to grow while the deduction remains fixed, the ratio gradually declines.

If the variable cash flow is considered as gross trading profit, and the fixed deduction as interest on debt, then (ignoring taxation) the residual cash flow represents equity earnings. Example 2.2 illustrates why the risk and growth potential of equity earnings in a geared company depend on the income-gearing ratio. If a firm is ungeared, i.e. has no debt and no interest payments, then equity earnings will vary at the same rate as trading profits.

The impact of gearing on the risk and growth potential of equity earnings can be illustrated by considering the returns to debt and equity as vertical slices of trading profit (see Figure 2.1).

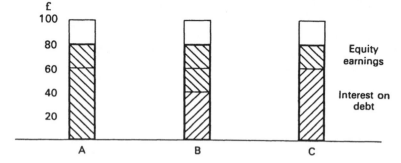

Figure 2.1   Returns to debt and equity as vertical slices of trading profit

Example 2.3

Three companies *A*, *B* and *C*, identical in all respects except in gearing, have all just announced a trading profit of £80. Company *A* is ungeared, so all trading profit is equity earnings. Company *B* has an income-gearing ratio of 50% (i.e., interest on debt shown as the bottom slice of profit in Figure 2.1 amounts to half of trading profit). Company *C* has an income-gearing ratio of 75% (i.e. the bottom £60 of profit is used to pay interest on debt). So if trading profit rises from £80 to £100, then for company *A* equity earnings increase by 25%, for company *B* by 50% and for company *C* by 100%. But if trading profit falls from £80 to £60, then company *A*'s equity earnings will fall by 25%, company *B*'s by 50% and company *C*'s by 100%.

Interest on debt is the secure bottom slice, and equity earnings is the relatively risky top slice portion of trading profit. If the interest rate is variable (as in the case of Fred Daly's debt) then equity earnings is potentially even more volatile as interest payments, the bottom slice, can vary upwards (or downwards). Note also that the level of gearing affects the risk of the return to debt as well as the return to equity. If company *C* has no reserves, then a fall in trading profit below £60 would result in an inability to pay the interest due. So,

● The level of a firm's income gearing affects the risk of the return to the *debt capital* as well as the risk and growth potential of *equity earnings*.

Risk to capital

Let us now return to Fred Daly. The principle of gearing explains why, although trading profits increased by 50% between Year 1 and 2, his equity earnings rose by a much greater proportion, and also why a 67% slump in profits the following year resulted in his equity earnings being wiped out. However, so far in Example 2.2 we have examined only the *returns* to the debt and equity capital. We must also consider the risk to the debt and equity capital itself.

Just as equity earnings is the residual after deducting interest payments from trading profit, equity capital is the residual after deducting debt from the value of assets. Similarly, just as the risk to equity earnings and interest on debt is a function of the income-gearing ratio, the risk to equity and debt capital depends on the capital-gearing ratio. This has already been illustrated in Example 2.1.

The risk to the equity and debt capital employed by Fred Daly thus derives from a fall in the value of his assets as well as through losses in his trading activities. Let us assume that after revaluation at the end of Year 3 of trading, Fred Daly discovered that his assets had fallen to £75 000, perhaps due to a fall in the value of his stock. With £50 000 still owed to the bank, this meant that his equity capital had fallen to £25 000 from the original £50 000.

Additionally, if losses in Year 4 exceeded £25 000, after allowing for interest due, then Fred Daly's business would be insolvent. Not only would Daly have lost all his equity capital, but assets would be inadequate to repay the £50 000 bank loan as well as interest due. The bank might therefore suffer loss, although as Mr Daly was in business as a 'sole trader' rather than as a limited company, the bank may be able to recover their loss from Daly's personal assets.

This extension to Example 2.2 has illustrated the following:

- Risk to capital (equity or debt) is a further consideration over risk to income, and factors that create risk to income will also tend to create *risk to capital*.
- Initially all losses are borne by the *equity capital*, as the repayment of debt is a legal obligation and a prior charge on the assets (that is why equity capital is often described as risk capital).
- Although debt capital is relatively secure compared with equity, it is not completely secure, as in cases of *insolvency or fraud*.
- The level of risk to debt capital, as well as the risk to equity capital, depends on the level of *capital gearing*.

At the end of Example 2.1 three categories of investment were identified. In Example 2.2, Mr Daly's interest is clearly a 'geared equity', but virtually all such ownership interests in business are geared in some respect, and it would be unusual to specify the equity interest as geared. The interest of the bank is similar to that of the building society in Example 2.1 – they own the debt and hold an 'interest bearing' investment.

By concentrating on the growth potential and risk of income-earning investments rather than considering capital value change in isolation, Example 2.2 has brought us closer to an understanding of investment prices, because the most important investments are income-earning investments, and it is the risk and the growth potential of income which largely determine investment prices.

3 Marketable Securities and the Stock Market

Fred Daly 'goes public'

Fortunately, Fred Daly's setback and decline as reported in Chapter 2 was entirely mythical. In fact his early success was the start of a long-term trend of continually rising profits, deriving largely from an expansion in the number of his shop outlets and diversification into records, toys, games and miscellaneous goods.

Although originally commencing business in his own name as a 'sole trader', Mr Daly's accountants soon advised him to form a private limited company, F. D. Newsagents Ltd, in which he and his wife became sole shareholders. The act of 'incorporation' has the effect of legally separating a business from its owners, and usually has favourable taxation implications. The limited liability status also means that, in the event of insolvency, Fred and Doris Daly could lose only their equity capital in the company, not their personal wealth, unless they had provided personal guarantees on loans made to the company.

As tends to happen with rapidly growing businesses, the expansion of F. D. Newsagents Ltd created requirements for new capital substantially in excess of the equity earnings which the two shareholders ploughed back into the company. Bank borrowing increased substantially, leading to an unhealthy rise in the firm's short-term debt, and thereby subjecting the business to increasing risk in the event of a trading downturn and rising interest rates. Furthermore Fred Daly's ambitions now included the opening of a number of major High Street retail outlets, an expansion requiring many million pounds, and even if the company's bankers had been prepared to lend such extra capital the new level of gearing would have been prohibitive.

Substantial *equity* capital was therefore needed. F. D. Newsagents Ltd, remaining as a private company, might have raised this finance from a merchant bank or a venture-capital fund in exchange for shares in the company. However, the main source of new equity capital is the stock market. By becoming a public company with a Stock Exchange quotation, substantial amounts of new capital can be raised by selling shareholdings to financial institutions and the investing public at large.

The process of 'going public' and obtaining a 'full listing' on the Stock Exchange involves satisfying the strict requirements of the Companies Acts and the Stock Exchange Council. A prospectus must be drawn up detailing, *inter alia*, the type of business undertaken, the history of the firm, its assets, past record and future prospects. With the involvement of accountants, lawyers, stockbrokers and merchant bankers, together with the expense of underwriting and advertising, the cost of a full listing might exceed £500 000. Clearly, this is not appropriate for firms with relatively small capital requirements. An alternative to a full listing for companies wishing to market their shares is the Unlisted Securities Market (USM), where the expense would be reduced substantially.

The twin requirements of F. D. Newsagents Ltd – namely, to raise substantial new capital and to 'degear' – are two of the principal reasons causing companies to 'go public'. Other advantages are the higher status of a quoted company, and the improved marketability of its shares which enables the owners to realise part of the value of their investment. On the other hand, by selling part of the equity (a minimum of 25% must be sold to the public under Stock Exchange regulations), the original shareholders are surrendering absolute sovereignty of their firm, although effective control is retained by a 51% share holding. The arguments for and against 'going public' are complex, with the correct decision being very personal to the needs of the individual company: but, as it suits our purpose, we shall assume that F. D. Newsagents Ltd goes public with a full Stock Exchange listing.

Let us assume that Mr and Mrs Daly decided to raise £100 million, and although the greatest need was for equity capital, they felt that some fixed-interest debt capital should also be raised in order to maintain a sensible level of gearing without the risks of short-term recall and rising interest rates inherent in bank borrowing. It was therefore agreed to raise £80 million of equity capital and £20 million of debt capital by the sale of ordinary shares and loan stock respectively.

It makes little difference to either the buyer or seller as to whether the £80 million of equity is raised by the issue of:

80 million ordinary shares at £1 each, or
800 million ordinary shares at 10p each, or
320 million ordinary shares at 25p each, or
any other combination totalling to £80 million.

However, we shall assume that 320 million shares were offered for sale at 25p per share, representing 40% of the equity and thus valuing the company's total equity at £200 million.

The figure of 25p per share is the price which, in the judgement of the merchant bankers in charge of the issue, the investing public will be willing to pay. Investors will be willing to buy only if they believe that their value, when traded on the stock market immediately after the issue, will equal or exceed the offer price of 25p. The price set by the market depends, in turn, on investors' view of the risk and future profitability of the company. In this case, 25p is also the 'nominal value' of the shares (the offer price and nominal value may be substantially different) and their formal title is 25p ordinary shares, F. D. Newsagents PLC.

The £20 million of debt capital could be raised by the sale of say:

12% debentures 1999–2005, or
13% unsecured loan stock 2020.

These are both fixed-interest bonds or loan stock which create a legal obligation on the company to pay interest (whether profit is being earned or not),
and to repay the debt at the specified time. However, whereas the capital
attributable to the debenture stock is secured against specific assets of the
company (often property), holders of unsecured loan stock do not have such
security. Debentures are often called 'mortgage debentures' because (as in
the case of a house mortgage) the debt can be repaid from the sale of the
assets in the event of default by the borrower.

The resultant risk differential partly explains the lower 'nominal rate of
interest' in the title of the debentures compared with the unsecured loan
stock but, as we shall see later, the duration of the loan is also important in
determining interest rates. The 'nominal interest rate' or 'coupon' quoted in the
title of the stock is the rate of interest paid per annum on each £100 of the
stock, and would tend to be the rate of interest that was just sufficient to
ensure the sale of the stock to the public, taking the repayment date and risk
into account.

The year quoted in the title of the stock is the year in which the debt must
be repaid, normally called the 'redemption date'. Where there is a range, as in
the debenture stock, the borrower has the right to select the most suitable
repayment date within the period quoted.

The story of Fred Daly, newsagent, has been extended into this chapter in
order to illustrate the principal types of financial securities issued by public
companies, and to explain the essential purpose and circumstances under
which these stocks and shares are issued. However, it should be appreciated
that this illustration has been simplified in many ways. Before arriving at the
situation where 'going public' becomes a sensible option, the corporate
structure of a firm is likely to be much more complicated than in the case of
F. D. Newsagents. There would usually be more shareholders than simply the
firm's founder and his wife, the parent company might have created a number
of subsidiaries responsible for different aspects of the business, and the firm's
debt would probably have been raised from a variety of sources on a variety
of terms and conditions. Again, a full explanation of the arguments for and
against 'going public' and the mechanisms by which new issues are offered to
the public has not been attempted as it is peripheral to the theme of this
book, but the reader is recommended to read one or more of the specialist
stock-market texts listed in Further Reading.

The purpose of this chapter is to introduce the principal financial securities
and the market in which they are traded. The analysis of these securities is left
to subsequent chapters. At this stage, it should be appreciated that the
characteristics of the debt and equity interests which we identified in

Chapter 2 are common to the debt and equity securities illustrated so far in this chapter – the difference being that the investments introduced in this chapter are marketable in the Stock Exchange, whilst those in Chapter 2 are not.

The essential differences between ordinary shares and loan stock will now be summarised.

Loan stock and ordinary shares compared

Both ordinary shares (colloquially referred to as 'equities') and loan stock are examples of financial securities, being legal claims to the profits that a company earns. As we have seen, they are sold by companies in order to raise capital to finance their business activities, and they are purchased by investors looking for income and, possibly, capital gain. Subsequent to their issue, both types of investments can be sold and purchased by investors in the stock market, indeed the large majority of financial securities will at any time be held by investors other than the original buyers. At this point, however, the similarities between the two investment types end. They repre-sent different interests and display fundamentally different investment char-acteristics under varying economic conditions.

- A share is an ownership interest in a company and the shareholders collectively own a company. Loan stock is the interest of the holders of debt capital who are merely creditors of the company.

As the company's owners, shareholders have the power to decide on policy by voting on resolutions at shareholders' meetings. Shareholders appoint directors to run the company, who may be 'executive' (i.e. involved in the day-to-day running of the company), or 'non-executive' (i.e. fulfilling a part-time advisory role). Loan stockholders cannot influence company policy, except that under certain circumstances their consent must be obtained before further borrowing is undertaken.

- Shares are regarded as perpetual investments whereas the overwhelming majority of loan stocks have a date (or dates) specified for redemption and therefore exist for a limited duration.

The life of shares may, of course, be ended by the company's liquidation or merger with another company.

- Shareholders receive dividends, the amount of which can vary annually. Loan stockholders receive interest which is normally fixed for the life of the stock.
- The return from shares is potentially high but risky, while the return from loan stock is normally lower but much more secure.

The high risk and return from shares arise primarily because equity earnings are a residual after all expenses, prior interests and taxation have been met. In the event of insolvency shareholders may lose all the value of their investment. On the other hand, the interest and capital repayment made to loan stockholders is limited to the contractually agreed amount, and has priority over payments made to shareholders. In the event of default, the stockholders can institute proceedings for the compulsory liquidation of the company's assets to enable any outstanding payment to be made.

● Shares are quantified in numbers but loan stock is quantified in amounts nominal.

For example, Mr X owns 5000 25p ordinary shares as well as £2500 nominal of 12% Debentures 1995 – 2005 in F. D. Newsagents PLC. The amount nominal is normally the capital repayable at redemption.

It is important to note that whereas the term 'stock' can be used to encompass all marketable securities including shares (Americans call ordinary shares 'common stock'), the word 'share' is specific to ordinary shares or preference shares (see page 71).

Rights issues

Existing public companies frequently wish to raise extra capital by the issue of new stock. In the UK the usual process by which new shares are sold is by 'rights issue', whereby existing shareholders are given the right to buy a certain number of the new shares in proportion to their existing shareholdings, at a price usually significantly below the market price of existing shares. Say the market price of ordinary shares in F. D. Newsagents PLC is standing at 43p and the company announces a 1 for 4 rights issue at 35p per share, then a shareholder holding 4000 existing shares has the right to buy 1000 new shares at the discounted price of 35p. Shareholders who do not have the financial resources available, or who do not wish to take up the offer, are protected from an effective loss by their ability to sell their rights allotment, as this itself will tend to have value so long as the price of the new shares is at a discount to the (identical) existing shares.

Raising new capital for existing quoted companies is generally a more important function of the stock market than raising capital for companies 'going public'. Equity capital raised by rights issue can vary from a few million pounds to several hundred million pounds.

British government bonds

Up till now, all the stock which have been introduced have been 'corporate' securities (i.e. financial securities issued by companies), but one of the most important categories of stock traded on the stock market is that sold by the government to help finance the government's borrowing requirement. These stocks are variously known as government bonds, British funds, 'gilt edged securities', or simply 'gilts'. Prior to the Second World War, most British governments aimed to balance the annual budget, but to finance any abnormally large expenditure, particularly in times of war, by the issue of these bonds. However, since the Keynesian revolution the public sector has usually spent much more per annum than has been raised in taxation, and although some of this deficit has been financed by various forms of national savings, overseas borrowing and short-term borrowing by the sale of Treasury bills, the large majority of the deficit has been funded by the issue of gilts. Consequently gilts collectively make up the majority of the national debt. Not only does the issue of gilts help to finance the central government's excess expenditure, but also a large part of the excess expenditure of nationalised industries and local authorities. The combined annual deficit of all three public sectors makes up the Public Sector Borrowing Requirement (PSBR), and it is fluctuations in this aggregate – including the need to refinance previous gilts at redemption – which largely dictates the amount of new gilt issues.

There are two principal categories of gilts, namely conventional fixed interest bonds and index-linked stock in which the investor's return is linked to the rate of inflation. Conventional gilts are similar to corporate loan stock, and as the issuing authority is the UK government rather than a company, the guaranteed interest and capital repayment are very secure.

Stock issued many years ago sometimes bear a title which indicates the reason for issue, e.g., 3 ½% War Loan. But the name of the stock is irrelevant to the investor, except to enable it to be distinguished from another stock of the same coupon or redemption date. Nowadays, new issues are usually given one of three titles – Treasury, Exchequer or Funding.

As in the case of corporate bonds, the nominal rate of interest (coupon) and redemption date is quoted in the title of the stock, but there are a small number of gilts which have no specific redemption date at all, the government having the right to postpone their redemption indefinitely. In fact these 'irredeemables' or 'undated' stock are unlikely to be redeemed until the cost of long-term borrowing drops below the rate paid to holders of the stock. The government is unlikely to redeem 3 ½% War Loan, for instance, until the cost of borrowing new money to repay the existing debt is less than 3.5%.

Conventional gilts are normally categorised according to the period that must elapse until redemption. The principal groups are short-dated stock (up to five years to redemption), medium-dated (5–15 years to redemption), long-dated (over 15 years to redemption), and irredeemables or undated stock. It is the period from the present until redemption that is relevant, not the life of the stock from its original issue; a short-dated stock may have been issued last month or 30 years ago. New issues may be shorts, mediums or longs according to the needs of the Treasury and the relative cost in interest payments, but no major issue of undated stock has been made since the 1930s.

The introduction of index-linked gilts in 1981 has been the principal innovation in the funding of the PSBR. The essential feature of these stocks is that both the interest paid and the redemption value are adjusted in line with changes in the RPI, thus providing investors with a return in real terms.

Stock-market investors

Investors in stock-market securities include charitable trusts, industrial and commercial companies, overseas investors and even some public sector bodies, but the two largest categories are the personal sector (individuals, executors and trustees) and the non-bank financial institutions (particularly insurance companies, pension funds, investment trusts and unit trusts). Without doubt one of the most important post-war trends in the UK investment market has been the growth of these institutions, particularly the growth of life assurance and pension funds, due to the huge expansion in contractual saving and occupational pension schemes. The increasing influence of these institutions in the investment market has followed from their need to find investment outlets for their enormous inflow of funds. Acquisition of investments by insurance companies and pension funds amounted to £38 billion in 1992, which is about £150 million for each working day.

The expansion in institutional investment has been coupled with a substantial decline in direct investment in stock-market securities by individuals. This has been due to a variety of factors, including the expansion of contractual investment schemes (e.g., life assurance), the growth of the unit-trust movement (enabling indirect investment in the stock market), the increasing relative attraction of house ownership as an investment, and the high levels of taxation imposed on the wealthy. The combination of institutional expansion and the decline in direct personal stock-market investment has resulted in a dramatic change in the relative influence of these two groups of investors. In the case of equity shares this is illustrated in Table 3.1.

The relative decline in share ownership by private individuals continued in the 1980s, despite the Thatcher government's policies of wider share ownership, lower personal taxation and the privatisation of government-owned companies and utilities. Although the number of shareholders in the UK rose from about 2.5 million in 1984 to over 11 million in 1991, over 75% of those hold shares in only one or two privatised companies. This is despite the introduction of schemes such as the Personal Equity Plan (PEP) which encourage equity investment by the provision of tax relief. Although private share ownership is greater in the USA and Japan, a similar trend towards declining personal share ownership was experienced in the 1980s.

The domination of the stock market by financial institutions and the enormous wealth controlled by a relatively small number of investment managers means that they tend to be 'price makers' rather than 'price takers'. With investment managers tending to make similar buy/sell decisions

Table 3.1   Ownership of UK listed equities

	1963 (%)	1975 (%)	1989 (%)
Individuals, executors, etc.	54.0	37.5	21.3
Public sector	1.5	3.6	2.0
Industrial and commercial companies	5.1	3.0	3.6
Overseas	7.0	5.6	12.4
Insurance companies	10.0	15.9	18.4
Pension funds	6.4	16.8	30.4
Unit trusts and investment trusts	12.6	14.6	9.1
Banks	1.3	0.7	0.9
Non profit-making bodies	2.1	2.3	2.0
Total	100.0	100.0	100.0

Sources: CSO; Stock Exchange.

in response to economic news, and to an extent subject to the 'herd instinct', substantial fluctuations in the level of stock prices tend to reflect the consensus views and actions of these fund managers. The larger the fund under management, the larger will share holdings in any company tend to be, and the larger the share holding the more difficult it is to trade without influencing the price. Selling shares in Company A to buy those of Company B will tend to cause a fall in the price of shares in Company A and a rise in those of Company B. This problem of marketability inhibits active management and discourages institutions from investing in small companies.

Political concern about the influence of the institutions results from their power to direct the flow of the nation's scarce capital resources, their ability to influence the management of industry, the lack of accountability of their trustees and managers, and the ability of a future government effectively to nationalise and control the bulk of UK industry by the relatively simple act of nationalising the financial institutions themselves.

The dealing mechanism

The system for trading stocks and shares in the UK was radically altered by 'Big Bang' in 1986. As the public was not permitted access to the floor of the Stock Exchange, the investor dealt through a stockbroker, acting as a professional agent. The broker would negotiate the best possible deal with 'jobbers', who were the dealers or 'market makers' in stocks and shares, buying shares through brokers acting for sellers, and selling shares through brokers acting for buyers. This 'single capacity' system meant strict demarcation between the functions and ownership of brokers and jobbers. The broker is a professional agent who charges a fee for his services, whereas the jobber was a dealer whose livelihood depended on making profits on his transactions. Consequently, at any point in time the price at which he offered to sell stock would be higher than the price he would bid to buy stock, the difference being the 'jobbers turn'.

Big Bang had many facets, but essentially it involved the Stock Exchange abandoning 'single capacity' in favour of 'dual capacity', i.e. allowing the same firm to undertake both broking and dealing business. It arose through the government's insistence that stockbrokers must abolish mandatory scale fees, and the assumption that unfettered competition between brokers would require them to be allowed to make deals in order to generate sufficient profit to survive. The outcome was a complete restructuring of the securities industry and the abandonment of face-to-face dealing on the floor of the Stock Exchange in favour of a system using computer screens and telephones. Instead of many relatively small firms of brokers and jobbers, the securities industry is now dominated by financial conglomerates, many owned by banks and overseas institutions, which typically undertake not only broking and dealing, but also retail banking, merchant banking, fund management and, in a few cases, property investment services.

From the perspective of the private investor, the process of buying and selling shares has changed little. The investor will use a broker to act on his behalf to negotiate the best price with market-makers (one of which may be an arm of the broker's own firm). However, major institutional investors who can afford SEAQ (the Stock Exchange Automated Quotation system, which lists stocks and their quoted prices) can deal directly with market-makers and thereby avoid the broker's fee.

The system for the settlement of share transactions remains unchanged. This involves the division of the year into 24 'accounts', i.e., periods normally of two weeks, but including four three-week periods when public holidays intervene. The exchange of share certificates and payment between the buyer's and seller's brokers normally takes place on 'settlement day' – usually the Monday ten days after the last day of the account (Friday). This system, which means that all deals made within an account are settled on the same day, provides scope for certain purely speculative transactions. Speculators nicknamed 'bulls' contract to buy stock which they do not intend to pay for, in the knowledge that before the end of the account they can 'cover' their position by contracting to sell the same stock, hopefully at a profit – hence the term 'bull market' when prices generally are rising. Conversely, 'bears' speculate on a fall in price by contracting to sell stock which they do not own, in the expectation that they will be able to buy back the same amount of stock before the end of the account at a cheaper price – hence the term 'bear market', when stock prices are generally falling and, unbelievably, 'bear covering' and 'bear squeeze' when rising prices force such speculators to cover their previous sales at a loss.

If the speculator has guessed correctly, then all he has to do is to collect his hard-earned loot on settlement day, but needless to say large losses can be made as well as profits. Although detracting from the stock market's image, such activity is tolerated in the belief that rather than creating instability, it has the effect of dampening down short-term share-price movements.

Here, it seems appropriate to introduce a third specimen of City fauna – the 'stag'. He applies to purchase part of a new issue of shares on public offer, in the expectation that when subsequently traded on the Stock Exchange he will be able to sell at a profit. In order to attract investors, a new issue will normally be priced somewhat below the price expected after the start of trading. That was particularly true of many privatisation issues of the 1980s, due to the size of the issues and the government's policy of attracting the public into share ownership. Stagging profits gave rise to accusations that state assets were being sold off too cheaply.

Functions of the stock market

Contrary to the impression that might be created above, the purpose of issuing shares is not to provide gambling chips for the indolent wealthy, nor is the Stock Exchange run as a casino to provide speculators with enormous unearned profits at the expense of the working man. That is not to deny that speculation exists, nor that enormous profits can occasionally be made, but it is more likely to be at the expense of some less fortunate speculator or investor, rather than the working man. In fact, the Stock Exchange Council, the regulating body of the Stock Exchange, is very sensitive about the market's image, and strict regulations are laid down in order to encourage market stability, outlaw dishonest practices and protect the serious investor.

The stock market is both a 'primary' market (i.e. a market in which new goods are sold for the first time), and a 'secondary' market (in which second-hand goods are traded). In its role as a market in new issues of stocks and shares, the stock market brings together those who require finance and those who wish to provide it. It performs a similar function to that of banks, except that the finance raised is long term rather than short term.

- By providing large amounts of long-term capital finance for British industry and the government, the stock market fulfils an important role in the economy.

The Stock Exchange's role as a secondary market is by far its most active with daily turnover averaging several billion pounds. The market fulfils the functions of providing a wide range of securities to investors, and enabling existing investors to liquidate cash tied up in stock. This secondary role is useful to the national economy in the following respects:

- The cost of capital finance to industry is reduced.

For example, in the knowledge that they can liquidate their investment, new investors in loan stock accept a lower interest rate than they would require if forced to hold the stock until redemption.

- It encourages the retention of earnings by firms, thereby providing further new capital for industry.

As we shall see, one of the main motives for investment in shares is the hope of capital gain. But if investors were unable to sell their stock, they would be unable to capitalise on a rise in value, and would tend to require maximisation of dividend payments. The capital gain that tends to result from the reinvestment of equity earnings encourages earnings retention, and retained earnings is a much larger source of corporate finance than issuing new stock.

- It encourages optimal allocation of capital resources.

A rising share price is an indication of a company's health and success, and should both facilitate and reduce the cost of raising further loan finance from both bank and market sources.

4 Analysis of Stock-Market Securities

Aims of investment analysis

The essential objective of investment is to maximise returns while minimising risk. However, investments giving high returns will tend to incur high risk, whilst low-risk investments will tend to give relatively low returns. Thus the investor must compromise. Investors with a high level of 'risk aversion' will seek low-risk investments and will be forced to accept a relatively low return, whereas those with less aversion to risk will tend to seek the higher returns available from higher-risk investments.

The basic aim of investment analysis is to assess the value of investments and to compare these with market prices, to enable sensible buy and sell decisions to be made. Investors will tend to buy those investments whose assessed value exceeds the market price by the greatest amount (i.e. those with the highest Net Present Value – NPV), and sell investments with a value less than the market price – negative NPV. The value of an investment depends essentially on its risk and expected return, and thus the principal problems of investment analysis are the estimation of risk and future return.

It is a relatively simple task to put a value on a gold nugget. Analysis would merely involve measuring the weight of the nugget and the purity of the gold. But the analysis of stock market securities, especially ordinary shares, is much more difficult because the two main considerations – risk and future return – are very difficult to assess. The fixed income nature of fixed interest bonds simplifies their analysis to an assessment of risk, but the variability of dividend income from equity shares, and the volatility of corporate profitability on which dividend payments ultimately depend, makes share analysis a complex process.

The objective of investment analysis is not to find the 'best' investment in terms of highest future income and lowest risk, it is to find the investment providing the best *value for money*. An assessment of expected return is of little use until related to the price of the investment. At the time of writing (1992) a share in Glaxo is priced at 679p while shares in British Steel are standing at 60p. The shares in Glaxo are highly priced as they are paying a dividend which is expected to rise steadily in the future. It is a well-managed company in a fashionable growth industry (pharmaceuticals) and has an excellent record of profits growth. On the other hand, British Steel is in a recession-prone industry, has recently reported losses and has halved its dividend. There is no doubt which is currently the more successful company, but it is a lot less obvious which of the shares will provide investors with the higher future return if purchased at their present price. That is the job of the investment analyst.

Analysis of ordinary shares

In the *Financial Times* share information service, the reader can find a number of figures, yields and ratios against each share, but no single unit which purports to measure either risk or future return. This is because the uncertainty of future return and the multifaceted nature of risk make precise calculation impossible, and different analysts would arrive at substantially different figures. The evaluation of risk and return relies ultimately on judgement – but judgement based on a comprehensive range of financial ratios, records and other information, none sufficient in itself but each illustrating a certain aspect of the company, such that an overall assessment can be made.

Detailed share analysis is beyond the scope of this book, but there are a small number of simple ratios which are sufficiently important to investment analysis in general, and whose concepts are so relevant to property analysis that their investigation is required here. In fact, we have already introduced one such ratio – the gearing ratio, an important indicator of both risk and growth potential. The others will be illustrated by Example 4.1.

Example 4.1

Amalgamated Marmalade PLC and Consolidated Jams PLC are trading in an identical industry, serve an identical market, are blessed with identical management skills and, in fact, are identical in virtually all respects except in size and capital structure. Analyse the figures on the opposite page, taken from their recently announced annual results, and explain which company's shares appear the more attractive investment at their current price level.

First, a word or two about these figures. Following from the assumption made about equal performance, both companies would be making equal use of their capital, so in each case trading profit is 20% of capital employed (debt plus equity). Interest is the interest paid to the loan stockholders (e.g., 8% of £10 million is £800 000), and dividends is the proposed total distribution to shareholders for the year, leaving in each case a significant sum to be retained by both companies.

The question is, which shares are the better buy? Given that investors are principally concerned with risk and return, any worthwhile analysis must tell us something about the risks and the return of the two shares. We already know that the gearing ratio affects both risk and potential return so we shall start with that.

	Amalgamated Marmalade	Consolidated Jams
Total assets	£33 million	£13 million
Current liabilities	£3 million	£1.75 million
Debt capital	£10 million	£2.5 million
	8% loan stock 2020	12% loan stock 1998
Equity capital	£10 million:	£5 million:
	40 million × 25p ord. shares	50 million × 10p ord. shares
	£10 million reserves	£3.75 million reserves

	(£)	(£)
Trading profit	6 000 000	2 250 000
Interest paid	800 000	300 000
Pre-tax profit	5 200 000	1 950 000
Corporation tax, say, 35%	1 820 000	682 500
Equity earnings	3 380 000	1 267 500
Dividends (to be paid shortly)	1 500 000	525 000
Retained profit	1 880 000	742 500
Current share price	**98p**	**32p**
Current price of loan stock (£100 nom.)	**£78.00**	**£102.50**

Gearing ratio

As previously defined

$$\text{Capital gearing} = \frac{\text{Debt capital}}{\text{Capital employed}} \times 100$$

Amalgamated Marmalade:

$$£\left(\frac{10\,m}{30\,m}\right) \times 100 = \textbf{33.3\%}$$

Consolidated Jams:

$$£\left(\frac{2.5\,m}{11.25\,m}\right) \times 100 = \textbf{22.2\%}$$

With Amalgamated Marmalade having the higher ratio, its equity capital is at greater risk to a fall in asset values. It might also lead one to expect that its earnings would be the more volatile. In fact, that is not the case because the lower interest rate payable on Amalgamated Marmalade's loan stock as compared with those of Consolidated Jams' compensates for the greater capital gearing of the former company. It is the *income-gearing ratio* which determines the risk and potential return to equity earnings:

$$\text{Income gearing} = \frac{\text{Interest paid}}{\text{Trading profit}} \times 100$$

Amalgamated Marmalade:

$$\frac{800\,000}{6\,000\,000} \times 100 = \textbf{13.3\%}$$

Consolidated Jams

$$\frac{300\,000}{2\,250\,000} \times 100 = \textbf{13.3\%}$$

As with several of the following ratios, it should be appreciated that there is no single 'correct' definition of gearing. In fact, capital gearing is frequently defined as the ratio of debt capital:equity capital, and a more relevant measure of income gearing would include not just interest payments but all priority charges faced by a company, such as rent and rates. When comparing ratios and yields in investment analysis, it is essential to know how the calculation has been made in order to ensure that like is being compared with like. Here we are primarily concerned with the concepts represented by the ratios rather than their calculation.

Price/earnings (P/E) ratio

For purposes of analysis it is simplest to measure earnings on a 'per share' basis, by dividing by the number of ordinary shares issued:

$$\text{Earnings per share} = \frac{\text{Equity earnings}}{\text{No. of shares issued}}$$

Amalgamated Marmalade

$$\frac{3\,380\,000}{40\,000\,000} = \textbf{8.45 p} \text{ per share}$$

Consolidated Jams

$$\frac{1\,267\,500}{50\,000\,000} = \textbf{2.54 p} \text{ per share}$$

It has been pointed out already that the object of share analysis is to identify the share that provides the best value for money. It would be absurd to buy Amalgamated Marmalade's shares simply because their earnings per share is greater, without considering the *price* of the shares. The ratio which relates earnings to price is called, not surprisingly, the 'price/earnings ratio', or simply the 'P/E ratio'. It is the current share price divided by the earnings per share, and is a 'years' purchase' multiple, indicating the relative expense of a share per £1 of equity earnings:

$$\text{Price/earnings ratio} = \frac{\text{Share price}}{\text{Earnings per share}}$$

Amalgamated Marmalade

$$\frac{98}{8.45} = \mathbf{11.60}$$

Consolidated Jams

$$\frac{32}{2.54} = \mathbf{12.60}$$

It is stressed that none of these ratios is a conclusive measure of worth. We see that it costs £12.60 to buy £1 of current equity earnings in Consolidated Jams, whereas it costs only £11.60 to obtain the same current earnings from Amalgamated Marmalade. So shares in Consolidated Jams are, in respect to current earnings, more expensive, but there may or may not be good reasons for this. The P/E ratio is one of the most widely quoted share ratios, but it is simply an indicator of a share's rating in the stock market – it does not reveal whether the rating is justified.

An alternative measure of the relationship between price and earnings is the *earnings yield*, being essentially the reciprocal of the P/E ratio expressed as a percentage return.

Dividend yield

Although earnings is theoretically the return to shareholders after all expenses and prior charges have been met, the inadequacies of traditional accounting techniques in times of inflation have meant that most manufacturing companies have had to plough a large proportion of earnings back into the company in order to replace worn-out machinery and equipment. Profit has been measured after allowing for depreciation of the historic (original) cost of equipment, but the rising cost of replacement has meant that more capital is needed to buy new equipment, and the main source of this is earnings. While retention of earnings is thus traditionally considered as providing for expansion or building up reserves, it has frequently been necessary for a company just to stand still. In such cases, it is obviously misleading to consider earnings as an accurate measure of return to shareholders.

Partly for that reason, and partly because an investor requires information about annual income as a percentage of price, analysis of dividends is also required. Again, dividend payments are reduced to a 'per share' basis:

$$\text{Dividend per share} = \frac{\text{Dividend payment}}{\text{No. of shares issued}}$$

Amalgamated Marmalade

$$\frac{1\,500\,000}{40\,000\,000} = 3.75\,\text{p}$$

Consolidated Jams

$$\frac{525\,000}{50\,000\,000} = 1.05\,\text{p}$$

Again, it would be foolish to select Amalgamated Marmalade's shares just because the dividend per share is higher. It is the amount of dividend received *per £1 spent on buying the shares* that is important. The relationship of share price and dividend is normally quoted as a percentage yield, called the 'dividend yield'.

Before calculating this yield, a brief word about taxation is required. The current system of corporation tax in the UK enables companies to pay out dividends net of standard rate income tax to their shareholders. So shareholders who pay income tax at the standard rate pay no tax on the dividend they receive, but investors subject to higher tax rates will be required to pay extra. Investors exempt from income tax are able to reclaim the tax already paid on their behalf by the company. As dividends are paid net of tax but percentage returns are normally quoted gross, the dividend yield on shares is normally calculated by 'grossing up' the net dividend so that direct yield comparison can be made with fixed interest bonds and other investments:

$$\text{Dividend yield (gross)} = \frac{\text{Net dividend/share}(100/[100 - T])}{\text{Current share price}} \times 100$$

where T = standard rate of income tax.

Assuming the standard rate of income tax to be 25%, the dividend yields for our two companies are:

Amalgamated Marmalade:

$$\frac{3.75(100/[100-25])}{98} \times 100 = \textbf{5.10\%}$$

Consolidated Jams:

$$\frac{1.05(100/[100-25])}{32} \times 100 = \textbf{4.37\%}$$

The dividend yield shows the current gross annual dividend (in £) that an investor is receiving for every £100 worth of shares. Income expressed as a percentage of the current price of an investment is a highly relevant unit of comparison for all income-earning investments, and a significant proportion of this book is devoted to explaining the pattern of income yields existing on different investments.

Just as the price/earnings ratio will vary in response to a change in either the share price or earnings, the dividend yield must vary according to changes in either share price or dividend. But whereas changes in dividends are made relatively infrequently (annually or six monthly), changes in dividend yields occur every time the share price changes. The dividend yield varies *inversely* with a change in price.

It should also be pointed out that both price/earnings ratios and dividend yields are either 'historic' or 'prospective'. If the figures are based on past earnings or dividend payments then they should strictly be described as historic, but (for instance, here) if the dividend has been announced but not yet paid the correct description of the yield calculated above is the 'prospective dividend yield'. Most P/E ratios and dividend yields published in the *Financial Times* and other journals are historic, being based on companies' last accounts or payments.

Dividend cover

A ratio which provides the investor with an indication of both the security of future dividend payments and the potential for increase is the 'dividend cover'. This is calculated by dividing the earnings per share by the dividend per share:

Amalgamated Marmalade

$$\frac{8.45}{3.75} = \textbf{2.25}$$

Consolidated Jams

$$\frac{2.54}{1.05} = \textbf{2.42}$$

Again, the name given to this ratio indicates its function. It is the multiple by which the dividend is covered by the earnings, earnings being the amount actually available for distribution to shareholders. If a company pays out all its earnings in dividends, then the cover is 1. If dividends exceed earnings (by drawing on reserves) then the cover is less than 1, and the dividend is said to be 'uncovered'. The greater the cover, the less is the risk that the dividend would have to be reduced in the future, and the greater is the likelihood of the dividend payment being raised.

Assets per share

Although it is the profit-earning capacity of a company which is normally the dominant factor influencing the market price of its shares, the value of the assets owned by the company is also important. This is particularly so in the case of property companies, investment trusts and companies which may become subject to a takeover bid, or which may liquidate their assets. Thus another useful ratio in share selection is 'net assets per share'. As the name implies, this ratio is the total assets of the company (normally excluding intangibles such as goodwill) minus liabilities, divided by the number of shares issued. It should approximate to the payment each shareholder would receive if the company went out of business, sold off all assets and repaid all debt. As with many of these ratios, precise definitions can vary – e.g., it can make a large difference whether assets are valued after allowing for capital gains tax (CGT) liability, and whether the assets are based on market values or book values (values as shown in company accounts):

$$\text{Net assets/share} = \frac{\text{Total assets} - \text{liabilities}}{\text{No. of shares issued}}$$

Amalgamated Marmalade

$$\frac{£33\,m - £13\,m}{40\,m} = \textbf{50 p}$$

Consolidated Jams

$$\frac{£13\,m - £4.25\,m}{50\,m} = \textbf{17.5 p}$$

A company's share is frequently quoted as being at a 'discount' or 'premium' to net assets. The share price of Amalgamated Marmalade (98p) is at a 96% premium to the net asset value per share (50p), whereas Consolidated Jams' shares (32p) are at an 83% premium to net assets of 17.5p.

Companies whose trading performance has been poor over a long period, but which own substantial property assets, can find that net assets per share substantially exceed share price, particularly after property revaluation. In such circumstances, the company may become subject to a takeover bid from an 'asset stripper' who, by buying a controlling interest (more than 50% of the shares), can then sell off the assets for their full market value. High net asset value can therefore prevent a fall in the share price even if the company's trading performance deteriorates, and can mean sharp gains if the company becomes subject to takeover. In stock-market jargon, the share would be said to have 'low downside risk' but 'high upside potential'.

Equity capitalisation

Now, a brief word about the value of companies. As already stated, the value of a share is largely dependent on the company's ability to earn profit and, except in a situation of takeover or liquidation, the share price will not normally be closely related to the value of the company's assets. The usual measure of the value of a company is its 'equity capitalisation' – that is, the number of shares issued multiplied by their price. The equity capitalisations of our two companies are:

Amalgamated Marmalade:

$$\text{(£)}$$
$$40\,\text{m} \times 98\text{p} = \mathbf{39\,200\,000}$$

Consolidated Jams:

$$\text{(£)}$$
$$50\,\text{m} \times 32\text{p} = \mathbf{16\,000\,000}$$

That is the value that the stock market puts on the companies. It would be wrong to add in the value of the debentures, as these are *liabilities* of the company, and the price of the shares is fixed in the knowledge that these liabilities exist.

Having analysed the relevant figures, let us conclude which of the two companies appears the preferable investment. Consolidated Jams is marginally more attractive on the basis of net assets per share, but this figure is insignificant in this case. The prices of the two shares are determined by earnings potential, not net assets. The capital gearing ratio is also less significant than the income-gearing ratio, and with this being identical for the two companies there is nothing to choose between them on that count. Amalgamated Marmalade, however, has both a more attractive price/earnings ratio and dividend yield. A relatively low price/earnings ratio means that the price of purchasing £1 of current earnings is relatively cheap, and a high dividend yield means that the return in the form of current dividends is relatively high.

Although the dividend cover of Consolidated Jams is marginally superior, Amalgamated Marmalade could have retained the same cover (by paying out only 3.49p per share), and still have provided a superior dividend yield (4.75%). Marginal differences in a firm's dividend policy such as this are not of major significance.

The most significant figures are therefore the price/earnings ratio and dividend yield, and on both these counts Amalgamated Marmalade is marginally superior. There is, however, one further consideration which has not been reflected in any of our ratios and which confirms the superiority of Amalgamated Marmalade. That is the date for redemption of the loan stock. Amalgamated Marmalade has borrowed cheaply on a long-term basis, and it will be well into the next century before it has to start worrying about repayment. Consolidated Jams, on the other hand, must repay its debt in 1998, and although equity reserves more than cover the amount of this debt, these reserves are unlikely to be in liquid form. The likelihood is that the company will have to raise new capital to repay the existing debt in 1998. Consequently, the company is vulnerable to the rising cost of capital – interest rates on new borrowing could be higher than the 12% paid currently. Equally, interest rates could be lower, but the requirement to repay this relatively short-term debt adds an extra element of risk to the company, making it less attractive to an investor in comparison with Amalgamated Marmalade.

Whilst we can confidently select Amalgamated Marmalade as the more attractive of the two investments, the reader should appreciate that the simple analysis undertaken is sufficient only because of the simplistic assumptions made about the similarity of the two companies. In reality, two companies would be bound to differ in an infinite number of respects, and a much more detailed analysis would be required to choose between them. Detailed investigations would also have to be made into the jam-making industry to ensure that it was likely to prove a profitable business, and therefore a suitable area for investment.

Analysis of corporate bonds

The fixed-income characteristic of bonds enables precise measurement of future returns to be made and substantially reduces the problems of analysis. Without the need to consider growth potential, the investor's concern is restricted to the ability of the company to maintain interest payments and repay debt at the redemption date.

In order to illustrate the principal ratios relevant to an analysis of corporate bonds, we shall again use the example of Amalgamated Marmalade and Consolidated Jams. The loan stock of both companies are deemed to be 'unsecured', and the security of the stockholders' income and capital thus depend on the financial status of each company.

Asset cover

The 'asset-cover ratio' indicates the ability of a company to repay debt (on liquidation). It is calculated by deducting prior ranking liabilities of the company (e.g., secured loans and preferential creditors, including rent, wages and unpaid tax) from total assets, and dividing by the debt in question plus any equal ranking liabilities of the company:

$$\text{Asset cover} = \frac{\text{Total assets} - \text{prior liabilities}}{\text{Nominal value of stock} + \text{equal ranking liabilities}}$$

Amalgamated Marmalade:

$$\pounds\left(\frac{33\,\text{m} - 3\,\text{m}}{10\,\text{m}}\right) = \textbf{3.0}$$

Consolidated Jams:

$$\pounds\left(\frac{13\,\text{m} - 1.75\,\text{m}}{2.5\,\text{m}}\right) = \textbf{4.5}$$

These ratios are satisfactory so long as the figure for total assets reflects their market value. Assets are well in excess of the amount needed to repay the debt. But if the value of assets is based on outdated book values, caution is required. Book values of plant, machinery, land and buildings may be substantially above or below their market values.

Interest cover

Whereas asset cover is an indication of the security of the loan capital, the 'interest-cover' ratio is an indication of the security of the stockholder's income. The concept is similar to the concept of dividend cover, a measure of the amount by which annual income available to pay interest covers the interest payable. All trading profits are available to pay the interest in this example:

$$\text{Interest cover} = \frac{\text{Trading profit}}{\text{Interest payments}}$$

Amalgamated Marmalade:

$$\pounds\left(\frac{6\,000\,000}{800\,000}\right) = \textbf{7.5}$$

Consolidated Jams:

$$\pounds\left(\frac{2\,250\,000}{300\,000}\right) = \textbf{7.5}$$

As the reader may have realised, this ratio is simply the inverse of the income-gearing ratio. The figures show that trading profits would have to fall by over 86% to cause the interest to be uncovered, and although that is always possible, the substantial net assets of both companies should enable interest payments to be maintained even if losses were incurred for several years.

Interest yield

The 'interest yield' is similar in concept to the dividend yield, being the percentage relationship of annual income to market price. But whereas with shares we calculate the yield on a 'per share' basis, with loan stock the unit adopted is £100 nominal of the stock:

$$\text{Interest yield} = \frac{\text{Annual interest per £100 nominal}}{\text{Current price per £100 nominal}} \times 100$$

So, taking the market values of the loan stocks originally quoted, the interest yields are:

Amalgamated Marmalade:

$$£\frac{8}{78} \times 100 = \textbf{10.26\%}$$

Consolidated Jams:

$$£\frac{12}{102.50} \times 100 = \textbf{11.71\%}$$

£8 is the annual income per £100 nominal of Amalgamated Marmalade's loan stock, as the stock has an 8% nominal rate of interest.

Redemption yield

The value of any good traded in a market can rise or fall, but whereas the future value of shares is very difficult to predict, the value of dated loan stock must be worth £100 per £100 nominal at the date of redemption, assuming no default on behalf of the borrower. Thus an investor purchasing either of these two bonds at their current market price can anticipate not just income, but also a capital change. At the quoted prices, a purchaser of Amalgamated Marmalade's loan who holds to redemption will gain £22 per £100 nominal, whereas a purchaser of Consolidated Jams' stock will lose £2.50 over a much shorter period.

The yield that takes account of this gain or loss together with the interest received, is called the 'redemption yield', being the investor's total return per annum in income and capital change, on the assumption that the stock is held until redemption. The redemption yield is a true measure of total return, an internal rate of return (IRR), for which there is no simple algebraic formula to enable precise calculation. However, the concept of the redemption yield can be illustrated (but *imprecisely* calculated), as shown below.

We shall assume that the loan stock of Consolidated Jams is to be redeemed on 31 December 1998, and that it is being analysed at a price of £102.50 per £100 nom. on 30 December 1995.

In each year of the investment, the investor will receive the interest, but over the three years he will make a loss of £2.50, that is an average of £0.83 per annum. So:

$$\text{Capital loss per annum} \quad \frac{0.83}{102.50} \times 100 \; = \; -0.81\%$$

Add interest yield	= +11.71%
Approximate redemption yield	**10.90%**

This calculation is inaccurate because an annual loss of 83p is not made, a loss of £2.50 is made after three years, which is not so bad, allowing for the time value of money. So the calculation above underestimates the return, and is shown here for illustrative purposes only. Assuming the interest is paid annually in arrears, the relevant cash flow is:

1995	1996	1997	1998
(£)	(£)	(£)	(£)
−102.50	+12	+12	+112

The IRR on this cash flow (calculated by trial and error or pocket calculator) is 10.98%, so:

Consolidated Jams

Redemption yield = **10.98%**

Similarly:

Amalgamated Marmalade

Redemption yield = **10.52%**

Note that in the case of Amalgamated Marmalade the redemption yield is *above* the interest yield, due to the £22 capital gain receivable in the year 2020.

On the basis of this analysis Consolidated Jams' stock appears the preferable choice as it provides higher interest and redemption yields, and has a superior asset cover. However, there are other considerations affecting the choice which we shall examine in Chapter 5, but even then the evidence is inconclusive and the choice between the two stocks must remain a matter of personal investment preference.

The various ratios introduced in this chapter are essentially units of comparison which indicate relative advantage or disadvantage and help sensible buy and sell decisions to be made. Each has little merit in isolation, but as part of a package of analytical tools each has a part to play. The ratios involving market price (especially the P/E ratio and dividend yield) are indicators of the rating given to the investment by the market, without explaining whether the rating is justified. Thus much more information is required in practice before sensible investment decisions can be made, particularly historic records and future profits predictions.

In introducing these various ratios we have identified the concepts of gearing, the price/earnings (years' purchase) multiple, cover and yield. It is these concepts which it is important to understand, because they are all crucially important to the analysis of property investments.

Treasury bills

Although traded in the short-term money market rather than in the stock market, and although scarcely a close substitute for long-term investments such as equities, gilts and property, Treasury bills play an important part in the investment market, and a brief description is appropriate here.

Whereas gilts are sold by the Bank of England in order to raise finance for the government on a relatively long-term basis, Treasury bills are issued to raise short-term money, usually three months. New issues are sold weekly by tender, to banks and other financial institutions. The issue and repurchase (rediscount) of these securities by the Bank of England is one of the most important ways in which the authorities have controlled short-term interest rates, because the Treasury bill discount rate influences bank lending rates and other short-term rates of interest in the economy.

Treasury bills do not pay out interest as such, but as they are purchased at a discount to their face value, they provide a return to the investor in the form of a capital gain over the life of the security. This return, quoted as a percentage yield, is called the *discount rate*.

Example 4.2

If a three-month Treasury bill with a face value of £10 000 is purchased for £9 750 what is the discount rate?

As the investor will receive the face value of the bill at redemption, his return over the three month period is:

$$\frac{250}{9750} \times 100 = \mathbf{2.5641\%}$$

but as yields are normally quoted on an annual basis, the annualised rate should be calculated. The discount rate on Treasury bills is conventionally annualised on a simple interest basis. In the case of this three month bill, the annual rate is therefore:

$$4 \times 2.5641 = \mathbf{10.26\%} \text{ p.a.}$$

If compounded quarterly, the annualised rate would be:

$$(1 + 0.025641)^4 - 1 = 0.1066 = \mathbf{10.66\%} \text{ p.a.}$$

Investment yields

Of all the units of comparison employed in the evaluation of investments, the yield is the most important. But there is a risk of the reader becoming confused about the various yields that have been introduced so far. In fact, only two broad types of yield have been mentioned:

(a)   income yield, e.g., dividend yield and interest yield,
(b)   internal rate of return (IRR), e.g., the redemption yield and the Treasury bill discount rate (when annualised on a compound interest basis)

While the former is merely the relationship between current annual income and current price, the IRR is a measure of total return taking account of both income (if any) and capital change (if any). In the case of a dated gilt valued at par (£100 per £100 nominal), the IRR (redemption yield) is the same as the current income yield (interest yield), because there is no capital change to redemption. In the case of Treasury bills, the IRR (discount rate) is merely the measure of capital change because there is no separate income, and in the case of a dated gilt valued above or below par, the IRR (redemption yield) is an amalgam of both income and the guaranteed capital change.

While the concept of the IRR is just as important to the share investor as it is to the investor in bonds (in that all investors are concerned with total return, not simply return in the form of income), no equivalent to the redemption yield is normally quoted for shares (or even for undated bonds), because they have an indefinite life, and their future income and price are unknown. The redemption yield on dated gilts can be precisely calculated only because it has a finite life and all future income and capital flows are known.

The reader who is unfamiliar with discounted cash flow (DCF) concepts and techniques is recommended to consult one of the many elementary textbooks on the subject but the principal points to remember about the IRR are:

(a) It is a true measure of total return from an investment, taking into account expenditure, income and capital change.

(b) It is a true return in the sense that it is a return over and above the cost of replacing the capital invested.

(c) If the original capital invested is not replaced, i.e. a loss is made, then the IRR is negative.

On the other hand, the current income yield is no measure of overall profitability. It is merely the percentage relationship between current income and current price, so a change in either income or price must tend to cause a change in the yield. In the short term, dividend yield changes tend to result from changing prices rather than changing dividends. Yields on fixed interest bonds can change only as a result of a change in price, because income is fixed, by definition. When it is said that relatively risky investments tend to give relatively high yields, that does not mean that risky companies strive to pay out higher dividends to shareholders than more secure companies; it means that the market prices of the securities issued by the risky companies are relatively low per £1 of dividend paid.

As illustrated here, these yields are measures of investment returns in money terms, and this is the use to which they are normally put. However, as stressed in Chapter 2, we must not lose sight of real (inflation adjusted) returns, and it is entirely appropriate for an investor to calculate an expected IRR or the historical IRR achieved from his stock after taking account of the anticipated or historical rate of inflation.

5 Gilt-Edged Securities – Prices and Yields

The greater the risk that investors perceive in an investment, the greater the yield that they will require from it. However, being guaranteed by the government, no significant risk is attached to the income and capital repayment on gilts. Yet if one examines the list of conventional fixed interest gilts shown in the *Financial Times*, interest and redemption yields are seen to vary substantially between one stock and another. This chapter investigates the major factors influencing yields on gilts, and identifies certain principles which help to explain yields on investments in general.

Being marketable securities like corporate stock, the price of gilts will vary from their nominal value according to the vagaries of market demand and supply, and being fixed-interest bonds, any change in price *must* bring about an inverse change in yield. At any time, a gilt is likely to have a market value different from its nominal value, consequently an interest yield different from its nominal rate of interest, and a redemption yield different again.

We shall now examine the impact of the redemption date on the price volatility and yield of gilts, commencing with an examination of the relationship between the price of undated gilts and long-term interest rates.

Effect of long-term interest rates on the price of undated bonds

Let us again use a hypothetical case for illustration. 2½% Consols, the oldest gilt still unredeemed, was issued in the nineteenth century, partly 'consolidating' a number of earlier issues. We shall assume that the stock was issued 'at par' (i.e. at a price of £100 per £100 nominal) and that 2.5% was therefore the going rate for such long-term borrowing at that time. The situation at issue per £100 nominal would therefore have been:

Stock	Income p.a. per £100 nom. (£)	Investors' required yield (%)	Market price per £100 nom. (£)
2½% Consols	2.50	2.5	100

The government had major new borrowing needs during and just after the First World War, so we shall assume that a new undated issue was made in 1920 – a time when, due to inflation in the aftermath of war, long-term interest rates had risen to 5%. In order to persuade investors to buy this hypothetical stock – let's call it 5% Treasury – the interest rate would have to be 5%, but with the availability of this stock, no rational investor would be willing to buy the old 2 ½% Consols at par. In fact, investors would be willing to buy 2 ½% Consols only if it provided a yield as good as they could obtain from 5% Treasury. Thus supply and demand imbalance would result in a fall in the market price of 2 ½% Consols to exactly £50 per £100 nominal, at which point its yield would be 5% and investors would be indifferent as between the two stocks.

Year 1920

Stock	Income p.a per £100 nom. (£)	Investors' required yield (%)	Market price per £100 nom. (£)
5% Treasury	5.00	5	100
2 ½% Consols	2.50	5	50

If the price of 2 ½% Consols fell below £50 to give a yield higher than from 5% Treasury then either rising demand would force its value back up to £50 (as investors bought it in preference to 5% Treasury), or falling demand relative to supply would cause a fall in price of 5% Treasury to bring its yield into line.

It is worthwhile specifically to state the following principle:

- If stocks are identical in all respects, except in their nominal rates of interest, then in a competitive market their prices will adjust so that their yields are identical.

Let us now move forward to the middle of 1974, when the government had a massive and expanding PSBR and, due to inflation accelerating apparently beyond control, long-term interest rates had risen to 15%. Again, we shall assume that the authorities sold another undated gilt (although in fact they did not, because they could raise the capital more cheaply by selling shorter dated gilts, and no government would wish to commit itself or its successors to paying such a high rate indefinitely). With long-term interest rates at 15%, the new stock (we shall call it 15% Funding) would have to give a 15% yield, and to enable existing holders of 2 ½% Consols and 5% Treasury to sell their stock, prices would have to fall to a level that would make their yield competitive with 15% Funding as in the table opposite.

The uniformity of yield on similar investments is due to the pricing effi-ciency of the stockmarket. In fact the market in gilts comes as close as any to the concept of the 'perfect' market. About £2 billion worth of gilts are bought and sold every day by a very large number of buyers and sellers, who have knowledge of the benefits, characteristics and prices of the various stock. There is therefore no chance of any individual seller persuading a buyer that his 2 ½% Consols are particularly attractive and actually worth, say, £20 when similar stocks are selling for £16.66.

Year 1974

Stock	Income p.a. per £100 nom. (£)	Investors' required yield (%)	Market price per £100 nom. (£)
15% Funding	15.00	15	100.00
5% Treasury	5.00	15	33.33
2 ½% Consols	2.50	15	16.66

The price changes shown here do not, of course, occur instantaneously on the issue of a new higher yielding stock. The changes take place over time, and occur whether new stock are issued or not. In fact, no new undated stock has been issued since the Second World War, and yet 2 ½% Consols were still yielding 15% in mid-1974. Nor is it the yield paid on a new stock which affects yields on existing stock, it is vice versa. Yields available on existing stock determine the yield which investors require on a new stock, and which the borrower must pay in order to sell the stock. That is one of the functions of the stock market – it shows borrowers the cost of raising new capital.

This illustrates a further principle:

● Although it is normal to say that a change in the price of a marketable investment causes a change in its yield, it is really vice versa. It is a change in investors' required yield that brings about the change in price. That is why a study of the determinants of yield is of such paramount importance to understanding investment prices.

It was the rise in investors' required yield from 2.5% to 15% (primarily due to inflation), that caused the price of 2 ½% Consols to fall from £100 to £16.66. The price change was brought about as a result of supply and demand imbalance. Existing investors felt that they were receiving an inadequate return compared with alternative investments, so increasingly tended to sell their stock, and higher yields were required to induce a sufficient demand to equate with supply.

We shall now advance to late 1982 when, as a result of progress in curbing inflation, interest rates on long-term borrowing had fallen sharply, causing yields on undated gilts to fall to 10%.

Year 1982

Stock	Income p.a per £100 nom. (£)	Investors' required yield (%)	Market price per £100 nom. (£)
15% Funding	15.00	10	150
5% Treasury	5.00	10	50
2 ½% Consols	2.50	10	25

We find that the market prices of the stocks have risen in proportion to the fall in the required yield. This illustrates another principle:

- The price of undated fixed-interest securities varies in inverse proportion to changes in their required yield and the general level of long-term interest rates.

It is not simply that price varies inversely with yield, that is true for all income-earning marketable investments. The point is that with perpetual fixed-income investments, price and yield vary in *inverse proportion*. The doubling of interest rates up to 1920 caused the value of 2½% Consols to fall by a half, the sixfold increase up to 1974 caused their value to fall to one sixth of their original price, and the one third fall in interest yields to 1982 caused a price rise amounting to one third of the resultant price. Despite the fact that income is guaranteed by the government, the market prices of irredeemable gilts are volatile in response to changing interest rates.

Price volatility and the term structure of gilt yields

In comparison with irredeemables, the existence of a redemption date on dated fixed-interest bonds has a stabilising influence on price movements. For example, assume that a hypothetical stock, Exchequer 10%, has one year to elapse before redemption and is priced at £100 per £100 nominal to give a yield of 10%.

In the unlikely event of yields doubling to 20%, rather than the price halving to £50 as would have been the case with an undated gilt, the price would fall only to about £91.70, at which:

$$(\%)$$

$$\text{Interest yield} = 10.9 \qquad \left(\frac{10}{91.7} \times 100\right)$$

$$\text{Approx. capital gain} = 9.1 \qquad \left(\frac{8.3}{91.7} \times 100\right)$$

$$\text{Approx. redemption yield} = \underline{20.0}$$

The price could not possibly fall by 50% because, apart from the 20% interest yield, investors purchasing at that price would also obtain a guaranteed capital gain of 100% over the one year to redemption. Conversely, in the event of market yields halving to 5%, investors would not obtain a 100% capital gain, as would be the case with undated gilts, but something much less.

The proximity of the redemption date therefore influences the price stability of bonds in response to changing market yields. The price of very short-dated stock will tend to be very stable, whereas the price of long-dated stock will be almost as volatile as undated gilts. The longer the period to redemption, the less is the influence of redemption on the stock's price. The reader is recommended to examine the list of gilt-edged securities in the *Financial Times* where, with stocks listed chronologically according to redemption date, the 'pull to redemption' is obvious. That is, shortest gilts have values relatively close to par, but the longer the date to redemption, the greater (generally speaking) is the variation from par value.

On the basis of this analysis, the price stability of short stocks must tend to make them a secure investment, whilst the volatility of long and undated stocks must render them relatively risky. Consequently, short-dated stocks would be expected to give relatively low yields, and medium and longs progressively higher yields, with undated stock yielding the highest of all. That indeed is the traditional 'term-yield structure' of fixed-interest bonds; upward sloping to the right (as at 31 January 1978, Figure 5.1). The variation in yield according to the term to redemption does not reflect liquidity – any of the stocks can be sold in the Stock Exchange within an hour or so on a normal working day, and the proceeds received within days. The yield difference reflects the risk of changing market prices, coupled with the probability that the longer the period to redemption the greater is the likelihood of the investor wishing to sell before redemption. If he is willing to hold to redemption, there is no monetary risk involved, assuming no risk of the government defaulting on its commitments.

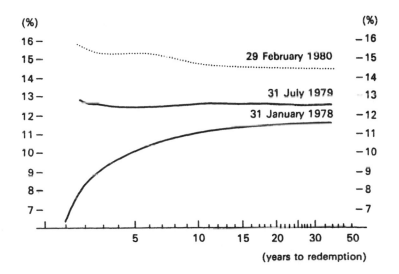

Source: Bank of England Quarterly Bulletin.

Figure 5.1   Term yield curves of British Government Stocks

However, the analysis above is incomplete in a number of respects and during the 1980s the term yield curve was frequently inverted (downward sloping to the right). The conclusion reached above − that market prices of short gilts are more stable than longer-dated stock − implies that yields on short and long stock are equally variable. However, in recent years short term yields have proved more volatile than long-term yields, thereby tending to even out the risk differential between different redemption terms. The volatility of short term yields has resulted from the government's increasing reliance upon manipulation of short term interest rates as a tool of economic management, and the relatively high yields at the 'short end' of the gilts market in the 1980s reflected a requirement to keep interest rates high in order to control demand for goods and services.

Investment yields tend to follow changes in the yields of close substitutes. A very short-dated gilt (say, with six months to redemption) is a close substitute for a Treasury bill. So a rise in the discount rate on Treasury bills (resulting from government action) will tend to cause a rise in the yield on very short gilts, as investors desert the latter for the attractions of bills. The effect of investors selling gilts will cause their price to fall and yield to rise in line with the Treasury bills.

A major influence on yields at the 'long end' of the gilts market is investors' expectations about inflation. Whereas short-term interest rates are largely determined by government intervention, long-term interest rates are largely a function of inflationary expectations. Relatively high yields on long-dated stock up until the late 1970s probably reflected not just the *risk* but the *expectation* of rising inflation and rising interest rates. Relatively low yields on longs during the 1980s reflected the perception that inflation was generally on a declining trend, and that long-term interest rates would eventually follow. Investors were willing to accept relatively low current yields (compared with short gilts) in the expectation that they would make a capital gain when long-term yields fell.

Other reasons for relatively low yields on long-dated gilts are:

(a) demand from life assurance companies and pension funds who look for long-term investments to match their long-term liabilities, and

(b) the lack of supply of new issues which have tended to concentrate on short and medium durations.

Like stock prices in general, the term yield curve is constantly changing. It has traditionally been upward sloping, but may be inverted. Sometimes it is steep (i.e. there is a substantial difference between yields on short and long gilts) and sometimes it is flat. In order to understand these changes one needs to understand the government's market activities and the impact of economic change on risk and return. Changes in price and yield come about only through changes in demand and supply, and whereas the government controls the supply of new gilts, demand will change according to investors' expectations and their perception of risk.

There are a number of salient points in this section worth restating:

- The proximity of the redemption date determines the price stability of a fixed-interest bond in response to any given change in market yields.
- *Ceteris paribus*, the closer the redemption date, the closer the price of a bond to its par value.
- The redemption yields of fixed-interest bonds will tend to vary from each other according to the proximity of redemption.
- The price stability of short-dated gilts relative to longs is one major reason for the traditional upward sloping term yield curve. However, government manipulation of short-term interest rates together with expectations of a decline in inflation can result in an inverted term yield curve.

Impact of taxation on gilt yields

We have already introduced the principle that stock prices will tend to adjust to bring about the yields required by investors, and thus if two stocks are identical in all respects except for their nominal rates of interest, their yields will tend to be identical. If this principle is correct, then why is it that two gilts with similar redemption dates clearly display substantially different redemption yields?

The following two gilts are deemed to have the same redemption date (2004), and to be identical in all respects except for their coupons:

	Price (£)	Interest (%)	Cap. Change (%)	Redemption (%)
Treasury 11 ½% 2001–2004	112.31	10.24	−0.86	9.38
Funding 3 ½% 1999–2004	67.25	5.20	2.51	7.71

Source: *Financial Times*, 1 July 1992.

Why are investors willing to buy Funding 3 ½% to obtain a redemption yield of 7.71% when they could buy Treasury 11 ½% and receive a significantly higher return? Should we not expect high demand for the 11 ½% stock to cause its price to rise and its yield to fall, and the converse to take place for the 3 ½% gilt, until the redemption yields come into line? The answer would be 'yes' – if it was not for the impact of taxation. While most investors are liable to pay income tax on interest received, unlike other investments gilts (and some corporate bonds) are exempt from capital gains taxation. Therefore, for most investors, 1% of capital gain is more valuable than 1% of interest.

The figures above show not only the annual interest and redemption yields guaranteed to an investor buying at the prices quoted, but also the return in the form of capital change (not specifically quoted in the *Financial Times*) which the investor must receive if he holds to redemption (this being the difference between the interest and redemption yields). It can be seen at a glance that whereas the 3½% stock provides investors with a significant amount of (tax free) capital gain, the 11½% stock provides its return in (taxable) interest as well as incurring a capital loss (which cannot be used to offset gains from other investments). This latter stock would subject most investors to a greater tax liability.

Low-coupon stocks give relatively low gross redemption yields because, with their price being relatively low in comparison with higher coupon stock, they provide a relatively large proportion of their return in the form of tax-free capital gain.

If we now deduct income tax at 33% from the interest yield and add the net yield to the return from capital change, we can see that the *net* redemption yields from the two stocks are similar:

	Price (£)	Interest (net) (%)	Capital Change (%)	Redemption (net) (%)
Treasury 11½% 2001–2004	112.31	6.86	−0.86	6.00
Funding 3½% 1999–2004	67.25	3.48	2.51	5.99

Of course, the 33% tax rate was chosen so that the redemption yields would nearly equate; it is impossible otherwise to judge what tax rate is appropriate, as different investors pay income tax at different rates. Many individual investors in gilts pay income tax at 40%, whereas insurance companies pay 33%, and pension funds are exempt.

This helps to illustrate a number of further principles:

- Investors are ultimately concerned about return *net* of tax, and indeed, net of any other expenses incurred.
- Investors are ultimately concerned about the *net total return (IRR)* to be received from an investment, and market price will adjust through the forces of demand and supply to provide a similar net redemption yield for stocks of similar risk.
- The income yield required from an investment is determined by deducting the return expected due to capital change from the total return required from the investment.

Note that although the market in general may be indifferent as between the two stocks at their current prices, individual investors are not. An investor paying a high rate of income tax would select 3½% Funding, whereas an investor paying the standard rate or less would find it more profitable to purchase the 11 1/2% stock. In order to satisfy the demand from investors paying high rates of income tax, the authorities occasionally issue new low coupon stocks at prices well below par.

Other influences on gilt yields

If the only factors affecting the gross redemption yields on gilts were the two so far examined – the period to redemption and the influence of tax-free capital gain – then all undated gilts would have an identical interest yield. They have no guaranteed redemption date, and thus there is no difference between them in risk or capital gain potential. However, a glance at the six undated stocks quoted in the *Financial Times* will show that their interest yields are all different. There are good reasons for these variations, although because of the relatively small amount of such stock in existence and the small number of investors trading in them, it is possible that minor yield and price anomalies sometimes exist.

3 1/2% Conversion is unique in that the authorities are committed to purchase a small proportion of the outstanding stock each year, so long as its average price within a six-month period remains below £90. The impact of this statutory purchase has tended to raise the price (and correspondingly reduce the yield) in comparison with other undated gilts.

Standard rate income tax is normally deducted from interest payments at source, but 3 1/2% War Loan is exceptional in that the interest is paid *gross*. This is advantageous both to nil taxpayers (in that the delay and bother of reclaiming the tax are avoided), and also to higher rate taxpayers (in that, although they will eventually be required to pay the tax, they have the use of the money in the meantime). This advantage must again tend to raise the price (and lower the yield) acceptable to investors in comparison with other stock. Certain dated gilts also pay interest tax free to overseas investors.

The timing and frequency of interest payments are other important factors affecting price and yield. Whereas interest on most gilts is paid in two equal segments each six months, 2 1/2% Consols is unique in that interest is paid quarterly. Furthermore, as the date on which interest is paid varies from one stock to another, the proximity of the next interest payment must vary, again resulting in variations in yield. For administrative reasons, shortly before interest (or dividends for shares) is due to be paid out, a stock is said to go 'ex dividend', indicating that subsequent purchasers will not be paid the forthcoming dividend, it being paid instead to the previous owner. When a stock goes 'ex dividend' excess supply over demand at the original price will tend to cause the price of the stock to fall by approximately the amount of the interest now lost to new buyers. The interest yields quoted for gilts in the *Financial Times* are calculated by deducting that part of the price which reflects the proximity of the next interest payment. On that basis, therefore, the interest yield will be unaffected by the proximity of the next interest payment.

These, then, are some of the principal factors influencing yields on fixed-interest stock, being in general relevant to corporate bonds as well as gilts. A corporate fixed-interest bond will tend to give a higher yield than an equivalent gilt because of the higher risk of default and the marginally higher transfer cost (market-maker's spread and broker's fee).

Index-linked gilts

Conventional gilts are inflation prone. At purchase, the investor 'locks into' a fixed income which cannot change during the life of the stock. Thus the purchasing power of the income (and the redemption value) are absolutely vulnerable to erosion by inflation. By contrast, index-linked gilts are designed to protect the investor from inflation. Their essential feature is that both interest payments and the redemption value are linked to the RPI (Retail Price Index), thereby retaining their purchasing power. If over the life of a stock inflation totals 75%, then the redemption value will be £175 per £100 nominal. Due to this inflation-proofing, coupons and real returns are low, although nominal (money) returns may be as high as, or exceed returns from conventional gilts.

A minor complexity is that interest payments and the redemption value are tied to the RPI eight months before the payment is due. Index linking begins eight months before the stock is issued and ends eight months before redemption. It is for this reason that the real redemption yield varies somewhat according to the rate of inflation over the actual life of the stock, as illustrated in the *Financial Times* share information service.

Due to the regular index-linking of interest and redemption value, market prices should tend to rise in line with inflation. However, as with any marketable investment, prices will vary according to economic change and market sentiment. The investor selling before redemption is not *guaranteed* inflation-proofing (or indeed any positive return) but if he holds in the medium or long term his return should exceed inflation.

Whereas index-linked stocks are likely to outperform conventional gilts in times of high and rising inflation, their relative performance is likely to be reversed in times of falling inflation. That was illustrated by conditions in 1982 when a sharp fall in both inflation and interest rates provided investors in medium- and long-dated conventional gilts with substantial capital gains and total returns in excess of 50%. In order to make a rational selection between conventional or index-linked, short-dated or long-dated, high coupons or low, the investor must not only take into account his own tax liability, income needs and risk aversion, but also take a view on future trends in inflation and interest rates.

As in the case of low-coupon conventional gilts, the high taxpayer is attracted to index-linked stock by the high proportion of the return likely to arise from tax-free capital gain. The investor should calculate the rate of inflation which would be sufficient to provide the same total return (net of tax) that he would receive from a conventional gilt of similar duration, and then make a judgement as to whether that 'break-even' rate of inflation was realistic. If he believed that inflation would exceed the 'break-even' rate he should select the index-linked stock, but if not he would obtain a higher return from the conventional stock.

Index-linked stock are also attractive to long-term investors such as life assurance and pension funds who seek inflation-proof investments to match their liabilities to pension and policy holders. The merits of the stock are obvious. They give an expectation of a positive long-term real return and provide the modern equivalent advantages that 2½% Consols provided to Victorian widows and orphans – a true 'gilt-edged' investment.

6 Ordinary Shares – Prices and Yields

A model of share-price determination

Equity shares differ fundamentally from dated fixed-interest securities, (a) by the ability of the dividend to vary and (b) due to the perpetual (or at least the indefinite) life of shares. Without the stabilising influence of fixed income and a terminal value, share prices must tend to be volatile, particularly as most share prices are closely linked to equity earnings and equity earnings tend to be volatile.

Owing to the greater risk of shares, investors will tend to require a relatively high return. If investors can obtain a guaranteed 10% per annum from investing in gilts, they are unlikely to invest in shares unless they can anticipate a higher total return (IRR), say, 15% per annum. This return will normally derive from both income and capital gain. If shares in Bluechip PLC, for example, are currently priced at 100p, but after one year investors expect a dividend of 5p and a rise in the share price to 110p, then:

$$\text{Investors' expected return} = \frac{5 + 10}{100}$$

$$= 0.15 \text{ or } \mathbf{15\%}$$

In calculating this return we have, in fact, solved the formula:

$$r = \frac{D_1 + (P_1 - P_0)}{P_0}$$

where r = expected return (IRR), D_1 = expected dividend in year 1, P_0 = current price and P_1 = expected price in one year.

However, in Chapter 5 we concluded that, rather than yields being determined by changing prices, stock prices are determined by investors' required yields. So if we know (or can estimate) investors' required return and the dividend and price in one year, then we can calculate the current share price. Using the figures above, and assuming that 15% represents investors' required IRR, then the price can be calculated:

$$P_0 = \frac{D_1 + P_1}{1 + r} \tag{6.1}$$

$$= \frac{5 + 110}{1 + 0.15}$$

$$= 100\,\text{p}$$

where $r =$ investors' required return (IRR).

Now, if Equation (6.1) is valid for determining the current share price, then the price in one year must be dependent on the expected share price and dividend in Year 2:

$$P_1 = \frac{D_2 + P_2}{1 + r}$$

By substituting $\dfrac{D_2 + P_2}{1 + r}$ for P_1 in Equation (6.1)

we can express the current share price in terms of the expected dividend in Years 1 and 2, and the expected price in two years:

$$P_0 = \frac{D_1 + \left(\dfrac{D_2 + P_2}{1 + r}\right)}{1 + r}$$

This reduces to:

$$P_0 = \frac{D_1}{1 + r} + \frac{D_2 + P_2}{(1 + r)^2} \tag{6.2}$$

So the current price of a share can be explained by reference to investors' expected dividends in the next two years, the expected share price in two years, and investors' required IRR. But again the price in Year 2 must reflect dividend and share price expectations in Year 3, and the price in Year 3 reflect expectations in Year 4, and so on. In fact, if we extend our pricing formula into perpetuity, future price expectations drop out entirely:

$$P_0 = \frac{D_1}{1 + r} + \frac{D_2}{(1 + r)^2} + \frac{D_3}{(1 + r)^3} + \dots \tag{6.3}$$

or,

$$P_0 = \sum_{t=1}^{\infty} \frac{D_t}{(1 + r)^t}$$

This expression states that a share's price is the present (discounted) value of expected future dividends. Consequently a share's price depends essentially on two major variables – expected future dividends and investors' required return (IRR).

This equation is a basic model which can be used by investment analysts to assess the intrinsic value of a share which, when compared with the market price, enables sensible buy and sell decisions to be made. However, due to the difficulty of estimating dividend payments beyond a relatively limited period, an estimate of the price at the end of this period would be made and incorporated into the pricing model, as shown after two years in Equation (6.2). Other refinements include the discounting of estimated future equity earnings rather than dividends, and the use of varying discount rates to reflect variation in the risk between one year's dividend and another.

The model applied to other investments

This model can be used as a basis for understanding market prices and for valuation. The principle, illustrated here in the context of ordinary shares, is applicable to all income-earning investments, particularly shares, gilts and property, and can be restated:

$$P_0 \text{ (or } V_0) = \frac{C_1}{(1+r)} + \frac{C_2}{(1+r)^2} + \frac{C_3}{(1+r)^3} + \dots \qquad (6.4)$$

where P_0 = current price of investment, V_0 = present value of investment, $C_{1,2,3}$ = expected cash flow in periods 1, 2, 3 and r = investors' required return (or target IRR).

This mathematical statement is a simple but extremely useful model of investment asset pricing or valuation, having an infinite number of uses in explaining investment prices, yields and other concepts. However innumerate the reader considers himself or herself to be, it is essential that the meaning of the expression is understood, as we shall be returning to it again and again throughout this book.

Expressed in words, the statement says that the price (or value) of an investment is the sum of future expected income flows, discounted over the period to elapse before each cash flow is received. More succinctly, the price (or value) of an income-earning investment is the present value of expected future income flows. Or again;

● The price (or value) of an income earning investment is a function of time, investors' income expectation and their required return.

A key word to remember here, particularly when relating this principle to shares or property, is the word 'expected'. Future returns from equity investments, whether in the form of periodic income or capital receipts, are uncertain and thus equity asset prices are based on expectations which may or may not be fulfilled. In fact, we could go further than this and say that virtually the only certainty in equity investment is that the expected return will not be received – it will inevitably be higher or lower than expected. So rather than saying that an investor *requires* a return of, say, 15% – which seems to imply certainty – it is more appropriate to say that he *requires an expectation* of 15%; more succinctly, his 'target' return is 15%.

This target IRR is the opportunity cost of the capital to be invested – in other words, the rate of return expected from an alternative investment of similar risk. It can be considered as having two components, viz., the rate of return currently available from riskless investments, plus a premium to reward the investor for putting capital at risk. Although (as we saw in Chapter 5) a long-dated gilt is not strictly a riskless investment, it is a lot less risky (in money terms) than the average ordinary share. It thus seems reasonable to suggest that the target IRR appropriate to an equity share might be the current redemption yield on long-dated gilts – say, 10% plus, say, 5% to cover risk – to make the 15% suggested at the start of this chapter. This is merely an indication of how the target IRR might be estimated (the subject is developed further in Chapter 8), because it is impossible to know for certain what total return an investor will require from an equity investment. In fact, many investors will not have a clear figure in mind themselves.

The model with constant growth assumptions

If constant dividend growth is assumed into perpetuity, Equation (6.3) can be restated as follows:

$$P_0 = \frac{D_1}{1+r} + \frac{D_1(1+g)}{(1+r)^2} + \frac{D_1(1+g)^2}{(1+r)^3} + \cdots \qquad (6.5)$$

where g = expected annual dividend growth rate.

However (provided r is greater than g), this series reduces to:

$$P_0 = \frac{D_1}{r-g} \qquad (6.6)$$

which states that share prices are a function of the *prospective dividend, investors' dividend growth expectation* and their *target IRR*.

But D_1/P_0 is the (prospective) dividend yield (d), so

$$d = r - g \qquad (6.7)$$

That is, a share's dividend yield is investors' target IRR *less* their expected dividend growth rate.

That is very similar to a conclusion reached in Chapter 5, which explained the determination of interest yields on dated gilts. Income yields are determined by investors' target returns, less returns expected from growth (positive or negative).

If we now substitute d for $r - g$ in Equation (6.6), we get:

$$P_0 = \frac{D_1}{d} \qquad\qquad (6.8)$$

which states that share prices are a function of their current dividend and dividend yield (a fact which follows from the definition of dividend yield itself). In other words;

- The price of a share is a multiple of its current dividend, the multiple being the reciprocal of investors' required dividend yield.

For example, the reciprocal of 5% is 20. So the price of a share paying a dividend of 10p and having a dividend yield of 5% must be 200p.

A share's price can therefore be regarded as being determined either by the current dividend and investors' *required* dividend yield (Equation (6.8)), or by future dividend expectations and investors' target IRR (Equations (6.3) or (6.5)). However, as investors' required dividend yield depends on their target IRR and future growth expectations, the essential pricing concept is the same.

Equations (6.6) and (6.7) are very useful abbreviations of our basic DCF pricing model (Equation (6.3)). It is unimportant that dividend growth will not be constant in the future, g should be considered as the (discounted) average expected growth rate which inevitably would be missed in some years but exceeded in others. Of course a totally different growth rate may be achieved in practice (or perhaps no growth at all), but what ultimately occurs is irrelevant to current prices; investment prices are based on *expectations* for the future, not on outcomes.

Note also that g is theoretically a growth expectation into perpetuity. Although it is virtually impossible to predict growth for more than a few years ahead, it is the growth expectation for the early years which is of dominant importance to investment pricing.

Let us now look at Examples 6.1 and 6.2, which illustrate and develop the principles introduced so far.

Example 6.1

Investment analysts investigating the ordinary shares of John Appleseed PLC are forecasting dividend payments over the next four years of 10p, 11p, 13p and 15p, and they predict a dividend growth rate of 10% p.a thereafter. Assuming a target IRR of 15%:

(a)   calculate the current value of the shares and

(b)   advise investors of the appropriate action to take in the knowledge that the current market price is 200p

We can predict the value of the shares at the end of Year 4 on the basis of the predicted dividend, growth rate, and the target IRR. So we shall assume that the shares are sold at that date, and calculate the current value by solving the following equation (based on Equation (6.2)).

$$V_0 = \frac{D_1}{1+r} + \frac{D_2}{(1+r)^2} + \frac{D_3}{(1+r)^3} + \frac{D_4 + V_4}{(1+r)^4}$$

First, we must calculate the expected value in Year 4:

$$V_4 = \frac{D_5}{r-g} \quad \text{(adapted from Equation (6.6))}$$

The expected dividend in Year 5 is

$$15\,p + 1.5\,p = \mathbf{16.5\,p}$$

So expected value in Year 4:

$$V_4 = \frac{16.5}{0.15 - 0.10} = \mathbf{330\,p}$$

and the current value:

$$V_0 = \frac{10}{1+0.15} + \frac{11}{(1+0.15)^2} + \frac{13}{(1+0.15)^3} + \frac{15+330}{(1+0.15)^4}$$
$$= 222.8, \text{ say } \mathbf{223p}$$

With the estimated value significantly exceeding current price (the NPV is 23p), a purchase would seem appropriate. Existing investors should be advised to hold, or perhaps buy more shares in Appleseed. However, shares in other companies with similar qualities and characteristics should also be analysed in case these provide an even higher NPV than Appleseed.

An alternative approach is to calculate the *expected IRR* to be received if the share is purchased at the current market price. This return is then compared with investors' *target IRR*, to enable sensible buy and sell decisions to be made.

The expected IRR is calculated by solving for *r* in the following equation:

$$P_0 = \frac{D_1}{1+r} + \frac{D_2}{(1+r)^2} + \frac{D_3}{(1+r)^3} + \frac{D_4 + V_4}{(1+r)^4}$$

$$200 = \frac{10}{1+r} + \frac{11}{(1+r)^2} + \frac{13}{(1+r)^3} + \frac{15 + 330}{(1+r)^4}$$

$r = 18.35\%$ (by calculator, or trial and error)

As this *expected return* significantly exceeds the *target return* (15%), investors would be advised to purchase the shares.

Note:

1. The discount rate used to calculate the present value of the investment can vary from year to year according to differences in risk. If it was considered that the income and capital value of the share in Year 4 was riskier than the dividend income in earlier years, it would be discounted at a higher rate. If a target rate of 19% is used, the value of the shares falls to 197.6p which, being lower than the current price, would indicate a sell recommendation.
2. In Example 6.1, recommendations are being made to investors in general. If the calculations were being made from the point of view of an individual investor, the dividend income and sale price should be adjusted to allow for his or her personal tax liability, and the discount rate should be the investor's net of tax target return.

Example 6.2

Two companies, United Shoes PLC and Associated Footwear PLC, are involved in an identical business activity and are identical in all respects except size and capital structure. United Shoes is ungeared while Associated Footwear has a 50% income-gearing ratio. Explain which of the company's shares would tend to give the lower dividend yield:

(a) when trading profit is expected to rise in the foreseeable future;
(b) when no profit growth is anticipated.

Say investors in United Shoes have a target IRR of 15%. Then, due to the greater risk of a geared company, the target IRR for Associated Footwear will tend to be higher, say 17%.

(a) Rising profit expected

Say trading profit is expected to rise by 5% per annum indefinitely, then United Shoes's equity earnings and dividends are also likely to rise by 5%. However, the 50% gearing of Associated Footwear will tend to result in a rate of earnings and dividend growth double that of profit growth, i.e. 10% per annum (so long as the 50% gearing continues) .

On the basis of these assumptions, we can use Equation (6.7) to calculate investors' required dividend yield on the two shares:

$$d = r - g$$

United Shoes:

$$d = 0.15 - 0.05 = 0.10 \text{ or } \mathbf{10\%}$$

Associated Footwear:

$$d = 0.17 - 0.10 = 0.07 \text{ or } \mathbf{7\%}$$

In times of rising profit, the superior growth expectation of the geared company will tend to cause its yield to fall below that of the ungeared company, despite the greater risk. Note again that the dividend yield is the *relationship* of dividend to share price. It is not a question of Associated Footwear paying out a lower dividend than United Shoes in times of rising profit, quite the opposite. Associated Footwear's dividend will tend to rise relative to that of United Shoes, but its share price will tend to be a higher multiple of the current dividend, resulting in a lower dividend yield.

(b) No profit growth expected

$$d = r - g$$

United Shoes:

$$d = 0.15 - 0 = 0.15 \text{ or } \mathbf{15\%}$$

Associated Footwear:

$$d = 0.17 - 0 = 0.17 \text{ or } \mathbf{17\%}$$

If no profit growth is anticipated, then no dividend or capital growth is likely, so the investors' total return can be derived only from the dividend yield. The gearing of Associated Footwear now confers no earnings advantage, but owing to greater risk, its target IRR and consequently (in the context of no growth) its dividend yield, will tend to be the higher.

Dividend yield and price volatility

The following points may help to summarise this discussion of dividend yields:

- A share's dividend yield is a function of investors' target return and growth expectation ($d = r - g$).
- Differences in the target return as between one share and another result principally from differences in risk.
- A share's dividend yield depends principally on *risk and growth expectation*.
- At any given level of growth expectation, the higher the risk *perceived* by investors, the higher will be both the target IRR and the dividend yield.
- At any given level of risk, the greater is investors' *growth expectation*, the lower will be the dividend yield required by investors.

Similarly, income yields on gilts and property are principally determined by risk and growth expectations.

This analysis of dividend yields partly explains the relative volatility of share prices in response to changing economic conditions, and the large price falls that can take place when previously successful growth stocks are unable to maintain a high rate of expansion ('ex growth' in stock-market jargon). In Example 6.2, the share price of Associated Footwear would tend to fall by just under 60% if the profit growth expectation in (a) was replaced by the no growth expectation in (b). Assuming no change in investors' target IRR, the dividend yield would have to rise from the original 7% to the new 17%. As the dividend is fixed in the short run, this rise in yield can come about only by a fall in the share price. Conversely, an increase in growth expectation can cause a sharp fall in the dividend yield required by investors and consequently a substantial rise in price.

Relationship of capital growth to income growth

Although many individual investors and speculators buy shares with capital gain as the main incentive, the dominant investors in the stock market – the insurance companies and pension funds – are more concerned with long-term income growth. In fact, except when investors' growth expectations change, capital and income growth tend to move in parallel. Given stable dividend-growth expectations in a stable market, dividend growth tends to be transmitted into capital growth.

Example 6.3

Beanstalk Enterprises PLC recently announced a dividend per share of 10p. The shares are priced at £2. Dividend growth of 10% per annum is forecast into the foreseeable future. If this dividend growth is achieved, what capital growth is likely over the coming year?

With a current dividend yield of 5% and dividend growth of 10% anticipated, a target IRR of 15% is implied. If in Year 1 a 10% increase in the dividend is paid out as anticipated, and the growth expectation of 10% and target IRR of 15% are unchanged, then the required dividend yield of 5% will also be unchanged. However, for the dividend yield to be 5% when the dividend payment is 11p, the capital value of the share must also have risen by 10%, to £2.20. Demand/supply imbalance at the former price will cause the price to rise so that the required dividend yield of 5% is maintained. When the dividend rises to 12.1p per share in Year 2 then, again assuming unchanged expectations and a stable market, the share price will tend to rise, to £2.42. As long as the dividend yield remains at 5%, any dividend growth achieved must be transmitted into capital gain, as the share price must remain a multiple of 20 times the dividend:

	Year			
	0	*1*	*2*	*3*
Dividend per share	10.0	11.0	12.1	13.3
Required dividend yield	5%	5%	5%	5%
∴ **Share price**	**200p**	**220p**	**242p**	**266p**

Such stability in the target IRR and dividend growth expectation would be unusual, due to changing yields on other investments and fluctuating economic conditions. But taking a medium- or long-term view, capital growth tends to move in line with income growth.

Summary

In this chapter, we have introduced two comprehensive but delightfully simple concepts of investment pricing — first that an investment's price is the discounted value of expected future income flows, and second that price is a multiple of current income, the multiple being the reciprocal of investors' required income yield.

Essentially the same concepts explain the pricing of gilts and property investments. The DCF concept is particularly useful in explaining certain price and yield phenomena introduced in Chapter 5, e.g., the 'pull to redemption' and the term structure of gilt yields. The two pricing models are also the bases of the two principal methods used for valuing property investments, namely the DCF and years purchase (YP) methods.

These pricing models do not mean that supply and demand theory is redundant, nor do the theories conflict. On the contrary, the pricing models help to explain changes in the supply and demand flows. Investors buy and sell according to income expectations and required returns, and the resultant supply and demand flows fix price.

For the sake of simplicity, such complications as taxation and the expense of buying and selling stock have been ignored in this chapter, but the importance of these should not be forgotten. Most investors in shares pay a lower rate of tax on capital gain than on income, therefore, as in the case of gilts, return in the form of capital gain is more valuable than income. With individual investors taking account of their personal taxation liability in their buy and sell decisions, such tax considerations will be reflected in market prices set by the resultant demand and supply flows. This was illustrated in the case of the low coupon gilt examined in Chapter 5.

7 The Investment Yield Spectrum

Yield relationship between gilts and equities

Traditionally, average dividend yields on ordinary shares were higher than yields on gilt-edged securities. This 'yield gap' – measured as the difference between the interest yield on 2 ½% Consols and the dividend yield on 'blue chip' ordinary shares – averaged around 1.5%, and could be explained and justified by the relative security of the two investment types. In the inter-war depression (a period when profit was hard to earn and bankruptcies frequent), the guaranteed interest payment on gilts was particularly valuable, especially as deflationary conditions between 1920 and 1935 caused the purchasing power of the fixed income to rise.

In the post-war period, however, while the average dividend yield on 'blue chip' equity shares has generally remained within a relatively narrow band of 4–6%, yields on gilts rose substantially. So virtually ever since 1959 there has been a 'reverse yield gap', i.e. yields on gilts have been significantly higher than dividend yields on 'blue chip' equities (see Table 7.1 and Figure 7.1).

Table 7.1   Reverse yield gap

	1 January		
	1930	1965	1992
Interest yield, 2 ½% Consols	4.7	6.3	9.9
Dividend yield, 'blue chip' equities	6.1	5.2	5.0
(Yield gap) or reverse yield gap	(1.4)	1.1	4.9

Sources: Barclays de Zoete Wedd; *Financial Times.*

The reverse yield gap is essentially a phenomenon of inflationary conditions. Whereas the inter-war deflationary period provided investors in fixed interest stocks with an income which was rising in real terms, the post-war inflationary trend has drastically eroded the purchasing power of fixed income. This, together with the upward trend in interest rates associated with rising inflation, caused a relentless rise in gilt yields, culminating at 1 January 1975 in a yield peak of over 17% for 2 ½% Consols when it seemed that the government of the day had abrogated its responsibilities to curb inflation. With the capital value of undated gilts varying in inverse proportion to changing yield, a yield of 17% implies a value of a mere £14.70, and despite a subsequent recovery the price of 2½% Consols in *real terms* is now less than 1.5% of its price in 1947 (the last date at which the stock stood at par value). That is what inflation has done to a government-guaranteed stock, once considered as the most secure and reliable investment available and an investment *sine qua non* for widows and orphans.

On the other hand, post-war inflation has generally enabled companies to achieve profits growth, leading to dividend growth and higher share prices. Although investors' target returns rose along with the rising yields available on gilts, higher growth rates made the relatively low dividend yields acceptable. In fact, insofar as dividends and share prices kept pace with inflation, dividend yields provided a return to investors over and above the rate of inflation.

UK GROSS REDEMPTION YIELD ON 20 YEAR GILTS
FTA ALL SHARE – DIVIDEND YIELD

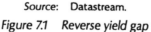

Source: Datastream.

Figure 7.1   Reverse yield gap

In terms of total returns, the large capital gains made by shares has resulted in equities massively outperforming gilts in the post-war period, despite relatively low dividend yields. On the other hand, the huge capital losses suffered by undated gilts meant that their annual returns were frequently negative.

An understanding of the reasons for the advent of the reverse yield gap is a useful test of the reader's understanding of some of the main principles developed so far in this section; it can justify a restatement and summary.

The 'yield gap' prevailed prior to 1959, because:

- Gilts were a secure investment offering a secure income, the purchasing power of which was stable or rising.
- Equity shares were a less secure investment, through the risk of dividend cuts, share price falls and even bankruptcy.
- Due to their greater risk, target returns from equities exceeded gilt yields, and any growth expectation from shares was insufficient to compensate, resulting in the yield gap.

The 'reverse yield gap' emerged in the post-war inflationary context, because:

- With the purchasing power of fixed income being eroded by inflation, investors required higher yields from gilts to compensate, and with rising yields causing falling prices, the risk of gilts increased thereby reinforcing the trend to higher yields.
- On the other hand, the mildly inflationary conditions of the 1950s and 1960s reduced the risk of corporate failure and increased the growth of shares.
- Although the target return from shares would have risen along with rising yields on gilts, this was compensated by rising growth expectations thereby keeping dividend yields relatively stable and low.

The demand for equity investments in the 1950s and 1960s was also increased by the growth of contractual savings through insurance companies and pension funds. The switch to equities was further boosted by the Trustee Investments Act 1961, which allowed extensive investment in equities for certain trusts previously debarred from such investments.

A somewhat different perspective of the 'reverse yield gap' is provided by Example 7.1.

Example 7.1

Say we have two investments A and B which are expected to earn the following annual cash flows:

Investment	Year				
	1	2	3	4	5
	(£)	(£)	(£)	(£)	(£)
A	10.0	10.0	10.0	10.0	10.0 to perpetuity
B	10.0	11.0	12.1	13.3	14.6 + 10% annual growth to perpetuity

If we assume initially that the risk difference between the two investments is negligible, then investors would clearly be willing to pay more for investment B than for investment A. In fact, if A is priced at £100, then B might be priced at £200.

Thus:

Current (prospective) income yield (%)

A   = 10% p.a. $\left(\dfrac{10}{100} \times 100 \right)$

B   = 5% p.a. $\left(\dfrac{10}{200} \times 100 \right)$

Yield difference = 5% p.a.

Whereas A is a perpetual fixed-income investment like an undated gilt, B is a growth investment, like an equity share in times of inflation. Thus, the yield difference is illustrative of the reverse yield gap.

Note that the IRR earned from each investment, if held in perpetuity, would be:

A   10% p.a. (interest yield only, no growth)
B   15% p.a. (5% dividend yield + 10% growth)

Investors have bid up the price of B, accepting a low initial yield in anticipation of growth, and if this growth is achieved they will receive a total return 5% higher than A. Although we started out by assuming similar risk, if A is an undated gilt and B is a share, the risk to B would be considered greater. The extra 5% represents the extra return required by investors to compensate them for this risk. Intuitively, in fixing a market price of £200 for B, investors have applied the formula:

$$d = r - g$$

Investors' target return is 15%, their growth expectation is 10%, so their required dividend yield is 5%. Given an initial income of £10, the price must be £200.

The above example emphasises the following points:

● An investment's income yield is the *relationship* of income to price. A low yield does not mean low income, it means high price relative to current income. A high yield does not mean high income, it means low price relative to current income.
● The total return (IRR) *achieved* from any investment is essentially composed of the initial income yield and growth (which may be positive, negative or nil).

- Investors' *target* return on any (risky) investment is *determined* by the return available on less risky investments plus an extra return to compensate for the extra risk (called the yield premium or risk premium).
- It is important to distinguish between the *target* return and the return ultimately *achieved* from an investment.

Other financial securities

So far we have examined ordinary shares, corporate bonds and gilt-edged securities, emphasising the fundamentally different characteristics of the two principal categories of stock – the fixed interest and the equity. However, there are a number of other financial securities which are also worthy of mention.

Preference shares

As with ordinary shares, the holder of preference shares owns part of the company, but unlike equities these securities are essentially fixed-interest investments. The name indicates that preference is given to holders of this stock over ordinary shareholders in the distribution of dividends and in the repayment of capital in the event of liquidation. Payments due on preferred capital must be met before any payment can be made to ordinary shareholders. In that respect, preference shares are similar to loan stock, but whereas interest and debt repayments are legal obligations on a company whatever its financial plight might be, dividend payments to preference shareholders are not. Thus in the hierarchy of payout, debt ranks first, preference capital second and equity capital last.

Most preference shares are 'cumulative', in that if a company has insufficient resources to pay the dividend one year, then the right to receive that dividend continues to the next year or indefinitely into the future, being payable before any dividend can be paid to ordinary shareholders.

Despite their relative security, the fixed-income characteristic of preference shares has made them unpopular with investors in times of inflation. They have also become unpopular with companies because, unlike interest on debt, dividends are paid out of profits on which corporation tax is assessed. It is therefore relatively expensive for a company to raise capital by the issue of preference shares and few such issues are now made. Being a fixed-interest liability, account should be taken of preference capital in calculating the effective gearing of a company's equity.

Participating preference shares

Some preference shares, as well as providing a fixed income, enable the investor to participate in the residual profit along with ordinary shareholders.

Whereas up till now all stocks introduced have been either interest bearing or equity type, 'participating preference shares' are part fixed interest and part equity. Where the fixed-income element is relatively large and the profit participation small, the stock would be nearly a fixed-income investment, but where the potential participation is relatively large these securities would be considered (and treated by investors) as being close to an equity. Such a stock which is neither purely interest bearing nor equity is termed a 'quasi-equity'. Participating preference shares are rare, and a more common member of this category is convertibles.

Convertible stock

Convertibles are hybrids, combining the security of fixed-interest stock with the growth potential of equities. As with a normal debenture, loan stock or preference share, a fixed payment is made, but the holder also has an option to convert his stock into a specified number of ordinary shares at a certain future date (or between certain future dates). If the option is not exercised before the final conversion date, then the stock reverts to being a normal fixed-interest stock. If the option is exercised, then the holder will receive a certain number of equity shares instead of the convertibles.

These stocks are a compromise. They are less risky than ordinary shares because of the secure interest payment which limits their potential fall in value, but if conversion seems likely to prove profitable, their price will tend to rise to reflect changes in the price of the company's equity.

Example 7.2

In 1990, Bagsoff Potential PLC issued 9% Convertible Debentures, which provided the option to convert every £100 nominal into 200 ordinary shares of the company in 1995. Explain the likely price and yield of the convertibles in 1993, if:

(a)   the company performs disappointingly and the share price in 1995 is thought unlikely to exceed 25p;

(b)   good profit growth is achieved and the share price in 1995 is expected to reach about 75p.

(a)   If profitable conversion is not anticipated, the stock would tend to be valued by the market as if it was, more or less, a normal debenture. If yields available on comparable unconvertible stock were 11% then, the price would not fall below £81.87, i.e. the price necessary to give a 11% yield to purchasers (on the simplifying assumption that the stock is irredeemable).

If the stock was to be converted in 1995 at a price of 25p then the value of the holding would be only £50, so clearly the investor would allow the option to lapse.

Without the prospect of profitable conversion, the price of the stock in 1993 would tend towards £81.87, yet rather above it, reflecting the hope that in the next two years profits might improve and conversion become profitable.

(b) If the share price in 1995 is 75p, then at that date the value of the convertibles must be very close to £150 and (assuming no substantial rise in the price of unconvertible stock) a major loss would be incurred if the option was allowed to lapse. The value of the stock in 1993 must therefore reflect their expected conversion value in 1995, and can be calculated as follows:

$$V_{1993} = \frac{C_{1994}}{1 + r} + \frac{C_{1995}}{(1 + r)^2}$$

$$= \frac{9}{1 + 0.11} + \left(\frac{9}{(1 + 0.11)^2} + \frac{150}{(1 + 0.15)^2} \right)$$

$$= £128.83$$

Note that a target IRR of 11% has been used here to value the relatively secure guaranteed fixed income, whereas a higher rate is used for discounting the relatively risky value of the conversion rights in 1995.

At this price the income yield is:

$$\frac{9}{128.83} \times 100 = 7.0\%$$

So if profitable conversion is expected, then the price of the convertibles will reflect the expected share price at conversion. But the best indication of the share price at the date for conversion is provided by the current share price, so the prices of the convertibles and the shares will tend to rise and fall in unison.

In fact, the value of convertibles will tend to be somewhat higher than the value of the shares into which they are to be converted. If the value of the convertibles in 1993 is £128.83, that implies a share price at that date somewhat less than 64p. This *premium* on the convertibles is due to their greater security in the event of a profit setback and the probability that their income is higher than that from the shares. Normally an option to convert extends over a number of years, and the date at which investors choose to convert tends to depend on the income receivable from the convertibles vis-à-vis the shares. Initially convertibles tend to pay the higher income, but if the company achieves good profit growth, then dividends may overtake the fixed interest and conversion may then be advisable.

We have seen that, depending on expectations for the future share price, convertibles may be valued in the market as being close to a fixed-interest stock or close to an equity. It can also be seen that the price of the convertibles will depend on the date for conversion. If conversion is likely to be profitable but the conversion date is many years ahead, then our pricing model explains that the convertible's price will reflect more of the fixed income and relatively less of·the distant equity than is the case in Example 7.2. So, depending on the share price and the conversion date, a convertible may be priced in the market as if it was virtually a fixed-interest stock or virtually an equity (or indeed, anywhere in between). Consequently, the convertible's income yield will reflect the proportion of the fixed-income and equity elements in the investment. In Example 7.2 the yield was 11% when the stock was priced as a fixed-interest investment, but relatively low (at 7%) when the price reflected a substantial equity content.

Thus rather than there being two distinct categories of stock – fixed-interest securities and equities, the former with high income yields and the latter with relatively low yields – we have a *spectrum*. Pure fixed-income investments are at one end of the spectrum, pure equities at the other, and in between are a variety of investments having an element of both fixed income and equity. Quasi-equity investments which are nearly fixed income will tend to have high-income yields, and those which are close to being equities will tend to have relatively low yields. This view of investments as being somewhere between the pure fixed income and pure equity is particularly relevant to property.

In times of inflation, it is this element of fixed-income/equity (in other words, the growth potential) which is the most important factor dictating an investment's income yield. Of course, risk is also relevant, but the importance of growth is illustrated by relative yields on conventional and index-linked gilts. Essentially there is one reason for this yield differential – growth expectation in times of inflation.

Let us now summarise the principal factors which determine differences in the income yields provided by marketable securities.

Factors affecting income yields

Risk

Our concept of risk must include both risk to income and risk to capital. Up to a point, the two tend to go hand in hand – any factor affecting income will tend to affect the price of a stock. However, all stock prices are vulnerable to other factors such as changing interest rates in the economy and stock-market trends in general, and thus income security does not guarantee capital security, especially in the case of undated fixed-interest stock.

Note that it is 'perceived' risk that affects yield. If investors are unaware of risk incurred in an investment, such risk will not be reflected in its yield.

Liquidity

The liquidity of an investment is essentially the *time* that it takes to realise the cash tied up in the investment. Investors have a preference for liquidity; *ceteris paribus*, they will choose the investment which enables them to recover their capital as quickly as possible when the need arises.

The impact of liquidity is demonstrated by the varying yields offered by building societies on deposits. Virtually the only factor causing the yield variations on such investments is the extra return which has to be offered to overcome depositors' liquidity preference.

Shares all have equal liquidity. Depending on which day of the account a stock is sold, the seller should receive his cheque within two to four weeks.

Marketability

This is best regarded as the ability to sell an investment at any time without suffering consequential loss. Gilts are very marketable, as are the shares of most large well-known public companies. There is constant two-way traffic in these stocks and the impact of selling a large block of stock (say, £1 million worth) would in itself be unlikely to affect the market price significantly. But the effect of selling £1 million worth of shares in a company with a small equity capitalisation would be to depress the price, thereby preventing the owner from realising their previous market value. That is one reason why the big institutions, who necessarily hold large blocks of shares, tend to prefer shares in companies with a large equity capitalisation.

Taxation liability

We concluded in Chapter 5 that investors are ultimately concerned with 'net of tax' returns. Thus expected loss through taxation will be taken into account in determining the gross yield required. Particularly important is the tax-free capital gain on gilts and the lower rates of tax normally paid on capital gain in contrast to income from equity shares.

Transaction (or transfer) cost

This comprises the various costs of buying and selling marketable securities, or investing in and realising non-marketable investments. Whereas there is no cost in making or realising an investment in a bank or building society, the purchase and sale of stock-market securities imposes significant expense. The major expenses of share transactions are the market-maker's spread, the broker's fee and stamp duty (an *ad valorem* tax payable on the purchase of shares).

As investors are ultimately concerned with net returns after all costs and taxation have been allowed for, then (*ceteris paribus*) the greater the transactions costs, the higher the gross yield investors will require.

Management cost

Another expense of investment is management and administration. Any investment requires constant reappraisal – witness the enormous real losses made by loyal investors in undated gilts over the post-war period. However, whereas money deposited in a building society creates little bother, the administration and continuing reappraisal of a portfolio of shares involves much time and effort.

Whilst the major investing institutions employ their own staff for these purposes, the personal investor must keep abreast with economic conditions, read the appropriate journals and stockbrokers' circulars, make buy and sell decisions, deal with such problems as rights issues, and try to cope with the tax consequences of investment actions. Continuing management is essential for successful stock market investment. The investor who has neither the time, knowledge or inclination would be advised either to incur the expense of having his portfolio professionally managed or to invest through unit trusts.

Growth expectation

Given a reasonable level of security, this is the most important factor influencing income yields on stocks and shares in times of inflation.

Taking a medium-term view, income and capital growth from equity investments tend to move in parallel. Fixed-interest investments, on the other hand, have no income growth potential but can achieve capital growth – either through a fall in investors' required yields, or through the 'pull to redemption' over time.

Frequency and timing of income

Income yield is the relationship between the *annual* dividend (or interest) and price. Price is a function of future dividends and the timing of their payment. So price and yield are influenced by the amount and timing of dividend payments.

Income yields tend to move seasonally according to the timing of dividend payments. Price will tend to rise (and yield fall) as the payment date approaches, then fall (and yield rise) when the stock goes ex dividend. This seasonal movement will be greatest where the dividend is paid in one lump sum, less if paid half-yearly and less again if paid quarterly. However, it is common in the case of gilts to deduct that part of the market price which reflects the proximity of the next income payment, thereby arriving at a yield (called the 'flat' or 'running' yield), which is unaffected by the approach of the interest payment.

These points can be related to our Equation (6.7), which explains the determination of the dividend yield for shares:

$$d = r - g$$

The first three points above are factors which determine investors' *net* target return, whereas the next three – being the expenses of investment – determine investors' *gross* target return. Investors' gross target return on an investment which is entirely exempt from tax and which involves no transaction or management cost would be the same as their net target return. The growth expectation does not directly affect the target return, only the dividend yield. Frequency and timing of income does not feature in Equation (6.7) because that is based on the assumption that income is received annually in arrears.

8 Modern Theories of Investment Pricing

Efficient market theory (EMT)

Methods of 'fundamental analysis', which attempt to assess the intrinsic worth of shares, have been criticised by some as a waste of time.

Fundamental analysis is founded upon the principles of investment pricing already introduced in this book, and mainly involves forecasting companies' profits and dividends with the aim of identifying underpriced or overpriced stock, so enabling sensible buy and sell decisions to be made (see Example 6.1). However it has been pointed out that the intrinsic worth of a stock is just one consideration influencing market price, and others – particularly investors' psychology – are also relevant. After all, it is not strictly the worth of a share that influences demand and supply, it is how valuable and attractive investors consider it to be.

Supporters of 'technical analysis' believe that future share price changes can be predicted by reference to historic movements in price, because certain patterns of price change appear to be repeated. So, rather than investigating the economic rationale behind a share's price, technical analysis largely consists of examining charts of the share's price movement, in order to identify signals which would indicate a future trend, and thereby enable a profitable buy, sell or hold decision to be made.

Although rejected by most academics, 'technical' or 'chart' analysis has gained many adherents in the UK, and the system is featured in many responsible investment journals. However, only the most rabid 'chartists' would entirely reject fundamental analysis, most would use it as a back-up system to confirm (or raise doubts about) the advisability of an action which appeared to be signalled by technical analysis.

The essential chartist tenet of predictability in share-price movements is in direct conflict with the 'random walk hypothesis'. This asserts that share prices move only in response to new information, and as news is entirely unpredictable (by definition), then share price movements themselves must be unpredictable and random.

The 'efficient market hypothesis' goes further than this and asserts that share prices accurately reflect all relevant available knowledge. If this is true, then anomalies of overpriced or underpriced stocks cannot exist, and unless an investor or analyst possesses relevant information unknown to the market in general, fundamental analysis is futile. If such analysis indicates that a share is underpriced or overpriced, it merely shows that the analyst's opinion of the share's risk and future return differs from the consensus view of market investors.

Efficient market theory (EMT) and the random walk hypothesis are supported by the observation that virtually no investment manager is consistently able to outperform the market. If shares are always correctly priced according to all information available, and if new information and circumstances are entirely unpredictable, then 'beating the market' must be merely a matter of chance.

Although the bulk of research evidence and academic opinion in the USA seem to support the concept of market efficiency, scepticism is rife amongst investment professionals in the UK. Not surprisingly, the theory was scarcely greeted with enthusiasm by the profession of investment analysts despite the fact that it bestows a considerable compliment on their efforts. EMT implies that investors (or at least the dominant investors) are so rational, knowledgeable and well advised, and the stock market so efficient, that share prices will discount the likely effect of new circumstances as soon as the information becomes available. However, if widely accepted, the theory is self destructive as investors will no longer be willing to incur the expense of expert analysis, and the absence of such advice would tend to result in the market becoming inefficient – a nice irony. Perhaps it is just as well that the level of credence afforded to the theory by investors in the UK is less than that of the academics. Note, however, that the theory does not imply that careful share selection is not important, but that rather than seeking out underpriced stock, the investor should select for features (such as security, high income, or growth potential) which are particularly appealing given his individual tax liability, level of risk aversion, needs or preferences.

It would be surprising if there is not an element of validity in each of the above theories, but particularly useful is the concept of the stock market as an efficient 'discounting machine' adjusting stock prices in response to new information affecting expectations of future investment returns. The newcomer observing the stock market for the first time is often mystified by price movements, both of individual stocks and the market at large. A sharp drop in a company's share price immediately after the announcement of a significant profit increase seems illogical, unless it is appreciated that the market was anticipating an even greater increase, and consequently expectations for the future share price and dividend have to be downgraded. The knowledge that the market possesses about conditions affecting each company's profit leads it to make profit projections (and to adjust prices) without information from the company itself. But on the announcement of annual or interim results investors will reappraise future prospects and buy or sell accordingly.

Observers of the stock market can produce unlimited examples which would appear to indicate relative efficiency or inefficiency. The share price of LASMO (a company involved in the exploration and development of oil in the North Sea) fell by 100p from 865p to 765p within two days of the announcement of a new supplementary tax on the flow of crude oil extracted from the

North Sea. Despite the relative complexity of the impact of this tax, LASMO's share price varied little over the next few days as analysts came up with assessments of the tax's impact on profits, apparently indicating that the market had got its sums right fairly quickly. However, on other occasions the market does appear to get things wrong, or to be overcome by sentiment rather than by economic logic. A sharp rise in share prices on the announcement of the engagement of Prince Charles and Lady Diana Spencer, for instance, was lamely attributed to the expected boost for tourism and the souvenir trades.

It may require undue faith to believe that all shares are 'correctly' priced according to available information, and that they always react instantly and appropriately to relevant news. But in a more moderate form EMT may be substantially valid. It is unlikely that major price anomalies exist in the shares of large companies due to the amount of analysis regularly undertaken. However, that may not be true for small companies as they receive much less attention from investment analysts and are much less actively traded.

Rather than possessing any mystical power to identify real value, the market prices stocks according to the *collective opinion* of interested investors. However, collective opinion is sometimes wrong and investors are influenced by volatile sentiments such as excessive optimism or pessimism, greed or fear, which can cause stocks to be over-priced or under-priced.

Risk and portfolio theory

So far, we have assumed that investors' target return, the appropriate discount rate to use in our DCF pricing model, is determined by the return expected from investments of similar risk to that being analysed, and is composed of a risk-free rate plus a premium to allow for risk. Although not incorrect, this analysis is simplistic. We have not yet defined 'risk', nor have we taken account of the benefits of portfolio diversification in reducing risk. Whilst detailed risk analysis and portfolio theory is outside the scope of this book, we can still make a significant improvement to this crude concept of the appropriate discount rate.

For the purposes of this chapter, we shall define the risk of an investment as the variability of its annual return from its expected return. This concept includes both risk to income and risk to capital, and as it encompasses variability above the expected return as well as below, it covers both 'upside potential' and 'downside risk'.

The notion that the appropriate discount rate depends on the risk of the individual investment particularly requires reappraisal, because investors seldom hold a single investment in isolation. They normally invest in a portfolio (or collection of different investments), in which any single stock is a relatively small part. The effect of diversification is to reduce the portfolio's risk well below the level which would be faced if all the capital was invested in one stock. Essentially the investor is concerned with the risk of his portfolio and his concern about the risk of any single stock is restricted to the effect that the addition of that stock will have on the risk of the portfolio as a whole.

The advantages of portfolio diversification and the irrelevance of the risk of a single investment are illustrated by Example 8.1.

Example 8.1

Suppose that an investor holds a single investment – shares in a commercial airline, a business which experiences significant changes in profitability as a result of changes in the cost of aviation fuel. Profit (and thus dividends and share price) tends to rise when the fuel price is low, and fall when the fuel price is high.

Say the return from the airline's shares varies as follows:

	IRR in times of:	
	Low fuel price	*High fuel price*
Airline company's shares	25%	5%

If we assume that low fuel price and high fuel price are the only possible scenarios and are equally likely, then each has a probability of 50% or 0.5. The expected return (which is the weighted average of possible outcomes) and the variability of return above and below the expected return are:

Expected IRR = $(0.5 \times 25\%) + (0.5 \times 5\%) = 15\%$
Variability   = $(25\% - 15\%)$ and $(5\% - 15\%) = \pm 10\%$

Let us now assume that our investor buys shares in an oil company. Its business is oil exploration, production and retailing, and its profits are highly geared to the price of fuel oil. It performs well in times of high fuel price but badly in times of low fuel price. Under these conditions, the anticipated returns are:

	IRR in times of:	
	Low fuel price	*High fuel price*
Oil company shares	−5%	35%

So,

Expected IRR = $(0.5 \times -5\%) + (0.5 \times 35\%) = 15\%$
Variability   = $(35\% - 15\%)$ and $(-5\% - 15\%) = \pm 20\%$

Whereas the expected return from the oil company's shares is the same as that from the airline, the variability is 20%, double that of the airline. So the oil company's shares are much the riskier and, in fact, incur a 50% probability of making a loss. The addition of such a risky investment might be expected to increase the risk of our investor's returns, but not so — in fact, quite the opposite. Assuming that the investor holds equal amounts of each investment, the variability of the combined portfolio can be shown:

	IRR in times of:	
	Low fuel price	*High fuel price*
Combined portfolio	0.5(25% − 5%)	0.5(5% + 35%)
	= 10%	= 20%

Expected IRR = (0.5 × 10%) + (0.5 × 20%) = 15%
Variability = (10% − 15%) and (20% − 15%) = ±5%

With the expected return from the oil company's shares being the same as that of the airline, the expected return of the combination is unchanged. But the variability of the portfolio is now only 5%, much less than that of either investment in isolation, and the 50% chance of a loss that would have to be faced if the airline's shares were held alone is eliminated.

So the addition of an investment, which in isolation may be more risky than the existing investment or portfolio, can reduce the risk of the resultant portfolio. The reduction in risk in Example 8.1 comes about as a result of the negative correlation between the investments. Returns from the two shares move in opposite directions in response to changes in the price of fuel.

Example 8.1 illustrates the rationale for holding a diversified portfolio of investments but is simplistic in many respects. For instance there are not just two possible levels of fuel prices, but an infinite variety. Also, there are many other factors affecting the return from both investments apart from the price of fuel, and the perfect negative correlation of return illustrated in the example would not hold when all these were taken into account in the real world. Nonetheless the importance of the price of oil to the companies in the example means that the illustration is generally valid, and it is interesting to note that shares of airlines and oil companies moved sharply in opposite directions when oil prices rose and fell on the advent and outcome of the Gulf crisis in 1990–1.

In the real world no two shares are perfectly correlated, negatively (as in the example) or positively. Nor is negative correlation between two investments necessary to reduce risk. The risk of a portfolio will be reduced by the addition of any investment which is less than perfectly positively correlated with the existing portfolio, and as perfect correlation between investments does not exist in reality, the addition of an extra investment will always reduce risk to some extent (so long as investments are equally weighted). Nonetheless, portfolio risk will be minimised by selecting investments whose returns are as independent or uncorrelated from each other as possible.

Modern portfolio theory (MPT)

Appropriate diversification reduces risk but it cannot eliminate it, hence the distinction in 'modern portfolio theory' (MPT) between 'specific risk' – which can be eliminated by diversification – and 'market risk' – which cannot. Specific risk (or 'unique' or 'unsystematic' risk) derives from factors which are specific to the individual company, and which are likely to be largely neutralised by other uncorrelated shares in a well-diversified portfolio. Market risk, however, derives from movements in share prices in general, which cannot be avoided.

Because of the relative ease with which the bulk of specific risk can be eliminated (a portfolio of 10 shares in equal proportions can remove over 80% of such risk), it is the *market risk* of a portfolio which matters most, and the market risk of a portfolio depends on the market risk of the constituent shares.

It is a feature of the stock market that share prices tend to rise and fall in unison, but shares are not equally volatile, and in every 'bull' or 'bear' market there will be some shares that manage to buck the trend. A profits recovery or

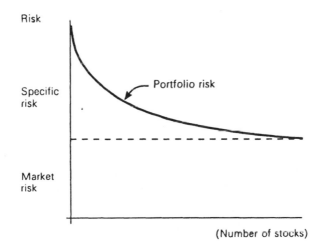

Figure 8.1   Risk reduction by diversification

takeover bid might cause the price of a share to rise when others are falling, or an unexpected profits slump might cause another share to fall when the market in general is rising. However, that does not mean these shares are unaffected by the market trend – the shares that fell would probably have fallen further if the market in general had not been rising. The risk deriving from such events is essentially specific risk which, as explained, is likely to be eliminated by other shares in the portfolio moving in the opposite direction. It can be confidently stated that all shares are influenced by market trends to some extent, but some are more sensitive to such movements than others. It is this sensitivity which is the nature of market risk and which is measured by the 'beta' (β) ratio.

β is the measure of market risk, so the share market as a whole necessarily has a β of 1. A share with a β of 1.5 is expected to vary by 15% for every 10% movement of the market, and a share with a β of 0.6 would tend to vary only 6% in such conditions. Shares or portfolios with a high β (termed 'aggressive' in investment jargon) will therefore tend to outperform the market in a 'bull' phase, but perform proportionally badly in a 'bear' phase. Conversely, shares or portfolios with a β less than 1 ('defensive' in investment patois) will tend to under-perform in a 'bull' phase, but prove relatively resilient in a 'bear' phase. By knowing the β of a stock its contribution to the market risk of the whole portfolio can be assessed, and by knowing the β of all stocks within a portfolio, an understanding of the risk of the portfolio can be gained – assuming the portfolio has been well diversified and specific risk effectively eliminated.

Factors determining the β of a share are complex and probably not fully understood, but the level of a company's gearing is one important factor, particularly the effective income gearing. Significant movements in stock market prices tend to reflect the national economic cycle, so the variability of a company's profits to the cycle is another factor which tends to determine a share's β. However, much of the risk to this factor is diversifiable, thereby coming within the definition of specific risk.

Thus because of the relative ease with which specific risk can be eliminated by diversification, the type of risk with which the investor is principally concerned in investment selection is market risk. As already explained, market prices adjust to give investors the yield they require, and if investors are essentially concerned with market risk and not specific risk, then market prices will reflect market risk only. In fact research has indicated that specific risk goes virtually unrewarded, and that investment returns reflect *market risk* only. According to the Capital Asset Pricing Model (CAPM) the relationship between risk and return in an efficient market is surprisingly simple – the yield premium provided by investments to compensate for risk varies in direct proportion to their β:

$$r_s - r_l = \beta_s(r_m - r_l) \tag{8.1}$$

where r_s = expected rate of return from investment s, r_f = risk-free rate of return, r_m = expected rate of return from the market and β_s = beta of investment s.

This statement says that an investment's yield premium (i.e. the extra return expected over that available from a riskless investment) is equal to its β multiplied by the yield premium for the market as a whole. Consequently, the appropriate discount rate to use in our DCF pricing model (investors' target IRR) is the risk-free rate of return plus the market's yield premium × the β of the share in question.

We have already seen that, with the exception of very short-dated stock, gilts are not risk free in terms of our definition of risk, and the best indication of a risk-free yield is considered to be the discount rate on Treasury bills. In both the UK and the USA the average annual yield premium earned by shares over and above the Treasury bill rate has been about 9%, so adopting this as the market's yield premium we can calculate the target IRR for any stock for which the β is available.

Example 8.2

Calculate investors' target return for the ordinary shares of J. Sainsbury and George Wimpey, given that their betas are respectively 0.76 and 1.27,[1] and that the current discount rate on Treasury bills is 10%:

$$r_s = r_f + \beta_s (R_m - r_f)$$

J. Sainsbury:

$$= 10 + 0.76 \,(19 - 10) = \textbf{16.8\%}$$

George Wimpey:

$$= 10 + 1.27 \,(19 - 10) = \textbf{21.4\%}$$

The market risk and target return for J. Sainsbury are relatively low, mainly because its business (food retailing) is not subject to large changes in demand over the economic cycle. On the other hand, as a building contractor George Wimpey is very vulnerable to the typical cycle of boom and slump in the building industry. High market risk means investors require the expectation of a relatively high return.

We now know more about r, investors' target return. If fundamental analysis indicates a higher expected return than that signalled by the CAPM, then investors should buy. If vice versa they should sell. Supporters of the extreme view of market efficiency who have implicit faith in the CAPM would say that such a situation is impossible, or that it simply proves the fundamental analysis to be incorrect, because according to EMT all shares must have a NPV of nil — share prices exactly reflect value. However, such an interpretation of EMT would have little support.

Note that the CAPM asserts that securities are priced by the market to reward the acceptance by the investor of market risk. The theory does not purport to tell the investor what precise return will be achieved, only what would be expected on the basis of market risk and past evidence of the market. The model can never be entirely proven, as it is concerned with expected return (which cannot be observed and measured) rather the actual return, but the supporting evidence is impressive.

Portfolio planning and management

In emphasising market risk and expected return, the special concerns of the individual investor are liable to be forgotten. Each investor will tend to have different needs and preferences which should be taken into account in selecting his own portfolio.

The individual investor's level of risk aversion and taxation liability have already been mentioned, but other considerations are a preference for high initial income or future growth. The amount of capital available for investment will also tend to limit choice, particularly in the case of a small personal portfolio, as will the need for liquidity and marketability, this last consideration being especially important to large institutional investors. Certain institutions such as trusts are also subject to legal constraints on their investment choice. There is more to portfolio planning than merely maximising returns at a chosen level of risk.

Modern portfolio theory — an imprecise title encompassing portfolio theory itself, EMT, and the concepts subsumed by the CAPM — was largely developed in the USA, where it revolutionised investment thought and action in the 1970s. By introducing simple measurement of portfolio risk (the market risk of a portfolio is the weighted average of the betas of constituent shares), it has substantially simplified the problems of portfolio selection and enabled the measurement of portfolio performance to be linked to risk.

Active portfolio management with the aim of outperforming the market can take the form of acquiring high β shares in 'bull' market trends and switching to low β stock in times of uncertainty. However, the increasing acceptance of market efficiency and thus the improbability of outperforming the market has led to the widespread adoption of 'index' or other 'passive' portfolio strategies on the maxim that 'if you can't beat them, join them'. Index funds are portfolios selected to mirror some key share index and, as with all passive portfolios, analysis, management and dealing expenses are reduced to a minimum. Little attempt is made to identify the 'best buys', and switching of shares is minimal. The value of the portfolio will tend to rise or fall in line with the market, or the section of the market that the index represents.

In the UK, MPT is regarded by the securities industry with a healthy scepticism. Much of it is controversial and may ultimately be rejected, but for our purposes this brief study of these simple and intuitively appealing concepts has provided a useful medium for gaining some basic understanding of risk analysis, asset pricing and portfolio theory.

We will conclude this chapter by summarising a few of the main points:

- Share prices represent the *collective opinion* of investors who are generally well informed by investment analysis, at least in the case of large companies. However, prices are influenced by sentiment which can lead to over-pricing or under-pricing.
- Share prices represent the discounted value of investors' expected future income flows, which are ultimately dependent upon profits, so prices will tend to move on *new information* which affects either companies' profits or investors' target returns.
- The risk of investment can be divided between risk that can be avoided by portfolio diversification (specific risk) and the remaining risk (market risk) which cannot be avoided. According to the CAPM, only the latter risk will be reflected in market prices and will provide an extra return to investors.
- According to the CAPM, an investment's target return is composed of the return available from riskless investments plus an extra return (risk premium) which is proportional to the investment's market risk (β).

9   Trends in Share Prices

Introduction

In order to enhance our theory of investment pricing and to provide some general understanding of the relationship between national economic conditions and the general level of investment prices and yields, we shall briefly examine significant trends in stock prices in the recent past.

Any good that is traded in a free market has its price determined by the forces of supply and demand. In a sense, nothing else is relevant – if a factor does not influence either supply or demand then it cannot influence price. However, there are an infinite number of factors affecting supply and demand, and by using our pricing model the dominant factors can be highlighted and price levels explained.

The fixed income nature of conventional bonds means that their prices vary mainly according to changes in investors' target return, but prices of equity shares are also heavily dependent on expected dividends. As dividends depend on equity earnings, so share prices depend critically on equity earnings (or, more generally, profitability). Corporate profitability and expectations for future profitability are crucial to understanding share price movements (see Figure 9.1).

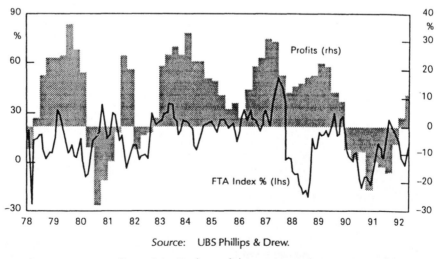

Source: UBS Phillips & Drew.

Figure 9.1   Profits and the equity market

Determinants of corporate profitability

Profit is essentially the difference between a firm's income from sales and its total costs. Income depends on the volume of sales and prices charged for goods or services. Costs comprise the costs of the factors of production – principally wages, interest on debt, raw materials, fuel, plant and machinery, rent, rates, etc. So anything which affects the volume of sales, the prices that a firm can charge, or any of the costs of production, will tend to affect profitability, dividends and share price.

The impact of certain costs will vary from one firm to another. A firm involved in a labour intensive activity will be badly hit by a sharp rise in wage levels, and a firm with a large amount of bank debt will be severely affected by a rise in short-term interest rates. Some firms may be unaffected by certain cost changes, and if income is rising faster than costs then profit will be rising despite the rise in costs. In times of inflation when most costs and prices are rising, it is the *relative* change in a firm's income and costs which will determine its profitability.

Factors determining a firm's profitability can be considered at three different levels – the economy, the industry and the firm.

The economy: international, national, local

As a result of increasing internationalisation of trade and finance, all firms in the UK must be affected in some way or another by changing conditions in the world economy. Particularly exposed are those manufacturing companies which export a high proportion of their output, or are dependent on imported raw materials, or are subject to competition from imported manufactured goods. These firms will be vulnerable to changes in the level of the pound sterling, as this affects the foreign-currency price of exports and the sterling price of imports.

Domestic economic conditions will be more important for the majority of companies. Changing demand for goods and services, resulting from changes in real disposable incomes, will influence not only the quantity of goods which firms can sell but also the prices which they can charge. Factor costs are also influenced by economic conditions, particularly interest on debt and wages. Government policies are of dominant importance to corporate profitability – not simply because the government influences the level of economic activity, but also because of its control of interest rates, taxation, public spending and legislation.

Firms which predominantly serve a regional or local market will also be affected by economic conditions specific to that area.

The industry

Although certain conglomerate companies undertake activities spanning different sectors of industry and commerce, the majority of firms are principally restricted to a single industry. Consequently their profitability is largely dependent on conditions within that industry. A company is more likely to achieve profits growth in an expanding industry (such as electronics) than in a declining one (e.g., shipbuilding or heavy engineering), and risk will tend to be greater in an industry facing cyclical demand (capital goods, textiles) than one in which demand is stable (food manufacturing). Some industries are particularly vulnerable to cuts in public expenditure (building and civil engineering, aircraft manufacture), others to foreign competition (motor cars, clothing), or to government-supported campaigns on health grounds (tobacco and drink). Each industry will have its own problems and advantages, and thus each firm within that industry will tend to suffer (or benefit) accordingly.

The company

There are an infinite number of variables influencing the profitability and risk of an individual firm, apart from those deriving from general economic conditions or the industry within which the firm operates. The importance of a firm's financial structure has already been mentioned, but other major considerations are the quality of management, labour relations, and the diversity of products and markets. The amount of a company's liquid finance or saleable assets, including property, will also affect its stability and security in times of trading difficulties.

The level of interest rates

Of all factors affecting stock prices and yields in the short/medium run, changes (or expected changes) in the level of interest rates is probably the most important. With interest rates affecting the opportunity cost of capital, corporate risk and profitability, this is clearly indicated by our pricing model. Interest on debt is a cost to all firms which borrow, but the level of interest rates also has a major impact on demand. The effect of rising interest rates is particularly severe in industries where the products are often purchased with borrowed money, e.g., construction and house building, and the manufacture of consumer durables such as electricals, kitchen goods and motor cars. Rising interest rates also tend to cause a fall in demand for goods and services through their impact on the net disposable income of households. A rise in bank base rates tends to have a knock-on effect on bank and building society mortgage rates, and with mortgage interest payments being a prior charge on the income of the average house owner, spending on non-essential goods and services tends to suffer. Over-borrowing for house purchase in the 1980s boom meant that the subsequent rise in interest rates had a particularly severe effect on consumer expenditure in the UK, and was one of the major reasons for the severity of the 1990–2 recession. Conversely, it remains to be seen whether the stimulating effect of falling interest rates in 1991–3 has been successful in ending the recession.

Taking into account the effect of interest rates on the cost of plastic debt, on decisions of industry to reinvest in capital goods, and on the incentive to save rather than spend, it is not surprising to see a correlation between the level of interest rates and share prices.

Stock issues and the 'weight of money'

One important influence on stock prices which is not clearly identified by the pricing model is the issue of new stock. New issues of shares or gilt-edged stock can be a significant element of market supply, and a surge in new share issues – either by companies 'going public' or by rights issue – can halt and reverse a 'bull' trend.

The higher are share prices the lower are dividend yields, and the lower are dividend yields the cheaper is a rights issue compared with alternative methods of raising new corporate finance. So a significant overall rise in share prices tends to induce an increase in the volume of new issues, particularly in conditions when firms lack liquid finance or are overgeared. This increased supply of new stock relative to demand tends to dampen or reduce share prices.

A crude but rational theory for predicting general market movements is the 'weight of money' argument. With institutional investors dominating the market and having a predictable inflow of funds, fairly accurate estimates can be made of the flow of new investment funds to be invested each year. There are four main investment media available to institutional investors – equities, gilts, property and liquid assets. So if, for example, the institutions are expected to invest a total of £50 billion of new funds, and liquid investments are expected to remain stable, property is expected to absorb £5 billion and £20 billion of new gilts are likely to be issued, then the remaining £25 billion must tend to be invested in shares. Therefore £25 billion is a rough measure of the expected net new demand for shares, and the greater is the volume of new issues, the less will be left over to buy existing stock that year.

Obviously the theory is crude, and in this simplistic outline it assumes personal and other investors will be neither net buyers nor net sellers. It also assumes that investment funds are trapped within the UK, but since the abolition of exchange controls, institutions invest substantial funds in over-seas equities. Conversely, overseas investors may be net buyers or sellers of UK stock, particularly gilts. However, the theory explains how private-sector fund raising can be 'crowded out' by the public sector. The government must finance its PSBR, and however reluctant investors may be to buy more gilts, they will eventually be tempted to take up all new offers. Gilt yields must rise to whatever level is necessary to coax investors into their purchase and, in order to compete, corporate securities must offer the expectation of even higher returns.

Impact of the economic cycle on share prices

During a reflationary or boom phase in the economic cycle, rising demand will usually enable a company to increase production and the price of its products, whilst the higher level of output will tend to reduce cost per unit, even although total costs may be rising. Conversely, in recessionary conditions low levels of production will tend to mean that labour, plant and machinery are not being used to capacity, so unit costs tend to rise and, with the low level of demand, prices cannot be raised sufficiently to cover increased costs. Early in a recession the fall in demand tends to cause an accumulation of stocks of unsold goods and raw materials, all of which have to be financed at a level of interest rates which tends to be high at such a stage in the cycle.

Corporate profitability is therefore closely tied to the national economic cycle and, traditionally, share-price movements have tended to mirror (in fact, lead) the cycle. Investors act on expectations, so share prices tend to rise or fall in anticipation of changes in profitability and the cycle. The early phase of a 'bull' market tends to coincide with a recovery in financial conditions and a fall in interest rates. But this is usually at a stage when firms are announcing falling profits, when unemployment is rising, and before there are any signs of real economic recovery. In fact, share prices and unemployment have frequently reached all time highs simultaneously, an irony not lost on trade unions, the press and politicians. Typically, shares tend to peak when the cycle is still in its recovery phase, and by the time industrial production has peaked, rising interest rates and the signs of an overheated economy have destined the market to a new 'bear' phase.

This typical stock market cycle has been less evident since the 1970s, perhaps partly as a result of the replacement of Keynesian demand management by more monetarist policies, yet the tendency remains.

Share prices and inflation

A glance at Figure 9.2 shows that, in the long run, share prices appear to have risen broadly in line with inflation. However, the influence of the trade cycle is reflected in the cyclical movements of the index prior to the 1980s, and the figure highlights the impact of the stock market crashes in 1973–4 and 1987.

In general, rising real incomes meant that firms faced a rising demand for goods and services, enabling them to recover increased costs by raising their prices. Consequently, profits and share prices tended to rise at around the inflation rate. In the 1950s and early 1960s inflation seemed to be caused predominantly by 'demand pull' pressures, whereby rising demand for goods

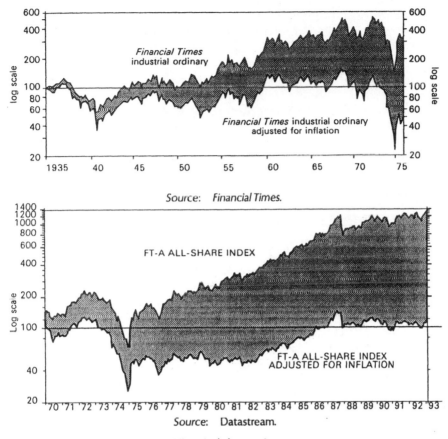

Figure 9.2   Historical share price movements

and services enabled firms to raise prices and make higher profits. Costs rose as well, particularly wages, but wage rises tended to *follow* the price rises and, in times of rising demand, cost increases could be recovered by further price increases and increased efficiency of production.

Over the post-war period, however, 'cost push' inflationary pressures gradually became more dominant. The devaluation of sterling in 1967 increased fuel, transport and imported raw material costs, but more important was the rising cost of labour. Instead of wages rising in response to high profitability and low levels of unemployment in times of boom, firms were increasingly forced to concede wage increases which could not be justified by current levels of profitability, and which pre-empted a rise in profitability in a subsequent economic upturn. Thus rising costs increasingly preceded rising prices. Firms depended on being able to raise prices in a reflationary phase to recover cost increases suffered in a prior recession. However, the benefit of rising demand in times of reflation was increasingly dissipated by an increasing propensity to import, and for twenty years from the mid-1960s the real profitability of UK industry suffered a relentless decline.

So, although share prices appear to have been a successful 'hedge' against inflation until 1972–3, it is altogether too simplistic to conclude that inflation is 'good' for shares. Whereas 'demand pull' conditions should enable profits and share prices to rise in real terms, 'cost push' pressures will tend either to cause falling equity prices or, at best, cause prices to rise at below the rate of inflation. Ultimately, however, share prices depend on corporate profitability, and trends in profitability cannot be explained merely by the rate of inflation – 'demand pull' or 'cost push'.

1973–4 stock-market collapse

The economic conditions leading to the financial crash in 1974, which featured not just a stock-market collapse but also a banking and property-market collapse, are fully described in Part VII, and will not be detailed here. 1974 is perhaps the most significant year in the story of post-war investment; it signalled the demise of the post-war 'cult of the equity' by revealing that a diversified portfolio of ordinary shares could no longer be considered as a guaranteed inflation hedge.

The reasons for this dramatic crash (a 73% fall in share prices from the May 1972 peak, as measured by the *Financial Times* index) are many and varied. It resulted partly from national economic mismanagement and the excesses of the previous boom, partly from the quadrupling of crude oil prices and the consequent worldwide economic shock, and partly from political forces. However, rather than investigating the underlying causes here, let us simply look at some of the factors which affected corporate profitability during this period.

The economic recession was introduced in the fourth quarter of 1973, when the Conservative government under Edward Heath introduced a series of deflationary measures, following the announcement of massive price increases for crude oil (then the UK's largest import item). Interest rates were raised to an all-time high, various controls on credit were introduced, public expenditure was cut and taxation increased. At a time when all their costs were escalating, firms were therefore faced with a substantial reduction in demand, both in the domestic economy and (as a result of the world recession) from overseas. Fuel costs spiralled in response to the rise in the price of crude oil, imported raw material costs were at an all-time peak and increased further as the pound sterling plummeted in response to the balance of payments crisis. The rise in costs was exacerbated when the new Labour government removed wage controls on taking office in February 1974, and wage rises in the region of 20–30% became the norm. Coupled with all these problems, firms faced price controls and effective tax increases.

The stock market tends to be blinded by sentiment, and carried away under its own momentum at both peaks and troughs. 1974 was no exception – the economic and financial conditions, although drastic, scarcely justified a level of share prices over 30% less in real terms than in the days of Dunkirk and the Battle of Britain. However, with crashes in banking, property, insurance and shipping, with a trade union movement able to disrupt government policies and bring down the Heath government, and with a new Labour administration apparently more intent on trade union appeasement than confronting economic reality, it must have seemed that capitalism's Armageddon was nigh. Such a prospect would be infinitely more likely to scare the pinstripes off a City broker than any number of Panzer divisions poised across the channel in 1940.

The stock market has always tended to be sensitive to political trends. This is inevitable with stock-price movements so dependent on the economy, and economic management inextricably linked with the political complexion of the party in power. With the Conservative party being allied to the concept of capitalism, but the Labour party more concerned with the welfare of the working man, the investment community in the City of London clearly has a right-wing bias. Ironically, however, investors have often fared better under a Labour administration, and the City and financial press are rarely uncritical supporters of a Tory government.

The 1980s boom and crash

A more detailed economic analysis of the 1980s is contained in Chapter 27, but it is worth highlighting here the principal trends and events affecting the stock market during the period of Margaret Thatcher's premiership.

The main surprise about the behaviour of stock prices during the 1980–2 recession was their stability. In many respects the problems of British industry were greater than in 1974–5, yet no share crash took place. Following the economic shock of the second oil price surge the world economy sank into recession, and the subsequent fall in demand faced by UK industry was exacerbated by the high level of sterling which resulted from the UK's self sufficiency in oil and the high level of interest rates maintained by the government in pursuit of its monetarist strategy. The new rise in fuel costs, another 'high' for interest rates and continued increases in wages, rents, rates and utilities might have been expected to replicate the stock-market conditions of 1974. The reasons why there was no 'bear' market in 1980–1 was perhaps firstly, that industry was better financed than in the mid-1970s, but more importantly the 'City' had confidence in the government's policies.

Essentially, Thatcher's economic strategy was to minimise government intervention in the economy and to create conditions in which competitive enterprise could flourish. That required a drastic reduction in inflation which the government sought to achieve by means of high interest rates to control money supply. The breakthrough came in 1982 with a sharp fall in the rate of inflation to 5% allowing in turn a crucial reduction in banks' base rate. This, together with a successful outcome to the Falklands war and the re-election of the Thatcher government in 1983 created the conditions for an economic revival and a 'bull' market in shares which continued until October 1987.

Shares massively outperformed alternative UK investments as the national economy recovered. The defeat of the coal miners after a year-long strike in 1985 signalled the government's final victory over the trade unions, and confidence in equities rose strongly. Institutional demand for shares was reinforced by the declining case for property investment, the fall in interest rates and eventually the end to new gilt issues when the PSBR became negative in 1987. UK and overseas equities became the principal home for the institutions' growing inflow of funds. Investment in shares by the personal sector also revived, stimulated by the privatisation programme and the government's encouragement of stock-market investment.

The long 'bull' market of the 1980s culminated with a further 50% surge in share prices in the year after Big Bang. The 'bullish' view in 1987 was that, with the trade unions and inflation under control, the objective of long-term growth with low inflation was being achieved. Having established a culture of entrepreneurial competition, the economy was being restructured and revitalised, and there was no reason why profits should not continue to grow. The UK was undergoing an economic miracle.

Unfortunately events have proved otherwise, but it was mainly concern about the US and the world economy which triggered the stock-market crash of October 1987. The London stock market has always tended to respond to significant trends on Wall Street due to the strong economic links between the two countries, and Monday 19 October was no exception. Shares had fallen heavily in the USA on the previous Friday, ostensibly over concern about the state of the US economy, in particular its enormous budget and trade deficits which threatened world economic stability. Following weekend press comment suggesting that the UK bull market could be over, shares plummeted on the Monday morning, and after Wall Street fell another 20% later that day, London followed with a further 10% fall on the Tuesday. Tokyo and other world stock markets suffered similar falls and the Hong Kong market closed in an attempt to stave off the panic.

What was dramatic and frightening about the 1987 stock-market crash was not its extent but its speed. The 37% decline in the FTA All-share Index from its July peak was small compared with 1973–4, and did no more than wipe out the gains of the previous year. But the speed of the fall (20% in the first two days) and its repetition throughout the capitalist world appeared to presage some dramatic world economic collapse akin to the depression which followed the Wall Street crash in 1929.

In retrospect we can see that the 1987 crash was pretty insignificant, except as a lesson on how markets act. Essentially it was a 'market correction'. Share prices were too high. They had lost touch with the fundamentals of earnings and dividends, and prices had to fall until sensible dividend yields and P/E ratios were re-established. Many investors realised that prices were too high but were 'hanging on for the ride', in the expectation that they would be able to identify the market turn when it arrived and sell in time. That's what investors tried to do on 19 and 20 October. The speed of the crash may also have been exacerbated by the introduction of electronic trading and the adoption of 'programme trading' and mechanistic buy/sell decision-making by US investors. Certainly the global nature of the crash reflected the internationalisation of investment in the 1980s, and the interrelationship between the three principal markets in New York, Tokyo and London.

The 1987 crash was not precipitated by any critical piece of economic news, such as a sharp rise in interest rates. The problem of the US deficits had been growing for years and was well known. So where does that leave Efficient Market Theory? Some have suggested that EMT has been disproved, at least as regards the general level of stock prices. Perhaps markets are better at fixing relative prices (i.e., the price of BP relative to Shell) than fixing the general level of stock prices in relation to the macro-economy. Certainly one lesson of the crash is that, rather than having a mystic ability to reflect true values or to predict the economy, stock markets are prone to over-price (and under-price) stocks. Investors are not always rational, and markets are influenced by their mass psychology. Markets are fallible.

II Property Investments –
Prices and Yields

10 Property Investments and the Property Market

Property interests

In order to understand the behaviour of property prices and yields under changing economic conditions, it is important to understand the nature and characteristics of the 'goods' being traded. The term 'property' throughout this book refers to land and buildings; what in England would be defined as 'real' property, as distinct from 'chattels', and in Scotland as 'heritable' as opposed to 'moveable' property. However, the 'goods' traded in the property market are not physical units of land and buildings, but legal rights over land and buildings.

In England and Wales, the highest form of land tenure under the Crown is the 'fee simple', or more generally, the 'freehold' estate. The freeholder in possession of land is vested with a perpetual right to use or dispose of the land as he wishes, subject to statute and certain inalienable rights of others. A freeholder may create lesser interests over his land, particularly a 'leasehold' interest, conferring on the 'lessee' or 'tenant' the right to possess and use the property for a specific period, usually subject to the payment of rent. Unless prohibited by the terms of his lease, this lessee may in turn create a subsidiary lease. In this case, he would be known as the 'head lessee' (or 'head tenant') and the occupier as the 'sub-lessee' (or 'sub-tenant'). The rent payable by the head tenant to his landlord (the freeholder and 'lessor') is known as the 'head rent', and that payable by the sub-tenant to his landlord (the head tenant) is known as the 'sub-rent'. In theory, there is no limit to the number of leasehold interests which may be created in this way over a single unit of land.

Whereas a freeholder, having a perpetual interest, may grant a lease for any period of time, even 999 years or more, the duration of any sub-lease cannot exceed the duration of the head lease. Unless security of tenure is provided by statute to an occupying tenant (as in the case of certain housing, farmland and business tenancies), the landlord can regain possession of his property at the expiration of the lease.

The values of such property interests depend crucially on the conditions of the lease contracts to which they are subject. The value of a freehold interest in a let property, for example, depends on the rent payable by the tenant and the duration of the lease remaining. If the head tenant has sub-let to an occupying sub-tenant, then the value of the head tenant's interest depends on the duration of both the head lease and the sub-lease, and the rent payable to the freeholder as well as that receivable from the sub-tenant. For the head tenant's interest to have value, rental income from the sub-tenant must normally exceed the rent payable to the freeholder, i.e. the head tenant must receive a surplus, called a 'profit rent'. For the sub-tenant's interest to have value, the rent payable to the head tenant must be less than the 'rental value', i.e. the annual rent that he would have to pay under a new occupation lease. For a leasehold interest to have a market value, it must be marketable, i.e. there must be no contractual or statutory prohibition on the sale of the interest.

Although the rent payable and the duration are important clauses in a lease, there are many others which are also critical in dictating the risk and return to the owner of a property interest. Sub-letting as well as sale may be prohibited. There may also be covenants restricting the use of the property, or prohibiting structural alterations. A lease contract will normally specify liability for repairs, insurance and reinstatement at the end of the lease. It may make provision for premature termination of the lease, specify redress for breach of contract and – crucially in times of inflation – provide for the review of rent periodically during the lease. Clearly, there is infinite scope for variation in the leases which create property interests, and consequently an infinite variation in property interests themselves.

It is useful to categorise property interests as follows:

1. Investment interests: where the holder receives a substantial net rental income from one or more subsidiary leaseholders, e.g.,
    (a) a freehold interest in a let property;
    (b) a head tenant's interest in a property sub-let at a substantial profit rent.
2. Occupation interests: these may be either
    (a) valuable, e.g., where the occupier is either the freeholder (owner occupier), or a leaseholder paying a rent significantly below rental value and with a substantial period of his lease still to run, or
    (b) no value or low value leasehold interests, where the tenant is paying a rent at, or close to, the property's rental value.

Interests in category 1 above can be considered as 'pure' investments. It is interests such as these which are traded in the property investment market, and which are the main subject of the analysis in Parts II and V of this book. However, the income of such investments is dependent on the rents which the occupying tenants (2(b)) are willing to pay for their right to occupy. The factors determining rents are analysed in Part III of this book.

Interests in category 2(a) are given little individual prominence in this book, but an understanding of their prices follows from our analyses of 1 and 2(b) because they combine the investment and occupational benefits of these latter categories.

Various other valuable interests can exist over property, e.g., a life interest terminating on the death of the life tenant, and the interest of the mortgagee (the lender) where a property is mortgaged as security for a loan. Such interests are rarely marketable and are not examined in this book.

Types of investment property

The following brief description is restricted to the types of property which are commonly acquired for investment purposes.

Farmland

The tenure of farmland is substantially influenced by the Agricultural Holdings Acts and related statutes, so that an occupying tenant is normally guaranteed security of tenure for life, together with a right to bequeath his tenancy. A landlord of a let farm may not regain possession of his farm for generations. As a tenant is normally debarred from either sub-letting or selling his interest, the large majority of investments in farmland are freehold interests, either let to the occupying tenant or held 'in hand' (owner-occupied). Although the number of 'in-hand' farms in the UK exceeds the number of let farms, higher demand for possession has resulted in an 'in-hand premium', i.e. the price of a freehold interest in an 'in-hand' farm can exceed the price of a freehold investment in a comparable let farm, often by 100%. Very few 'in-hand' farms are now let due to the consequent loss of this premium and the inability to regain possession. Freeholders who do not wish to farm the land themselves may appoint a manager, or enter into a partnership or other joint venture arrangement with an active farmer in order to avoid the formal creation of a legal tenancy.

Although the ownership of farmland in the UK is still dominated by private individuals and family companies and trusts, large areas of farmland are owned by the Crown, charitable trusts, religious institutions and public authorities. A few large insurance companies and pension funds invest in farms, but since the early 1980s, institutional investment has decreased substantially. Farmland varies in quality from barren hill land to prime arable, and it is mainly this latter class which is the subject of institutional investment, particularly units in excess of 200 hectares.

Woodlands

Unlike farmland, investment in woodlands traditionally involves freehold occupation of the land. So, rather than the investment being in land and buildings, it is in the land and the growing crop of timber, which may take 60 years or more to mature. The investor will receive no income from his initial costs of establishing and managing a plantation until, at best, first thinning after 20 years or so. Thereafter, further thinning may produce three or four tranches of income before clear felling.

An investment in woodlands is occasionally based on a conventional land-lord/tenant relationship, with the investor owning the land and leasing it for an annual rent to a tenant who will gain the direct profits of the timber growing. Although this provides a regular income for the landlord, it tends to create problems for the tenant due to the irregularity of income from timber growing. Unless he is a major grower such as the Forestry Commission, owning many different plantations, he is unlikely to be generating regular income with which to pay an annual rent.

Institutional interest in woodland investment has engendered a variety of joint venture schemes whereby two parties (such as a financial institution and an estate owner) share the profits of timber growing. Such schemes can take maximum advantage of the institution's capital availability, the taxation liabilities of the two parties, their individual investment needs, and the aver-sion of institutions to becoming actively involved in management.

The majority of woodland investment is in 'softwood' or conifer plantations in hill or upland areas in the western side of the country, where the higher rainfall and relatively mild climate provide adequate returns from faster growing species such as Sitka spruce.

Commercial property

Freehold and long leasehold interests in office and shop property constitute the large majority of the property portfolios of the financial institutions. It is commercial and industrial property which forms the principal subject of this book. As quality and location are critical factors determining the risk and return from such property, institutional investment is primarily restricted to modern buildings in good urban locations. The majority of such property in the UK is owned by the financial institutions and property companies.

Certain other commercial property types, e.g., prime hotels, are also sub-ject to pure investment, but the ownership of public houses and petrol filling stations is dominated respectively by the brewers and oil companies as a means of promoting the sale of their products.

Industrial property

Industrial property has generally been a less attractive investment than shops and offices, largely due to its poorer growth record and vulnerability to economic recession. Nonetheless, modern well located factories and ware-houses constitute on important element of institutional property portfolios. On the other hand, most older property — particularly large purpose-built factory buildings in declining industrial areas — is still owner occupied, and would not be considered an attractive subject for investment.

Residential property

About 90% of housing stock in Great Britain is either owner occupied or owned by public authorities. Most of the remainder is owned by housing associations, charitable trusts, property companies or employers who lease the property to employees under service tenancies.

Housing is not a popular investment medium for institutional investors and is not considered in detail in this book. It is too politically and socially sensitive, is expensive to manage, and seems liable to remain subject to rent control.

Special characteristics of physical property

Having introduced the principal interests and types of property relevant to our study, we must now briefly examine the general characteristics of the medium over which these interests exist, namely the physical land and buildings. Property has certain almost unique characteristics which distinguish it from most other commodities. Although mostly obvious, these are of profound significance, and require to be clearly stated. Only by understanding the nature of both the intangible interest and the tangible property can a sound understanding of property prices and yields under changing economic conditions be achieved.

Dual components

Any developed property consists of two elements, land and buildings – or, more strictly, land and capital improvements which may be roadways, fences, drains, etc. as well as buildings. In some cases (e.g., urban offices) the property consists mostly of building and a smaller amount of land (by area and by value) whereas in other cases (e.g., farms) the land content is the greater. The dual nature of physical property complicates its analysis as the economic characteristics of land and buildings are very different.

Durability

Pure land (as the earth's surface) is totally durable, and buildings and other capital improvements are relatively durable compared with most other goods. This durability enables the right to use property to be separated from its ownership, and allows a variety of interests to exist over the same property unit at the one time. Ultimately, however, buildings must deteriorate, and the long-term investor must anticipate either expenditure on repair or replacement, or depreciation in value.

Fixed location

All real property is fixed in location, by definition. If it is moveable it cannot be real property. It is this characteristic which, unlike moveable goods such as motor cars, results in similar properties in different locations having substantially different values. Property in areas of low demand cannot move physically to satisfy high demand in another location.

Note, however, that although immobile physically, property is relatively mobile between certain different *uses*.

Heterogeneous

Each physical unit of property must be unique because it is fixed in location. Even similar bungalows in a row, or flats in a multistorey block are unique in respect of location. Most buildings will also tend to vary according to size, age, use type, standard of construction and repair, etc. This, together with the heterogeneous nature of each legal interest, means that (unlike homogeneous shares in any company), the value of each property interest is unknown to the market and must be individually assessed.

Stock elasticity

The total amount of land in the world, in any country, or in any location, is essentially fixed. However, the significance of this characteristic is liable to be exaggerated because the stock of land available for any individual use, as well as the intensity with which land is used, can vary. Furthermore, the second component of a property – the building – being constructed by man, is relatively elastic in stock in the long run.

The elasticity (variability) of stock of any property type depends on the pure land requirements of that use, and the proportion of total land stock in that location currently employed in that use. For example, farmland stock in Lincolnshire cannot be significantly increased because farming is the dominant land use in that county and farming requires a lot of land. Conversely, however, the long-term stock elasticity of office property in towns and cities is much greater, due to the relatively small proportion of land devoted to office use, the relatively small amount of land required for office development, and the availability of land which is transferable from other uses. Additionally, the stock elasticity of dairy farms will be greater than that of farmland in general, and the stock elasticity of supermarkets greater than retail property in general.

So, despite the overall fixed stock of land, the stock of commercial and industrial property is elastic in the long run, although it is relatively inelastic compared with most other goods, due to planning constraints and the overall relative land scarcity in the UK. However, in the short run, the stock of the principal property types is very inelastic due to durability and the time involved in the property development process. At any point in time, existing stock tends to dominate the market and is unable to vary in response to a change in space needs.

The property market and its imperfections

The above characteristics, in particular the infinite diversity of both the physical land and buildings and the legal interests existing over them, result in a uniquely complex market. In fact, rather than a single entity, the property market is a conglomeration of sub-markets. Occupation interests are traded in the letting market and, as rent is the price of occupation, the level of rental values is determined by the forces of supply and demand for property to let. Similarly, the price of property investment interests is determined by investment demand and supply in the investment sector. As different factors determine occupation demand and supply from investment demand and supply, these two markets require a separate analysis. Similarly, the development sector requires an independent analysis. In that sector old interests, both investment and occupational, are extinguished, and new interests are created in new properties.

Although each of the three sectors requires a separate analysis (see Parts III, IV, and V), they are closely linked. The rental value of occupation interests influences the income and value of investment interests. In turn, the value of investment interests is a major determinant of site values and development activity in the development sector. Like the Stock Exchange, the property market is both a primary market (in which new goods are sold for the first time) and a secondary market (in which secondhand goods are traded). However, because of the durability of property, the majority of interests changing hands tends to be in existing or 'standing' (as distinct from newly developed) properties.

Within the three main market sectors, there are an infinite variety of subdivisions, defined, e.g., according to use type, location and quality. There is the prime office letting market in the City of London, the prime farmland investment market in East Anglia, the prime industrial letting market in Reading and, doubtless, secondary shop markets in Bootle, Cleethorpes and Clacton on Sea. Each sub-market will be subject to its own unique economic conditions, with buyers who may not consider another area as a close substitute.

The property market is ubiquitous; it has no formally organised market place where prices are quoted and deals publically witnessed. That is just one of many features which contribute to its imperfection. Lack of detailed freely available information is endemic to the property market. Not only do many deals and their prices go unreported, but many deals involve some form of consideration apart from the price, so that the price agreed does not provide reliable evidence of market value. Property for sale or let may also be inadequately marketed so that buyers are unaware of what is available, and lack of knowledge is accentuated by the uncertainties created by legislation, particularly in the areas of planning, taxation and land tenure.

Probably the most important consideration leading to imperfect knowledge in the market is the complexity and diversity of the interests themselves. The type, location, size, age and general condition of a building may be known, together with the principal conditions of the lease to which the interest is subject, but apparently minor aspects of the physical structure (e.g., inadequate provision of fire escapes to satisfy the Fire Precautions Act), or of the lease contract (e.g., a badly worded rent review clause) can have a substantial impact on market price. Detailed knowledge of property interests and thorough analysis of rents and prices is necessary to enable buyers and sellers, whether investors or tenants, to understand rental and price levels for different property types in different locations. That is the economic *raison d'être* of the property valuer and agent.

The problem of assessing market rents and prices is accentuated by the small number of deals which take place. Changes in market conditions are difficult to perceive. Whereas hundreds of millions of pounds' worth of shares are being bought and sold in the Stock Exchange every day, evidence of only a handful of reliable property transactions might be available in any sub-market. This problem is particularly acute in the farmland market, where new lettings are a rarity and any individual farm may remain in the same family for centuries.

The diversity of property, particularly in respect of location, provides sellers or lessors with an element of monopoly power. The absence of a close substitute property available on the market at the same time, together with a lack of knowledge of the appropriate rent or price level, may enable the seller or lessor to achieve a figure higher than true market value.

The complexity of property interests and the property market makes it essential for buyers and sellers to employ professional experts, particularly surveyors and solicitors. The cost of these experts, together with the sheer length of time involved in the sale process, discourages short-term trading or frequent 'in and out' operations.

In comparison with stocks and shares, investment interests in property are highly priced and indivisible, and instead of large numbers of buyers and sellers, a relatively small number have sufficient financial resources to invest. Because of the large sums of money required for direct property investment, the market is dominated by financial institutions and property companies. Unlike the stock market, private individuals have little direct influence in the commercial and industrial sectors of the market, although they do have in farmland and, of course, in housing.

Clearly, the property market fails to meet any of the main prerequisites of the concept of a 'perfect market'. The 'goods' are highly priced and indivisible, consequently there are relatively small numbers of buyers and sellers, transactions costs are high, and the heterogeneity of property interests results in a pervasive obscurity about their qualities and true values. This contrasts with the Stock Exchange where information is freely available and where the market in gilts must come as close as any to the 'perfect market' concept.

The relative perfection of the stock market means that stock prices are sensitive and respond quickly to new information or a change in sentiment. In contrast, the manifest imperfection of the property market is one reason for the relative stability of property prices. Property prices do not normally react to short-term changes in market conditions, and the market seems slow to react even to fundamental change. Owners are frequently willing to retain their properties on the market unlet or unsold for substantial periods, rather than accept a rent or price below that which they hope to achieve.

However, it is not only market imperfection which results in price stability, but the constraints imposed under standard lease agreements. The relatively long-term nature and inflexibility of most commercial and industrial occupational leases (20–25-year terms are common) restrict the ability of occupiers to give up occupation, in turn restricting the supply of property for relet in times of economic recession, and tending to keep rental values stable. Similarly, the stability of rental values and the lengthy periods between rent reviews (five years is common) lead to stability of investment income and, consequently, stable investment prices.

It is important not to confuse the notional concept of a 'perfect market' with the realistic concept of an 'efficient market'. A 'perfect market' would be perfectly 'efficient', but an 'efficient market' need not meet the criteria for a 'perfect market'. The concept of efficiency is much less restrictive than that of perfection, and the many imperfections of the property market do not preclude the possibility that the property market is efficient. Indeed studies[1] suggest that the investment sector is efficient (in a relatively weak sense) indicating that prices in general reflect publically available information. That is an assumption implicit in the theory of property pricing that we will now develop.

We shall highlight a number of salient points from the above introduction to the property market.

- The value, risk and potential return of a property investment is dependant upon the terms of the leases to which the interest is subject, and upon the physical property over which the legal interest exists.
- The property market is a ubiquitous conglomeration of interrelated sub-markets in which prices are determined. The principal categorisation is into the letting, investment and development sectors, with further subdivisions according to, e.g., use-type, location, quality and size.
- The property market is very imperfect, particularly in contrast with the stock market, and values are slow to respond to changing market forces. The imperfection derives partly from the substantial value of most property interests, but principally from the heterogeneous nature of each interest.

11 Property's Yield and a Pricing Model

Property's rental yield

As concluded in Part I, an investment's yield serves both as a unit of comparison and as an aid to understanding price. The dividend yield, for instance, is widely used to compare the stock market's rating of shares, and a share's yield determines the multiple by which its price exceeds the current dividend. That multiple is the reciprocal of the required dividend yield. So if investors' required yield is 5%, the share's price must be 20 times the current dividend.

The same is essentially true for property. The rental yield is the most important unit for comparing the market's rating of property investments, but due to certain unique features of property investments, the relationship between price and current income is sometimes more complex than for stock market securities. In the first part of this chapter, these features are investigated and the rental yield explained.

In this and the remaining chapters of Part II, we are concerned essentially with pure investment interests in property, e.g., freeholds and leaseholds in business property subject to tenancies from which the investor is receiving a regular income. But it is pedantic always to include the term 'interest' when describing a property investment. It is common to describe a property as being sold when, strictly speaking, it is the investor's interest in the property which is sold, and that simplification will be frequently used in this text.

The significance of rent review

One feature of property investments is that rather than income being variable annually, rental payments normally remain fixed for a period of years. The timing and frequency with which rental payments can vary is a critical feature determining the characteristics, price and yield of an investment. The rent payable can be changed either when an existing lease expires and a new one commences, or as provided under a lease contract. Long leases are still in existence which make no provision for rent review, particularly ground leases, i.e. leases of urban sites which the tenant has subsequently developed and sub-let to occupying tenants.

A long lease without provision for rent review is unlikely to be granted nowadays, due to the impact of inflation on fixed-income investments and the tendency for rental values to rise in times of inflation. Just as equity shares gained popularity as a hedge against inflation, investors in property sought protection against inflation by introducing provision for rent review into lease contracts. Whereas in the immediate post-war period rents would frequently be fixed for the duration of a lease, in the 1950s provision was made in most new leases for a review of rental value after, say, 21 or 33 years. In the 1960s, 14-year review periods became accepted, and then in the late 1960s and early 1970s seven-year, five-year and occasionally three-year reviews were introduced into new commercial leases. Nowadays 20- or 25-year leases subject to five-year rent reviews are common.

In explaining property yields, we must distinguish between 'rack-rented', 'reversionary', and fixed-income investments. The term 'rack-rented' describes an investment in which the rent paid to the investor is the property's rental value. A 'reversionary' investment is one in which current rent differs from rental value, and in which a review is due to take place within a reasonable time. Rent is normally reviewed to the property's rental value at the date of the review. A fixed-income investment is one where any scope for rent review is so far in the future that it has a negligible effect on present value.

The price of an investment depends on income expectations, and the period of time to elapse before that income is receivable. Thus, the price of a 'reversionary' investment will reflect both the current level of income as well as the change expected at review (the 'reversion'). The longer the period to elapse before reversion, the greater will be the impact of current income on price, but as the reversion draws closer the price will increasingly reflect the income change to take place at reversion. The price of properties with distant reversions will be little affected by changes in rental value, but the closer is reversion, the more investment prices will reflect rental growth.

As rental values have generally risen in the post-war era, rental income has normally increased substantially at reversion. An indication of value trends within the rent review period is shown in Figure 11.1. This assumes that the property has been let at its rental value at the start of the lease, with the rent subject to review in Year X. The rental value is assumed to grow at a constant rate throughout the period, thereby being indicated by a straight line when drawn to a logarithmic scale (a curve if drawn to an arithmetic scale). Initially, or immediately after review, an investment's value will tend to rise at a rate substantially below the rate of rental value growth, but as the reversion draws near, capital growth tends to exceed rental value growth. In fact, immediately before reversion, the investment's value will tend to rise even if rental value is static, and possibly even if rental values are falling slightly.

In inflationary conditions, rental values are generally expected to rise, thus investors purchasing reversionary investments will anticipate three elements of return (a) current income, (b) capital gain deriving from rental value growth, and (c) capital gain deriving from the passage of time to reversion, sometimes called 'uplift'. This latter gain results from previous rental growth and is somewhat similar to the capital growth of a low coupon gilt as it approaches redemption, but whereas such growth in a gilt is essentially fixed and

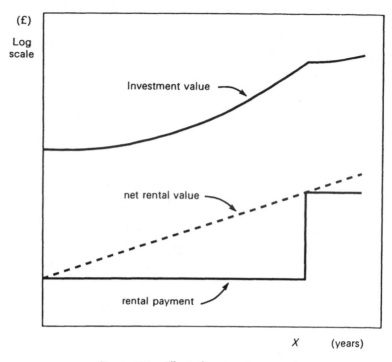

Figure 11.1   Effect of rent review on value

guaranteed, in the case of property it is variable. In effect, rental growth from earlier years has been stored up, and is being released as a capital gain as the reversion approaches.

The three elements of return can be illustrated by putting figures into Figure 11.1. Let us suppose that one year before reversion in Year X, the rent paid is £12 000 per annum, and the rental value is £50 000 per annum. We shall also assume that if it had been let at its rental value, the capital value of the investment would have been £1 million, indicating a capitalisation multiplier ('years' purchase') of 20 and a yield of 5%. However, as the reversion to rental value is one year ahead, the current value of the investment must be somewhat less than £1 million. Let us assume that the investment has just been purchased at its market value of £963 810.

At purchase, the income yield is therefore:

$$\frac{12\,000}{963\,810} \times 100 = \mathbf{1.245\%}$$

But, on the assumption that rental values and market yields remain unchanged over the coming year, then the investment must be worth £1 million in one year's time, representing a capital gain (uplift) of £36 190.

This gain, expressed as a percentage return, is:

$$\frac{36\,190}{963\,810} \times 100 = \textbf{3.755\%}$$

The addition of this capital gain return and the initial income yield is exactly 5%, being the same as the income yield of the property if let at its rental value:

$$\frac{50\,000}{1\,000\,000} \times 100 = \textbf{5.0\%}$$

The combination of the initial income yield and the gain from uplift is normally called the 'equivalent yield', presumably because it is equivalent to the income yield on a rack-rented property. A rack-rented property can give no uplift. The current rental yield from a rack-rented property and the equivalent yield from a reversionary property would constitute the total return (IRR) that investors would receive on the assumption of unchanged rental values and market yields. The equivalent yield, like the redemption yield on a dated gilt, is an IRR, but whereas the redemption value of a gilt is fixed, the rental value of a property is expected to rise in times of inflation to give investors a further return.

The unit commonly used to compare rack-rented property investments is therefore the current rental income yield, and in the case of reversionary investments, the unit of comparison is the equivalent yield. The rental income yield on a rack-rented property would tend to be similar to the equivalent yield on a comparable reversionary property, but not identical as in this illustration. This is because, like a low-coupon gilt, a reversionary investment gives a higher proportion of its return in the form of capital gain. Most investors would pay less tax on capital gain than on income, and so less tax on a 5% equivalent yield than on a 5% income yield. The price of £963 810 was used in this example because it is the price which would provide an investor with an equivalent yield of 5%. However, because of the lower tax liability imposed by this investment in comparison with a rack-rented property, there is a case for suggesting that investors would accept a somewhat lower yield, implying a marginally higher price than £963 810.

The third element of return anticipated by the purchaser is the return deriving from a rise in rental value. If, over the year to reversion, the rental value grows by 10% to £55 000, the value of the investment at reversion will rise to £1.1 million to give a total IRR of (just over) 15%. Note that the full benefit of this rental growth is received at the end of that year because of the rent review then taking place. A further 10% rental growth in the following year would not provide a 10% gain in that year because of the lengthy period to elapse before the next review. Part of the growth is stored up to provide uplift as the subsequent review approaches.

Although the capital value of equity-type freehold investments must ultimately follow trends in rental values, the effect of rental income being fixed for periods of several years is to increase the stability of capital values. If reversion is several years ahead, investment values are protected from falling rental values by the fixed income, and if reversion is close at hand, investment values have generally been protected from a short-term fall in rental values by the uplift accruing from previous rental growth. The rent review system has meant that even in times of recession (such as in 1980–2 when rental values rose only marginally), a portfolio of property investments could provide respectable returns due to the release of uplift deriving from rental growth in earlier periods of boom.

The relationship between rental value, rental payment and the capital value of a property investment let on regular rent reviews is shown in Figure 11.2. Note that the investment-value profile assumes a constant market yield. As in the case of stock-market investments, property values may also rise or fall as a result of a change in the level of yields in the market. Note also that, unlike the illustration, prime investment properties are normally let on the basis that rents can only be reviewed upwards, i.e. if there is a net decline in rental value over the period between reviews, the rental payment would remain unchanged.

In conditions of rising rental values, tenants will normally be paying rents below rental value, but when rental values are on a sustained downward

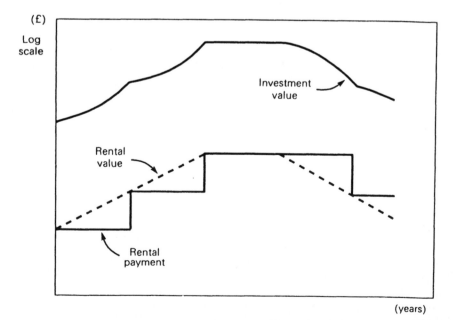

Figure 11.2   Value trend and rent review

trend, rental payments would tend to exceed rental values. In the inflationary conditions of the post-war period, rising rental values and the system of rent reviews have meant that income from property investments has rarely fallen, in contrast to dividend income from shares which, being variable annually, has been more volatile. It requires a sustained period of falling rental values to cause a rent reduction at review. That occurred in the central London office market in the 1990–2 recession when most properties were 'over-rented', but investors were protected to an extent by the standard upward-only review clause in most leases.

One further complication can arise in the calculation of a property's yield. Unlike an investor in shares or bonds, a property investor may be required to pay certain unavoidable recurrent expenses, such as maintenance, repairs and insurance of buildings, together with rent collection and certain other management costs. The liability of an investor to pay such periodic expenses depends on the lease conditions, but whereas in most modern leases the burden is placed on the occupying tenant, in many older leases the responsibility rests with the landlord. If the investor is liable for such items, the annual cost is deducted from the gross rental income when calculating the rental yield.

Rental yield – leasehold investments

As a lease can be granted only for a finite period (sometimes very long), leasehold investments must ultimately come to an end. However, unlike a dated gilt, the interest can have no value at its termination, thus ultimately a leasehold investment is a depreciating asset. As the market value of a leasehold reflects the length of the lease still to run, then if its rental yield was the simple relationship of current rent to current value, the yield would vary according to the remaining term of the lease. The yield would tend to rise as the value fell as the end of the lease approached. Consequently, direct yield comparisons could be made only between leaseholds of similar duration. The dearth of sales evidence of leasehold investments renders such a comparison inadequate, so traditionally leaseholds have been compared by the rental yield after deducting the annual sinking-fund instalment required to replace the value of the investment over the remaining term of the lease.

A purchaser of a leasehold is deemed to set aside in a sinking fund that part of his annual profit rent which would be exactly sufficient to replace the purchase price of the investment over the remaining period of the lease. The sum accumulated at the end of the lease would therefore be sufficient to purchase another leasehold identical to the first, and so on in perpetuity. By this concept, leasehold investments are notionally converted into perpetual investments, thereby enabling their yields (net of the annual sinking-fund instalment) to be comparable with yields on freeholds and leaseholds of different duration. The yield traditionally used for comparing leasehold investments (sometimes called the 'remunerative rate') is therefore the relationship between the current net profit rent, less the annual sinking-fund instalment, and the current market value of the investment, assuming it is sub-let at full rental value.

For a variety of reasons,[1] this yield is a potentially unreliable unit of comparison and there is a strong case (especially for relatively short leases) for using the expected IRR as an alternative.

We will conclude this section by restating the yields appropriate to each case.

- The yields commonly used as units of comparison are as follows:

    (1) Rack-rented and fixed-income freeholds:

    Rental income yield %, which is:

    $$\frac{\text{Current annual net rent} \times 100}{\text{Market value}}$$

    (2) Reversionary freeholds:

    Equivalent yield %, which is the annual IRR deriving from both the net rent and the capital change which arises from the passage of time to reversion (assuming that the rental value and market yield remain constant).

    (3) Leaseholds (rack-rented):

    Remunerative rate %, which is:

    $$\frac{\text{Current net profit rent} - \text{Sinking-fund instalment} \times 100}{\text{Market value}}$$

The yields defined above are sometimes called the 'all-risks yield' or simply 'the yield'. In each case it is the rate used by valuers when using the traditional Years' Purchase (YP) method of valuation. When the net rental income from a rack-rented freehold is capitalised at a rate of 5% (a YP of 20), the valuer is calculating the capital value which gives investors an *income yield* of 5%. When the current income and rental value of a reversionary property are capitalised at 5%, the valuer is calculating the value which gives investors an *equivalent yield* of 5%.

A property pricing model

In Chapter 6, a DCF pricing model was introduced which was appropriate to all income-earning investments (Equation (6.4)). This can be restated to apply specifically to property investments:

$$P_0 = \frac{R_1}{(1+r)} + \frac{R_2}{(1+r)^2} + \frac{R_3}{(1+r)^3} + \cdots \qquad (11.1)$$

where $R_{1,2,3}$ = expected net rental income in future periods 1, 2, 3; r = investors' target return (IRR) p.a. and P_0 = current price or market value.

This basic model will now be adapted to explain the pricing and rental yields of freehold investments subject to a variety of rent review arrangements.

Fixed-income freeholds

In the case of a freehold investment in a property let on a very long lease without provision for rent review, the rental income is fixed, and Equation (11.1) can be simplified to:

$$P_0 = \frac{R}{r} \qquad (11.2)$$

Expressed in words, this states that the market value of a fixed-income freehold is the net rent receivable divided by investors' target return.

But

$$\frac{R}{P_0}$$

is the rental yield (quoted as a decimal), which we shall give the symbol y, so for fixed-income freeholds:

$$y = r \qquad (11.3)$$

This expression states that the rental yield of a fixed-income freehold equals investors' target return. That is the same relationship as between the interest yield and investors' target return on an undated gilt, although in both cases the relationship implies an expectation of stable market yields. If investors purchased either investment in expectation of a change in yield, then they must anticipate a capital gain or loss which would result in a total return above or below the income yield.

Example 11.1

On the assumption that investors anticipate stable market yields, and that their target return is 15%, estimate the value of a freehold interest in a city centre site let for 150 years in 1950 at a net rent of £10 000 per annum (fixed):

$$P_0 = \frac{R}{r}$$

$$\frac{10\,000}{0.15} = \textbf{£66\,667}$$

The reversion to rental value in the year 2100 is so far distant that it will have virtually no present value. Virtually all the return from the investment derives from the £10 000 of fixed income.

Freeholds with annual rent review

If a freehold investment is subject to annual rent review then, assuming a constant rate of rental value growth, the basic DCF model can be restated as follows:

$$P_0 = \frac{R_0}{1+r} + \frac{R_0(1+g)}{(1+r)^2} + \frac{R_0(1+g)^2}{(1+r)^3} + \cdots \qquad (11.4)$$

which simplifies to:

$$P_0 = \frac{R_0}{r-g} \qquad (11.5)$$

where R_0 = current rental value and g = expected rental value growth rate p.a. But as,

$$\frac{R_0}{P_0} = y \quad \text{(the rental yield)}$$

then

$$y = r - g \qquad (11.6)$$

Expressed in words, the yield of a freehold investment let on a long lease with annual rent reviews is investors' target return less their expected rental value growth rate per annum.

This relationship between income yield, target return and growth is basically the same as for ordinary shares (where $d = r - g$).

Note that the rent received by the investor in any year is deemed to be the rental value at the start of the year. The rent received in Year 1 is thus the rental value in Year 0. Rent is deemed to be received annually in arrears.

Example 11.2

Estimate the market value of a freehold interest in a prime city-centre shop recently let at a rent of £50 000 subject to annual review. Assume investors' target IRR is 15%, and rental growth is expected to be 10% per annum:

$$P_0 = \frac{R_0}{r-g}$$

$$= \frac{50\,000}{0.15 - 0.10} = \text{£1 000 000}$$

Freeholds with regular review periods exceeding one year

Very few investment properties are let on annual review, and the large majority are subject to review at regular intervals of five or seven years. If a property was let on a long lease subject to rent review at three-year intervals, the basic DCF model could be restated as follows:

$$P_0 = \frac{R_0}{1+r} + \frac{R_0}{(1+r)^2} + \frac{R_0}{(1+r)^3} + \frac{R_0(1+g)^3}{(1+r)^4} +$$

$$\frac{R_0(1+g)^3}{(1+r)^5} + \frac{R_0(1+g)^3}{(1+r)^6} + \frac{R_0(1+g)^6}{(1+r)^7} + \cdots \qquad (11.7)$$

which simplifies to:

$$P_0 = \frac{R_0}{r\left(\dfrac{(1+g)^n - 1}{(1+r)^n - 1}\right)} \qquad (11.8)$$

where R_0 = current rental value (start of lease or at rent review) and n = interval between rent reviews (years).

But as

$$\frac{R_0}{P_0} = y,$$

then

$$y = r - r\left(\frac{(1+g)^n - 1}{(1+r)^n - 1}\right) \qquad (11.9)$$

This expression states that yields of freehold property investments let on regular rent reviews depend on investors' target return, their rental growth expectation, and the period between rent reviews. As in the case of Equation (11.6), the yield is determined by investors' target return *less* a growth element, but rather than the growth element being simply investors' annual rental growth expectation, it is that growth rate *reduced* by the effect of the rent review period delaying the receipt of higher income.

Example 11.3

On the assumption that investors anticipate 10% rental growth and have a target IRR of 15%, estimate the market value of a freehold interest in a city centre commercial property just let on a long lease at a rent of £50 000 subject to five-year reviews.

We shall solve this question in two stages – first we shall calculate investors' required yield and then the investment's value:

$$y = r - r\left(\frac{(1 + g)^n - 1}{(1 + r)^n - 1}\right)$$

$$= 0.15 - 0.15\left(\frac{(1 + 0.10)^5 - 1}{(1 + 0.15)^5 - 1}\right)$$

$$= 0.0595 \text{ or } \mathbf{5.95\%}$$

$$P_0 = \frac{R_0}{y}$$

$$= \frac{50\,000}{0.0595}$$

$$= \mathbf{£840\,336}$$

Impact of the rent review period on property yields

Note the effect that the five-year rent review has had on the yield and value of the property in Example 11.3 in contrast with that in Example 11.2. In both examples, the target return and rental growth expectation were the same, but the yield in Example 11.3 is almost 1% higher, and the value almost £160 000 lower, purely because rent reviews are at five-yearly intervals instead of annually. The effect on investors' returns of the five-year reviews is illustrated by the different expected income from the two investments:

Expected rental income (£)
Year

	1	2	3	4	5	6
Annual Review	50 000	55 000	60 500	66 550	73 205	80 526
5-year review	50 000	50 000	50 000	50 000	50 000	80 526
Difference	—	**5 000**	**10 500**	**16 550**	**23 205**	—

Whereas the two investments will provide the same income in Years 1 and 6, an investor in the property let on five-year review will lose out on substantial amounts of income in Years 2, 3, 4 and 5 in comparison with what he would have received if the property had been let on annual review. If the two properties had the same yield, investors would anticipate a higher total return from the property let on annual review. This would lead to an excess demand over supply for such properties, resulting in their prices rising and their yields falling until the yield differential indicated above came about.

If the two investments are considered to be of equal risk and investment quality, investors' target return will tend to be the same for each. But because of the effect of the five-year rent review on future income, investors will require a higher initial income yield from that property to give them the same total IRR as they could get by investing in the property with annual review. 5.95% is the yield required to give investors an expected IRR of 15%. Consequently, although the initial rental income is £50 000 in each case, the value of the property with five-year review must be only £840 336 in contrast to £1 000 000 for the property let on annual review.

● In times of generally rising rental values, the longer the period between rent reviews (*ceteris paribus*) the higher will be the yield required by investors. The market forces of demand and supply will bring about the yield differential.

The reader should be aware of certain simplifying assumptions made in the foregoing analysis. First, rental income is deemed to be received annually in arrears, whereas it would normally be received quarterly or half-yearly in advance. Second, the rent review period in Equations (11.8) and (11.9) is deemed to remain constant in perpetuity. Third, the equations are valid only if no changes in market yields are anticipated, so that expected capital growth must ultimately equal expected rental growth. Fourth, the rental growth rate is deemed to be constant in perpetuity. Despite these limitations, the various equations neatly encapsulate (for non-reversionary freeholds) the essential relationships between price, rental income, yield, target return, growth expectation and the rent review period.

Reversionary and other investments

In cases where the above assumptions are not valid, and in the case of leasehold investments, the full DCF model can be applied with appropriate adjustment. In the case of reversionary freeholds, price can be explained by a combination of the simplified expressions and the full DCF model.

Example 11.4

Estimate the market value of a freehold interest in a city-centre commercial property let on a 33-year lease 30 years ago at a fixed rent of £5000. It is expected that, at the expiry of the current lease, the property will be relet on a five-year rent review basis. The current net rental value is £50 000 and, as before, investors' target return is assumed to be 15% and their rental growth expectation 10% per annum.

The following equation encapsulates all the information in the question which can influence its present value:

$$P_0 = \frac{R_1}{(1+r)} + \frac{R_2}{(1+r)^2} + \frac{R_3 + P_3}{(1+r)^3}$$

We know the target IRR and the rent receivable over the next three years, so the main problem is to calculate the expected price on the assumption of a sale of the investment on reversion at the end of Year 3:

$$P_3 = \frac{R_4}{y}$$

The rental income in Year 4 is the expected rental value (RV) at the end of Year 3, which is the current rental value subject to 10% growth per annum over three years.

> Expected RV in 3 years $= 50\,000\,(1 + 0.10)^3 = $ **£66 550**
> Expected yield at reversion $= $ **5.95%** (see Example 11.3)

$$P_3 = \frac{66\,550}{0.0595} = \text{£1 118 487}$$

So:

$$P_0 = \frac{5000}{(1+0.15)} + \frac{5000}{(1+0.15)^2} + \frac{5000 + 1\,118\,487}{(1+0.15)^3} = \textbf{£746 840}$$

Property pricing model – summary

In our analysis of stock-market investments (Chapter 6) we concluded that stock prices could be considered as either:

(a)   the present value of expected future income flows, as represented by the full DCF model. In the case of equity shares:

$$P_0 = \frac{D_1}{(1+r)} + \frac{D_2}{(1+r)^2} + \frac{D_3}{(1+r)^3} + \cdots$$

or

(b)   current income divided by the current income yield. For shares:

$$P_0 = \frac{D_1}{d}$$

However, it was shown that, given constant growth assumptions, (b) was merely a simplified version of (a), the link between the two models being the expression:

$$d = r - g$$

Virtually the same concept applies to property pricing. Property values can be considered as the discounted value of expected future net rental income flows (DCF model):

$$P_0 = \frac{R_1}{(1+i)} + \frac{R_2}{(1+r)^2} + \frac{R_3}{(1+r)^3} + \cdots$$

or as the current rent divided by the rental yield (non-reversionary investments):

$$P_0 = \frac{R_1}{y} \quad \text{(the YP model)}$$

Given constant rental growth assumptions, the link between the two models is the expression:

$$y = r - r\left(\frac{(1+g)^n - 1}{(1+r)^n - 1}\right)$$

The YP model can therefore be considered as merely a simplified version of the full DCF model. When using the full DCF model, the rental growth expectation, rent review period and target return are *explicitly* stated, but in the YP model these three variables are *implicitly* reflected in y, the income yield. For freehold investments let on regular rent reviews, Equation (11.8) most neatly encapsulates the four principal variables determining price, and it is these variables which we must therefore examine in our quest to explain the price of property. Although Equation (11.8) is not strictly valid for reversionary or leasehold interests, the values of these investments are also determined by the same four variables. Additionally, the price of reversionary investments is determined by the period to elapse before reversion, and leaseholds by their duration and the liability to pay a head rent.

These two models also represent the two property valuation methods normally used in practice. When using the DCF method, the valuer must attempt to quantify the market's rental growth expectation and target return. As these two variables can never be precisely known, only estimated, the YP model has the advantage that hard evidence of current rents and yields is available from transactions taking place in the property market. That makes the YP model the more popular for the valuation of relatively standard investments, whereas DCF is probably superior for the valuation of more complex investments, particularly short leaseholds and reversionary investments where growth potential is complex, where good market-sales evidence of comparable properties is unavailable and where the yield is difficult to determine.

The purpose of valuation is usually to *assess* the market value of a property, a problem deriving essentially from the heterogeneity of property interests. Our purpose in this book is to *explain* property values; to explain why different property investments have different values, and why the general level of values moves over time. In the pursuit of that objective we shall be addressing ourselves essentially to Equation (11.8) and the variables contained therein, although in this Part we shall restrict ourselves to explaining rental yields according to Equation (11.9). In the next two chapters, we shall therefore examine the characteristics of property investments which determine investors' target return and growth expectations – two major variables in our pricing model.

We will conclude this chapter with the following points.

- The market value or price of a property investment can be considered as:
  (a) the present value of expected future net rental income, or
  (b) a multiple of the current net rent. In the case of non-reversionary freeholds the multiple is the reciprocal of investors' required income yield.
- The yield of a rack-rented freehold subject to regular rent review depends on investors' target return, their rental value growth expectation and the period between rent reviews.

- *Ceteris paribus*, the higher the investors' target return, or the lower the investors' rental growth expectation, or the longer the period between rent reviews, the higher will be a property's yield.
- In the case of freehold property subject to a very long lease without provision for rent review, the yield will tend to equate with investors' target return.

12 Property's Risk and the Level of Yields

In Chapter 11 we introduced a model of the determination of property's yield (restated below). In this chapter the principal variables in the model will be investigated and the level of yields in the property market explained.

$$y = r - r\left(\frac{(1+g)^n - 1}{(1+r)^n - 1}\right)$$

The model shows (for rack-rented freeholds with regular rent review) the mathematical relationship between a property's yield, rent review period, investors' growth expectation and target return. The expression cannot be used to calculate the yield appropriate to any property investment because two of the variables – investors' target return and growth expectation – are always unknown. Nonetheless, by examining the characteristics of property which determine these variables, we can tentatively quantify or 'guesstimate' their values, thereby helping to explain the level of yields (or changes in yields) occurring in the property market. We shall first examine the determinants of investors' target return, represented by the symbol r in the equation above.

In Part I we concluded that investors' target return from any investment is composed of the return available from alternative relatively riskless investments plus a premium to compensate investors for the extra (market) risk of the investment in question. Additionally, the target return must reflect differences in liquidity, marketability, transaction cost, management cost and taxation. These aspects of property investments will now be examined in comparison with those of stock-market investments.

Risk

The individual investment

In Chapter 8, an investment's risk was defined as the variability of its annual return (IRR), and as the return varies as a result of changes in both income and price, this concept of risk encompasses risk to income as well as risk to capital. The risk characteristics of fixed-income freeholds must be similar to those of undated gilts. Most tenants subject to fixed head rents benefit from substantial profit rents, and it is unlikely that they will default on their rental payments, as this might result in the loss of their own valuable interest. Thus, as in the case of gilts, fixed-income freeholds must tend to be very secure and the principal risk must derive from changes in the level of long-term interest rates and the rate of inflation.

The risk characteristics of equity property investments must be somewhat akin to equity shares. In both cases, income can vary over time, and may even cease. A company may declare no dividend and a property investment may suffer from tenant default or a rent void. The variability of both dividends and rents can lead to a proportionately greater variability in price, due to changes in the growth expectation on which yield and price is based. Despite these similarities, however, property is innately a less risky investment than ordinary shares.

An ordinary share is a claim over an intangible and potentially ephemeral asset – the profit-making ability of a company. As explained in Part I, corporate profitability is dependent on a large variety of factors, some of which are critically dependent on good management, and others which are beyond management control. Property investments, on the other hand, are rights over land and buildings, tangible and very durable assets. Property values and rental income are less dependent on management ability, and if a tenant goes bankrupt the investor should suffer a relatively minor loss – perhaps a brief rent void and the expense of finding and leasing to a new tenant. Whereas corporate bankruptcy can mean that shareholders lose all their capital invested, the loss to the company's landlord is likely to be minimal, partly because rent is normally paid in advance, partly because it is a priority payment in the event of bankruptcy, but principally because the property is durable and can be relet to another tenant.

In circumstances less extreme than bankruptcy, a company in difficulty will stop paying dividends before it stops paying rent. Rent is a contractual obligation like interest on debt, dividends are not. Furthermore, much prime property is let to public authorities who are unlikely to default on their payments, and who will tend to remain as tenants over long periods, thereby again reducing the risk of voids and the expense of reletting.

Prime commercial and industrial property is largely free of two of the three risk 'strata' to which company shares are subject (see Chapter 9). It faces little risk from the problems of the individual firm, and also from the problems of a specific trade or business type. This is because property is mobile between user and, to a certain extent, between use. Shops, offices, factories and warehouses can be used by many different firms and types of business, and the problems of one firm or business type should not normally cause a prime property to be left unoccupied for a long period. That is why investors are reluctant to buy purpose-built factories – if versatility is reduced, the risk of rent voids increases.

On the other hand, property is vulnerable to national and local economic recession and to a slump in certain broad categories of industry and commerce. For instance, shop investments are vulnerable to a decline in consumer expenditure and the problems of the retail trade, and factories are vulnerable to a slump in manufacturing activity. Property also suffers the disadvantage of being fixed in location, thereby being vulnerable to rent voids or falling rental values arising from a localised recession. That is partly why the bulk of the property portfolios of the major institutional investors are located in the more economically healthy parts of the country.

Property which is subject to institutional investment is usually of such quality and in such a location that there is little risk of long-term rent voids. If a property is unoccupied over an extended period it often means that the landlord is holding out for too high a rent, rather than indicating an inability to find a tenant. However, such property is not riskless, it is still vulnerable to falling rental and capital values.

The investment category

So far this discussion has been concerned largely with the risk of individual properties vis-à-vis individual shares. But a substantial part of these risks can be avoided by portfolio diversification. Just as the risk of holding shares in any company can be reduced by investing in other shares, so (e.g.) the risk of localised recession faced by individual properties may largely be avoided by investing in other locations. These risks may be of little consequence to the investing institutions because they hold diversified portfolios of each invest-ment type, and due to the dominance of these institutions in the stock and property markets, such risks will be of little significance in determining market prices and yields. We will therefore proceed to examine the *relative* risk of separate *portfolios* of gilts, equities and property.

Here it is important to point out the problems of comparing returns from property with stock-market securities. With stock prices being recorded daily and dividends widely reported, it is a simple matter to accurately measure returns. But there are major difficulties in measuring property returns, arising primarily from the heterogeneous nature of property and the small number of sales which take place. This means that property performance indices have to be based on valuations rather than sale prices, and valuations are fallible. In particular, there is a tendency for the valuation of the index constituents at one date to be influenced by the valuation at the previous date, so that the index underestimates the periodic fluctuations in market prices and returns. This problem of 'smoothing' is greater the more frequently returns are measured and valuations made.

Another problem in comparing investment risk is defining and measuring the risk that really concerns investors and which is reflected in market prices. Can risk be adequately represented by the variability of annual returns? Should it be measured in real terms rather than money terms? Should we just measure downside fluctuations in returns rather than variability upwards and downwards? Over what period should returns be measured? Is a year relevant or is it just used for convenience? Perhaps investors are more

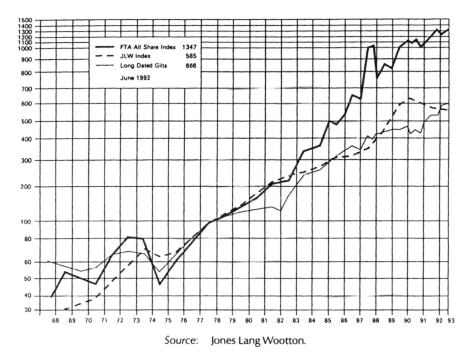

Source: Jones Lang Wootton.

Figure 12.1   Overall performance of property, gilts and equities

concerned with fluctuations over shorter or longer periods such as three or five years.

These are just some of the questions posed by this kind of study and which, like performance measurement, go beyond the scope of this book. However, an indication of property's low risk relative to gilts and equities is given in Table 12.1, which shows the results of a study[1] of the relative performance of long-dated gilts, equities and property over the 25-year period 1967–92. The data source for this study was the JLW Property Index. The function of this index is to measure the performance of a typical institutional property portfolio, diversified according to property type and location, containing both prime and secondary property and measuring total returns which reflect the impact of, e.g., rent voids and depreciation.

Table 12.1 shows mean returns and a variety of risk measures calculated in both money (nominal) terms and in real (net of RPI) terms, over three-year and five-year periods as well as annually. The reason for calculating returns over the longer periods was twofold. First, the possibility of understating fluctuations in property's annual returns (due to the smoothing effect of valuations) is unlikely to be perpetuated over three- or five-year periods. Second, it seems possible that, due to the long-term nature of their liabilities, the investing institutions are less concerned with risk over one year than over these longer periods.

Table 12.1   Risks and returns 1967–92 (June to June)

Types of returns	Property	Long gilts*	Equities[†]
Annual money returns			
Mean return %	13.8	10.7	17.7
Standard deviation %	11.2	12.3	21.3
Downside semi-variance	69.1	80.2	256.2
'Beta' coefficient	0.11	0.34	1.00
Annual real returns			
Mean return %	4.5	1.7	8.2
Standard deviation %	10.8	12.7	20.9
Downside semi-variance	72.1	78.2	219.6
Downside real-variance	41.8	64.2	126.5
'Beta' coefficient	0.16	0.39	1.00
Triennial money returns			
Mean return %	50.5	37.3	61.0
Standard deviation %	27.8	28.4	46.6
Downside semi-variance	366.9	387.8	1107.4
'Beta' coefficient	0.12	0.50	1.00
Triennial real returns			
Mean return %	15.3	5.5	24.8
Standard deviation %	22.5	25.6	42.1
Downside semi-variance	291.9	308.9	801.6
Downside real-variance	101.8	207.8	300.6
'Beta' coefficient	0.20	0.52	1.00
Quinquennial money returns			
Mean return %	98.4	72.9	126.7
Standard deviation %	38.1	44.4	87.0
Downside semi-variance	541.2	922.1	3497.3
'Beta' coefficient	0.03	0.43	1.00
Quinquennial real returns			
Mean return %	25.6	10.8	48.5
Standard deviation %	27.4	36.0	71.9
Downside semi-variance	346.4	544.4	2000.9
Downside real-variance	48.1	296.2	340.0
'Beta' coefficient	0.14	0.45	1.00

Correlation coefficients	Property/ gilts	Property/ equities	Gilts/ equities
Annual money returns	0.02	0.21	0.59
Triennial money returns	0.06	0.19	0.82
Quinquennial money returns	0.02	0.08	0.83
Annual real returns	0.15	0.29	0.63
Triennial real returns	0.20	0.35	0.87
Quinquennial real returns	0.19	0.34	0.90

Note

Standard deviation is a measure of the dispersion of returns around the mean.

Downside semi-variance measures the variability of returns below the mean.

Downside real variance measures the variability of real returns below a nil real return.

It measures an investment's ability to keep pace with inflation.

'Beta' coefficient is a measure of the variability of returns relative to equity shares (FT-A All-share index). It is not a true beta which could be legitimately used in the Capital Asset Pricing Model.

* Measured from Phillips & Drew 25-year gilt index until December 1975 and the FT-A over-15-year gilt index thereafter.

† FT-A All-share index.

Data source: JLW Property Index.

Table 12.1 shows property as having less risk than either gilts or equities on all 21 measures. Property's risk advantage over equity shares is substantial, but over gilts it is relatively small, particularly in terms of standard deviation and downside semi-variance measured over annual and triennial periods.

The stability of property's returns relative to equities is no great surprise. On occasion, returns from shares have fluctuated dramatically, in particular from −50% in 1974 to +148% in 1975,[2] although these years were exceptional. It is property's stability relative to long gilts which is more surprising, although these have fluctuated from −15% to +51% in the worst and best years. In contrast, until the 1990s, there has been only one calendar year (1974) in which property's returns have been negative.

The mixed portfolio

But we still have not focused on the risk that is of real importance to the institutional investor. It is not the risk of each investment type that is important but the risk that each brings to a combined portfolio. As institutions hold portfolios composed principally of property, equities and gilts (and other fixed income investments whose returns tend to move in concert with gilts), the institutions will be concerned with how returns from each of the three categories tend to co-vary, or correlate with each other. It is therefore interesting to find that returns from property show a much lower correlation with both gilts and equities than the correlation of gilts with equities (see Table 12.1). This appears to hold true whether returns are measured in real or money terms and whether calculated over one, three or five years. This highlights the merits of property as a diversification for portfolios dominated by equities and gilts.

The low risk of property relative to gilts and equities derives both from the innate characteristics of property investments and the imperfection of the market in which it is traded. Rental values have been more stable than corporate profitability, rental income more certain than dividends and property values more stable than share prices. The volatility of returns from equities is principally due to the volatility of share prices which, in turn, derives from the volatility of corporate profits and their sensitivity to economic and political trends. The volatility of returns from gilts derives from the sensitivity of their prices to changes in inflation and interest rates. Although property's returns are also affected by economic trends and changing interest rates, it is a good hedge against inflation and prices are stabilised by long leases and lengthy rent review periods.

The low correlation of property's returns with gilts and equities can be partly explained by the tendency of returns from gilts and equities to *lead* the economic cycle whereas property has tended to *lag*. A rise in gilt prices has tended to precede a bull market in shares, which in turn has tended to peak before the height of economic activity. On the other hand, rental growth from commercial and industrial property tends to lag economic activity, and the effect of lengthy rent review periods is to cause a delay before rental growth is converted to higher investment income. The property investor may gain from a rise in income when equities are suffering from the impact of the next recession. Thus property has tended to provide a stabilising influence over the economic cycle to portfolios dominated by equities and gilts.

Liability matching

One further aspect of risk that we must address is the ability of investment returns to match the liabilities of investors. This is of particular importance to the life assurance and pension funds whose essential function is to pay out pensions and benefits to their members. As the principal concern of these institutions is to meet these liabilities, it seems probable that they are less concerned with the variability of investment returns *per se* than the variability of returns vis-à-vis their liabilities. This is reflected by a policy of matching their liabilities with investments of similar characteristics. The long-term nature of the institutions' liabilities and their links with inflation and the level of wages suggests that the measure of risk in Table 12.1 that comes closest to reflecting their concern is the 'downside real variance' of returns over five years. That measures the risk of failing to keep pace with inflation over five-year periods, and property's superiority on that measure generally seems to confirm its risk advantage over the other investment types.

Liquidity

In terms of liquidity, property is clearly at a disadvantage in comparison with stock-market securities. Shares can be sold on the stock market within a few minutes of the decision being made, and the seller should receive the proceeds within two to four weeks. On the other hand several months may elapse before the completion of a property sale. Time is involved in drawing up particulars of sale and in advertising. Interested parties must be allowed to inspect the property and legal documents, and sufficient time must be given for valuations to be undertaken, finance arranged and the legal formalities completed.

Although investors have a preference for liquidity, this may not be a major factor determining property yields. The life assurance and pension funds which dominate the property investment market have little need for liquidity from property. Such needs as they have can be met either by their inflow of funds or from their other investment assets, and they have traditionally regarded their property holdings as a long term 'lock-away'.

On the other hand, property's illiquidity can create difficulties for specialist property funds such as property unit trusts and property bonds when facing large encashments by unit holders. It is also a disadvantage to all investors striving to manage portfolios in the face of market change. The investor who decides to sell property because of fear of a market downturn may be unable to sell before the downturn arrives and prices fall.

Marketability

Property investments of a quality acceptable to institutional investors have normally been very marketable, particularly during the period 1967–82 when the institutions were actively increasing their property portfolios. However, during the market slumps of 1974 and 1990–2 property became difficult to sell. Property which is not acceptable to financial institutions tends to be particularly difficult to sell in times of high interest rates, as buyers of such investments generally purchase with the help of borrowed money.

In comparison with gilts and equities, property is clearly less marketable. In fact, one of the fundamental differences is that, whereas stocks and shares can always be sold instantly on the stock market, a property can sometimes languish unsold on the property market for months. In the stock market prices move quickly to equate demand with supply, but in the property market demand and supply can be unbalanced for months or even years before market prices move to a 'market clearing' level. By that time demand and supply have probably changed again, so that market prices tend to lag changes in buying or selling pressure. That is one feature of an imperfect market.

Taxation liability

Standing property investments (as distinct from property developments) are taxed on much the same basis as ordinary shares. The investor is normally subject to tax on investment income and capital gain (in excess of inflation) realised on sale. Gilts and certain corporate bonds are exempt from CGT but interest is taxable. Despite this concession, most investors pay more tax on an investment in gilts than on shares or property, because with gilts the majority of the return tends to derive from income rather than from capital gain. Although an investor such as a life assurance fund or an individual may face the same nominal tax rate on income and capital gain, effectively capital gain is more valuable due to the indexation allowance and the fact that payment of the tax is postponed until sale. Historically, equities and property have given the bulk of their returns in capital gain rather than income, thus they have faced less tax than gilts per 1% of return.

Transaction costs

The complexity and heterogeneity of property investments in comparison with stocks and shares necessarily means that more expert advice is required by both seller and purchaser. The main expenses of the purchaser are legal fees, valuer's fees and stamp duty, whereas the seller normally faces legal fees and selling agent's fees and expenses. These amount to much more than the costs of buying or selling the same value of stocks and shares, particularly in the case of gilts which are exempt from stamp duty and where dealing costs are very low for large deals. However, as property tends to be held for much longer periods than gilts, the relative *annual* transaction costs incurred through holding a portfolio of each becomes much less significant. Nonetheless property is still at a disadvantage.

Management costs

In the case of property where the annual liability for repairs and insurance is borne by the tenant, management duties include the following:

(a) rent collection, accounting and ensuring that lease covenants are being complied with;
(b) portfolio management, annual revaluation and performance analysis;
(c) non-annual negotiations at rent review and at the end of leases.

The annualised cost of these items is estimated at not less than 0.35% of the value of the portfolio. The cost of managing a portfolio of gilts or equities is variable but normally less, particularly in the case of gilts.

Property's target return

We can now reach some tentative conclusions about investors' target return from property. The target return is normally compared with the redemption yield on conventional long-dated gilts (valued at par). Although long gilts are not riskless, they provide a better comparison than Treasury bills because they are a closer substitute for property for the long-term investor, and there is a closer relationship between their yields and property yields over time. Long gilts are also considered to be a better comparison than undated gilts because the market in longs is larger and less speculative, and their redemption yields are believed to provide a better indication of the opportunity cost of long-term investment capital. In fact, the investing institutions use gilt yields as a yardstick for comparing returns with other investments.[3]

It is conventional to assume that the target return on good quality property investments is 2% above the redemption yield on long-dated gilts. The evidence for this 2% premium probably originates from the yield premium over gilts which was available from prime commercial property in the non-inflationary conditions of the inter-war period, as well as from the yield premium generally provided by fixed-income ground rents in recent times. In neither of these situations would rental growth be significant, so market yields provided good evidence of investors' target return. However, the existence of a 2% yield premium on non-growth property investments does not prove that a similar (or any) premium is appropriate for growth investments. This is because (e.g.) fixed-income investments,

(a) fail to benefit from the low taxation of capital gain relative to income,
(b) lack the ability to reduce portfolio risk by providing returns with a low correlation to gilts and equities, and
(c) cannot reduce risk in real terms or match the inflation-linked liabilities of the investing institutions.

Market evidence of the relative movement of yields on gilts and property over the 1980s suggest that there is no constant relationship between gilt yields and property's target return. In fact, it seems that the yield differential has varied over a range of 4% or more, which would be consistent with property's target return moving from a 2% premium to a 2% discount and back again.[4] As previously explained, it is not possible to precisely identify property's target return or the yield differential with gilts, nor can it be proved that property has traded on a yield discount to gilts, yet a 2% yield discount would be a *possible* outcome to our investigation of the relative merits of gilts and property and might be arrived at as follows:

	%
Risk	−2.50
Liquidity and marketability	+1.00
Taxation liability	−1.00
Transaction costs	+0.25
Management costs	+0.25
Yield difference	−2.00

The above figures tentatively quantify the relative costs and benefits of investing in a portfolio of property compared with a similar sized portfolio of long-dated gilts. For instance, it is suggested that property's poorer liquidity and marketability would tend to cause investors to require an extra 1% IRR, but that property's lower taxation liability would compensate by the same amount. The figures illustrate how property's yield differential with gilts *might* have been negative, but they also indicate why the differential will constantly be changing. Transaction costs of gilts have changed since Big Bang, and the relative taxation liability of the two investments has changed and will continue to change according to (a) changes in the proportion of return which derives from income and capital gain, and (b) changes in the rates of tax charged.

By far the most difficult figure to estimate is the allowance for the relative risk of the two investments, because it is investors' *perception* of risk which will be reflected in the target return, and that perception will be constantly changing. The investigation of the risk of gilts and property illustrated in Table 12.1 may or may not be accurate (depending largely on whether the JLW Index is a good representation of returns from property), and the 2.5% discount for risk suggested above may or may not be a fair interpretation of it. But even if the analysis is accurate, it may not reflect investors' *perception* of the relative risk. An additional complication is that the study is *historical* whereas investors are making buy/sell decisions for the *future*. The risk of gilts seems unlikely to be as great in the next twenty years as it has been in the past twenty years, due to a lower and less volatile outlook for inflation. It is investors' *perception* of the relative *future* risk of gilts and property which influences property's target return, yield and price at any point in time.

Property's target return differential with gilt yields is a measure of the investment market's relative rating of the two investments and must inevitably vary with economic trends and sentiment. At the time of writing, property is in the doldrums and the yield premium is likely to be high, perhaps over 3%. But henceforth in this book we shall assume that, for good-quality commercial-property investments, the conventional 2% yield premium is correct, i.e. that the target return is 2% above the redemption yield on long-dated gilts. However, it is important to appreciate that the premium will not only vary over time, but will vary also between one investment and another (see Chapter 13).

Before proceeding to investigate the growth variable in our model of yield determination, we will specify a number of conclusions from this chapter so far, and include simple examples to help consolidate an understanding of the material.

- There are difficulties in assessing property's risk relative to other investments and in defining the risk that concerns the dominant investors and which will be reflected in market prices. However, it seems probable that

property has generally proved a less risky investment than either equities or long-dated gilts since the late 1960s.
- The low correlation of property's returns with both equities and fixed-income investments makes it a valuable diversification for portfolios dominated by equities and gilts.
- Property's target return is best estimated by reference to the redemption yield on long-dated gilts and is conventionally assumed to be 2% above the gilt yield. However, the yield premium is a variable not a constant and probably varied over a range of at least 4% in the 1980s.
- The risk that is reflected in the target return and market prices is not historic risk, but investors' perception of future risk.

Example 12.1

In Example 11.3, we saw that if investors' target return was 15% and their growth expectation was 10%, then the rental yield of a property let on five-year rent review would tend towards 5.95%. Calculate the change in yield which would tend to take place if the target return fell from 15% to 14%, on the assumption that the rental growth expectation was unchanged:

$$y = r - r\left(\frac{(1+g)^n - 1}{(1+r)^n - 1}\right)$$

$$= 0.14 - 0.14\left(\frac{(1+0.10)^5 - 1}{(1+0.14)^5 - 1}\right)$$

$$= 0.048 \text{ or } \mathbf{4.8\%}$$

So a fall in the target return will tend to cause a (marginally greater) fall in property yields. Conversely, a rise in the target return will tend to cause a rise in property yields. The change in target return could result from a change in either or both the gilt yield or the yield premium. However property yields do not respond to every change in gilt yields. First, gilt prices and yields are far more volatile than those of property, and property yields tend to follow gilts only when a significant trend is taking place (see Figure 12.2). Second, the influence which was responsible for causing a yield change on gilts may also cause a change in property's growth expectation. If a rise in gilt yields resulted from a rise in inflation, for example, this would also tend to cause a rise in investors' rental growth expectation, and the changes in the two variables would tend to cancel each other out to leave the yield unchanged. That helps to explain why yields on property have tended to remain relatively stable in comparison with yields on fixed-income investments.

Example 12.2

What might be the effect on the yield of the property in Example 12.1 if a fall in the growth expectation from 10% to 9% per annum had coincided with the fall in the target return?

$$y = r - r\left(\frac{(1+g)^n - 1}{(1+r)^n - 1}\right)$$

$$= 0.14 - 0.14\left(\frac{(1+0.09)^5 - 1}{(1+0.14)^5 - 1}\right)$$

$$= 0.0585 \text{ or } \mathbf{5.85\%}$$

Although a marginal fall of 0.1% is indicated, it is unlikely that any discernible yield change would take place in reality.

Investors' growth expectation

We shall now examine the second major variable in our model of yield determination – investors' growth expectation as represented by the symbol g. This requires some clarification. First, it represents an annual *rental value* growth rate (not growth arising from changing yield or uplift, as the model assumes that the property is rack rented and there is no expectation of yield change). Second, it represents investors' (or the market's) *expectation* for future rental growth. Yields and prices are based on expectations even in the knowledge that the outcome may be very different. Third, given the inevitability that rental growth will fluctuate, g must be considered as an *average* growth rate, in fact a *discounted* average growth rate *into perpetuity*, meaning that g will be strongly influenced by the rate of growth expected in the near future and less influenced by growth expected in later years. Fourth, as rental values may fall as well as rise, g may be *negative* as well as *positive*.

Impact of depreciation

An important factor affecting the yield and price of growth investments in property is depreciation through obsolescence. Whereas land is a truly perpetual investment buildings must depreciate, and the value of the building element substantially exceeds the value of land in most commercial and industrial properties. Obsolescence affects property gradually over time, but rather than causing an actual fall in value in times of inflation, it works as a depressant on growth. Consequently, depreciation is best regarded as the extent by which rental growth on actual property falls short of growth on equivalent (hypothetical) property which is brand new, and which (notionally) remains new permanently.

As investors will take account of the inevitability of depreciation in their buy and sell decisions, prices and yields must reflect their expectations for depreciation. Thus the symbol g in the yield model must represent growth *after* allowing for the expected rate of depreciation. That means that g has two components,

(1) rental growth expected from new property, and
(2) negative growth due to depreciation.

As these two components are interacting growth rates, their mathematical relationship with g in the yield model is represented as follows:

$$g = g_m - d - dg_m$$

where g = rental growth rate, actual property; g_m = rental growth rate, perpetually new (modern) property; and d = rate of depreciation.

A simple example will help to clarify this analysis.

Example 12.3

On the basis of the past performance of an index of hypothetical new property (e.g., *Investors Chronicle* Hillier Parker Rent Index), future rental growth for offices is predicted to average 8% p.a. Assuming a target return of 12%, five-year rent reviews and a 2% rate of depreciation, what would be the lowest yield on which offices could justifiably be bought?

First, calculate the growth rate appropriate to actual offices which is equivalent to 8% for hypothetical new offices:

$$g = g_m - d - dg_m$$
$$= 0.08 - 0.02 - (0.02 \times 0.08)$$
$$= 0.0584 \text{ or } \textbf{5.84\%}$$

Then use this growth rate to calculate the yield required to give an IRR of 12%

$$y = r - r\left(\frac{(1+g)^n - 1}{(1+r)^n - 1}\right)$$
$$= 0.12 - 0.12\left(\frac{(1+0.0584)^5 - 1}{(1+0.12)^5 - 1}\right)$$
$$= 0.068 \text{ or } \textbf{6.8\%}$$

Note that we have used the formulae here as tools of investment analysis. However, *if* the figures in the question reflect the expectations and target return of the market, then office yields will tend towards 6.8%.

Note also that the growth rate on actual property is similar but not identical to the growth rate on equivalent new property *less* the rate of depreciation (5.84% is rather less than 8% −2%). The formulae used here show correct mathematical relationships which can be used to calculate to any number of decimal points, but that is pointless as none of the variables can be precisely identified and neither in reality can the yield. The purpose of the model is to help explain the level of property yields and how they are influenced by changes in the variables. It also helps to quantify resultant changes in yield, but to calculate to more than one decimal point is pointless and misleading.

Market's implied rental growth expectation

One interesting and useful exercise in property investment analysis is to restate the yield model in terms of g in order to calculate investors' implied rental growth expectation:

$$g = \left(\frac{(r - y)(1 + r)^n + y}{r} \right)^{1/n} - 1 \qquad (12.1)$$

where g = market's implied rental growth expectation.

It seems somewhat less problematic to estimate investors' target return than their growth expectation so, in the knowledge of rental yields in the market (y), Equation (12.1) can be solved to find the market's implied rental growth expectation on the assumption that investors are rational and the market is efficient.

Example 12.4

Freehold investments in prime rack-rented office property let on long leases subject to five-year rent reviews have recently been selling on yields of 5%. On the assumption of a 12% target return, calculate investors' implied rental growth expectation.

$$g = \left(\frac{(r - y)(1 + r)^n + y}{r} \right)^{1/n} - 1$$

$$g = \left(\frac{(0.12 - 0.05)(1 + 0.12)^5 + 0.05}{0.12} \right)^{1/5} - 1$$

$$= (1.4447)^{1/5} - 1$$

$$= 0.076 \text{ or } 7.6\% \text{ p.a.}$$

The annual rental growth expectation required to justify the purchase of the property is 7.6%. That is the rental growth which would provide the investor with his target return of 12%. If investors felt that such a growth rate was unlikely, they would not buy the property at such a low yield, but buy gilts instead, thereby causing the property's price to fall and yield to rise to the level required by investors. Conversely, if investors anticipated a higher growth rate, property would be in greater demand, price would rise and yield fall to the level just considered acceptable. Thus, assuming that investors' target return is indeed 12%, 7.6% is exactly the rental growth anticipated by the market.

We have now digressed somewhat from our original objective. Instead of explaining how market yields are determined by investors' growth expectation, we have illustrated how market yields can be used to quantify the market's rental growth expectation. However, if we now suppose a change in investors' growth expectation from that calculated in Example 12.4, we can use our model to illustrate the yield change which would tend to result.

Example 12.5

If investors' rental growth expectation for the properties in Example 12.4 fell from 7.6% to 7% per annum, what change in yield would tend to take place, assuming no change in investors' target return?

$$y = r - r \left(\frac{(1+g)^n - 1}{(1+r)^n - 1} \right)$$

$$= 0.12 - 0.12 \left(\frac{(1 + 0.07)^5 - 1}{(1 + 0.12)^5 - 1} \right)$$

$$= 0.057 \text{ or } 5.7\%$$

The properties' yield would tend to rise to 5.7% as a result of the fall in growth expectation.

We conclude this section by highlighting the following points.

- A fall in growth expectations will tend to cause a rise in yields, and a rise in growth expectations will tend to cause a fall in yields.

- The rental growth expectation represented by the symbol g has two components (both of which are variables) namely (1) rental growth expected from hypothetical new property, and (2) the expected impact of depreciation through obsolescence.
- *Ceteris paribus*, the higher the growth expectation or the lower the expected rate of depreciation, the lower will be the yield

Impact of the rent review period

This is best illustrated by Example 12.6.

Example 12.6

If, instead of five-year rent reviews, the properties in Example 12.4 had been let on a long lease subject to 14-year reviews, what effect would that have tended to have on the yield?

$$y = r - r\left(\frac{(1+g)^n - 1}{(1+r)^n - 1}\right)$$

$$= 0.12 - 0.12\left(\frac{(1+0.076)^{14} - 1}{(1+0.12)^{14} - 1}\right)$$

$$= 0.065 \text{ or } \mathbf{6.5\%}$$

The effect of the less frequent reviews would be to cause the property's yield to rise from 5% to 6.5%. A higher yield is required by investors to compensate for the lower return resulting from the long review period, despite the fact that rental value growth is unaffected. Generally speaking, the less frequent the rent review, the higher will be a property's yield.

It could be argued that the investor's income is more secure than on a five year review basis, and that therefore the target return should be below 12%. In contrast, however, such investments have proved relatively unmarketable and thus no adjustment to the target return is proposed here.

Frequency and timing of income

Whereas most gilt-edged securities and equity shares pay interest or dividends half yearly, the majority of modern lease contracts stipulate that rent is paid quarterly or half-yearly in advance. As already stated, most equations in this book are based on the assumption that income is received annually in arrears. So to be strictly valid for a property on which rent is received quarterly in advance, our yield model in Equation (11.9) must be amended as follows:[4]

$$y = \frac{4(\sqrt[4]{1+r} - 1)}{\sqrt[4]{1+r}} \left(\frac{(1+r)^n - (1+g)^n}{(1+r)^n - 1} \right) \qquad (12.3)$$

Example 12.7 illustrates the impact that this factor would tend to have on property yields.

Example 12.7

What would tend to be the effect on the yield of the office property in Example 12.4 if rent was payable quarterly in advance instead of annually in arrears as previously assumed?

Using Equation (12.3):

$$y = \frac{4(\sqrt[4]{1+0.12} - 1)}{\sqrt[4]{1+0.12}} \left(\frac{(1+0.12)^5 - (1+0.076)^5}{(1+0.12)^5 - 1} \right)$$

$$= 0.047 \text{ or } \mathbf{4.7\%}$$

So the effect is to reduce the yield from 5% to 4.7%.

The yield model revised

Before relating our theory of yield determination to the experience of yield trends over the last twenty years, we will summarise the conclusions reached so far.

The basic model (11.9) indicates that property yields are determined by three variables, namely, investors' target return, their rental growth expectation and the period between rent reviews. However, the target return and the growth expectation each have two components, thus:

- Property yields are determined by five variables, namely redemption yields on long-dated gilts, investors' required yield premium (or discount), rental growth expectations for new property, expectations for depreciation, and the rent review period. Furthermore, if the assumption is dropped that rent is paid annually in arrears, the frequency and timing of rental payments constitutes a further variable.

Historical yield trends

In relating our theory of yield determination to market evidence of yield trends, it will be assumed that there have been no significant changes in either the rent review period or the frequency of rental payments. In fact in the 1970s, yield movements can largely be explained by changes in just two of the variables, gilt yields and rental growth. Figure 12.2 illustrates a clear correlation between property yields and the gilt yield over the period 1971–7 inclusive. Although less stable, strong upward and downward trends in the gilt yield are generally mirrored by similar trends in property. Moreover, the periods during which gilt and property yields diverged (1972–3 and 1978–9), were periods of sharply rising rental growth. If rental growth (and the growth expectation) is rising to compensate for a rise in the gilt yield, then property yields would tend to remain relatively stable, as they did during the above periods. The yield trends in the 1970s also illustrate a traditional cyclical trend, rising on the advent of a recession (1974) and falling in times of economic recovery and boom (1971–3 and 1977–9).

In contrast with the 1970s, property yield trends in the 1980s appear perverse. On the basis of previous trends, a significant rise in yields would have been expected over the two-year period, late 1979 to late 1981, due to the combination of the rising gilt yield and the fall in rental growth expectations associated with the slide into recession. Yet yields remained obstinately stable. Conversely, a fall in property yields might have been expected in 1982 (due to the sharp fall in the gilt yield) followed by a continuing downward trend as the economy recovered and rental growth increased. In fact, property yields *rose* sharply in 1982 and continued to rise until 1987, despite rising rental growth. These trends can be explained by reference to significant changes in property's yield premium relative to gilts, and investors' perception of depreciation through obsolescence.

Property yield trends in the 1980s are more realistically represented in Figure 12.3 than in Figure 12.2. The divergence between the two figures is due to the Healey and Baker chart representing prime property whereas Hillier Parker measures average yields for property acceptable to institutional investors. The definition of prime property narrowed significantly in the early 1980s, so that although the Healey & Baker series is a fair representation of investment yields in the 1970s, it represents only the very best quality property in the 1980s.

So how can the movement of property yields over the period 1980–7 be explained? First, we will take the period late 1979 to 1981 inclusive, which started after the peak of the 1978–9 boom. During this period gilt yields rose by about 2.5% while the UK economy sank into its deepest recession since the 1930s. The recession would inevitably have reduced rental growth expectations, by an amount estimated at 1.5% p.a. in the case of offices.[5] This combination of the rising gilt yield, falling growth and stable property yields implies a reduction in the differential between the gilt yield and property's target return of about 4%, consistent with property's target return moving from a 2% premium to a 2% discount on the gilt yield.

A 2% yield discount on gilts accords with the investigation of property's risk and target return earlier in this chapter, and seems feasible in the economic and investment market context of the time. This two-year period

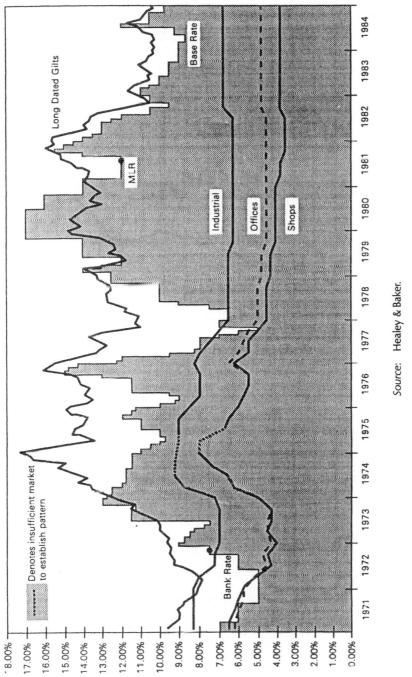

Source: Healey & Baker.

Figure 12.2 Prime commercial property yields

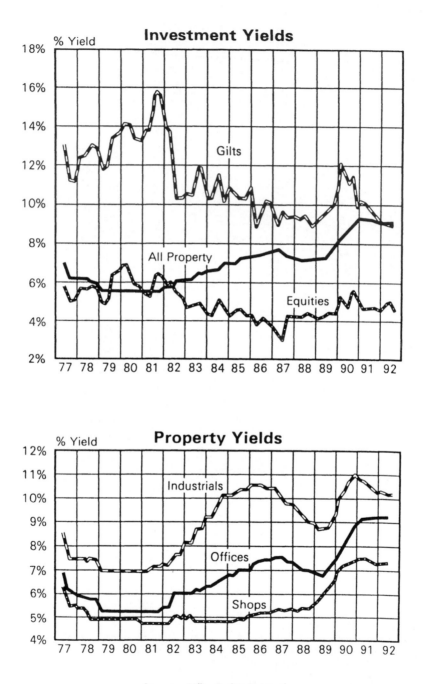

Source: Hillier Parker Research.

Figure 12.3   Average yields

featured conditions which were remarkably favourable to property compared with both gilts and equities. Gilts proved vulnerable to the high level of interest rates required by the government's monetarist policies, a PSBR rising out of control and an upsurge in inflation in the wake of the second oil price shock. Equities looked risky as bankruptcies soared and profits plunged in response to record interest rates, an overvalued currency, the world recession and ever-rising fuel and labour costs. This was the classic 'stagflationary' context in which property had tended to outperform gilts and equities in earlier periods, and with new evidence of out-performance and its counter-cyclical qualities, it seems quite rational for institutional investors to have purchased property on a target return discount to gilts.

Whereas the *divergence* of gilt and property yields over 1979–81 is explained by a fall in property's target return differential with gilts, the *convergence* of gilt and property yields over the period 1982–7 is explained by an opposite trend, together with a sharp increase in investors' perception of property's vulnerability to depreciation. In 1982, the economic fundamentals moved beneficially for gilts and equities and adversely for property. By the end of the year the battle against inflation appeared to have been won. The inflation rate fell to 5% bringing about a dramatic fall in gilt yields and providing investors with returns of over 50% for the year. Equities also responded well to the fall in interest rates and the prospect of economic recovery, but property's popularity came to an end and prices fell for the first time since 1974. The case for investing in a hedge against inflation sank with the decline in inflation and property's case was further undermined by the introduction of index-linked gilts (see Chapter 27).

The convergence of property yields and gilt yields over 1982–7 when (at least latterly) rental growth expectations must have been rising, implies a sharp rise in the target return differential with gilt yields, reflecting investors' reassessment of the relative risk of the investments. Rather than a rise in the perception of property's risk, it could be explained by a perception that the risk of gilts had been much reduced by the decline of inflation, and by the reduced portfolio attractions of property in view of the availability of index-linked gilts, overseas investments and the improved prospects for UK equities.

The rise in yields over 1982–7 also reflects a sharp increase in the market's perception of depreciation, particularly in the case of office property. This arose from the obsolescence suffered by many offices as a result of the widespread introduction of computers, and the need for redevelopment or extensive refurbishment in order to maximise rental value.

The rise in property yields came to an end late in 1987 after the stock-market crash had reminded investors of property's merits as a portfolio diversifier, and the economic boom of the late 1980s produced dramatic rental growth. However, the improving trend was reversed by the onset of the recession and the rise in gilt yields in 1989. Plummeting rental values caused a sharp increase in property yields until Hillier Parker's all-property average yield uniquely coincided with the gilt yield in 1992. This coincidence of yields reflected not only property's high target return premium over gilt yields and falling rents, but the long time lag expected before any upturn in rental growth.

This review of yield trends over the last twenty years highlights the relevance of the four main variables subsumed by the yield model, but also emphasises the importance of viewing property in the context of a mixed asset portfolio. Property's target return differential with gilt yields depends not only on the market's perception of property's risk relative to gilts (as well as liquidity, marketability, etc.), but on its portfolio attractions relative to all alternative investments including index-linked gilts and overseas investments.

Finally, although we have stressed that market prices are based on expectations, it often seems that the property market seldom looks far ahead. Instead of property values moving according to rental growth *expectations*, experience indicates that prices and yields move mainly on *evidence* of changing rents.

13 The Spectrum of Property Yields

In Chapter 12, we explained how the investment characteristics of property determine its yield and how the level of yields changes over time. But different property investments can have substantially different yields, mainly because of variations in their risk and growth potential. So now we shall examine the three main facets of property investments which determine their risk and growth potential, thereby explaining yields on individual investments. These three facets are (a) the investment interest, (b) the type of property over which the interest exists, and (c) the quality of the investment.

The investment interest

In Part I, we investigated the pricing of stock-market securities in some detail, largely because the characteristics which explain stock prices and yields are also present in property investments. Property investments can also be fixed-income, equity or quasi-equity, geared or ungeared, risky or secure, perpetual or of limited life. We shall now illustrate how property investments may be compared with stock-market securities, enabling their yields to be understood by reference to the yields of their stock-market counterparts.

In Part I, stock-market investments were grouped into three main categories according to the ability of their income to vary – fixed-income, equity and quasi-equity investments. We saw that income yields on fixed-income investments tended to be high, yields on equities tended to be relatively low, and yields on quasi-equities varied from high to low according to the fixed-income/equity characteristics of the investment. In fact, it was suggested that rather than three separate categories, we had a spectrum with pure fixed-income stock at one end, pure equities at the other and in between, the quasi-equities varying from the almost fixed-income to the almost pure equity. We concluded that, given a reasonable element of security, an investment's income yield would be largely determined by its position within that spectrum, because of the importance of growth potential to the determination of yields.

This concept of investments as being located somewhere within the fixed-income/equity spectrum is particularly relevant to property, because although some pure fixed-income and pure equity interests do exist in property, the large majority of investment interests are quasi-equities, falling somewhere between the extreme ends of the spectrum.

As explained in Chapter 10, the characteristics of a property interest originate from the legal contracts to which the interest is subject. The characteristics of a freehold investment, for example, being unburdened by any higher interest, depend on the conditions of the lease granted to the tenant, but the characteristics of a head-leasehold investment depend both on the conditions of the head lease and the conditions of the sub-lease. Of particular importance to this analysis is the length of the leasehold interests created, and the provision for review of rent. Freehold investments will be considered first.

Freehold interests

The unencumbered freehold in possession (the interest of the owner occupier) endows the freeholder with a perpetual right to the full benefits of occupying property. In the case of business property, that is the right to the full profits of undertaking business activity on the premises without the liability to pay rent. The notional annual return from this interest is the rental value of the property (i.e. the annual amount that tenants would be willing to pay for occupation), and as this will tend to vary according to changes in the profitability of the business activity for which the property is best suited, the freehold in possession is a pure equity interest.

However, if the property is let, then the nature of the freehold interest depends on the conditions of the lease. If let either on a one-year lease or on a long lease with provision for annual review to rental value, the freehold is still an equity interest, at least to the same extent as an ordinary share which declares its dividend annually. On the other hand, if a property is let on a long lease (say, 66 years or more to run) without provision for rent review, the freehold is virtually a fixed-income investment. The reversion to the full rental value is so distant that it will have a minimal present value, and therefore virtually all the value derives from the right to receive the fixed income.

Although the rent of retail property is occasionally linked to the tenant's sales turnover, annual reviews are exceptional for business property in the UK, and although some fixed-income investments remain from leases granted in the pre-war or early post-war years, the overwhelming majority of property investments lie somewhere between the extreme ends of the fixed-income/ equity spectrum. A reversionary freehold subject to a lease with 50 years to run without provision for rent review has a small equity element because the reversion is close enough to have some current value, and each year the property's value will tend to change to reflect both the declining period to reversion and changes in the rental value. The value of properties with shorter reversions will be more responsive to changing rental values, and as the period to reversion shortens, such freeholds will more and more take on the attributes of equity type investments.

In the case of properties let with provision for rent review, the longer the period between each review, the closer is that investment to a fixed-income type, and the shorter the review period, the closer it is to an equity. Freeholds benefiting from three-, five-, or seven-year reviews are not strictly pure equity investments, however, they are regarded as effectively being equity types, and it would be pedantic to consider them as quasi-equities. On the other hand, investments subject to 14-, 21- or 33-year reviews should be considered as quasi-equity investments. A large proportion of the equity is lost, and the annual growth potential is significantly affected.

As in the case of stock-market securities, freehold investments may thus be located at either end (or anywhere within) the fixed-income/equity spectrum, and in times of inflation their position in this spectrum will largely determine yield. Fixed-income investments will tend to have high yields because of their lack of growth potential, equity type investments will tend to have relatively low yields, and the (equivalent) yields of quasi-equity investments will lie somewhere in between, according to the relative value of their fixed-income and equity elements.

The investment characteristics of a fixed-income freehold ground rent are similar to those of a preference share or undated bond, although the comparison with a preference share is more strictly correct because a freehold is an ownership interest. Like both these securities, a freehold ground rent is a perpetual investment, and its income is fixed and very secure because the head tenant's rental payment will normally be covered several times by his sub-rental income. Due to these similarities, yields on such freeholds tend to remain close to the yields on undated bonds and preference shares, but somewhat above, as explained in Chapter 12.

The investment characteristics of equity property interests are broadly similar to equity shares, and consequently the average dividend yield has normally been close to the average rental yield on equity interests in prime commercial property. Both are perpetual growth investments which benefit or suffer from changes in the profitability of their underlying assets.

A reversionary freehold is comparable to a convertible preference share or debenture which has a conversion date similar to the date of the freehold's reversion to rental value. In either case, current income is fixed, but the price of the investment will reflect the reversion to a more valuable income at the conversion/reversion date. If that date is far in the future, the equity element will be small, the price will mainly reflect the fixed income and the (equivalent) yield will be high. But if the date is close at hand, the majority of the price will reflect the value of the equity reversionary interest, and the (equivalent) yield will tend to be low.

When the current lease on a reversionary investment comes to an end, the freeholder must be assumed to relet on a frequent review basis. So as the reversion approaches, the investment gradually converts to an equity type, and investors' required equivalent yield will fall. However, in the case of a freehold let on a very long lease with lengthy review periods (e.g., 14 or 21 years), the essential nature of the investment is unaffected by the approach of a review. The value of the investment will rise as the review approaches and correspondingly the current income yield must fall, but the equivalent yield will tend to remain unchanged. Such investments remain quasi-equities until the lease nears its end.

Leasehold interests

Leaseholds must tend to be more complex and dissimilar than freehold investments (a) because of their limited lives, and (b) because their investment characteristics depend on the terms of both the head lease and the sub-lease. First the implications of the limited lives of leaseholds will be examined.

Ultimately all leasehold interests must come to an end with a nil value, consequently an investor holding to the end of a lease must suffer a capital loss. That does not imply that such an investment is necessarily unprofitable, merely that the expected income to be received over the period of ownership must be sufficiently high to compensate for the loss of the investor's capital. As all the return from such an investment must come in the form of income, and as income is effectively taxed at a higher rate than capital gain (for most investors), a leasehold held to its termination must incur a higher level of taxation (per 1% IRR) than an equivalent freehold.

On the other hand, although they must ultimately depreciate, equity-type long-leasehold investments may have substantial growth potential over much of their lives, in some cases a greater growth potential than a freehold over a similar property. The values of leaseholds do not decline steadily throughout their lives, they tend to show a parabolic profile. This is illustrated in Figure 13.1, where the value profiles of two leasehold investments, both with 50 years to run, are compared with that of a freehold. All three investments are deemed to have an initial market value of £1 million, and the properties to be subject to identical constant rental value growth. For simplicity, the effect of rent reviews has been omitted, so in each case the profiles assume that rental income is variable annually.

The profit-rental income of a leasehold investment is the difference between the rental income received from sub-tenants and the head rent payable to the landlord. Thus, if the head rent is substantial and fixed throughout the duration of the lease, the leasehold investment must be geared. Because the head rent is a fixed deduction from a growth income, the residual profit rent must grow at a rate faster than the growth of the sub-rental income, and also faster than the income growth of a comparable freehold. On the other hand, due to the limited life of leaseholds, the capital value of the investment may not grow at as fast a rate as the income.

Figure 13.1 assumes constant market yields, thus as the freehold's income growth must be transmitted into a similar capital growth, the value profile of the freehold investment also illustrates the rental income growth trend for both the freehold and the ungeared leasehold. The ungeared leasehold is deemed to be subject to a 'peppercorn' (negligible) head rent, such that its

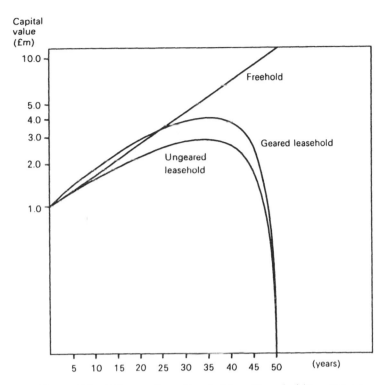

Figure 13.1   Value profiles of freehold and leasehold investments

profit rent grows at the same rate as the rental income of the freehold. On the other hand, the geared leasehold in Figure 13.1 is subject to a fixed head rent which is initially 33% of its sub-rental income, so throughout its life the profit rental income of this investment must grow at a rate faster than that of the other two investments.

Note that:

(1) Although the incomes of both the freehold and the ungeared lease-hold are growing at the same rate, the capital growth of the leasehold is substantially lower, even when the lease has 50 years to run.

(2) The superior net income growth of the geared lease enables its capital value to grow initially at a faster rate than both the ungeared lease and the freehold. However, as time passes, the fixed head rent declines as a proportion of rental income, the capital growth rate falls, eventually leading to a fall in value.

(3) In times of substantial rental growth, the fall in value of equity type leasehold investments tends to be restricted to the last 15 years or so of the investment.

All but relatively short leases may be growth investments.

It follows from this that an equity-type leasehold investment could be regarded as a growth, non-growth, or depreciating investment, depending on the duration of the lease remaining, and the period over which the investor intends to hold the investment. Not only do different leasehold interests have markedly different characteristics, but the same interest will have different characteristics at different stages in its life. An investor requiring a growth investment might well buy a long leasehold investment, but with the intention of selling it before its value starts to decline. Another investor (particularly one with a nil taxation liability) might well find a short leasehold attractive. The high income over the remaining period of the lease should provide a return more than sufficient to compensate for the capital loss.

The terminable nature of leasehold investments tends to make them less popular than freeholds with the major investing institutions, who are principally looking for long-term growth investments. It can also create an additional risk of rent voids as the lease nears its end. A leaseholder cannot grant a sub-lease for a period longer than the remaining term of his head lease. So if the existing sub-tenant quits two or three years before the end of the head lease, the head leaseholder might have difficulty in reletting the property for such a short and inconvenient period. No sub-tenant means no rental income for the leaseholder, but he must still pay the head rent to the freeholder; there is therefore a risk of suffering a negative cash flow.

This highlights the risky 'top-slice' nature of leasehold investment income, and illustrates that the risk, like the growth potential and other qualities of leaseholds, derives from the duration and conditions of both head lease and sub-lease. As the profit rent is frequently a geared residual, then if the sub-rental income falls (e.g., through falling rental values, rent voids or default), the effect on the profit rent will be proportionally greater than it would be for a freeholder leasing directly to the same occupying tenants.

Examples 13.1–13.5 illustrate the disparate nature of leasehold interests. In each case, it is assumed that the head lease has many years to run.

Example 13.1

A leasehold interest in which the head rent is subject to frequent review to full rental value.

In this case, the leaseholder's profit rent must be extinguished at each review, and only a small profit rent could build up between reviews. This interest could therefore not be a valuable investment. To have a significant value, leaseholds must be subject either to a fixed head rent lasting for a considerable period, or to a head rent which is reviewable to a level significantly below rental value. Additionally, to be considered as a pure investment interest, the property must be sub-let (or be capable of being sub-let), and be marketable – that is, there must be no restriction in the head lease against assignation (sale).

Example 13.2

A leasehold interest subject to a fixed head rent and sub-let for the whole of the remaining term of the head lease at a fixed rent.

As the sub-lease expires on the same date as the head lease, there can be no reversionary increase in the profit rent. The profit rent is fixed for the whole of the remaining life of the interest, consequently it is a pure fixed-income investment. Its yield (after deducting the sinking fund instalment necessary to replace the capital at the end of the lease) would therefore tend to reflect the yield on long-dated gilts and fixed-income freehold investments, but be somewhat higher than the latter due to the top-slice risk and terminable nature of the leasehold.

Example 13.3

A leasehold interest subject to a 'peppercorn' head rent, and a sub-lease which has provision for frequent rent review.

Due to the insignificant head rent and the variable sub-rent, this invest-ment is an ungeared equity type. The profit rent will therefore have much the same risk and growth characteristics as the income of a freehold over a similar property which is subject to a similar rent review pattern. However, as illu-strated in Figure 13.1, its capital growth potential will tend to be less than for the equivalent freehold. The leasehold's yield (after allowing for a sinking fund) will tend to reflect yields on similar freehold interests, but be somewhat higher due to the lower growth expectation and the disadvantage of being a terminable investment.

Example 13.4

A leasehold interest subject to a substantial fixed head rent and a sub-lease which has provision for frequent rent review.

This leasehold is a geared equity. The leaseholder's profit rent will depend not only on the property's rental value growth, but also on the income-gearing ratio, i.e. the ratio, head rent/sub-rental income. The higher is the head rent as a proportion of sub-rental income, the greater is the growth potential of the profit rent, and also the greater is the risk of falling rental values and rent voids due to the 'top-slice' nature of this profit rent.

Example 13.5

A leasehold interest where the sub-rents are reviewed regularly to rental value, and the head rent is reviewed at the same time to a fixed proportion of rental value.

This is an equity-sharing relationship under which both the freehold and leasehold interests are equity investments. Confusingly, such a leasehold is sometimes called a 'geared' lease — in the sense that the head rent is geared or linked to changes in the rental value – but it is not a geared investment in the sense used in this book. At rent review, the profit rent and the head rent will both move in proportion to changes in the rental value.

This investigation has indicated the general investment characteristics and approximate yields of some long or medium-length leasehold investments. However, as a lease nears its end accelerating capital depreciation means that the investment bears little comparison with any other investment type, and the anomalies inherent in assessing yields on the traditional 'net of sinking fund' basis become increasingly significant. Instead, the increasing ability to forecast the profit rent throughout the remainder of the lease makes comparison, analysis and valuation on the basis of the full DCF model more appropriate.

The property type

This is the second facet of a property investment which is responsible for determining its risk and growth characteristics. It is subsidiary to the legal interest, because a fixed-income investment can have no growth potential whatever the property type may be, and because the income security of most fixed-income investments usually makes the property type irrelevant. Property type is only relevant to explaining yields on investments with an equity element. Therefore, we shall restrict this investigation to good-quality equity freehold investments in the principal types of investment property.

Farmland

Unlike commercial and industrial property, the value of farmland is crucially dependent upon whether it is owner-occupied or let. A freehold interest in an 'in-hand' farm may exceed the value of an equivalent tenanted farm by 100%. As the rental value of equivalent farms would be the same, the 'in-hand' premium implies that the yield on the let farm may be double that of the 'in-hand' farm.

The high price and low yield of 'in-hand' farmland must be due in part to non-financial considerations of the wealthy individuals who still dominate that sector of the market. There is the enjoyment and prestige of owning rural property, farming is considered by many as a fulfilling occupation, and some individuals may be induced to pay high prices because of the difficulty in obtaining a farm tenancy. However 'in-hand' farmland is not a 'pure' investment, and as most institutional investment is in tenanted farms, we shall concentrate on these.

Until the 1980s the post-war growth performance of prime arable land was impressive, perhaps surpassing that of any other income-earning investment. The growth derived from the rising profitability and efficiency of farming in the UK, helped by the declining stock of arable land which resulted from urbanisation and motorway construction, and the 'roll-over' relief from CGT when land was sold for development purposes. Growth is enhanced by the minor influence of depreciation in comparison with offices and industrial property, and the three-year rent review periods laid down by the Agricultural Holdings Acts.

Farmland has been regarded as a very secure investment, due not so much to the indestructibility of land, as to its invulnerability to economic recession. With the demand for food being relatively stable, the returns from farmland should be largely uncorrelated with returns from most other equity investments, thereby making it an attractive addition to a portfolio. Farmers rarely default on rental payments, but in that event a landlord could easily relet or benefit from the higher value by retaining the farm 'in-hand'.

Farmland's growth record and low risk resulted in yields falling to as low as 2% in the early 1970s when many institutions were seeking to increase the farmland content of their portfolios. But in the 1980s growth faltered and yields rose to 6% for good quality arable, with higher yields for poor quality and upland farms. Over the nine years to December 1990 farm values fell by a total of 33%, and over the six year period to 1990 institutional ownership of let farmland has halved.[1]

The main source of the growth of farmland values in the 1970s was rising prices for farm produce, particularly after Britain's entry to the EEC. However, the fundamental problem in the 1980s was food surpluses and the reduction in price support from the EC. Through its impact on farming profitability, this affected rental values and investor's returns (see Part III).

Woodlands

An investment in woodlands differs from an investment in farmland and other property types in a number of respects. The investor is traditionally an owner-occupier, the subject of the investment is both the land and the growing crop of timber and, unless the plantations include a broad range of tree ages, there will be no regularity of income.

The major part of the value of a plantation is normally in the growing trees rather than in the land, and as trees are at risk to fire, disease and windblow, woodlands would normally be considered to be a more risky investment than farmland. Although risk through fire is insurable, it is uncommon and difficult to insure against disease and windblow.

The principal attraction of woodlands from the point of view of the institutional investor is the growth expectation. It is difficult here to avoid a pun — woodlands are a growth investment in both a physical and a value sense, and have proved to be an excellent inflation 'hedge'! In fact, not only are woodlands a good inflation hedge, but they are also an excellent hedge against a fall in the value of the pound sterling and UK economic decline. With 90% of UK's timber-needs being imported, the price of timber in the UK will be set in world markets. So if the value of sterling falls relative to other currencies (particularly the currencies of timber exporting countries), the sterling price of imported timber will tend to rise. Consequently, the price of home-grown timber will tend to rise, as it is a relatively insignificant element of total supply and a substitute for imported timber.

With a relentless fall in the area of mature forests in the world, and a growing demand for timber, it is forecast that the price of timber will rise at a rate in excess of inflation, making woodlands an attractive long-term investment prospect.

Commercial property

The two components of a commercial or industrial property investment are in fundamentally different proportions to that of a farmland investment. Although both consist of land and buildings, a farm is essentially land with a relatively small amount of buildings and other fixtures (physically and by value), whereas commercial and industrial properties are composed mainly of buildings with a relatively small amount of land. Whereas the stock of farmland cannot increase significantly, the stock of commercial and industrial properties is elastic in the long run because buildings are created by man.

This is significant in two respects. First, the ability to develop new commercial and industrial properties increases the risk of oversupply and reduces growth potential in the face of rising demand. Second, because obsolescence affects buildings but not land, depreciation is significantly greater for commercial and industrial property than for farms. As a building's obsolescence increases, its attractiveness to tenants declines. So not only is its growth potential reduced but the risk of rent voids tends to rise.

Another reason for commercial and industrial property being viewed as more risky than farmland is that the business activities which occupy such property are more vulnerable to national macroeconomic trends than is the case with agricultural property. In times of recession or slump, users of shops, offices, hotels and other commercial property will all tend to be affected by the decline in demand, resulting in lower profitability and reduced space requirements, leading in turn to the risk of rent voids and falling rental values.

Despite these disadvantages, the performance record of commercial property investment in terms of both risk and growth has been good. The rental and capital growth of office property has derived from the long-term trend in the UK economy away from industrial activity towards service activity. There has been a massive expansion in both private-sector commercial activity and public-sector administration. The growth in shop property has derived from the post-war rise in real incomes which, by expanding consumer expenditure, has increased the demand for shop property and enabled retailers to pay higher rents.

The above characteristics of commercial and industrial property relative to farms helps to explain the traditional hierarchy of yields in the property market. Farms have provided the lowest yields. Shops have been next, normally yielding less than offices due probably to their superior growth record and the perception that they are less vulnerable to rent voids and to depreciation. In the case of prime High Street shops, a large proportion of value tends to be in the land rather than in the building, and the burden of refitting and modernisation is frequently borne by the tenant rather than the landlord.

Industrial property

The triple disadvantages of urban property compared with farmland – elastic stock, vulnerability to recession, and greater depreciation – are probably even more important to industrial than commercial property. In particular, the relative speed and ease with which new industrial development can respond to a rise in demand restricts its growth in boom conditions, and increases the risk of oversupply in a subsequent economic recession. Manufacturing industry is particularly vulnerable to economic fluctuations, and factory premises tend to be at greater risk to rent voids than other property types. Factory and warehouse property are usually perceived as having a shorter building life than shops and offices, and the high proportion of value normally attributable to the building rather than land tends to increase the impact of depreciation.

These investment disadvantages and the generally inferior growth record of industrial property has resulted in yields remaining significantly higher than those of shops and offices, usually by a margin of 2–3% (see Figures 12.2 and 12.3).

Investment quality

The third major facet of a property investment which determines its yield is quality. This relates to both the legal interest and the physical property. The principal features of the legal interest which distinguish its quality are:

(a)   length of lease and rent review provision;
(b)   repairing covenant;
(c)   tenant.

The significance of rent review has already been explained. Investors also prefer a lease to contain a 'full repairing and insuring' covenant, under which the tenant is responsible for all such expenses. Although the rent payable by the tenant would be reduced, this arrangement minimises the investor's management expense and the risk of such costs accelerating faster than the rent received.

A landlord will also minimise his management cost by leasing each property (particularly an office block) to a single tenant, and the value of an investment can be enhanced by having a well-known company as a tenant. Public authorities or large stable public companies are favoured tenants, as they are unlikely to default on their rental payments or other commitments.

The principal features of the physical property which influence its quality are:

(a) age or modernity, and building quality;
(b) design, layout and size;
(c) location.

The quality of a building will not only affect the attractiveness of the property from the tenant's point of view (and therefore the rent he is willing to pay), but it may also influence the rate of obsolescence and the future growth of the property's value. Additionally, there is usually an optimal size for every property which will influence its rental value and yield.

Finally, apart from farm property where soil fertility is crucial, location is probably the most important factor determining quality. It is the location of a shop relative to pedestrian flow, the location of offices vis-à-vis a city's commercial centre, and the location of industrial property close to transport facilities and a population centre which largely determine the growth potential and risk of an investment, and consequently its yield and value.

The institutions usually restrict their investment to good quality property (but not necessarily prime), and their demand relative to the restricted supply of such property has led to a significant yield differential with lower-quality investments.

Application of price theory

In order to consolidate an understanding of property yield and price theory, we shall now examine a variety of investments and estimate the yields and/or prices which would tend to be set by the market. For the purpose of this exercise, it is assumed that long-dated gilts are yielding 10%.

Example 13.6

Estimate the yield and price of a freehold interest in a prime city centre office property, recently let for 25 years on a five-year rent review basis to a public authority at a rent of £500 000 per annum (net).

This investment is the right to receive £500 000 per annum for five years followed by an income which may vary every five years according to the property's rental value at each review date. The frequent reviews identify the investment as an equity type, and as it is a freehold interest in prime office property let to a reliable tenant on a relatively long occupation lease, the investment would be considered as a highly marketable and relatively secure growth investment. The target return might be 2% above the current yield on gilts, but due to the growth expectation, the yield would be low. Traditionally, the yield on such investments would have tended towards 5%, and we shall assume that to be appropriate in this case.

As the £500 000 rent is also deemed to be the current rental value, a yield of 5% implies a price of £10 million:

$$P_0 = \frac{R_0}{y}$$

$$= \frac{500\,000}{0.05} = £10\,000\,000$$

Example 13.7

Estimate the yield and market price of a freehold interest in a prime city centre site let for office development purposes in 1951 on a 999-year lease at a fixed rent of £5000 per annum (net).

This is a fixed-income ground rent of £5000 per annum effectively into perpetuity. The reversion is far too distant to have any current value, so all the value of the investment is in the fixed income. The tenant has erected an office block on the site (see Example 13.8), therefore the head rent is very secure, being covered 200 times by the sub-rental income. However, despite this security and despite the investment being in a prime commercial property, the yield must be high because of the absence of income growth potential. Owing to its higher risk, poor liquidity, marketability etc, relative to gilts, we shall assume that investors require a 2% premium over the current yield available on gilts. Thus the target return is 12%, and as a perpetual fixed-income investment, the yield will be the same. This implies a price of:

$$P_0 = \frac{R}{y}$$

$$= \frac{5\,000}{0.12} = £41\,667$$

Example 13.8

Estimate the yield of the head leasehold interest in Example 13.7. The offices have been sub-let to a variety of occupiers on 25-year leases subject to five-year reviews for a total net rent of £1 million.

This interest is the right to receive the sub-rental income subject to the payment of the fixed head rent. This profit rent, currently £995 000, will change regularly as sub-tenants' rents are reviewed to rental value, so the investment is an equity type and, although leasehold, it has so long to run that it is effectively perpetual. The less reliable tenants compared with Example 13.6 (and perhaps also the stigma of being a leasehold rather than a freehold interest), would tend to result in a marginally higher yield than for the investment in Example 13.6, say 5.5% or 6%.

Example 13.9

Estimate the yield on a freehold interest in a 200 hectare prime arable farm in East Anglia. Although the original lease expired just over three years ago, the tenant remains in occupation.

As the tenant will have security of tenure under the Agricultural Holdings Acts, he will be liable for rent review every three years. We shall assume that the landlord gave the appropriate notices, and that the rent was recently raised to the rental value. This is an equity-type freehold in a good-sized prime farming unit. Investors' target return on such investments might be lower than on commercial property due to their security and portfolio attractions, so that when coupled with the growth expectation deriving from rental growth and the frequent review, low yields result, say 5–6% in this case.

Example 13.10

Estimate the yield on the tenant's interest in Example 13.9.

The tenant's interest can have no market yield, for three good reasons. First, as he is paying a rent at or near the rental value, he can have no significant profit rent. Second, we have been concerned here exclusively with pure investment interests, and as the tenant is debarred from sub-leasing under the Agricultural Holdings Acts, his interest is an occupation interest, not an investment one. Third, as he is debarred from selling his interest by the Agricultural Holdings Acts, it can have no market value and no market yield.

Example 13.11

Estimate the yield of a freehold interest in a secondary estate of industrial property let to a variety of occupying tenants on 21-year leases subject to seven-year reviews.

Although this is an equity investment, the yield required by investors will tend to be much higher than for any of the investments so far considered. The market's target IRR will be high, perhaps 20%, because industrial property is less secure than other types and the secondary quality indicates a further substantial level of risk from voids and default. There is no law in land economics which states that rental value growth of property in secondary locations need be any less than that in prime locations, but if the quality of buildings leads to a high rate of depreciation then the growth expectation must be affected. A yield of 15% is tentatively suggested here.

Example 13.12

Estimate the yield on a freehold interest in a recently refurbished prime city centre office property, let 40 years ago on a 42-year lease at a fixed rent of £2000 per annum (net). The net rental value is now £100 000.

This investment is the right to receive £2000 per annum for two years, then the reversion to rental value when the freeholder must be expected to relet on frequent (say, five-year) reviews. Thus, despite having been subject to a fixed rent for 40 years, the investment is unquestionably an equity type. Only the future income is relevant to the investor, not the historic income.

Despite the age of the property, the recent refurbishment and prime location indicate that investors' required yield will be similar to the property in Example 13.6, i.e. 5%. However, in this case 5% would be the equivalent yield; the current income yield must be very small. Whereas all previous equity investments considered here have been let at rental value, this is a reversionary investment.

If the reversion to rental value was due immediately rather than in two years' time, then on the basis of a 5% yield the value of the investment would be £2 million (£100 000 × 20). So currently the value must be somewhat below £2 million, and thus the current income yield must be somewhat above 0.1%. The value of the investment mainly reflects the proximity of the large reversionary income, not the small current income.

A purchaser of this investment will anticipate three elements of return over the next two years – an income yield of just over 0.1% p.a., a capital gain due to the approach of reversion (uplift) of just under 4.9% p.a., and further capital gain deriving from growth in rental value.

Example 13.13

Estimate the price of a freehold investment similar in all respects to that in Example 13.12 but let 40 years ago on a 66-year lease. The rent paid is also £2000 per annum and the rental value £100 000 per annum.

This investment is the right to receive £2000 per annum for 26 years and then the reversion to rental value. As in Example 13.12, we must assume that the investor will relet the property on a frequent review basis at the expiry of the present lease. Due to the long period of fixed income before reversion, the investment is clearly not a pure equity, but neither is it a pure fixed-income investment. The reversion is sufficiently close to have a significant present value, and the investment's value will tend to vary each year according to changing rental values and the approach of reversion. The investment is therefore a quasi-equity on which investors must require an equivalent yield somewhere between the 5% and 12% yields already determined for equity and fixed-income investments over similar property. Market evidence of yields on other similar reversionary investments would be rare, and the pricing of such investments is better understood by reference to the full DCF pricing model.

Assuming a target IRR of 12%, the market's implied rental growth expectation for the property in Example 13.6 is 7.6% per annum (this was calculated in Example 12.3 for another property with a 5% yield and five year reviews). Therefore if we assume that the property in this example is of similar quality to that in Example 13.6, then investors must also impliedly be expecting 7.6% growth. Using that growth rate, we can calculate the expected value of the investment at reversion in 26 years, on the assumption that it will then have a yield of 5%, because at that date it will be an equity investment similar to the property in Example 13.6.

In order to calculate the present value of this investment, we shall assume that the property is sold immediately after reversion. We must therefore solve the following:

$$P_0 = \frac{R_1}{(1+r_1)} + \frac{R_2}{(1+r_1)^2} + \cdots + \frac{R_{26}}{(1+r_1)^{26}} + \frac{P_{26}}{(1+r_2)^{26}}$$

$$\text{Expected rental value year 26} = 100\,000(1+0.076)^{26}$$
$$= £671\,610$$

So,

$$P_{26} = \frac{671\,610}{0.05} = £13\,432\,200$$

Investors' expected income is therefore £2000 per annum for 26 years plus the sale price of £13 432 200 in Year 26.

The value of that cash flow, using a rate of 12% to discount the income and 10% for the sale price, is **£1 142 800.**

It would be incorrect to discount both the income and the expected price (Year 26) at the same discount rate, because the two elements of return face different risk and are taxed at different rates. Although the expected price is much less certain than the income, it has been discounted at a relatively low rate reflecting the low tax on capital gain. The income has been discounted at the return deemed to be required on fixed-income property investments. Note that due to the relatively small amount of the current income, the large majority of the value of this investment derives from the reversion despite the long period to elapse before it is received.

Example 13.14

Estimate the price of a leasehold investment in a prime office property with 16 years to run and subject to a fixed head rent of £20 000. The property has been sub-let for the remaining term of the head lease to a public authority on a seven-year review basis. The next review is in two years, the current rent is £100 000 and the rental value £150 000 per annum (net). Freehold investments over similar property let on five-year review have recently sold on a yield of 5%.

Although the seven-year rent review arrangement means that this investment has income growth potential, and the substantial fixed head rent provides an element of gearing, the relatively short life remaining means that the capital value of the investment must shortly start to decline. Rather than long-term capital growth, this investment can have no value in 16 years. As with Example 13.13, pricing is best understood by reference to the DCF model:

$$P_0 = \frac{R_1}{(1+r)} + \frac{R_2}{(1+r)^2} + \ldots + \frac{R_{16}}{(1+r)^{16}}$$

where $R_{1,2}$ etc. = expected net profit rent in years 1, 2, etc.

In order to calculate the investor's expected profit rent over the remaining life of the lease, we must calculate the expected rental value at the rent review dates in two years' and nine years' time. The rental value at these dates determines the sub-rental income, and thus the investor's profit rent for the subsequent seven-year periods. As similar properties with five-year reviews are selling on a yield of 5%, we can again assume a rental growth expectation of 7.6%.

Expected profit rent:

Years		£
1–2	100 000 − 20 000 =	80 000
3–9	150 000(1 + 0.076)² − 20 000 =	153 666
10–16	150 000(1 + 0.076)⁹ − 20 000 =	270 002

The NPV of this cash flow using a discount rate of 17% = **£824 682.**

A target return of 17% has been adopted here, as it must tend to be higher than the 12% used to discount the income in Example 13.13, due to the 'top-slice' risk imposed by the income gearing and the short life of the investment. All the return from this investment must come in the form of highly taxed income.

It should be appreciated that although this study has implications for property valuation, these examples are intended as practical illustrations of our pricing theory, not as examples in valuation methodology.

In Chapters 11–13, the principles of investment pricing previously identified in our study of the stock market have been applied to the pricing of property investments. This is justifiable because the same investors – the large financial institutions – dominate both markets, and they apply the same general criteria in selecting property investments as they do in selecting stocks and shares. The property investment market is merely one sector of the overall investment market.

However, our pricing theory is not yet complete. We shall return to it again in Part V, once we have learnt more about the needs of property investors and the behaviour of rental values under different economic conditions. Our study of property pricing so far has merely revealed something about the relationship of price to rental income, or the amount that an investor is willing to pay per £1 of current rent. We have not yet investigated the determinants of rental value or rental growth. That omission must now be rectified.

III   The Determination of Rental Value

14 The Concept of Rent as a Surplus

Introduction

In seeking to explain how the market determines rental value, we shall address the following three questions:

(a) What causes rent to be paid for the use of property?
(b) What determines the amount of rent paid for the use of a property?
(c) What causes rental value to change over time?

We shall start the analysis with a simple example in the context of farmland, then introduce a more rigorous theoretical examination, and finally convert to the practicalities of urban property.

The theory of land rent

Let us suppose that a 100 hectare low-ground farm is being offered to let on the open market by the freeholder, on the following assumptions:

(a) the tenant will provide and maintain all buildings, fences, roads and other fixed equipment;
(b) the lease is on a year to year basis, i.e. the lease can be terminated by either side at the end of any year, and the rent may be reviewed annually (For the purpose of this discussion, the Agricultural Holdings Acts and related legislation have been repealed);
(c) the two most profitable uses of the farm are (i) livestock production and (ii) cropping (although the former use will include some cropping and the latter some livestock in order to gain the benefits of rotation and integration of the two activities). The expected revenue and costs per hectare of the two uses are shown in Table 14.1.

If these figures reflect the expectations of the most competent and efficient farmers, then:

(a) the rent to be paid to the landlord for the one-year lease of the farm would tend towards £100 per hectare (£10 000 for the farm);
(b) the land would tend to be used for cropping rather than for livestock;
(c) the farm would tend to be let to the most efficient farmer, or a less efficient farmer who was willing to accept lower profits.

In other words, assuming a competitive market and that farmers strive to maximise profit:

- the rent paid for the use of land will tend towards the surplus remaining after deducting the costs of the optimally employed factors of production from the revenue expected from using the land for its most profitable use;
- land tends to be allocated to its most profitable use;
- land tends to be allocated to one of the most efficient users or to a less efficient user willing to accept a lower level of profit.

Table 14.1   Farm income, costs and surplus

	Livestock enterprise (£)		Cropping enterprise (£)	
Expected revenue from sales (per hectare)				
Livestock	545		200	
Crops, etc.	250		650	
		795		850
Expected costs (per hectare)				
Labour – wages, inc. tenant's labour	200		210	
Capital				
livestock; feeds, etc.	140		50	
seeds, fertilisers, sprays	80		140	
machinery; repairs, depreciation, fuel	80		125	
buildings; repairs, depreciation, insurance	40		40	
finance; interest on tenant's capital	35		35	
Enterprise – tenant's required profit	150		150	
		725		750
Expected surplus (per hectare)		**70**		**100**

All three of these hypotheses are dependent on competition between land users to obtain the use of the land. If we imagine that the tenancy is to be granted to the farmer offering the highest rent at public auction, then less efficient farmers will gradually drop out of the bidding as the rent bids rise above the level which they can afford. Perhaps due to poor crop husbandry the inefficient farmer may achieve a poor grain yield, by poor marketing he may fail to maximise his income, by wasteful use of seed, fertiliser, machinery and labour his costs may be excessive, and generally in an infinite number of ways he may fail to maximise the difference between revenue and costs. As a potential tenant cannot afford to offer a rent greater than his expected surplus of revenue over costs (including required profit), he must drop out when bidding rises above that level. Consequently, a farmer who intends to use the land for livestock production will drop out of the auction after bids rise above £70 per hectare, unless his level of required profit is less than the £150 envisaged here.

Assuming that all farmers require the same level of profit, the farmer who is willing to offer the highest rent must intend to use the land for cropping, and must tend to be the most efficient. He would offer a rent marginally higher than the surplus expected by the second most efficient farmer, who would then drop out of the auction, leaving the most efficient farmer as the success-ful bidder.

On the assumption that the figures in Table 14.1 represent the expected revenue and costs of the second highest bidder, then the rent that would be paid to the landlord would be (marginally above) £100 per hectare. We shall call this sum 'land rent', being the economic return to (or earnings of) pure land, and which we shall define as *the residual after deducting the expected cost of the optimally employed factors of production from the revenue expected from using the land for its most profitable use.*

It should be clear from Table 14.1 that the farm's land rent is dependent on:

(a) the volume of produce from the cropping enterprise
(b) the price at which this produce can be sold
(c) the amount of productive factors employed
(d) the cost of these factors
(e) the level of profit required by the farmer

Land of poorer fertility or subject to a less suitable climate will tend to produce a lower output and, thus, a smaller surplus. Likewise, land situated at a distance from a marketplace will tend to have a lower land rent than land close to the market, due to the cost of transporting the produce to the market, or the lower price that will be offered by merchants at the farm gate.

Note that the surplus earned by any single land use is a geared residual. Relatively small changes in either revenue or costs will tend to cause propor-tionally greater changes in the surplus. Here, a 16% fall in the income expected from crops would wipe out the surplus from the cropping enter-prise. However, the land rent is less volatile than the surplus earned by any individual land use, because in the event of a fall in the price of crops, the livestock enterprise would become the most profitable use, thereby restricting the fall in land rent (assuming that livestock prices remained unchanged).

If such a fall in the price of crops occurred unexpectedly, the land rent need not change at all, because land rent is based on expectations, not on out-comes, and farmers' expectations for the following year may remain unchanged. It would be farmers' profits which would bear the brunt of the fall in income, not land rent. On the other hand, if it was felt that the price of crops had fallen permanently, then the land rent would tend to fall. Thus although the surplus earned by any crop in any year is potentially very volatile, land rent is relatively stable because it is based on farmers' expectations, not outcomes, and because the use of the land can be changed in the event of the first becoming unprofitable.

Farmers' expected surplus from any crop will take account of all possible outcomes for revenue and costs, such as the risk of a poor harvest, the volatility of market prices and changes in factor costs. Such risks will also be reflected in the level of profit required by the farmer. In estimating the level of rent which he can afford to pay, the farmer is undertaking a very similar exercise to that of an investor assessing the price he can afford to pay for a share. Both face risk and uncertainty, and just as the return that an investor achieves is likely to be substantially different from his target return, so a farmer's profit in any one year is likely to prove different from his required, or target, profit level.

Before we can fully answer the three questions posed at the start of this chapter we shall have to relax or modify the various simplifying assumptions. Only then can we explain the relationship between the theoretical concept of land rent and the level of rent paid for business property. However, the reader may already have realised that the concept of land rent is essentially the rental value of pure land, i.e. the annual rent which would tend to be paid for the right to occupy the land if offered to let on the open market. We can now answer the three questions as applied to pure land, rather than to land and buildings.

What causes rent to be paid for the use of land?

Rent is paid:

(a) when prospective tenants consider that the income-earning potential of the land exceeds all factor costs including sufficient profit, and
(b) when competition exists between tenants for possession of the land.

Consequently no rent will be paid for land which is incapable of profitable use (e.g., land liable to regular flooding), or where there is no land scarcity (e.g., the American Western frontier in the early nineteenth century).

What determines the amount of rent paid for the use of land?

The amount of rent is determined by the amount of surplus expected from using the land for its most profitable use.

The profit required by the tenant will depend on profit available on alternative but similar land which, in turn, will depend on the intensity of the competition to obtain possession of such land. The level of required profit will also depend on the risks involved in the use of the land, and such non-financial considerations as pleasure or prestige obtained from its occupation. The greater is the competition to obtain possession of land, the lower will be tenants' target profits, and consequently the higher will be the rent that tenants are willing to pay.

What causes rental value to change over time?

The rental value of land changes over time due to changes in the expected surplus of income over the cost of using the land. This in turn results from changes in the productivity of the land, the market price of produce, and the productivity and costs of the factors of production. For example, the rental value of arable farmland has risen substantially over the post-war period due to the rising price of farm produce, increases in productivity due to improved seed varieties, weedkillers and fertilisers, a fall in the cost of labour due to the introduction of efficient machinery, and the improved knowledge and management skills of farmers.

Before explaining the link between land rent and the rent actually paid for the use of a property, we will examine the conditions under which factors of production are optimally combined.

Land rent and the theory of factor combination

The theory of factor combination derives from the 'law of diminishing returns', which states that 'when successive units of a variable factor are combined with a fixed amount of another factor, then eventually the resultant increments in output (per unit of the variable factor input) will decrease', i.e. the marginal product will eventually diminish.

In illustrating this principle, it is appropriate to imagine land as the fixed factor with which successive units of capital – the variable factor – are being combined. The principle is illustrated in Figure 14. 1. The total product curve traces the output of the land resulting from the combination of varying units of capital with the land. The principle is illustrated by changes in the increase in output (the marginal product) which result from the use of each additional unit of capital. The marginal product is shown hatched, and is also plotted as a separate schedule from the base line. The principle of diminishing marginal returns is seen to operate after the use of three units of capital, because thereafter the marginal product declines with the addition of each successive unit. Note that the total product must continue to rise so long as the marginal product is positive.

If the fixed factor is assumed to be a hectare of farmland (not shown in Figure 14.1) and the variable factor as seed, then the total product curve shows the output of grain cropped as a result of varying units of seed being used, and the marginal product curve illustrates the extra grain cropped as a result of the use of each extra unit of seed.

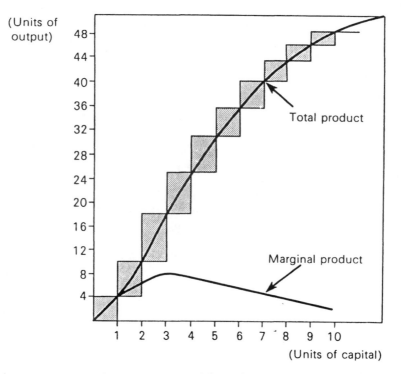

Figure 14.1   Law of diminishing returns

Although Figure 14.1 illustrates the principle of diminishing returns, it does not explain how much capital to combine with the land. To do that, we must ascribe money value to the output and introduce the money cost of the factor used. Consequently, in Figure 14.2 the marginal product curve has been given a price dimension – i.e. instead of representing the marginal physical product in units of grain, it represents the marginal revenue product (MRP), being the money value of that produce. We have also introduced a schedule showing the cost per unit of the capital, and as it is likely that the unit cost of capital will be constant no matter the amount used, the schedule has been drawn parallel to the base line. As the total product is merely the sum of the marginal products, that schedule has been omitted and the scale of the diagram has been enlarged for clarity.

We now have sufficient information to explain the optimal amount of capital to combine with the land. If the user of the land employs less than OX units of capital, the marginal revenue earned by an extra unit exceeds its cost, consequently it is profitable to employ additional units of capital up to OX units. If more than OX units are employed the cost of the last unit exceeds the revenue it earns. OX is therefore the profit maximising number of units of capital to combine with the land.

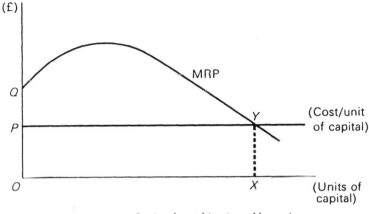

Figure 14.2   Optimal combination of factor inputs

Thus, we have a theory of the optimal combination of a variable factor with a fixed factor. The optimal amount of the variable factor to employ depends on its unit cost and its marginal revenue productivity when combined with the fixed factor. However, in reality, productive activity involves more than two factors, neither of which need be fixed. It takes buildings, machinery, labour and enterprise to farm or to undertake virtually any business activity on land, and just as there is an optimal combination of factors with land, there is also an optimal combination of all factor inputs with each other.

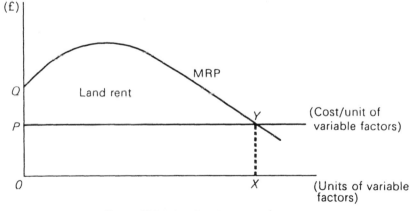

Figure 14.3   Land rent as a surplus

So we shall now assume that the cost and revenue curves in Figure 14.3 represent the cost and marginal revenue earned when a *package* of optimally combined variable factors is employed with the land. The package would include all factor inputs necessary for efficient farming, including buildings and the farmer's labour, management and enterprise, as shown in Table 14.1. With the MRP curve representing the extra revenue to be earned from the use of each successive unit of the package of factors, the profit-maximising number of units to combine with the land is again OX units. The total revenue to be earned by the use of OX units is represented by the figure QYXO, but as PYXO represents the total costs of OX units of the variable factors (including the farmer's required profits), then QYP represents the surplus of revenue over cost from using the land. If the revenue and cost schedules represent the most profitable use of the land (cropping in our original discussion), then QYP is the land rent as previously defined, i.e. 'the surplus remaining after deducting the costs of the optimally employed factors of production from the revenue expected from using the land for its most profitable use'.

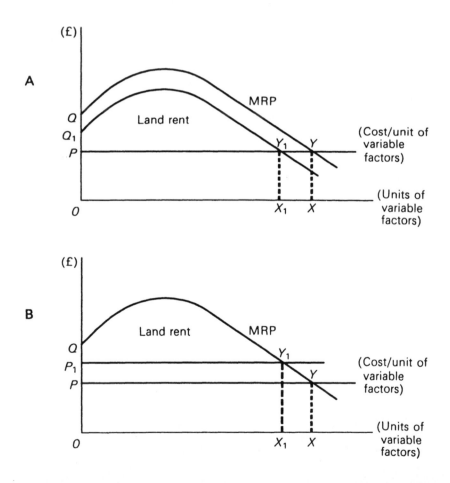

Figure 14.4   The effect of changes in MRP and costs on land rent and the intensity of land use

The relative surpluses earned by cropping in comparison with livestock are represented in Figure 14.4A. If it is assumed that the unit costs of cropping are similar to those of livestock (*OP*), the lower marginal revenue productivity of livestock (Q_1Y_1) in comparison with cropping (*QY*) results in a lower surplus (Q_1Y_1P instead of *QYP*), as well as in the use of fewer units of the variable factors (OX_1 instead of *OX*). That could explain why in Table 14.1 higher costs per hectare were ascribed to cropping compared with livestock. It is not because unit costs of cropping were considered to be higher than for livestock, but because marginal productivity theory suggests that profit-maximising farmers would employ more units of the variable factors for the cropping enterprise. In other words, farmers would use the land more intensively for cropping than for livestock production.

Figure 14.4A also illustrates the effect of a change in the MRP of the most profitable land use, say as a result of a change in the price of crops. The downward-sloping profile of the MRP curve indicates that, assuming stable costs, changes in the MRP (represented by vertical movement of the whole MRP curve) will tend to affect both the land rent and the intensity with which the land is used. Similarly, changes in the unit costs of the factors will tend to affect both the land rent and the intensity with which the land is used. Figure 14.4B shows the effect of a rise in unit costs from *OP* to OP_1, on the assumption that the MRP remains stable. Land rent will fall from *QYP* to QY_1P_1 and the amount of the variable factors employed will fall from *OX* to OX_1.

So the land rent depends on the MRP and unit costs of the (optimally employed) factors involved in using the land for its most profitable use. Land rent will change over time as a result of changes in the MRP and factor costs.

As well as providing a graphical representation of the original example, this more theoretical study has enabled us to derive a theory about the *intensity* of land use, which is important both to the study of rent as well as to our later study of property development. The amount of variable factors used in combination with land depends on their cost and marginal productivity when combined with land. The higher the productivity of land, the more intensively it will tend to be used. That is why farmland which is particularly fertile or advantageously located near a population centre will tend to be farmed more intensively than remote or less fertile land, and why land in city centres is more intensively developed than land in more peripheral urban locations.

Up till now, we have assumed that the amount of land under consideration is fixed in size, but this need not necessarily be the case. Where land is variable, the condition for optimal combination is fulfilled when the MRP to be earned from the use of an extra £1 worth of the land is exactly the same as the MRP to be earned from the use of an extra £1 worth of each of the other cooperating factors. The amount of each factor used will depend on its cost and MRP when combined with the other factors. As factor costs change so will the optimal combination. If land is cheap, it will tend to be used liberally. If expensive, it will be used intensively.

This condition for optimal factor combination explains why rent per hectare varies according to farm size. Factors are not available in £1 units, but are largely indivisible. The indivisibility of factors such as buildings, labour, combine harvesters, and the management potential of farmers, tends to lead to an optimal farm size which varies according to the type of farm. The land rent per hectare of a 200-hectare arable farm will tend to be significantly higher than that of a similar 100-hectare holding. In the larger farm, factor combination can be closer to the optimal and factor cost per unit of output minimised.

Relationship between land rent and rental value

We shall now remove the simplifying assumptions made at the start of this chapter and thereby explain the relationship between land rent and the rental value of property. On the basis of our assumptions, the rental value of the farm is the same as the land rent. Tenant farmers would be willing and able (indeed forced by competition) to offer up to £100 per hectare to the landlord. However, the terms of the lease are unrealistic. First, property subject to a lease normally includes buildings and other fixed equipment, and second, leases of business property are rarely on a year to year basis. Rent is rarely a single payment for one year of occupation, it is usually a sum paid annually for a longer period of occupation. Under the Agricultural Holdings Acts and related legislation, tenant farmers have security of tenure for life, and are subject to regular rent review.

We shall now investigate the impact on rental value of (first) lease conditions and (second) the provision of fixtures with land under a lease contract.

Effect on rental value of lease conditions

Security of tenure, even for a limited period and whether provided by statute or under a lease contract, must tend to affect the rent that tenants are willing to offer under competitive conditions. Tenants will take a longer-term view of the use of the land, and will take account of benefits to be received from any improvements they make to the property, or losses to be suffered from its misuse.

The period between rent reviews will also affect rental value, particularly in times of inflation. Rather than taking a view on revenue and costs over a single year, a potential tenant will bid a rent which reflects his expected revenue and costs over the period in which the rent will be fixed. Theoretically, the rent offered will tend towards the (discounted) average expected surplus per annum over the rent review period. If profit is expected to rise in line with inflation, the longer the period between rent reviews the higher will be the rent that tenants will be willing to pay. Under a three-year review arrangement tenants should be willing to increase their rent bids, and therefore accept lower profits in the first year than they would accept under an annual review arrangement, in the expectation of making higher profits in Years 2 and 3. If that seems dubious, there can be little doubt that a tenant subject to 14-year reviews would be willing to offer a significantly higher rent than if faced with annual reviews (in times of inflation).

It is therefore not simply the physical quality of a property, but the terms or conditions of the lease which affect its rental value. Other relevant conditions are whether rent is paid in advance or arrears, and whether landlord or tenant is responsible for the repair and insurance of the fixtures.

The security of tenure provided to farming tenants, the keen competition to obtain the few farms available for let, and the basis on which farm rents are reviewed has led to the situation where rents offered on the open market are occasionally well above the level that could be justified on the grounds of farming profitability. What is being offered on such occasions is an extra amount in the form of a premium, called 'key money'. This is offered in the hope of obtaining the tenancy and the associated security of tenure, in the knowledge that at subsequent reviews the rent will be adjusted to the market rental value. The payment of 'key money' implies that rents agreed at rent review tend to be below what many tenants would be able to pay, and it reflects the fact that the tenancy virtually guarantees an attractive self-employed business for the tenant and his family in succession. Key money is not exclusive to farm property, it is also a feature of prime shop property in times of buoyant trading. Retailers may be willing to offer key money in order to ensure possession of a shop location which is considered critical to their business.

Key money would not be paid on a year to year tenancy. It is paid only because security of tenure is guaranteed for a long period, either under a lease contract or by statute.

Effect on rental value of the provision of fixtures

Whereas land rent is a payment for pure land, let property normally includes buildings and other fixed equipment such as fences, drains and roadways. Thus the rent normally paid by a tenant to a landlord will include a payment for such fixtures, as well as for the land itself.

It is not easy to distinguish the return attributable to buildings from the return attributable to land at any point in time. In the short run, a landlord would be willing to lease existing buildings as long as the rent received for them covered his short-run supply costs, e.g., repairs, insurance and management. However, buildings would not be redeveloped when obsolete unless the landlord anticipated that he would receive a rent for them which would cover both the short-term supply costs and a sufficient return on the capital spent on the redevelopment. The extra rent (above that payable for pure land) which is just sufficient to induce the development of the buildings is the annual long-run supply cost of (or long-run economic return to) the buildings and fixtures.

The annual costs of the buildings and fixtures in Table 14.1 can be considered as being the long-run supply costs, as they include a figure for depreciation. Thus if the buildings were let with the land, and if the landlord was responsible for repairs and insurance, then the rental value of the farm would tend towards £140 per hectare. That is a land rent of £100 plus £40 for the buildings and fixtures.

Although such a theoretical division can be made between the rent attributable to the land and the rent attributable to the fixtures, it tends to be artificial and largely irrelevant. What we are interested in is the rental value of the whole property, land and fixtures combined, and at any point in time, the rent that tenants are willing to pay for fixtures will depend on their contribution to the profitability of the farm as a whole. Furthermore, in the case of modern urban property of investment quality, the existing buildings are likely to have a long projected life span. Except in the very long run, the buildings and fixtures are not variable, they are almost as fixed as the site on which they stand.

Therefore, instead of assuming that buildings and fixtures are variable factors, we shall now regard the whole property – land and fixtures combined – as the fixed factor, with which the tenant occupier can combine variable amounts of labour, capital and enterprise in order to undertake his business activity (see Figure 14.5).

If Figure 14.5 represents the same property as Figure 14.3, then the MRP schedule will be unchanged, but this time the cost per unit of the variable factors excludes the supply costs of the buildings and fixtures, and consequently *OP* in Figure 14.5 is lower than in Figure 14.3. *OQYX* represents the tenant's total revenue from using the property for its most profitable use, and *OPYX* represents the total cost of the factors he provides, including his target profit. Therefore *PQY* is the surplus of revenue over costs – being the rent that efficient tenants would be willing to pay – and represents the property's rental value.

The rental value *PQY* in Figure 14.5 must be greater than the land rent *PQY* in Figure 14.3 because it includes a return to the buildings and fixtures as well as the return to pure land. If the landlord pays all the costs of the fixtures, *PQY* in Figure 14.5 represents gross rental value, but if the short-run supply costs (such as repairs and insurance) are paid by the tenant and are therefore included in *OPYX*, then *PQY* represents the property's net rental value.

This analysis provides us with a more useful concept of rental value than the land rent analysis:

(a)   because the property (land plus fixtures) is regarded as a single fixed factor under most circumstances (except when taking a very long-run view, or in the case of a property ripe for redevelopment);

(b)   because it separates the factors provided by the landlord, for which rent is paid, from the factors provided by the tenant (labour, materials, enterprise, etc.) which really are the variable ones.

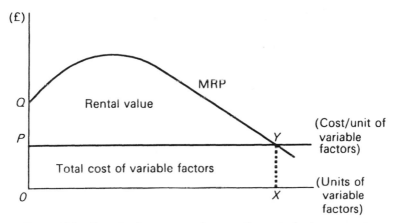

Figure 14.5   Rental value as a surplus over the cost of using property

Reverting finally to the three questions posed at the start of this chapter, we will conclude that:

- rent is paid for the use of property when prospective tenants in competition consider that the revenue-earning potential of carrying on a business activity on the property exceeds the costs of the factors which they must provide (including normal profit);
- the amount of rent paid for the use of a property (rental value) will tend towards the surplus expected by efficient tenants after deducting their expected business costs (including normal profit) from the revenue they expect from using the property for its most profitable use;
- the rental value of a property will change over time according to changes in the expected surplus of revenue over costs.

The following conclusions are also worth stating:

- The surplus concept envisages rental value as an 'expected super-normal profit', which competition forces tenants to pay to the landlord.
- Rental values will tend to vary according to changes in the profitability of the type of business for which the property is best suited.
- A property's rental value will depend not only on the physical land and buildings but on the terms of the lease, including, e.g., the length of the lease, rent review period and repairing covenants.
- The greater the rental value of a property, the more intensively it will tend to be used.

15 Rental Value – a Demand and Supply Analysis

Introduction

Rental value is the market price (per annum) of occupying property, and market prices are determined by the interaction of demand and supply. So, rental value is determined by demand and supply, specifically by occupation (or tenant) demand and the supply of property to let.

The concept of rent as a surplus is essentially a demand-side theory. Rather than providing a full explanation of rent determination, it helps to explain *occupation* demand and the *maximum* rent that a tenant might be willing to pay. Nonetheless, the surplus concept is particularly useful in explaining the rental value of farmland and prime High Street shops, because in these cases supply tends to be very inelastic and rent is essentially demand determined. However, in the cases of office and industrial property, the supply side is much more important and an understanding of rent determination requires a detailed insight into both supply and demand.

Using conventional static analysis, rent determination is illustrated in Figure 15.1A. From an equilibrium level of rental value, R, occupation demand rises from D to D_1 (say as a result of an upturn in economic activity after a recession), and with short-run supply being inelastic (curve S_{s1}) rental values rise to R_1. By increasing the profitability of development, rising property values induce an increase in supply, but only after a time lag, as represented by the (relatively elastic) medium-run supply curve (S_m). So rental values would tend to settle back to R_2, as indicated by the intersection of curves D_1 and S_m, assuming no further change in demand.

The normal experience of office rents in any individual town is that, whereas rents can rise quite sharply on an economic upturn, they tend to level off rather than fall when the supply of new property subsequently increases. That implies a further rise in occupation demand during the development period (to D_2, see Figure 15.1B) to match the increased supply and maintain rents at R_1.

However, in certain circumstances, the combination of a substantial increase in supply through development and a levelling off in demand in a subsequent recession can cause a substantial fall in rental values. If (see Figure 15.1C) the rise in tenant demand to D_1 caused rental values to rise to R_1, that could induce a rise in supply from S_{s1} to S_{s2}, which could cause rental values to fall back to R_3, almost as low as where they started.

Something like this happened in the City of London office market in both the mid-1970s and the early 1990s (see Chapter 16). A sharp rise in demand in

183

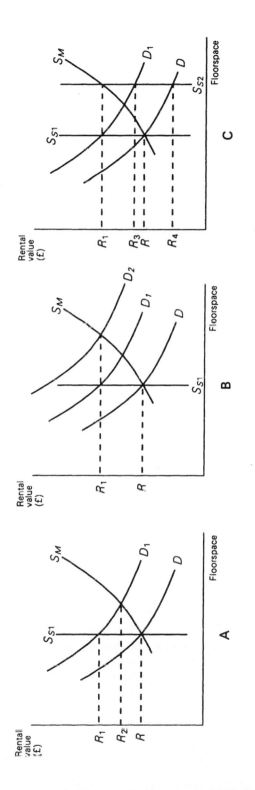

Figure 15.1 The determination of rental value

the preceding boom caused rents to escalate, which together with a relaxation of development control, induced a development boom. When the resultant supply increase met the relatively stable (or slightly falling) demand in the subsequent recession rents fell dramatically.

If demand fell back from D_1 to D, then rental values could end up at R_4, well below where they started, because although office supply is moderately elastic *upwards* in the medium run (through property development) in response to a *rise* in values, it is virtually inelastic *downwards* in response to a *fall* in values (because of durability).

These illustrations provide some basis for the analysis of rent determination. The concepts illustrated by equilibrium analysis can be useful, but they are simplistic. With its many imperfections and its endemic time lags, the property market is seldom in equilibrium, and the full complexities of the market's pricing of property cannot easily be conveyed by graphics.

We will now proceed to examine the demand- and supply-side forces at work in the letting sector of the property market, drawing on relevant principles from elementary price theory. However, a word of caution may be in order beforehand. The significance of some of this content may be obscure to the reader without some understanding of elementary price theory. In particular, the reader should appreciate the significance of the elasticity of demand and supply, and be able to distinguish between changes in demand and supply which result from a change in price (movement along a curve) from changes in demand and supply resulting from a change in some other variable (a shift in the curve itself). Although care has been taken to explain most of the concepts, reference to an elementary economics textbook is recommended for the reader whose understanding of elementary microeconomics is shaky.

Occupation demand for business property

The principle of derived demand

From the point of view of the tenant, land and business property are factors of production and, as in the case of all factors, demand depends on their ability to produce goods and services when combined with other factors of production. Therefore, the demand for a factor is a *derived demand*, derived from the demand for the products of the factor. For example, the occupation demand for dairy farms depends on the demand for milk and dairy products, the occupation demand for shops derives from the demand for retail goods, the occupation demand for factories is derived from the demand for manufactured goods.

So, through its influence on occupation demand, the demand for goods and services must influence rental value. That principle is implicit in, and illustrated by, the surplus concept of rent explained in the last chapter.

However, the surplus concept does more than illustrate the principle of derived demand. For instance, it shows how any exogenous change in factor costs (i.e. costs other than land) will tend to affect occupation demand without any change in the demand for the products. But, although the principle of derived demand does not provide a complete explanation of demand change, it does explain the dominant influence on occupation demand for property. Changes in demand for the goods and services provided by business tenants will affect both the level of output and the prices which they can charge for their produce, the two together determining the revenue and largely determining the expected surplus to be earned from using property.

When the rent of arable farmland was rising simultaneously with a sharp rise in the price of corn during the Napoleonic Wars, it was assumed that the rising price of corn was being caused by landlords increasing rents charged to tenant farmers. It was the economist David Ricardo who pointed out that it was the rising demand for corn to feed the troops that had caused the price of corn to rise which then, by increasing tenant demand, was transmitted into rising rents

Generally speaking, it is the aggregate power of consumers which determines tenant demand and rental values. Despite the element of monopoly power arising from the uniqueness of any individual property, landlords rarely have the power to raise rents autonomously.

Income elasticity of demand

With occupation demand for property being derived from the demand for the goods or services provided on the property, and with the demand for goods and services being sensitive to changes in disposable incomes, another useful concept in understanding occupation demand is *income elasticity of demand*. Essentially this is a measure of the responsiveness of demand to changes in people's incomes, defined as follows:

$$\text{Income elasticity of demand} = \frac{\%\ \text{change in demand}}{\%\ \text{change in incomes}}$$

Property is said to have a strongly positive income elasticity of demand – in other words, changes in incomes tend to have a substantial direct effect on the occupation demand for property. Increasing real incomes over the postwar period have ultimately been the principal cause of rising property values in the UK. However, different categories of property will have different income elasticities. Occupation demand for factories is more income elastic than for farms, because the demand for food is more stable than the demand for manufactured goods in response to changing incomes. Occupation demand for prime shops may be less elastic in response to a fall in average real incomes than is the demand for secondary shops. It is even conceivable that very old tenement flats may have a negative income elasticity of occupation demand, i.e. be an 'inferior good' for which demand declines in response to a rise in incomes.

The income elasticity of occupation demand is a major determinant of both the risk and growth potential of property investments. The variability of real incomes over the economic cycle has meant that occupation demand and rental growth for commercial and industrial property have followed a cyclical pattern. The greater the income elasticity of demand for a particular category of property, the greater will be its rental growth potential in times of economic recovery and boom, and the greater will be its vulnerability to falling rents and voids in times of recession. Conversely, there is evidence to indicate that the relatively stable demand for food results in relatively stable occupation demand and rental values for supermarkets and food stores.[1, 2]

In seeking to explain occupation demand for business property, emphasis has been given to the concepts of derived demand and surplus profitability. That may be somewhat simplistic, e.g., demand for office and industrial space will also be affected by technological change. The widespread introduction of microcomputers into most office-based activities in the 1980s is likely to have had an effect on floorspace demand for reasons apart from its effect on corporate profitability and the demand for goods and services, either because the efficiency of computers reduces the need for office staff and (hence) floorspace, or because the requirement for computers increases the floorspace requirements per employee. However, need which is not backed up by purchasing power has no effect on demand, hence the emphasis given to how the financial power of the consumer tends to be converted into occupation demand by the producer.

Price elasticity of demand

Until now we have been concerned with the *position of*, and *shifts in the position* of the demand curve. In turning to (price) elasticity of demand, we are now concerned with the *shape* of the demand curve. Price elasticity of demand is a measure of the change in demand which results from a change in price:

$$\text{Price elasticity of demand} = \frac{\%\text{ change in quantity demanded}}{\%\text{ change in price}}$$

In the context of rent determination, it refers to the responsiveness of occupation demand to a change in rent. Does a rise in rent cut off demand and cause tenants to vacate property? Does a fall in rent attract a rise in demand? The concept is important to understanding property's risk and growth characteristics. It helps to explain why rental values may continue to rise in buoyant conditions, rather than flagging after a brief spurt.

Economic theory tells us that the elasticity of demand for a factor depends on the elasticity of demand for its product. The inelastic demand for food again explains the inelastic occupation demand for farms and foodstores. An inelastic demand for his product implies that it is relatively easy for a tenant to pass on rising costs by raising prices for the goods or services he provides, thereby enabling him to sustain his rental payments.

The elasticity of demand for a factor also depends on the price and availability of substitutes. There is no substitute for land and property in a general sense, neither are the major categories of property close substitutes for each other; an office is not a substitute for a shop. Although a factory, office or shop in one area might seem to be a close substitute for a similar property in another area, the critical importance of location to property is a fundamental reason for the perception that property in general has a very inelastic demand. Precise location is particularly important to retailers. A shop on the 'wrong' side of a street, or beyond a few metres of 'dead' frontage, would not be regarded by retailers as a sufficiently close substitute for a shop in a prime location. The concept of demand elasticity helps to explain the large disparities in rental value between similar shops in different parts of the High Street.

The individual nature of each building (e.g., in terms of size, design and layout) and the specific accommodation needs of different businesses accentuates the lack of substitutability of one property for another. Offices without air-conditioning are not regarded as an acceptable substitute for air-conditioned premises by most firms in the financial services business in the City of London, nor is a suite of 50 000 ft^2 a close substitute for a suite of 200 000 ft^2. There is also evidence that the demand for new industrial property is less sensitive to rent than the demand for secondary property.[3] Many tenants do not regard old property as a sufficient substitute for new and are willing to pay higher rents for new property.

However, publicly owned property to let is clearly a close substitute for similar privately owned property. So where ample factory accommodation is made available by a local authority at restricted rents, tenant demand for any nearby privately owned accommodation would prove price elastic. Small rent increases in the private sector would encourage tenants to lease the local authority premises in preference, thereby preventing any sustained rental growth.

In seeking to explain rental values, it is the demand to lease property that is relevant, but we must acknowledge owner occupation as the alternative means of occupation. Thus the cost and availability of owner-occupied premises will tend to affect the demand for rented accommodation. Firms which regard buying as an alternative to leasing will take account of the relative costs, particularly the cost and availability of finance (for purchase), expectations for future rental growth, and taxation relief on rent and interest payments.

The elasticity of demand for a factor depends on the scope for using it more (or less) intensively. As rents rise, tenants will strive to occupy less space. Yet in the case of business property there will be a limit to such savings if efficiency is not to be impaired.

The elasticity of demand for a factor also depends on its cost as a proportion of total factor costs. So, the higher that rent becomes as a proportion of business costs, the more elastic will be occupation demand. For most occupiers of industrial and office property, rent is a relatively small proportion of total costs, again helping to explain the perception that occupation demand is relatively inelastic. However, the cost of occupation to a business is not only rent but rates, service charges and (usually) repairs and insurance and, in the case of prime High Street shops, rent and rates together tend to be an unusually high proportion of total business costs. The dramatic increase in the rates burden faced by many retailers in the recession of 1980–2, together with rent increases arising from the previous boom, had a particularly severe effect, forcing many retailers out of business and leading to a sharp increase in empty shops.

When selecting a property to let, business tenants are making a long-term strategic decision of critical importance to the profitability of their business. While the level of rent is important it will frequently be outweighed by other considerations, and once in occupation the costs of moving (including possible loss of business goodwill) are a major disincentive to vacating existing accommodation.

Before turning to the supply side of the price equation we will summarise the main principles identified so far.

- Rental value is determined by the interaction of occupation (or tenant) demand and the supply of property to let.
- Occupation demand derives primarily from the demand for the goods or services which the property is suited to provide, together with the expected profitability of that business activity.
- With demand for goods and services being dependent on household incomes, particularly real disposable incomes, occupation demand is sensitive to changes in incomes and tends to vary over the economic cycle.
- The demand for most property appears to be relatively price inelastic, probably due primarily to the lack of substitutability of one property for another, and to the fact that for most tenants rent tends to be a relatively small proportion of total costs.

Supply of property to let

Market supply and stock

For simplicity, the illustrations at the start of this chapter were made by a consideration of changes in *stocks*. Demand was treated as the total amount of floorspace demanded by tenants (i.e. floorspace occupied by sitting tenants as well as demand from tenants seeking tenancies), and supply as floorspace stock. But, more strictly, prices are determined by *market flows*. Rental values at any point in time are determined by demand from tenants actively seeking accommodation, and the supply of floorspace being offered to let on the market. Market supply is neither stock, nor new additions to stock, nor net changes in stock. It is property for which tenants are being sought, and which will normally consist of both existing property being offered for relet and new property being let for the first time.

The significance of the stock of property is in explaining long-term market supply, and consequently the general level of property prices over time. In the long run, supply depends on stock, but in the short-run supply can vary independently of changes in stock.

The link between stock and market supply can be usefully illustrated by an analogy with gilt-edged securities. Over the post-war period the stock of gilts has varied substantially, reflecting changes in the government's borrowing requirement. New gilts are regularly being issued, and old ones redeemed. If new issues exceed redemptions in any year, stock must be increasing, and if redemptions exceed new issues, stock must be declining. If records of market transactions in gilts are investigated, it will be found that the amount of gilts being traded annually has varied roughly in line with changes in stock. So long-term supply is a function of stock. However, the volume of transactions day to day, or week to week, will vary independently of changes in stock, because investors' decisions to sell and buy are made in response to changes in variables such as inflation and interest rates.

Similarly with property. The difference between development completions and properties demolished represents net changes in the stock of physical property. The long-run supply of property to let will tend to vary in line with long-run changes in stock, but the supply in any week, month, or even year will rise or fall not in response to changes in stock, but according to changes in such variables as consumer expenditure or the level of economic activity.

The analysis is complicated by the fact that we cannot equate the physical stock of property with a stock of tenanted properties. The stock of both tenanted property and property investments can vary independently of changes in physical stock because of the existence of owner-occupied property. In the post-war period, for example, the stock and long-term supply of tenanted farmland has been declining at a rate faster than the decline in the physical stock of farmland. Landlords have been reluctant to relet farms which become vacant, due to the loss of the 'in-hand' premium.

Conversely, over the same period, an opposite trend has taken place in prime commercial and industrial property. The stock of tenanted property and property investments has expanded at a rate greater than the expansion in the stock of physical commercial and industrial property. Taxation is very important in determining the relative cost to an occupier of owner occupation compared with leasing, and one important reason for the trend towards leasing commercial and industrial property is that rent is an allowable expense against profit for corporation tax purposes.

The two elements of supply

The market supply of commercial and industrial property to let at any point in time normally consists of *existing property* being offered for relet (or trans-ferred from owner occupation) and *new property* being let for the first time. The ratio of existing supply to new supply will vary from place to place and from time to time, but due to the durability of property, existing supply tends to dominate. The annual supply of new offices to let in the City of London consistently averaged about one third of the total annual supply over the period 1973–80,[4] but exceptionally in the late 1980s new supply exceeded the supply of existing property due to the development boom. In other locations and for other property types new supply would normally constitute a smaller proportion of the total.

As existing offices are a close substitute for new offices of the same quality, tenants may largely be indifferent between them, and they are taken together as far as our demand analysis is concerned. However, in a supply-side analysis they must be examined separately, because the two elements of supply are subject to different influences.

The supply of *existing property* being offered for relet at any point in time will depend on the number of tenants who have recently decided to vacate property. Tenants' decisions to vacate, like decisions to take up a lease, depend principally on their expectations for the future profitability of business activity. Thus, the supply of existing property for relet tends to vary inversely with changes in occupation demand. In times when economic activity and busi-ness profitability are rising, occupation demand will tend to rise and the supply of existing property for relet will tend to fall, as sitting tenants continue in occupation. Conversely in recessionary conditions demand will tend to fall and supply to rise.

The supply of existing property for relet is likely to be more stable than demand, as in most cases existing tenants would vacate at a break or at the end of a lease. The lengthy terms of most business leases in the UK tends to increase the stability of supply.

The supply of *new property* to let at any point in time depends on decisions to develop new property, normally taken some time previously. A full analysis of the determinants of development activity must await Part IV, but essen-tially the volume of development activity depends on the level of expected development profit. The profitability of development depends on the differ-ence between the value of the completed property and the total cost of development. Thus, when rental and capital values are rising relative to development cost, the amount of new projects will tend to increase.

It is rising demand for commercial and industrial property which induces an increase in new supply, but after a time lag. The substantial time involved in development projects means that supply cannot respond immediately to changes in demand. The development period varies according to the type of property, but very approximately it will vary from a minimum of six months for industrial property to five' years or longer for major city centre commercial developments (the National Westminster Bank headquarters in the City of London took over 10 years from inception to completion). This long time lag before new supply can respond to increased demand makes it essential to introduce a time dimension into our analysis.

Supply in the short run

In the short run, both the new and existing elements of supply tend to be relatively inelastic.

$$\text{Price elasticity of supply} = \frac{\%\ \text{change in quantity supplied}}{\%\ \text{change in price}}$$

The short-run supply inelasticity of *new property* results from the time involved in site acquisition, design, obtaining statutory approvals and competitive quotations and the construction process itself. We shall define the short run as the period which must elapse between the date that the decision is made to go ahead with a project, and the date when the property is completed and is available for occupation. So if new developments have to be completed before being offered to let then, by definition, the supply of new property is *inelastic* in the short run in response to changing price or other market conditions.

However, an element of elasticity is introduced by the ability of developers to market property to let before completion, in fact even before the work has started. In times of rising occupation demand and rental values, developers tend to delay leasing until the project is nearing completion, whereas in times of falling demand developers tend to market projects early in order to reduce the risk of a rent void at completion.

Although the supply of new commercial property is relatively price *inelastic* in the short run (meaning that an increase in values cannot induce a quick increase in supply), that does not mean that the short-run supply of new property is *fixed*. The supply of new property to let depends on development decisions taken some time previously, and at any point in time new supply may be on a rising or falling trend as a result of an increase or decline in development starts initiated at some previous date.

The short-run supply of *existing property* to let also tends to be relatively inelastic to changes in rental value. Tenants do not normally reduce their space usage as a result of short-term rental-value increases, they are much more likely to reduce their space demand in response to failing consumer demand or profitability. One reason is the relative unimportance of rent in the total costs of most firms, another is the infrequency of rent review, which shields tenants temporarily from rental-value increases. The expense of moving to alternative accommodation is also a deterrent to giving up a lease.

However, rises in total occupation costs including rates appear to have caused an increase in the supply of existing shop property in 1980–2, and in both the early 1970s and the late 1980s dramatically rising rental values of offices in the City of London caused a substantial trend towards decentralisation. Whilst some firms moved out of the City entirely, others made space savings by moving those members of staff whose presence in the City was unnecessary, retaining a smaller staff in reduced accommodation.

Despite these examples it appears that, as in the case of new property, the supply of existing property is relatively price *inelastic*, and consequently the composite supply function must be relatively *inelastic* in the short run. Additionally, as noted earlier, the supply of existing property for relet is relatively *stable*, due partly to the influence of lengthy lease contracts. This indicates a relatively *stable* composite supply of property to let in comparison with the more volatile occupation demand, and we must therefore conclude that significant short-term rental-value changes normally result principally from changes in occupation demand.

Supply in the medium run

Whereas the short run has been defined as the time taken to develop new property, the medium run is probably best regarded as the period spanning the end of the short run to the length of an economic cycle, say up to ten years. Within this timespan both the new and existing components of supply are much more elastic than in the short run, and tend to vary cyclically. The supply of *existing property* to let will tend to increase in times of recession as tenants cut back their activities, close branches or go out of business. Conversely, existing supply will tend to decline in times of economic upturn and boom as business becomes more profitable.

The supply of *new* commercial and industrial property tends to vary as a lagged response to changing values over the economic cycle. Due to the length of the development period for city centre office property, there is a tendency for developments which were initiated during an economic upturn or boom to be completed and made available to let during a subsequent downturn. Such trends will be examined in further detail in Chapter 16.

Supply elasticity in the long run

The significance of long-run supply elasticity is in the relationship between market price and development cost. In the notional case of perfect elasticity, supply can instantly respond to any increase in demand, thereby keeping price stable. More realistically in the case of manufactured goods, an elastic supply implies that price will *tend towards* production cost (including normal profits for producers). This is because market production ultimately depends on the existence of profit. A temporary availability of super-normal profit (due to market price exceeding production cost) will induce an excess of supply over demand, thereby causing price to fall back towards production costs. Conversely, an absence of normal profit will tend to result in a fall in supply relative to demand causing price to rise towards production cost.

The longer the production period and the more durable the product, the more important is a time dimension in the analysis. For instance, it is not possible to increase the stock of supertankers in response to a short-term surge in demand, and their durability resulted in a worldwide glut after demand for oil fell in the wake of the oil price shock of the 1970s. Thus, within the short to medium term, existing stock tends to be inelastic and price is mainly demand determined. But after a year or two in a rising market new supertankers can be built to meet demand, and even in a falling market new ships will eventually be required as existing stock wears out or becomes obsolete. So, market price must *ultimately* tend towards production cost.

In the case of goods with a perfectly inelastic supply there can be no link between production cost and market price, except insofar as demand may be affected by the availability of a substitute good with an elastic supply. The price of a Rembrandt has no link with production cost (except insofar as potential buyers may regard the work of modern painters as a substitute).

In translating these concepts to property, the analysis is complicated by its dual components, building and land, each having very different economic characteristics, e.g.:

(a)   the overall stock of land is fixed whereas that of buildings is elastic;
(b)   land is perpetually durable whereas buildings deteriorate and become obsolete.

Whereas land is a finite natural resource, buildings are essentially a manufactured product somewhat like supertankers. They have a lengthy production period and, although relatively durable, they ultimately become obsolete and require replacement.

It follows from the above that the proportion of land and buildings which comprises a property will tend to have a significant effect on its supply elasticity and value. The mix varies according to property type, location and quality. Farmland and prime High Street shops consist mainly of land (by value) whereas offices and industrial property are normally composed mainly of buildings.

In the case of traditional farms, land is clearly the essential element. The buildings (and other capital improvements such as fences, roads etc) are adjuncts which improve the efficiency of the land use. As the stock of land is inelastic, it follows that the supply of farms must be inelastic, even in the long run. Tenant demand must therefore provide the principal explanation for rental value and we cannot expect any direct relationship between value and building costs.

The stock of prime High Street shops is also very inelastic, even in the long run. This is because of the importance of location relative to pedestrian flow, and the inability to satisfy demand in that location by either spatial or vertical development. Demand is principally for the area fronting the street at street level (the so-called Zone A) and that space cannot be significantly increased. Prime Zone A space is as inelastic as the frontage of the prime shopping pitch in any town. Thus, the demand side of the equation must provide the principal explanation for rental value, and there will be no direct relationship over time with building costs.

Although the stock of shop floorspace in any prime High Street location will tend to be inelastic, the stock of shops in general in any town or city will be much more elastic. In particular, the development of covered shopping centres and the trend towards out-of-town shopping pose a major threat by providing a more attractive or convenient alternative to the shopper. The traditional prime shopping pitch is also vulnerable to changing transport facilities or town centre redevelopment which can change established patterns of pedestrian flow. The inelastic stock of prime traditional shops does not, therefore, guarantee rental growth in the context of rising consumer expenditure. The availability of an attractive substitute with a relatively elastic stock (e.g., shopping centres) could result in a decline in occupation demand.

In contrast to farms and prime shops, the stock of office and industrial space is much more elastic in the long run. Within the constraints of planning control, office demand can be met by building vertically and by transferring land from other urban uses. In the case of industrial property precise location is normally less critical, and adequate land with planning permission is normally available to satisfy demand. This stock elasticity means that the supply side of the price equation is much more important than for farms and shops, and in the long run one would expect values to show a close relationship with development cost.

However, the supply elasticity of office and industrial property will vary from one location to another. In places such as Mayfair in London where office development is strictly controlled, values will be demand determined. Similarly, in fully developed urban areas, the scarcity of land and the inability to satisfy industrial demand by vertical development will result in an inelastic supply of industrial property. Only in locations where supply is elastic can we expect values to have a close long-term link with development cost. Yet even in the examples above the link is not entirely broken because tenant demand will be affected by the availability of cheaper accommodation in substitute locations where supply is elastic.

The supply elasticity of offices and industrial property over the country as a whole provides the long-term link between market values and inflation. The dominance of construction cost in total development cost, and the close link between construction cost and the rate of inflation, means that the value of office and industrial property will tend to keep pace with inflation in the long run. But in the cases of farmland and High Street shops, any link with inflation must have a demand side source, e.g., disposable incomes or consumer expenditure.

A close long-term link between development cost and market value can only exist for modern or modernised properties, whereas any individual property's value must decline through obsolescence. Furthermore, the link requires a generally stable or rising demand for floorspace. In the context of *falling demand*, all property has an inelastic supply due to durability. If there is a surplus of floorspace there can be no link with development cost, and inflation cannot provide a support to values, except in the very long run. Ultimately, all property will become obsolete and will need to be replaced, so values must tend towards development costs again. But ultimately the individual property is obsolete, so in the context of falling demand, no property is a guaranteed hedge against inflation.

We will conclude this supply-side section with the following salient points.

- Market supply is the amount of space being offered to let which, at any point in time, will normally consist of two components, new and existing property.
- In the short run, the supply of the four main property types tends to be inelastic, and rental values are primarily demand determined..
- This applies also in the cases of farms and High Street shops in the long run. However, the relatively elastic supply of office and industrial property in the long run means that there should be a long-term relationship in these cases between values and development costs.
- The post-war investment performance of prime shops can be explained by the rental growth arising from the combination of a strongly positive income elasticity of demand and a long-term inelastic supply.
- In the cases of office and industrial property, the long-term link between value and development cost in the context of rising demand has tended to make such property a hedge against cost-push inflation.
- In the context of falling demand, the link with development cost is broken and inflation will not provide a support to values..
- We have developed two conceptual parameters to our theory of rent determination, (a) the demand-side (surplus) concept, which sees rental value as a super-normal profit, and (b) the supply-side concept, which envisages rent as an annualised development cost. In most circumstances, the explanation for a property's rental value will lie somewhere in between.

Cross-sectional analysis

It is important to distinguish between *cross-sectional* and *time series* analyses. The former seeks to explain *differences in values at any point in time*, e.g.,

(a) between one property and another in the same location;
(b) between one location and another.

Time series analysis seeks to explain value *trends over time,* e.g.,

(a)   for any individual property;
(b)   for any sub-market;
(c)   for UK property as a whole.

The concepts discussed so far in Part III are relevant to both forms of analysis, and their application is illustrated further in Chapter 16. However, in this section factors explaining rent differences between individual properties and different locations will be identified.

The rental value of any individual property depends on the demand for it from prospective tenants, and the demand depends on its efficacy in fulfilling the function for which it is used. That follows from the concept of rent as a surplus. The value of a business property will be maximised when its size, layout and design maximises the difference between revenue productivity and user cost. In other words the rental value (per ft^2) of a commercial or industrial property will be maximised when it maximises the tenant's profit. The building may be required to attract business customers, it should provide the services essential to efficient use, and be of such construction as will minimise recurrent expenses such as heating and maintenance.

Of dominant importance in understanding the demand for any urban property is its location, both in a regional as well as a local sense. Once built, a property cannot move to where demand for its services is high. It is dependent on attracting demand where it stands. If all business activity was transacted by telecommunication, location would be of minimal importance, but business frequently involves the transfer of goods or face to face contact between people, and the movement of people and goods is both expensive and time consuming. Location is critical to business property, because it determines the convenience and travel costs of customers and employees, and the transport costs of goods and raw materials.

More specifically, the proximity of a labour force and road, rail (and perhaps sea or air) transport facilities is important to the profitability of manufacturing or wholesaling, and thus to the value of factory and warehouse premises. Similarly, the proximity of urban transport facilities and the volume of pedestrians in an adjacent street is crucial to retail turnover, profitability and the value of shops. The proximity of transport for customers and workers, and the availability of car parking, is important to office property. With a traditional radial transport network, the most accessible part of a town is normally the centre. Consequently, shopping and commercial activities have been attracted there, and that is where property values tend to be highest.

Whereas a general store in a residential area might benefit from being isolated from competition, most commercial businesses enjoy a symbiotic relationship with other similar or related businesses. Shops will tend to locate beside other shops in order to take advantage of the custom attracted there, even if in direct competition, e.g., jewellers often locate beside other jewellers, and shoe shops beside other shoe shops. Although not so dependent on passing trade, the professions and certain other businesses benefit from the complementarity of their activities. Accountants, solicitors, surveyors, and bankers are to some degree interdependent and gain from close physical contact. Perhaps the ultimate example of interdependence influencing business location is in the City of London, where stockbrokers and securities traders are attracted by the presence of the Stock Exchange, insurance companies and brokers are attracted by Lloyds (the insurance market), and banks are attracted by the Bank of England and the money markets.

A detailed examination of urban values can reveal subtle and sudden changes which might at first seem inexplicable, particularly in the case of shop property. Shops on one side of a street may have rental values substantially different from similar shops on the other. Even on the same side of the street, shop values can change dramatically within a few metres. A busy urban street can prove a subconscious barrier to pedestrian shoppers, discouraging a look at shop windows on the other side, and a few yards of 'dead frontage' interrupting a continuous succession of shops will deter investigation beyond. With much city centre shopping being undertaken on impulse or in response to window display, the volume of pedestrians on the adjacent street is crucial to a shop's turnover, and the volume of pedestrian flow can change markedly within a few metres.

At an inter-urban or regional scale, shop rental values will vary primarily according to differences in the spending power of the local population, which in turn will depend upon the health of the local economy. But the value of shops in certain locations, e.g., Central London and Edinburgh, can also be substantially affected by the impact of spending by tourists.

There is a wide variation in prime High Street shop rents in towns and cities across Britain. That is what one would expect. With an inelastic supply, shop values are primarily demand determined, and demand will vary from town to town according to the size and wealth of the local population. However, the same disparity of values across the country is not seen for prime industrial or even for prime office property. That supports our theory of the significance of supply elasticity. If industrial and office values are *ultimately* related to development costs, and if development costs vary little from one location to another, then one would expect to see some similarity of values across the country for properties of similar quality.

The reader who found this chapter confusing is recommended to continue on to the next chapter before reading this chapter again and, if necessary, referring to an elementary textbook on price theory. The practical illustrations in Chapter 16 should help to consolidate an understanding of the rather theoretical concepts in this chapter.

16 Rental Value and the Sub-Market

Introduction

So far in Part III we have examined the theoretical background to rent determination, identified pricing concepts and explained their relevance. While emphasising, e.g., the significance of time lags and elasticities in the property market, little attempt has been made to quantify these because they will vary from one type of property to another, from place to place and from time to time. The objective is for the reader to understand the concepts, recognise their application and thereby make judgements about their significance to rent determination in any particular circumstance.

The property market is not a single entity but a system of diverse but interrelated sub-markets. Trends in UK property are merely an aggregation of trends in an infinite number of sub-markets, distinguished according to, e.g., use type, location, quality and size. The value of any individual property or sub-group of properties is determined by the forces of demand and supply acting in its own sub-market. The theory of rent determination developed in Chapters 14 and 15 will now be applied to explain rental values in the individual sub-market, with particular emphasis on the three principal types of investment property – shops, offices and industrial property.

Farmland

It should be clear from Chapter 14 why the rental value of farmland varies from one farm to another. Soil fertility is clearly of dominant importance because fertility primarily determines the crop which can be grown, its yield and quality. Consequently. the most fertile land tends to have the highest rental value per hectare. The location of a farm is also important, due partly to variations in climate which affect productivity, and partly with respect to markets and centres of population, which affect transport costs and the level of local demand. Although improvements in transport have substantially reduced the impact of location on farm rents since the time of von Thünen, ferry costs are still a significant factor determining the use and rental value of agricultural land in the Northern and Western Isles of Scotland. Small changes in rental value can sometimes be observed when a sugar-beet factory or barley-malting plant opens up or is closed down in an area, as this will tend to affect the most profitable crop of local farms, and the surplus which can be earned.

A farm's rental value per hectare will also be affected by its size (highest rents tend to be paid for arable farms in excess of 200 hectares), the compactness and layout of land and buildings, and the adequacy and condition of the farm buildings, fences, land drains and other fixtures. All these and other factors must influence rental value as they will affect the surplus which can be earned by using the farm.

In view of the inelastic supply of farmland, rental value trends will depend on changes in revenue productivity relative to farming costs. The post-war growth of values was due to the rising profitability of farming through, e.g., the introduction of improved seed varieties, pesticides and weedkillers which increased the volume and quality of crops, and improvements in livestock breeds, animal health and husbandry which increased the output of dairy and livestock enterprises. Mechanisation has reduced harvest losses and the real cost of labour, and grain drying and crop storage systems have enabled farmers to gain from the higher prices which prevail beyond the harvest season. These and many other factors, including improved knowledge and farm management skills, have all contributed towards a rise in the surplus to be gained from farming land, and consequently a rise in occupation demand.

Of dominant importance to farm rents are the prices received for the sale of farm produce, and whereas the relatively high prices set by the European Community for grain, meat and dairy products boosted UK farming after Britain's entry to the EC, a decline in prices relative to farming costs has resulted in a significant fall in rental values since the mid 1980s. Future trends in farm rents and investors' returns from farmland are likely to be primarily determined by the level of prices set by the EC. However, different farms will be differently affected. Rents of low-ground cropping farms will vary with the price of cereals and other crops, rents of dairy farms will be closely related to the price of milk and dairy products, and rents of upland farms will depend on the prices of beef and mutton.

Retail property

Cross-sectional analysis

Before turning our attention to shop property, it is worth considering the case of petrol filling stations. These do not occupy a major place in the property investment market because, just as the ownership of public houses has been dominated by the major brewers, the large multinational petrol companies own the majority of prime filling stations to make petrol retailing an integral part of their business. However, petrol stations are worthy of attention because they provide a peculiarly simple illustration of the relationship between location, sales turnover, profit and rent.

The figures below represent the annual income and returns from two similar filling stations, and illustrate how the concept of rent as a surplus can help to explain rental value differences between one property and another. Although station B has half the turnover of A, its rental value is only one third, because the factors of production provided by the tenant are being used less efficiently, and operating costs are therefore a higher percentage of revenue.

	Station A	% of gross profit	Station B	% of gross profit
Throughput (gallons p.a.)	1 000 000		500 000	
Gross margin per gal., say	15p		15p	
Gross profit	**£150 000**		**£75 000**	
Operating costs, say	£60 000	40%	£37 500	50%
	£90 000		£37 500	
Required net profit, say	£45 000	30%	£22 500	30%
Rental value	**£45 000**	**30%**	**£15 000**	**20%**

In fact, this probably underestimates the rent differential between the two stations. The gross profit margin per gallon of petrol would tend to be greater for the larger station due to the discount offered by petrol companies for bulk sales. Also, in contrast to station B, the throughput of station A is sufficient to attract petrol companies to bid for the tenancy, and petrol companies are willing to accept lower profits on petrol sales than would be acceptable to other operators, thus enabling them to offer higher rents. The required net profit here should be considered as including interest on capital.

According to the theory of optimal factor combination, the higher revenue productivity of station A means that the site would tend to be developed more intensively. It would tend to be more fully modernised and have a greater number of pumps, bigger storage tanks and a larger forecourt. Total operating costs would therefore tend to be higher than for station B, but operating costs per gallon sold would be lower, leaving a higher residual available to pay in rent.

Despite petrol companies' propaganda, quality varies little between brands, and in the modern self-service station there is little service provided. Petrol stations essentially provide a single, virtually identical product, and customers tend to buy principally according to need, convenience and price. It is the stations with the largest throughput which will be best able to provide motorists with the keenest price, and stations with the highest throughput are those located adjacent to the greatest volume of traffic. Therefore by far the most important factor determining the rent of a petrol station is its location relative to traffic flow and other competing petrol stations.

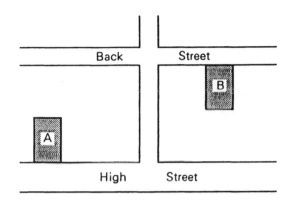

Figure 16.1   Shop location and pedestrian flow

Similarly, in the case of traditional High Street shops it is location relative to the volume of pedestrian traffic in the adjacent street which is outstandingly the most important determinant of turnover and rental value per ft^2. Two shops, even in close proximity, can have completely different values depending on the volume of pedestrian flow in the street on to which they front. The two shops (A and B in Figure 16.1) are deemed to be identical in every respect except that A fronts on to the busy High Street, and B on to the quieter Back Street. The relationship of turnover and rental value can again be explained by the surplus concept, as illustrated below:

	Shop A (£)	*% of turnover*	*Shop B (£)*	*% of turnover*
Sales turnover (exc. V.A.T.)	1 000 000		500 000	
Gross profit	**300 000**	**30%**	**150 000**	**30%**
Operating costs wages, rates, etc.	150 000	15%	100 000	20%
	150 000		50 000	
Required net profit	50 000	5%	25 000	5%
Rental value	**100 000**	**10%**	**25 000**	**5%**

As with the petrol station, these figures should be taken as being merely illustrative of the relationship of turnover to rent. Turnover, gross margins and profit levels vary substantially according to the type of retail business. However, the example shows that the differential in rent tends to be greater than that of the turnover of the two shops. Shop A has double the turnover but four times the rent, and with a sharply different investment yield as between prime and secondary locations, the capital value of Shop A could be eight times that of Shop B.

In contrast to filling stations, shops do not offer identical products, nor is the quality of service uniform. To a greater extent than the motorist, the shopper will seek out a specific shop because of its reputation, or due to previous experience or loyalty. Nonetheless, as the shopper will wish to avoid excessive travelling and walking, convenience of shops to transport facilities is important, and as many purchases are made on impulse or as a result of window display, the volume of pedestrians on the adjacent street is crucial to sales. High rents are thus usually paid around bus or train termini or underground stations, particularly by such retailers as newsagents, fruiterers and florists.

As already mentioned, most shops enjoy a symbiotic relationship with each other, i.e. they benefit mutually from close proximity as they feed off each other's custom. Because of the drawing power of such national multiple traders as Marks & Spencer and Boots, highest rents are often paid for shops in close proximity to such 'magnet' traders, and despite the high rents payable, these multiples seek occupation of the best trading pitches in order to maximise turnover and profit. The presence of 'magnet' traders, a good mix of retail type, and the minimisation of 'dead frontage' (i.e. premises occupied by banks, building societies and betting shops), are factors crucially important to the success of modern shopping developments.

Rental values vary from one pitch to another within a street, from one street to another within a town, and from one town to another. The general level of shop rental values in any town centre must tend to be determined by the stock of shops in relation to the spending power of the population in the catchment area served by the town centre. The retail spending power of a population depends on the size of the population, its wealth and level of disposable incomes.

- Generally speaking, the larger the town and the greater its prosperity, the higher is the level of prime shop rental values.

Time series trends

The performance of shop rents in real terms over the twenty-year period 1972–92 is shown in Figure 16.2 in relation to retail sales volume and retail profits. The impact of economic cycles on both rents and retail profits is clear, both being much more volatile than the volume of retail sales which is also influenced by the cycle. There is a close coincidence between the trends, peaks and troughs in retail sales and shop rents, at least until the early 1980s. During the recession of 1980–2 it was the policy of many retailers to maintain sales volume at the expense of profit margins, and it may have been the need to rebuild profit levels which delayed until 1984 the upturn in rents in response

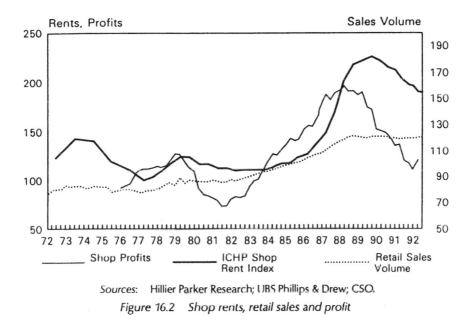

Sources: Hillier Parker Research; UBS Phillips & Drew; CSO.

Figure 16.2   Shop rents, retail sales and profit

to the rise in retail sales. Generally, retail rents appear to have lagged trends in profits somewhat since the 1970s and also lagged the 1988 peak in retail sales.

Not only is the national level of rents constantly changing but the inter-town and intra-town structure of rents is also dynamic, resulting in substantially different growth performances for shops in different locations. The rental growth of the individual shop will be influenced by retail spending in its immediate location. That, in turn, will depend on local, regional and national economic trends, together with any local changes in shopping habits, or the pattern of pedestrian flow arising from, e.g., street pedestrianisation or the development of a new shopping centre. As the property investor is primarily concerned with future rental growth, he has plenty to think about when selecting shops for his portfolio.

Highest growth in retail sales will tend to take place in towns with both a rising population and a growing economy. Of particular importance to any town or region is the performance of its base industries. Towns whose econo-mies are dominated by a single industry, or where employment is largely in declining industries such as mining or shipbuilding would not provide an attractive context for retail investment.

One interesting aspect of this subject is how rental growth varies according to town size. Over the period 1965–78, the Hillier Parker research team found that shop rental growth in medium-sized towns in England and Wales consistently outperformed rents in both smaller and larger towns.[1] However, over the period 1977–86, their sample of smallest towns emphatically out-performed the three other size categories.[2] Furthermore, since the early 1970s shops in large cities (excluding London) have performed best in economic booms and relatively badly in recessions, producing volatile growth trends in comparison with shops in smaller towns. Similarly, Healey and Baker[3] found that their largest category (major regional centres) performed worst in the recession of 1980–3 and best in the recovery of 1983–6. Conversely, the smallest category (smaller sub-regional centres) performed best in the recession and worst in the upturn.

These trends must all have their foundations in economics, socio-economics and demographics, but proving their cause is not easy, nor is it obvious which trends are 'one off', temporary or long-term. The volatility of rental growth in cities might be explained by their industrial base and their relative vulnerability to the economic cycle compared with the more rural based economies of small towns. A long-term underperformance of shops in large cities (excluding London) may be due to a combination of population decline, the problems of manufacturing industry, traffic congestion and inadequate car parking in city centres or, more recently, the development of 'out of centre' shopping. The rising burden of rates has also fallen particularly heavily on prime shops in cities.

Shop rental growth in central London has occasionally followed a different trend from the rest of the country, illustrating a negative correlation with UK retail sales in the early 1980s. Both Hillier Parker[4] and Healey & Baker[5] have identified a positive correlation between central London shop rents and the number of visitors to London. The number of overseas visitors is particularly affected by the strength or weakness of the pound sterling. In times when the pound is weak relative to other currencies, overseas tourists are attracted by the cheapness of British goods and a holiday in the UK. Visitors are particularly attracted to Oxford Street and the other main shopping streets of the West End of London, where changes in tourist expenditure have been reflected in a change in rents after a time lag of about a year.

Another interesting comparison is rental growth for prime shops compared with secondary. According to Hillier Parker,[6] secondary shops outperformed prime in the first half of the 1980s in all locations measured except for parts of inner London. It would be dangerous to ascribe reasons for this trend, but in the case of shops the quality classification is essentially due to location, and there is no law in land economics which states that rental growth in prime locations need exceed that elsewhere.

Trends in retailing

The 1980s saw widespread changes in the business of retailing which have enormous significance for retail property. This section will briefly outline some of the more important trends and discuss their significance.

Perhaps the most important trend in the 1980s was the move to 'out-of-town' or 'out-of-centre' locations by retailers of food, 'do-it-yourself' (DIY) and bulky items such as furniture, electrical and 'white' goods (e.g., refrigerators, washing machines), together with a growing dominance of national traders at the expense of 'independents'. The trend out-of-centre was founded on the expansion of car ownership, traffic congestion in town centres and the relatively low cost of land in peripheral locations. This allows extensive car parking and large floor areas which, in turn, enable retailers to provide wider choice and price discounts due to economies of scale.

The move out of centre by food retailers coincided with a demand for flexible shopping hours and 'one-stop' shopping due to an increase in the number of single-person households and housewives with daytime jobs. These trends resulted in the development of shopping centres at the expense of local neighbourhood shops and a sharp reduction in the number of High Street supermarkets. Whereas, out-of-centre provision for food retailing has typically been in the form of 'superstores' of some 50 000 ft^2, retailers of bulky goods have been housed in retail warehouses, normally within an integral 'retail park', designed for the person shopping by car, enabling him to take away his purchases rather than depend on subsequent delivery.

The 1980s saw the continued development of covered shopping centres, in town centres, out-of-centre and out-of-town, providing greater comfort for the shopper, facilitating one-stop shopping and, particularly at the level of 'regional' centres, exploiting the trend towards mixing shopping with leisure. Arguably it is major regional or sub-regional centres such as those at Brent Cross in north London and the Metro Centre at Gateshead which pose the greatest threat to the traditional town centre. As well as extensive shopping facilities, they provide many of the leisure attractions of the town centre, such as restaurants, cinemas and ice rinks. With the facilities in a warm and comfortable ambience, these centres are an attractive alternative to the town centre for a 'day-out' for families and young people.

The move out of town reversed an earlier post-war trend which had resulted in a reduction in the number of suburban and local shops and a concentration in town centres. However forecasts of continuing decline and the ultimate demise of traditional shops are probably exaggerated. Development of regional centres is likely to be tightly controlled by planning authorities, and the out-of-town trend may be mainly restricted to the retailing of food and bulky goods. This implies that out-of-town shops will satisfy need and convenience, whereas town centres will provide pleasure and 'comparison' shopping, e.g., for clothing, fashion and jewellery. However, to compete with out-of-town locations, many town centres will need to improve accessibility, and provide a more attractive environment and enhanced facilities.

The alternative of continuing decline for town-centre shopping would prove disastrous for shop values. Whereas the inelastic supply of prime traditional shops boosts rental growth in times of rising demand, the effect is reversed in times of falling demand. There would be no support for values in the event of a major decline in town-centre shopping.

Property type and rent determination

In the cases of farmland, petrol stations and traditional shops, we have illustrated the determination of rental value by the theory of surplus. In fact, farmers and retailers often assess the rent that they can afford to pay by deducting expected costs from expected revenue, in much the same way as we have shown. Surplus theory is particularly relevant to these property types because of supply inelasticity, the element of scarcity, and the close relationship between the individual property and the earning capacity of the business appropriate to it. To a greater extent than office or industrial property, the occupation of a farm, filling station or a shop virtually guarantees to the competent tenant a certain level of income. In other words, the profitability of farming and retailing (in a prime location) is closely tied to the land. But the profitability of carrying out a business in office and industrial property is less dependent on the property occupied. In these cases, a demand and supply approach is more appropriate.

The surplus theory should not be interpreted too literally. In deciding what rent to offer, the prospective tenant will be influenced by rents paid for comparable properties. He is not likely to offer more rent than he considers necessary to win the tenancy.

The surplus theory assumes strong competition between tenants to obtain a tenancy. Thus, with competition greatest for prime locations, the theory may provide a more valid explanation for prime rents than for other locations, and for prime High Street shops than for shops in general (where supply is much more elastic). With shop rents more flexible upwards than downwards, it is probably also a better explanation for rising rents in times of boom than when rents are static or falling. Intense competition between retailers in the period 1986–9 was a major cause of the rental boom and, arguably, caused rents in some locations to rise too high at the expense of retailers' profits.

The dominance of national multiple retailers in prime locations, and their willingness to offer rents beyond what could be justified on the basis of short-term trading prospects, may seem to raise doubts about the theory's applicability. In contrast to independent retailers, the national and international multiples frequently offer whatever rent they consider necessary to locate in a prime pitch, in apparent disregard to surplus profit. In fact, such policies do not refute the surplus theory. The multiples are merely taking a longer-term view than would be taken by independent traders. The multiples are taking strategic decisions to occupy the locations which they feel will provide attractive profits in the long term. As established traders (and public companies), they have the financial resources to sustain short-term low returns from some of their outlets in the cause of maximising longer-term profits. Frequently, however, the multiples will also be able to outbid independents on a short-term view due to their economies of scale, including bulk purchasing of goods from manufacturers or suppliers.

Measuring market forces

Before proceeding to examine the determination of office rents we need to look briefly at the mechanism by which property changes hands. In the stock market, buyers and sellers do not deal with each other but with specialist dealers. Because sellers don't need to seek out a buyer before trading (or vice versa), there is no delay in transactions. Prices are quickly sensitive to even minor changes in supply and demand as market makers respond to increased buying or selling pressure by raising or lowering prices.

The dealing mechanism is radically different in the property market. There is no equivalent of the market maker, primarily because of property's hetero-genous nature. The unique characteristics of any property interest means that a potential tenant or investor must spend time and money investigating whether a property meets his needs and, if so, what he should pay in terms of rent or price. A double transaction, from seller to dealer and from dealer to buyer, is not financially viable.

The time necessarily involved in a tenant finding a suitable property means that it may be months before a transaction takes place. Thus even in an active and healthy letting market there must tend to be a considerable pool of property available to let (i.e. the supply of property to let). Equally, there will be temporarily frustrated tenants looking for suitable property to occupy (occupation, or tenant, demand). If supply and demand are broadly in bal-ance (in terms of floorspace), rental values will tend to be stable in real terms, and rising gently in times of inflation.

Whereas the supply of space available to let may be quantified through advertisements and literature provided by letting agents, occupation demand at any point in time is difficult to measure because firms do not normally advertise their space needs. Changes in the balance of demand and supply can best be identified by changes in the amount of extra space being offered to let ('additional supply'), and the amount of space successfully let ('take-up') within the same period. Take-up is not a measure of demand, it is a measure of letting transactions or satisfied demand. However, a rise in take-up in condi-tions of ample supply would tend to indicate a rise in demand. If additional supply exceeds take-up, then supply is rising, and probably rising relative to demand. If take-up exceeds additional supply, then supply is falling, and demand is probably exceeding supply. Take-up and additional supply (which includes existing, new and refurbished property) are the two dynamic indica-tors of market trends.

This analysis, which is particularly relevant to office and industrial property, is illustrated in Figure 16.3 for City of London office floorspace. When addi-tional supply exceeds take-up, total floorspace availability (supply) is rising, and vice versa. Figure 16.4 illustrates the correlation between changes in rental growth and 'market balance', i e the balance between take-up and additional supply. Rental growth trends mirror changes in market balance, but

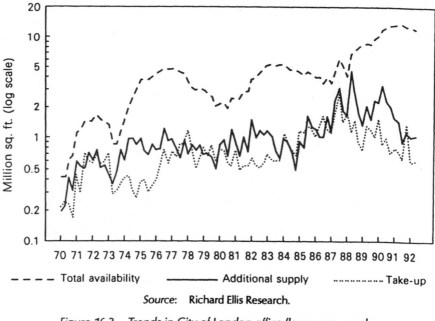

Source: Richard Ellis Research.

Figure 16.3   Trends in City of London office floorspace supply

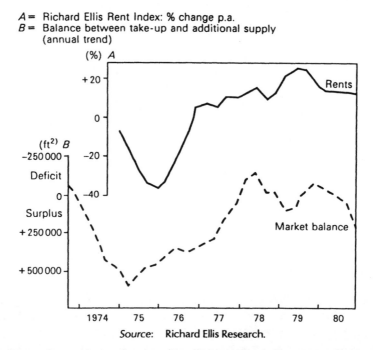

A = Richard Ellis Rent Index: % change p.a.
B = Balance between take-up and additional supply
    (annual trend)

Source: Richard Ellis Research.

Figure 16.4   City market cycle – trend in office rental growth compared with market
               balance

with a time lag of over six months – the period required for changes to become apparent to the market. In periods when take-up has exceeded additional supply, rental values have tended to rise sharply, and when additional supply has substantially exceeded take-up (as in 1974–6 and 1990–2), rental values have fallen.

Office property

Whereas a shop is a place to display and sell goods, an office is a place to house personnel who undertake administrative services. The quality of the building is more important for offices than for shops. The building should promote working efficiency and comfort, and minimise running costs. It should provide the necessary services and enable flexible sub-division of floorspace. The provision of car parking is also important to value, as is location. Location relative to other offices, and to transport facilities for customers and staff makes the town centre the traditional location for offices, but traffic congestion and lack of car parking help to explain the trend to out-of-centre business parks.

Cyclical influences on office rents

Office occupiers cover a diverse range of functions, and include both the public sector and the private sector, the professions and trade, financial services and manufacturing. Office-based activities serve all aspects of the economy, and demand for these services reflects the level of economic activity. Thus, occupation demand and rental values tend to follow a cyclical trend.

Figure 16.5 illustrates the relationship between GDP and the rental growth of prime offices in 15 major UK office centres monitored by Richard Ellis[7] over the four economic cycles from 1961 to 1981. Economic upturns in 1962–3, 1968, 1972–3 and 1977–8 resulted in an acceleration in rental growth as rising demand met a short-run inelastic supply. The rising values tended to induce an increase in office development contributing to a decline in rental growth when, after a time lag, the increased supply of new space coincided with falling demand when the economy subsequently went into recession (1964–5, 1970–1, 1974–5, 1981–2).

In none of the 15 centres included in the Richard Ellis research did office rental growth manage to consistently avoid a cyclical trend. Nor did any centre consistently outperform or underperform over the 20 years of the survey. However, the duration of each cycle and the growth performance within it have varied substantially from centre to centre. In any individual centre, rental values typically followed a stepped pattern, rising sharply due to demand/supply imbalance on an economic upturn then stabilising on a plateau for two years or more.

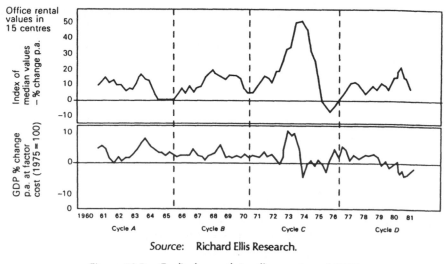

Source: Richard Ellis Research.

Figure 16.5   Cyclical growth in office rents and GDP

These cyclical trends in office rents have occurred within a long-term expansion in service activity and office stock in post-war Britain. The secular trend away from manufacturing employment towards employment in office-based service activity continues. Indeed during the twelve years of the Thatcher leadership, service employment rose by 2.6 million at the expense of some two million jobs in manufacturing, and in the South East region, service activity is estimated to account for 78% of employment (June 1990).[8]

Rental trends in the City of London

It might be assumed from the above that although rental growth rates would vary from location to location, trends would be in the same direction. Figure 16.6 shows that that is not necessarily the case. In the boom/bust cycle of the Thatcher period, as well as that of the 1970s, office rents in the City and in Scotland followed different trends. However, taking a longer-term view, in both cycles Scottish rents followed the trend in London, but after a two- to three-year time lag.

We shall now examine rental trends in the City of London in the two boom/ bust cycles in order to consolidate a practical understanding of the forces which determine rents. By analysing the City office market, we gain an understanding of a uniquely dynamic market, highly significant on the inter-national stage as well as at national level. This brief case study also provides a useful preface to the analysis of the two boom/bust phases of the property market which are detailed in Chapters 26 and 27.

Our theory of office rent determination has stated that rental values are demand led, and that demand is derived from the demand for the services provided. Thus it is important to appreciate that business activity in the City is dominated by financial services. London is the financial capital of Europe and, along with New York and Tokyo, is one of the three leading financial centres of the world. It is also important to understand that the City is merely a district of central London, which should be distinguished from other central London areas such as the West End. It is located at the original heart of the city and comprises about one square mile.

Apart from the Stock Exchange, the City contains the banking and money markets governed by the Bank of England, and the insurance market dominated by Lloyds. There are also markets in foreign exchange, commodities, gold and precious metals, shipping, financial futures and options. However, in the central core of the City, banking, insurance and investment services dominate. Therefore it is the demand for these services that must explain tenant demand and office rental values in this location.

One feature of City offices worthy of mention is the importance of location to an extent unusual for office property. Market operators are willing to pay high rents in order to be close to their market, for both practical purposes and for prestige. Banks prefer a location close to the Bank of England, insurance companies and brokers prefer to be close to Lloyds. The importance of location would indicate a price-inelastic demand for office space, thereby explaining a substantial rent differential with less attractive locations on the City fringe, and contributing towards what (until the 1980s) used to be the highest office rents in the world.

City office rents 1970–7

Strong rental growth of City offices in the late 1960s derived from a combination of expansion in demand and restriction in supply. The rising demand originated principally from an expansion in both domestic and international banking. The growth in domestic banking was due to rising living standards, the increased flow of savings, and growth in the demand to borrow from the personal, corporate and public sectors of the economy. But of greater significance was the dramatic expansion in the short-term money markets, particularly the Eurodollar market. Together with the dominance of Lloyds in international insurance, it was the growth of foreign-currency borrowing and lending which was chiefly responsible for the City's growth as an international financial centre. The expansion of international banking attracted a steady influx of foreign banks to London, creating a rising demand for top-quality floorspace. In 1990, there were 480 foreign banks with offices in London, more than in any other financial centre in the world and a fivefold increase since the mid-1960s.

The other dominant factor responsible for rental growth in the late 1960s and early 1970s was the control of development. Although the planning authority had restricted development for many years, the incoming Labour

212

1969–1977

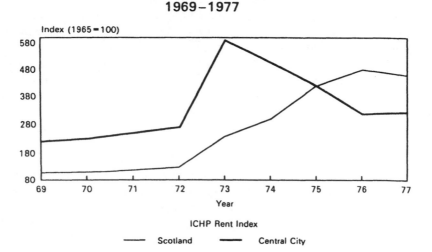

Index (1965 = 100)

ICHP Rent Index

———— Scotland   ▬▬▬ Central City

1985–1992

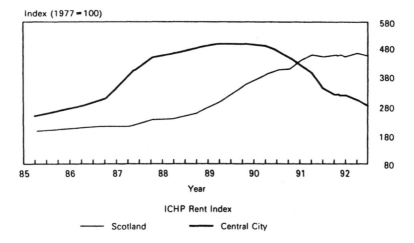

Index (1977 = 100)

ICHP Rent Index

———— Scotland   ▬▬▬ Central City

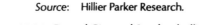

Source: Hillier Parker Research.

Figure 16.6   Central City and Scotland office rents

government imposed a virtual freeze on development in November 1964. Due to the 'Brown Ban' (after George Brown, the minister responsible) supply was unable to satisfy the rising demand, thereby contributing towards the high rate of rental growth in the late 1960s, and providing a base for the escalation in rents which occurred in the boom years of 1971–3.

After two years of recession, in 1971 the Conservative government commenced a reflation of the economy so that over the next two years the economy expanded dramatically. The domestic boom coincided with a world boom and caused a huge expansion in the money markets and 'secondary' banking in the UK. This, together with an influx of European banks into the City due to Britain's entry to the EEC, conspired to create a surge in office demand which, interacting with the fixed stock, resulted in central City rents doubling within a year. Paradoxically, this rental spiral was exacerbated by a government-imposed freeze in business rents (see Chapter 24).

The 43% fall recorded by the ICHP rent index over 1973–6 approximated to 70% after adjusting for inflation – probably the largest real fall in rents recorded in any sector of the UK property market. The circumstances creating this collapse are examined in Chapter 26 and are only briefly summarised here, but the explanation is provided by the forces of demand and supply.

At the end of 1973 a domestic and international recession was triggered by a quadrupling of crude oil prices. The speed and severity of the government's deflationary measures, coupled with the mismanagement of a number of secondary banks, led to a major financial crisis including widespread bankruptcies in secondary banking. The glut of floorspace which resulted from the financial crisis was exacerbated by a trend towards decentralisation set off by the previous rental boom. This trend (which illustrates a certain price elasticity of supply) was encouraged by a 'quango' called the Location of Offices Bureau (LOB) which was able to provide financial assistance to firms relocating. Firms which were unable to justify the expense of a City location reduced their costs by relocating all or part of their staff to other parts of London or provincial towns.

However, the principal cause of the fall in rents in the mid-1970s was the surge in development completions. One of the first actions of the Conservative government on coming to power in 1970 was to relax office development controls. Thus, development activity in the City increased dramatically in the boom period causing a surge of completions some three years later. The supply of offices to let was further increased by the early marketing of developments undergoing construction. Under these influences the supply of vacant office space rose to well above 10% of City floorspace stock. A deeper and more prolonged rental decline was avoided by the banking activity which resulted from the recycling of OPEC 'petrodollars' through the London money market.

City office rents 1985–92

The story of this period starts with 'Big Bang', the soubriquet given to the deregulation of the financial markets in October 1986. Big Bang had many facets, including (a) an end to 'face-to-face' trading in the Stock Exchange in favour of a system using computers and telephones, (b) the internationalisation (globalisation) of securities trading, and (c) the creation of a new regulatory system for investor protection. However, perhaps the most important change was (d) the creation of financial conglomerates.

New financial conglomerates typically involved a major bank (clearing bank and/or merchant bank) taking over a stockbroker and stockjobber. Many of the major groups also acquired a fund management arm, frequently a money market operation and, in two or three cases, a property agency. The majority of groups also have overseas subsidiaries and some of the largest groups are owned by American, Japanese, Swiss, German or French institutions. Thus the structure of the City's financial services industry was transformed from a large number of independent firms, most of which had previously undertaken a single clearly defined function, to a smaller number of integrated groups each striving to provide a broad range of financial services, frequently at an international level.

The changing structure of the financial services industry coincided with a substantial increase in both domestic and international investment activity and the move to a computer-based system of stock trading. This revolution, together with the introduction of microcomputers into most office-based activities, brought about fundamental changes in the specification, quality, unit size and amount of office accommodation required in the City. A particular need arose for large undivided floor areas, air conditioning and floating floors which could house the cabling required for electronic equipment. Whereas just two or three years earlier the dominant demand in the City had been for small office suites, the new financial groups required large buildings, in excess of 100 000 ft². Although it was not usually practicable to collect all their operations in one building, they wished to house a major element of their business under one roof, e.g., their securities trading arm or fund management operation.

As Big Bang approached, the type of accommodation required by financial conglomerates was in very short supply in the City. By far the largest single development taking place was the Broadgate scheme on the eastern boundary of the City, designed by the developers Rosehaugh Stanhope specifically to meet the requirements of the financial services industry. However, this single development could not hope to meet the burgeoning floorspace needs in either amount or timing, and the large financial groups were forced to look elsewhere in central London, particularly the West End and to London Bridge City on the South bank of the Thames. The combination of the inadequate supply and quality of accommodation, together with occupation costs which were the highest in the world threatened the future of the City as an international financial centre.

It was in this context that the hugely ambitious office scheme at Canary Wharf in the derelict London docklands was conceived. Helped by the absence of planning controls and the relief from rates accorded by Enterprise Zone status, this development envisaged an entirely new financial centre amounting to some 12 million ft², costing over £3 billion. In view of its location just 2.5 miles east of the Bank of England, the threat posed by this project was sufficient to persuade the City planning authorities to relax their density restrictions.

Occupation demand in the City had been growing steadily in the years prior to Big Bang in response to economic recovery, a buoyant stock market and expansion in financial services. However, in the twelve months following Big Bang in October 1986 City office rents rose dramatically. Rising demand meeting an inadequate supply of suitable accommodation drove vacancy rates down to just 2% of floorspace stock, and led to a rate of rental growth reminiscent of 1972.

The first threat to City office values came with the stock-market crash of October 1987, just one year after Big Bang. The dramatic fall in share prices caused a sharp reduction in share trading and a fall in the numbers of staff required in the securities business. The decline in staff numbers meant a decline in floorspace needs and, although no dramatic reduction in occupation demand was evident, the market underwent a significant change in sentiment. The urgency to obtain new accommodation lost its edge and tenants' willingness to force rents upwards disappeared as the profitability of securities trading collapsed. Although rental values continued to grow over the next two years at a much reduced rate, potential tenants gradually realised that within a relatively short time there would be an ample choice of accommodation.

As in the 1970s it is principally on the supply side that the reasons for the dramatic decline in City office rents in 1990–2 are to be found. Whereas office redevelopment had been continuing at a modest rate prior to Big Bang, the level of activity increased dramatically thereafter, particularly on the north and east fringes of the City. In the three years 1987–9 alone, developments totalling over 20 millon ft^2 of office floorspace were started, about one third of existing floorspace stock. The boom reflected the high projected profitability of development, resulting not only from rising values and relaxed density controls, but also from the acceleration of obsolescence which necessarily widened the gap between the value of an obsolete office block and that of modern offices designed for the electronic age.

Whereas development starts in the City peaked in 1988, completions continued to rise until 1991 when over 8 million ft^2 of space was finished, most of which was available to let. That year also saw the completion of the main tower of Canary Wharf, but a slight decline in completions in the West End. The outcome was some 40 million ft^2 of offices available to let throughout central London comprising new, second hand and floorspace under construction. The glut of space arose not only through redevelopment but as a result of relocation of office jobs from central London. In a similar response to the rise in office rents in 1972–3, the number of jobs being relocated increased by a multiple of four from 1985 to 1990. The cost of property was the principal reason for this trend, but other significant factors were high wage costs, transport congestion and the poor quality of life in central London.

With positive occupation demand and a sharp decline in both development completions and relocations, the City office market started to stabilise in 1992. However, revival in the letting market was hampered by the inflexible structure of the traditional lease. Tenants wishing to move to larger or newly developed premises experienced difficulty in assigning existing leases, particularly in cases where the rent payable exceeded rental value. Despite rental values in real terms being below their lowest level following the 1970s collapse, the huge glut of office space in central London seemed to preclude any early recovery in rents.

Industrial property

Essentially, industrial property is space for the manufacture or storage of goods prior to distribution. Building size and specification can vary enormously from 'nursery' units for small and start-up businesses to giant regional warehouses of over 250 000 ft^2, used by major retailers. Retail distribution has undergone dramatic changes in recent years. 'Electronic point-of-sale' (EPOS) information is relayed to computerised stock-control systems enabling order lists to be assembled on the basis of 'just-in-time' (JIT) delivery. Building specification will depend on function, but major considerations include – eaves height to enable the use of automatic racking systems, floor areas unobstructed by piers and stanchions, floor reinforcement to take heavy loads, insulated roofing and space heating to enhance workers' comfort, adequate loading and parking space, ancillary office accommodation and staff facilities. Functional efficiency is critical but so is the adaptability of buildings. As in the case of all business property, value will depend primarily on the property's ability to maximise the profit of potential occupiers.

Light industrial use was merged with offices under the B1 use class in the 1987 Town & Country Planning Use Classes Order. This allowed the development of many 'business parks' of 'hi-tech' buildings mostly having a large office content. It enabled companies to combine their administration and sales with their production or distribution activities, and was particularly attractive to companies in such high-technology areas as electronics, computers, chemicals, pharmaceuticals, research and development. These buildings are generally finished to a higher specification than traditional industrial property and would normally provide substantially more car parking, together with extensive landscaped areas, often occupying an area in excess of 40 hectares, as at Stockley Park, West London.

Traditional industrial premises rarely need to attract customers to their door, nor do they normally benefit from an immediate proximity to other related businesses. Thus precise location is less important to value than for shops and offices. But uncongested accessibility to motorways or other transport facilities is critical, as is proximity to a centre of population and a skilled workforce. Modern factory and warehouse premises will normally be contained within an industrial estate where the above considerations have been met.

Although relatively high rents for industrial property surround most British cities, proximity to London is the most important influence on industrial rents in England, with values heavily concentrated towards the south and east of the country. Highest rents have been paid to the west and south of London, particularly either side of the M4 motorway to Heathrow airport (and beyond) and south by Gatwick airport to Brighton on the south coast. However, development in the 1980s of the M25 orbital motorway around London seems to have partially restored the balance to the north and east of the capital. Proximity to a motorway is clearly advantageous to industrial property and high rent corridors tend to lie alongside motorways, particularly in urban areas. However, exceptionally high rents will only be sustained where land scarcity prevents supply responding to demand.

Time series trends

As in the case of both shop and office property, the general level of industrial property rents is influenced by economic trends. In fact, the impact of the national economic cycle on tenant demand would tend to be exaggerated in comparison with the other two property types due to the effect of the stock or inventory cycle.

During a recovery phase in the trade cycle, retailers will tend to increase their orders from wholesalers by an amount greater than their increased sales, in order to build up stock to a level commensurate with their higher level of sales. Similarly, wholesalers will tend to increase orders from manufacturers by an amount greater than their (increased) sales to retailers, and manufacturers may also raise output to a level higher than the (increased) level of orders, if a further rise in demand is anticipated. So in times of rising demand, manufacturing output will tend to rise by a greater proportion than the rise in consumption, as stocks of goods are built up. Conversely, in a recessionary phase of the economic cycle, manufacturing output will tend to fall by a greater proportion than consumption as retailers, wholesalers and manufacturers attempt to reduce stocks.

Whereas retailers, wholesalers, distributors and importers can (up to a point) pass back the burden of reduced sales, the manufacturer is at the end of the line, and may be faced with substantial cutbacks in production during the destocking process. This may involve temporary or permanent closure of sections of his business, thus bringing vacant property on to the letting market. Wholesalers, importers and distributors will similarly require less warehouse accommodation, occupation demand will fall and existing supply increase, tending to cause either a fall in rental value or, at least, a decline in rental growth. The rate of destocking will depend on the rate by which demand is falling, expectations for the future, and the level of interest rates. Interest rates tend to be high early in a recessionary phase of the cycle, and as

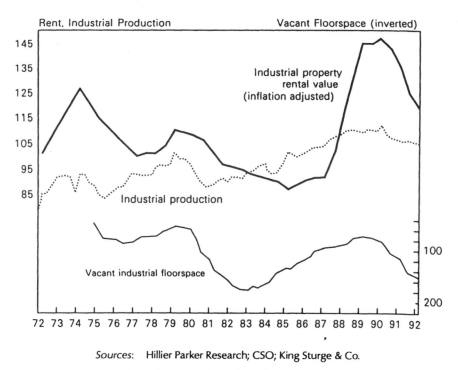

Rent, Industrial Production   Vacant Floorspace (inverted)

Sources: Hillier Parker Research; CSO; King Sturge & Co.

Figure 16.7   Industrial rents, industrial production and vacant floorspace

the excess stocks have to be financed, the level of interest rates is a significant factor determining the speed and severity of the destocking process.

Figure 16.7 shows the relationship over the twenty-year period 1972–92 between industrial production, vacant industrial floorspace and the ICHP industrial rent index adjusted for inflation. A very close correlation between the three series could not be expected as they are not entirely compatible, e.g., the index for industrial production relates to the UK, whereas, vacant industrial floorspace covers England and Wales only, and the ICHP rent index is restricted to good-quality industrial property in Great Britain. Nonetheless, there is a clear correlation between the trends shown by the three indices, especially a coincidence of the timing of the peaks of the booms.

In contrast however, there have been substantial time lags between the troughs in industrial production and subsequent troughs in real industrial rents. This can be explained by (a) the excess floorspace capacity of tenants at the bottom of a cycle which must be absorbed before tenants require more space, and (b) the large supply of vacant floorspace to let. Only when occupation demand starts to exceed the supply of property to let will rents start to rise strongly, and this has only occurred during boom periods, e.g., 1972–3, 1978–9 and 1987–9.

IV The Theory and Finance of Property Development

17   Site Values and Development Activity

One conclusion already reached is that because existing stock tends to dominate the property market, it is mainly the demand for (and supply of) *existing* property which determines price at any point in time. It is the level of prices fixed in this 'secondary' market which influences the supply of new developments. It has therefore been logical to embark on our quest to explain the price of property by emphasising the market in existing property. However, the supply of new property must also affect price, so it is to the development sector of the property market that we must now turn our attention.

Development and the developer

Generally speaking, land development is the process of improving the productivity of land, something which may be achieved without extensive construction work. However, in the context of commercial and industrial property, development normally implies the creation of new buildings, either as a result of undeveloped land being built on for the first time (new development), or as a result of the replacement of existing buildings by new structures (redevelopment), or through substantial conversion or modernisation (refurbishment) of existing buildings.

In each of these cases development would normally involve the following tasks:

Site identification and appraisal

Finding a site with the potential for profitable development. In order to assess the viability of the project, the developer would have to select the use, size and form of development which would maximise profitability (subject to planning and other constraints). He would have to assess the expected value and demand for the property on completion and estimate all development costs.

Site acquisition

In the case of a major urban project encompassing a number of existing properties, site assembly may take several years. Normally all existing legal interests must be acquired, and in the short run many owners and occupiers may be unwilling to sell, even at prices well above existing use value. Acquisition is simplified if the land to be developed is held in a single ownership.

Planning permission

Obtaining planning permission and other statutory approval. Ideally, outline planning permission should be obtained prior to site acquisition, as restriction on use and density may render a project unprofitable.

Financing

Finance will normally have to be raised to pay for the site, construction and other development costs.

Design and construction

The developer will normally appoint such specialists as an architect, quantity surveyor and structural engineer to undertake design, costing and detailed management of the building work.

Letting and sale

Many developments are not sold, but retained as long term investments by the developer. From the point of view of assessing the profitability of a project, the date of completion of a development is best defined as the date at which it becomes fully let; thereafter, ownership should be regarded as an investment in the completed project.

A full description of the development process is not attempted in this book, nor is a study of methods of development appraisal. The objective of Part IV is (a) to explain the economic forces which affect site values, (b) to explain changes in the volume of development activity – as by affecting supply, this will affect the rental and capital value of existing property – and (c) to investigate financing methods and to analyse the risks and returns accruing to the various interests involved in development.

The six components of the development process listed above are ultimately the responsibility of the developer, although much of the work may be undertaken by professional agents. The developer is the party that motivates, coordinates, makes the crucial decisions and bears the main financial risk of the project. Although the majority of prime city centre commercial development in the post-war period has been undertaken by property companies, much has also been undertaken by owner occupiers (especially banks, insurance companies and some major retailers), certain large national building contractors and by life assurance and pension funds. In the public sector, local authorities, new town development corporations, and certain other public sector agencies have been active, particularly in the development of industrial property.

The developer is the agent who, within the imperfections of the price mechanism, is helping to make optimal use of scarce land resources. In that respect, as well as by providing the offices, shops, factories and warehouses required by the economy, he is carrying out an important economic function for the community.

Although most private-sector development is undertaken for profit, there are exceptions. Owner occupiers requiring specialist buildings may be willing to undertake development at a loss in order to create a profitable outlet for their trading activities. Similarly, large building contractors occasionally take on projects of doubtful profitability in order to create construction work for themselves in times of low demand. The profit motive is also less important in the public sector, especially in the case of local authorities, new-town development corporations, and regional development agencies, who have the broader responsibility to promote the economy of their area.

In the case of investment property, however, the profit motive is paramount in explaining development activity and site values. Unless otherwise stated, it is assumed in this book that the main concern of the developer is profitability, and that the developer is a property company or financial institution specialising in such activity. A development is a form of short-term property investment, and the readiness of developers to undertake such projects will depend on the returns expected and the risks perceived. We shall now investigate the sources and determinants of the risk and return from property development.

Risks and returns from property development

Table 17.1 shows a simple budget for the redevelopment of offices on a prime city centre site. The site can be purchased immediately for £2million, it is expected that construction work will start in six months' time, and that the project will be completed and fully let in two years. After taking account of expected demand/supply conditions, the rental value (net) of the completed property is expected to be £600 000 and the market yield 6%. Construction costs, fees and expenses have been carefully estimated at the amounts shown.

Total cost is the cost of all factors of production employed over the development period. These must include the cost of financing each item of expenditure, whether the capital used is borrowed or is the developer's own equity. The interest rate adopted here is 15% per annum but the finance costs have been calculated on the assumption that interest is charged half yearly at half the annual rate (7.5%). As the site is purchased at the start of the development, that cost must be financed over the full two-year period. The finance costs of construction have been calculated on the basis that these costs are spread evenly over the 18 month period of construction, and that

Table 17.1   Budget schedule for office redevelopment (£)

			£
Expected value on completion			
Net rental income		600 000	
Years purchase at 6% in perpetuity		16.667	
Expected capital value (or sale price)			10 000 000
Expected development cost			
Site cost			
Purchase	2 000 000		
Acquisition fees and expenses, say	70 000		
	2 070 000		
Finance, 7.5% half yearly	694 420		
		2 764 420	
Construction cost			
Demolition and construction	4 500 000		
Architect's and QS fees	562 500		
	5 062 500		
Finance, 7.5% half yearly	389 180		
		5 451 680	
Disposal Cost			
Fees and expenses, say		83 900	
			8 300 000
Expected profit			**£1 700 000**

the contractor is paid at the end of each six months, i.e. he is paid one third after 12 months, one third after 18-months and one third after 24 months. The last instalment is paid at the completion of the project and, as in the case of the disposal cost, does not require to be financed.

On the basis of these figures, the expected profit is £1 700 000, which we shall assume is just sufficient to persuade the developer to go ahead with the project. This being so, what are the principal variables which could bring about a change in the level of profit ultimately achieved? Although the cost of the site constitutes a significant proportion of total cost, once purchased it cannot subsequently affect the level of profit directly. Besides, as we shall see, rather than changing site value being a determinant of development profitability, it is vice versa – the value of a site is dependent on the expected profitability of its development. Likewise, as the various professional fees are relatively stable percentages of other major variables, these are also unimportant as determinants of profitability.

On the cost side, this leaves construction and finance costs as the important variables, but as total finance cost depends on both the interest rate and the length of the development period, there are really three principal cost variables. As we have defined the development period as the time elapsing from initiation until the property is fully let, this variable encompasses delays prior to, and during, construction, as well as rent voids after completion of the building. Such delays mean that the capital invested in the project must be financed over a longer period, and the receipt of income is postponed.

On the revenue side, the two variables are the rental value and yield at completion. Thus there are five principal variables which may bring about a change in the profitability of the project – the rental value and yield at completion, construction cost, annual finance cost, and the length of the development period. It is changes in these variables which create the majority of risk in development projects.

Let us now investigate the impact of changes in these crucial variables in the context of our development. The profitability of development, as with any project, is a geared residual, so that a relatively small change in these variables can bring about a proportionately large change in the residual profit. Simple calculations show that a 17% fall from the forecast net rental income, or a 17% rise in the yield on completion would, if either occurred independently, wipe out all profit from the project. Conversely, an equal but opposite change would cause profit to double. The project is therefore said to be very sensitive to changes in either variable. The project is less sensitive to a change in construction cost – it would require a 31% rise to extinguish profit – and even less sensitive to changes in finance cost – a 33% rise in the interest rate to 20% would reduce profit by only 23%. But note the impact that a year's delay in letting would have. Assuming all other variables remain the same, the increased cost of financing the site purchase and construction over one extra year raises total cost by £1 278 631 and reduces profit by 75%.

Generally speaking, the greater is any variable as a proportion of the project's total value, then the greater is the project's sensitivity to that variable. Also, the longer the development period, the greater the impact of finance cost. Thus larger projects taking longer to complete tend to be more vulnerable to rising finance cost.

We can see, therefore, that a development project such as this is vulnerable to adverse changes in a number of variables, but our analysis so far is simplistic in the respect that these variables are unlikely to change independently. Each is dependent on national macroeconomic conditions which will tend to influence most or all of the principal variables *concurrently*. For instance, in the short run, rental values are primarily dependent on changes in occupation demand, but property yields are also dependent on occupation demand, as it affects risk and expected rental growth. As occupation demand also affects the ability to let a development, it can also influence the development period (see Figure 17.1).

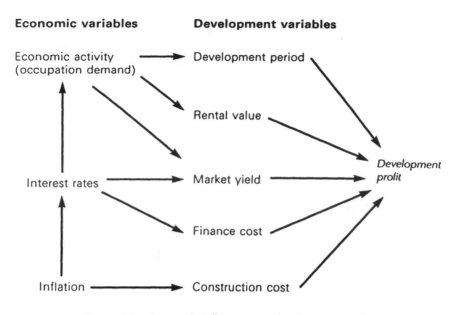

Figure 17.1   Economic influences on development profit

Similarly, changing interest rates in the economy will affect both finance cost and property yields directly and, as a significant trend in interest rates will tend to affect economic activity, a change in this variable could affect four out of the five development variables. A rising trend in interest rates may *simultaneously* cause a rise in finance cost, a rise in yields, a fall in rental income received at completion and, by delaying the letting of completed projects, prolong the development period. A combination of relatively small adverse changes in these variables would normally be sufficient to extinguish any profitability and, conversely, favourable changes could dramatically improve profit.

As the rate of inflation is a major determinant of the cost of construction, it can be seen (Figure 17.1) that there are three macroeconomic variables on which development profit is principally dependent. Ultimately the bulk of the risk of major development projects derives from changes in these three macroeconomic variables.

The timing of a development project is likely to prove critically important to its profitability, and the developer should attempt to forecast economic conditions at project completion. Reflationary conditions, by causing an upturn in occupation demand, will tend to cause not only a rise in rental values and a reduced risk of rent voids at completion, but possibly also a fall in yields, all factors tending to increase the profitability of development. Furthermore, early in a recovery phase of the economic cycle interest rates and inflation (and thus the rise in construction costs) will tend to be low. Under such conditions, therefore, all the principal variables could move favourably.

Conversely, under recessionary conditions the same variables will be tending to move in an adverse direction. Early in a recession the customary high level of interest rates and inflation will tend to cause an acceleration in building and finance costs. At the same time, falling occupation demand will tend to dampen rental growth and create problems in the letting market. The combination of a 10% rise in total cost and an 8.7% fall in the value of the completed property would be sufficient to extinguish all profit in our development. Note that we are not suggesting an actual 8.7% fall in the value of such property in the market, but an 8.7% shortfall from the value anticipated when the development appraisal was made two years previously, a perfectly realistic outcome.

The reader who remembers our discussion in Chapter 8 will have recognised that the bulk of the risk identified above is *market risk* rather than *specific risk*. Most of these risks cannot be avoided by diversification, because other developments (and most other investments) will be similarly affected by the same macroeconomic variables over the economic cycle. However, insofar as economic activity and occupation demand vary according to location, some risk reduction will arise through regional diversification of development projects. There are also other risks specific to individual projects which can be diversified away, but it seems probable that the majority of development risk is unavoidable.

Although the risk of property development is closely related to that of (standing) property investment, development risk is much the greater. According to one traditional method of appraising development projects, the yield relationship between the expected net income on completion and total cost should normally be 1.5–3% above the investment yield on the completed property. In our case, such a development yield is only 7.23% (£600 000/£8 300 000×100), being only 1.23% above the market yield on the completed property (6%). On other traditional criteria, our expected profit appears acceptable, but nonetheless this project should probably be considered as being in the lower range of what would normally be considered acceptable. On a DCF calculation, the expected IRR from the project is 37.5%, a return which would seem attractive on all but the riskiest projects. However, this is a return, not pure profit as no deduction has been made in the calculation for the wages and expenses of the developer and his staff, nor any allowance for the cost of finance or taxation.

Mitigating the risks of development

A developer is able to take certain actions to mitigate the risk of development. First, he should estimate costs and future return as accurately as possible by using techniques of demand assessment, taking account of other competing developments in progress, and by using forecasting services such as those for building costs published by the RICS[1] Building Cost Information Service. Second, the risk of development will generally be minimised by completing a project as quickly as possible. We have seen that the principal risk of development derives from changes in national economic conditions over the development period. As such changes take time, the risk of development must derive from the length of the development period.

The developer can also take action to fix certain variables, particularly those to which the project is most sensitive. In fact, the risk of adverse change in all main variables can, theoretically, either be avoided or reduced by contract. The direct risk of rising finance cost, for example, can be avoided by borrowing on a fixed-interest basis, the risk of escalating building cost may be reduced by arranging a fixed-price contract with the builder, and risk of construction delay may be mitigated by the introduction of a clause in the building contract under which the contractor would be liable for loss due to avoidable delay. The crucial risk of rent voids at completion can be reduced by arranging to 'prelet' the property (i.e. prior to going ahead with a project a lease is agreed with the future tenant), and the risk of falling rental value during the development period can be avoided by preletting at a specific rent. Finally, the risk of rising market yields can be avoided by a 'forward sale' to an investor at a prearranged yield or price.

Unfortunately for the developer, the probable impact of shifting the risk onto other parties in this way is to make the development unviable. In larger contracts with long construction periods, few contractors would be willing to take on a fixed-price contract, and if they did they would charge a higher price. Similarly, an extra charge would result from the inclusion of a damages clause, fixed-interest finance is normally more expensive than variable interest, and a forward sale would tend to be concluded at a yield somewhat above the probable market yield at completion.

Substantial preletting of larger commercial developments is usually regarded by developers as at least highly desirable, and often as an essential precondition for going ahead. Frequently, and particularly in periods of economic uncertainty, the ability to prelet is the crucial factor which makes development risk acceptable, and on which a decision to proceed with a project finally depends. In every case, the developer should identify the risks to which the project is most vulnerable, assess the cost of limiting these risks by contract, and after weighing up the risks avoided against the resultant reduction in expected profit, make a judgement on what action to take.

Ultimately, the principal risk of development derives from the length of the development period over which cost and value variables are liable to change. In the case of projects taking longer than two or three years, it becomes impossible for the developer to take a confident view of economic conditions at completion. In this situation, preletting is both more important and more difficult to achieve as few occupiers wish to commit themselves so far ahead. Such developments tend to remain the province of the larger public companies and institutions, which would be able to sustain the impact of a project incurring major losses. Despite the ability to contract out of certain risks, at every level development tends to be a risky business, but one for which an attractive return can be earned under favourable circumstances.

Another aspect of development risk is that involved in assembling a large site consisting of a number of properties, in each of which a variety of interests may exist. Acquisition of all interests may take many years, and the risk is considerable because the developer may be required to pay substantially in excess of existing use value in the knowledge that ultimately one or a small number of existing owners may render the project unviable by refusing to sell. Alternatively, the last owner to sell may use his monopoly power to extract a price from the developer well beyond the intrinsic value of the property itself. Not only may the developer find that he is unable to go ahead with the project and that its value is below the price paid, but much of the property may be vacated, therefore paying little or no rent and falling into disrepair. In the meantime, the finance costs of purchase will be constantly mounting.

Similarly, if a developer acquires a site prior to obtaining planning permission then he is taking the risk that permission may not be granted for the use, or at the density which would make the project viable. Alternatively, if he applies for planning permission first, existing owners may become more aware of the site's development potential, and accordingly bargain for a higher price. Both these situations illustrate the potential benefits of undertaking major projects in co-operation with the local authority, which has the ability both to use its planning powers for the benefit of the project, and to use its compulsory purchase powers to aid site assembly.

We will summarise this section by reiterating the following points:

- There are five principal variables which determine the profitability of development projects, viz., cost of construction, annual cost of finance, duration of the project (until fully let), rental value and yield at completion. It is changes in these variables which are the main source of risk and return.
- Whereas for any individual project each of these variables may change independently, they all tend to be influenced simultaneously either in an adverse or beneficial direction according to macroeconomic trends over the economic cycle.
- Risk arising from national economic conditions is principally market risk (as distinct from specific risk). Thus a large part of the risk of development cannot be avoided by diversification into other development projects.
- A developer may reduce the risk of a project by fixing the main variables by contract, but this will reduce the project's potential profitability and may render it unviable.
- The risk of the individual project varies with its size and duration. The larger the project, the longer the development period and the greater is the risk of costs and values moving adversely.

The theory of site value

We can state two necessary preconditions before a development project will be initiated, both of which follow from an assumption that developers and property owners seek to maximise profit.

(a)   The expected value of the completed development must exceed the cost of the site and all development costs, including a sufficient level of profit for the developer.
(b)   The value of the site for development purposes must match (or exceed) its value for existing use.

If this latter condition is not satisfied, then the developer would be unable to purchase the site for a price at which he could make an adequate profit. The existing owner would be unlikely to sell to the developer for less than he could get for existing use purposes. Even if the developer already owned the site, he would maximise profit by selling it off at its market value or by retaining it in its existing use.

In order to explain the conditions under which new development will take place, it is therefore necessary to explain the determination of site value.

Site value as a residual

This theory is similar to the (surplus) theory of the determination of land rent (Chapter 14), except that now we shall consider an unencumbered freehold interest and investigate the capital value of a development site rather than the annual value of a tenant's interest in land. The concept of site value as a residual can be illustrated by inverting the data in Table 17.1. Whereas in Table 17.1 the site cost was deemed to be known and the residual represented the expected profit, in Table 17.2 the developer's required (target) profit is assumed and the residual represents the amount which the developer can afford to pay for the site. Assuming competition between developers to acquire the site, and that this residual represents the highest price which the most efficient developers would be willing to pay, then it can be regarded as the value of the site for development purposes. Assuming also that development (as distinct from existing use) represents the most profitable use of the site, then the residual represents the land rent of the site (in capital terms), as previously defined, e.g., 'the surplus after deducting the expected costs of the optimally employed factors of production from the revenue expected from using the land for its most profitable use'.

Table 17.2   Site value as a residual (£)

		£
Expected value on completion		
Net rental income	600 000	
Years purchase at 6% in perpetuity	16.667	
Expected capital value (or sale price)		10 000 000
Expected development cost		
Construction cost		
Demolition and construction	4 500 000	
Architect's and quantity surveyor's		
fees	562 500	
	5 062 500	
Finance, 7.5% half yearly	389 180	
		5 451 680
Disposal cost		
Fees and expenses		83 900
Developer's target profit		
(17% of capital value)		1 700 000
		7 235 580
Residual available for site acquisition		2 764 420
Finance cost of site purchase	694 420	
Acquisition fees & expenses, say	70 000	
		764 420
Residual indicating development value of site		**£2 000 000**

The parallels between the data in Tables 14.1 and 17.2 should be clear. Just as the rental value of land represents the expected annual surplus a tenant can earn from using the land, the development value of a site represents the expected surplus the developer can earn over the development period.

Site value as a development's NPV

The development value of a site can also be regarded as the net present value (NPV) of the project's expected cost and revenue flows. If the developer's target profit is treated as a cost paid out at the completion of a project then, using the cost of finance as the discount rate, the NPV represents the site's development value. In our case, the six month cash flows are:

			Months		
	0	6	12	18	24
Acquisition fees	−70 000	—	—	—	—
Construction	—	—	−1 500 000	−1 500 000	−1 500 000
Architect's and quantity surveyor's fees	—	—	−187 500	−187 500	−187 500
Disposal cost	—	—	—	—	−83 900
Profit	—	—	—	—	−1 700 000
Value at completion	—	—	—	—	+ 10 000 000
Net cash flows	−70 000	—	−1 687 500	−1 687 500	+6 528 600

Discounting these cash flows at 7.5% half yearly:

$$NPV = C_0 + \frac{C_1}{1+r} + \frac{C_2}{(1+r)^2} + \frac{C_3}{(1+r)^3} + \frac{C_4}{(1+r)^4}$$

$$= -70000 + 0 + \frac{-1687500}{(1+0.075)^2} + \frac{-1687500}{(1+0.075)^3} + \frac{6528600}{(1+0.075)^4}$$

$$= £2\,000\,000$$

Alternatively, the target profit could be omitted and the cash flow discounted at a target IRR which reflects risk and the developer's required profit. So long as the target IRR (here 17.34% per six-month period) is consistent with the cost of finance and the target profit (£1 700 000), the NPV (the site value) must again be £2 000 000.

Note that we adopted cash-flow periods of six months to avoid the over-simplicity of annual figures. In practice, shorter periods — say, three months — would be more appropriate. Note also that 7.5% per six months is not strictly equivalent to 15% per annum, but in fact finance is frequently provided on the basis that interest is charged half yearly at half the nominal rate.

This example shows that the residual concept illustrated in Table 17.2 and the NPV concept are really the same. The result of the two calculations must be identical, provided that the finance cost is accurately calculated as in Tables 17.1 and 17.2, instead of an approximation being made.

Site value and development density

According to our theory of land rent, land value is the surplus on the assumption of optimal combination of all factors with the land. The developer will strive to optimise his use of resources, because only by doing so can he maximise his profit. The property developer is faced with a myriad of resource-use decisions on all matters from the structural and architectural form of the building to the services, fixtures and finishings to be provided. In fact, most of these decisions will be made by the architect, quantity surveyor, structural engineer or other specialist, but the developer will lay down general guidelines in his brief to the architect.

The ultimate principle which must tend to underlie such decisions is that of the maximisation of discounted returns. The developer will neither strive to minimise total cost, nor maximise the value of the completed property, but to maximise the (discounted) difference between them. This principle will also dictate whether a developer should refurbish or redevelop. With less structural work involved and a shorter development period, refurbishment will normally be cheaper than complete redevelopment, but the value of the completed property is likely to be less. A decision on which is preferable will be based on which scheme provides the higher expected NPV or IRR.

Let us now investigate the theory determining the optimal size of building to erect on a cleared urban site of fixed size, and explain the relationship between this and site value. As we are investigating the optimal combination of factors of production, the solution is again based on the principle of diminishing returns. In Figure 17.2 the MRP curve QY represents the extra revenue to be earned (extra value of the completed property) from the addition of each successive unit of accommodation (e.g., each extra storey or unit of floorspace) to the fixed area of land. The curve must ultimately slope downwards, as eventually extra accommodation can be provided on a fixed site only by building upwards, and the extra value accruing to the property from the addition of each (higher) storey tends to fall significantly from ground to first floor, and marginally thereafter.

The marginal cost curve, PY is shown as declining initially, but rising thereafter. Although development cost per unit of accommodation may well initially decline from, say, a single storey to a two-storey building, eventually marginal cost must tend to rise (a) because of the need for more expensive foundations and structural framework for taller buildings, (b) due to requirements for fire escapes and successively more expensive lifts, and (c) because the taller the building, the longer it will take to build, thereby creating higher finance cost and greater risk, in turn leading developers to require higher profit.

It should be appreciated that the curves QY and PY merely represent general trends in marginal revenue and cost. In any individual development, the shapes of the curves would vary, being stepped rather than evenly curved as shown.

Provided that all costs are contained within the marginal cost curve, including finance cost and the developer's target profit, then the optimum (profit maximising) amount of accommodation to provide on the site is OX units, and PQY represents the price that the developer would be willing to pay for the site. In competitive conditions with adequate knowledge, PQY would represent the capital value of the site for development purposes.

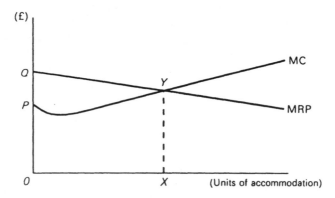

Figure 17.2   Site value and the density of development

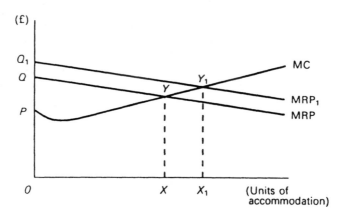

Figure 17.3   The impact of changes in the level of property values on site value and the density of development

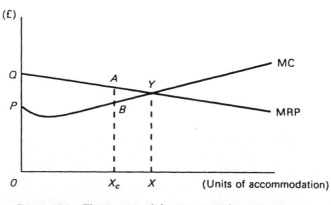

Figure 17.4   The impact of density control on site value

Note that site values and the optimum density of development are simultaneously affected by changes in costs and revenue. A rise in property values while development costs remained constant would cause an increase both in site values and in the optimal density of development. This is shown in Figure 17.3. An upward shift in the MRP curve to Q_1Y_1, results in a higher optimal development density of OX_1, and an increased site value of Q_1Y_1P. A fall in development costs (downward shift in PY), while property values remained constant, would have a similar effect, whereas conversely either a rise in development costs or a fall in property values would reduce site values and the optimal amount of accommodation to develop on a site. Thus changes in site values do not affect the optimum density, nor vice versa, they are both simultaneously affected by changes in development costs and property values.

Figure 17.3 can also be used to represent differences in site value and building density in different locations. If Q_1Y_1 represents the MRP of a development in a prime location then, due to the lower level of property value, QY would represent the MRP of a similar development in a secondary location. Assuming the development cost in both locations is similar, then Q_1Y_1P represents the value of the prime site and QYP the value of the secondary one. OX_1 represents the optimal size of the building in the prime location and OX the optimal size in the secondary location. That, of course, is the situation commonly observed in practice; sites in city centres tend to be more valuable than in peripheral locations and in city centres buildings tend to be taller. It is the higher occupation and investment demand for property located in prime positions which makes it profitable for developers to build to a higher density, and the extra surplus earned by building higher enables them to offer a higher price for such sites.

Note also the impact of use or density controls on site values. The imposition of controls prohibiting the most profitable use of a property would be to restrict the MRP from say, Q_1Y_1 in Figure 17.3 to QY, thereby reducing both site value and development density. Conversely, the removal of such a control would have the opposite effect. The impact of density controls is shown in Figure 17.4. If the density of development is restricted by the planning authority to OX_c units of accommodation, then the direct effect is to reduce site value by the amount of AYB. At a density of OX_c, the development's value is $OQAX_c$, and total cost $OPBX_c$. Thus $PQAB$ is the surplus available for site purchase.

In our analysis of the determination of rental value, we followed up a simple illustration of rent as a surplus by linking it with the condition necessary for the optimal intensity of land use. We have now done the same for the capital value of development sites. Like Figure 14.3, Figure 17.2 illustrates this condition of optimal factor combination, as well as providing a graphical illustration of the residual concept. In each case, it should be clear that if either expected revenue or any component of expected cost changes, then site values will tend to change, and as values and costs are continuously changing, site values must similarly tend to be in a state of flux.

It should be emphasised here that, strictly speaking, site values are dependent on *expectations* of costs and revenue over the development period, rather than current costs and property values. But, any change in current costs and values will tend to influence expectations. Before any individual site is purchased and the development initiated, the site value is the residual reflecting *expected* costs and revenue. Once the site has been purchased and the development started, it is the developer's profit which is the residual reflecting changes in *actual* costs and revenue.

Site value – a demand and supply analysis

In practice, surplus theory probably gives a better indication of the maximum or ceiling price which a developer would be willing to offer, than providing an entirely sufficient explanation for the price paid for development land in the market; it gives a better explanation of demand than of market price. As in the case of developed property, price is ultimately determined by the forces of demand and supply.

Supply is the amount of land available and capable of profitable development. The stock of such land in any town or location is limited geographically. It will also be limited by planning controls and, in certain situations, market supply may be further restricted by elements of monopoly ownership or control, either private or public.

The concept of site value as a surplus implies that, in times when property values are rising relative to development costs, site values will rise to the level which just provides developers with adequate profit, and when development costs are rising relative to property values, site values will correspondingly fall to a level which still enables profitable redevelopment to take place. In competitive conditions the former may be generally true, but at least in the short run the latter is not. Site values seem to be more flexible in an upward direction when the expected surplus is rising, than in a downward direction when the surplus is falling.

In part, this results from inflation. Price rises of most goods have been more dramatic than price falls. But there is more to it than that. Perhaps the most important reason is that site values (urban and green field) are supported, or underpinned, by existing use values. We have already explained that, under an assumption that property owners and developers seek to maximise returns, development will be initiated only if the development value of a site exceeds its existing use value. If that is not the case, then owners would not sell sites to developers and therefore the supply of sites would be nil.

In fact, the development value of a site will normally have to be substantially greater than the existing use value in order to persuade existing owners to sell. Developers cannot normally wait until existing owners wish to sell, so they will have to offer a price which is sufficiently high to persuade them to sell, to overcome the owners' 'inertia'. Such a price will have to be sufficient to make the owner feel better off after the sale, so if the existing owner is in business in the property, the price will normally have to cover, *inter alia*:

(a) cost of acquiring and, if necessary, converting new premises in at least as attractive a location as before;

(b) any loss of profit or goodwill which may be suffered as a result of the move;

(c) taxes such as CGT which may become payable on the sale, but which would otherwise have been indefinitely postponed;

(d) all expenses and professional fees involved;

(e) an additional sum to compensate for intangibles such as the worry and bother involved in the move.

Furthermore, the subjective value that most owners put on their property often tends to be above its market value. Thus the developer will normally have to pay a price significantly higher than existing-use value. So if the surplus available from the development falls, the amount available to pay existing owners falls and the less likely it is that this will be sufficient to cover the existing-use value plus the premium necessary to overcome the inertia of existing owners.

Another reason for the downside inflexibility of site values probably results from the reluctance of owners to sell for a price less than what they could have obtained previously. Normally existing owners neither have to sell nor particularly wish to sell, and rather than accept what they might consider as a relatively low price they will tend to hold on in the expectation that conditions will improve and that they will be able to obtain a more favourable bargain in the future (see Figure 17.5).

This would indicate that the short-run supply curve for development sites is significantly more elastic below the current price level than above it. A sharp rise in demand due to a rising expected surplus from development activity tends to cause a sharp rise in site values, but a similar fall in demand seems to cause a relatively small drop in price. This is illustrated in Figure 17.5 – a rise in demand from D to D_1 causes a rise in price from OP to OP_1, but a fall in demand from D to D_2 would reduce price only to OP_2. The bottom of the supply curve would coincide with the existing use value of the land.

Having explained that site values *normally* seem to be more volatile upwards than downwards, dramatic falls of as much as 80% took place in central London in the market slumps of 1974–5 and 1990–2, when development became unviable. Aside from excessive values in the previous booms, such dramatic price falls can be explained by the absence of a significant support from existing use value, as these sites will have been either cleared of buildings or vacated by tenants (and be incapable of reletting without refurbishment). In terms of Figure 17.5, the supply curve would not have been elastic below price P, and it would have shifted to the right, representing an increase in supply due to developers being forced to liquidate their assets in order to

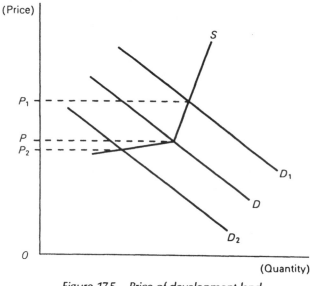

Figure 17.5   Price of development land

repay debt and avoid insolvency. As site values are a geared residual, they must tend to be more volatile than the value of developed property.

Another reason for regarding the surplus theory with caution is that the assumption of a competitive and knowledgeable market frequently does not exist. Of the three principal sectors of the property market the development sector is substantially the most imperfect. Whereas properties for sale or rent are widely advertised in the press, owners are often unaware of the develop-ment potential of their property, and development opportunities have to be discovered by the developer himself. There is a widespread lack of knowledge about what sites might be available for sale, whether planning permission would be granted, and under what conditions. Potential developers lack knowledge about the terms of the lease of an occupying tenant and any other interests in a property which might make redevelopment impracticable. In many cases, it may not be obvious whether a site has any potential for viable development until a detailed appraisal has been made. Uncertainty and risk are endemic in property development, different developers will have markedly different proposals for the development of any site, and markedly different offers are likely to be made. The uniqueness of each site (and the secrecy often prevailing in the market about prices paid) makes an assess-ment of site value difficult, and there is frequently widespread disagreement on price between developers and agents.

The following points are worth restating:

● For a development to be financially viable, the value of the site for development purposes must exceed its value for existing use.

- The development value of a site can be regarded as either (a) the NPV of the cash flow of a profit-maximising project, or (b) the expected surplus of income over the costs of a profit-maximising project. The essential concept is the same.
- In the absence of density controls, the value of a site and the optimal density at which to develop it will both vary simultaneously in response to changes in development costs and the value of developed property.
- As the development value of a site is a geared residual, site values are more volatile than the values of developed property.
- Normally, site values seem to be more volatile upwards than downwards, because (a) the market value of any site is underpinned by its existing use value and (b) sellers are reluctant to accept a price below that which they could previously have accepted. However, the value of *cleared* sites have fallen by as much as 80% in times of market slump.
- As in the case of rent determination, the surplus theory may frequently be a better indication of ceiling price than market value, and a better explanation in times of rising values than when values are falling.

Obsolescence

Let us restate the conditions necessary for private sector development to take place. First, development will be undertaken only if the value of the completed property is expected to exceed the cost of the site plus construction and all other costs of development, by a margin sufficient to give a developer his required profit. Second, the development value of the site must exceed its value for existing use purposes.

Taking account of the cost of building a completely new structure under modern conditions, for these two preconditions to be satisfied the value of the completed development requires to be very much greater, in fact a significant multiple of the value of the existing property. In Table 17.2, the expected value of the completed new property must be over five times the existing use value of the existing property. For such a large value differential to exist, most urban redevelopment involves either a change to a more profitable use or redevelopment to an effectively higher density than that already existing. In any case, the existing property must be subject to substantial obsolescence.

Obsolescence in property may be categorised as physical, functional or economic, any one (or any combination) of which may cause the value of a property to fall to a fraction of the value of its potential replacement. *Physical obsolescence* is the physical deterioration of the various elements of a building, through age and use. It will reduce the value of a building because of the increasing expense of repair and maintenance, and the building's limited future life.

Functional obsolescence is the decline in the usefulness or suitability of a building for modern purposes, deriving from either:

(a)   declining demand for the use for which the building is designed, e.g., warehouses located at a closed rail terminal;
(b)   inappropriate design, layout, fixtures or services, e.g., industrial property with insufficient door or eaves height to enable efficient use of forklift trucks.

In the former case, the obsolescence derives from the building's use type, in the latter case from inappropriate or outmoded design. Functional obsolescence and physical obsolescence are likely to be present to some degree in most buildings, even modern ones, and can be partly overcome by alteration, renovation or refurbishment.

Additionally a building may be redeveloped because it under-utilises its site. An office building of, say, five storeys in a city centre may be physically excellent and be fully modernised, but if it occupies a site which has planning permission for redevelopment to a higher density then redevelopment may be profitable. It is neither physically nor functionally obsolete, but it is *economically obsolete*.

The bulk of city-centre commercial redevelopment in the post-war period has come about as a result of a combination of physical, functional and economic obsolescence. The rising real cost of maintenance and repairs has given an impetus to the replacement of traditional buildings by structures which minimise such costs. Higher standards of accommodation which combine efficiency with worker comfort have been demanded by occupying firms, thereby providing scope for both refurbishment and redevelopment, whilst the huge rise in the demand for office space in the post-war period, together with the ability to construct multistorey buildings with steel and reinforced concrete, has enabled redevelopment to a higher density in prime locations.

It is the relative decline in the existing use value of property through obsolescence compared with the surplus available from development which brings about the conditions for profitable redevelopment. As obsolescence occurs gradually over time, one might expect that the volume of development activity would also be spread evenly over time. In fact, the level of development activity varies cyclically because the demand for space and the cost of providing it is subject to cyclical trends.

Cyclical trends in development activity

In order to explain changes in the level of private-sector development activity we must explain changes in (a) the availability of viable development opportunities, and (b) the expected profitability (and risk) of development. The former is the opportunity, the latter is the motive. Both are dependent on relative changes in the values of existing property and the costs of development.

In Part III we saw that the rental value of commercial and industrial property varied according to changes in the level of economic activity. In a reflationary or early boom phase in the economic cycle, rental (and capital) values can rise sharply due to rising occupation demand and relatively inelastic supply, while at that stage in the cycle construction and finance costs tend to be comparatively low and stable. Consequently, being a geared residual, the development value of sites will tend to rise at a rate faster than the rise in the existing use value of existing property. More properties will therefore satisfy the conditions necessary for redevelopment to take place.

The increased supply of viable development sites will tend to reduce the intensity of competition between developers, resulting in a rise in the level of available profit. At the same time, the apparent risk of development will be falling, particularly the risk of rent voids at completion. Developers will therefore tend to expand their activities, and new developers will be attracted into the business. In terms of our residual calculation in Table 17.2, the development value of sites will rise as the value of completed new property rises relative to development cost, but the rise in site value will be mitigated by a rise in developers' target profit due to the prolific number of alternative sites available.

The opposite trend will tend to occur in times of falling economic activity. During a recessionary phase in the economy, a fall in occupation demand relative to supply will tend to cause a decline in the rate of rental growth (or possibly a fall in rental values), in contrast with the level of development cost which at this stage will tend to be rising fast, due to high levels of cost inflation and rising interest rates. The surplus from development will therefore tend to decrease at a rate faster than any decline in the existing use value of property, fewer development projects will therefore be viable, and the downward inflexibility of site values will exacerbate the declining trend in development activity as developers are unable to acquire sites at a price which enables them to make a profit. Competition for the few viable sites will increase, expected profit levels will fall, most developers will reduce their activities, and others will go out of business when existing projects are complete.

The cyclical variation in development activity is probably exaggerated by the relative ease with which developers can expand (or reduce) their activities. They often have relatively few staff overheads and a lull in development activity enables them to concentrate on the management of their portfolio of property investments.

A simplified illustration of cyclical changes in development viability is shown in Table 17.3. In current conditions, the development value of the site is significantly lower than the existing use value, so development is not viable. But after a 25% rise in rental value (while development cost remains stable) the development value of the site substantially exceeds the existing use value,

Table 17.3   Effect of changing value and development cost on the viability of redevelopment

	Current conditions	After 25% rise in RV	After 25% rise in cost
Existing use value			
Current rental value	£100 000	£125 000	£125 000
Years purchase in perpetuity at 10%	10.00	10.00	10.00
Existing use value	£1 000 000	£1 250 000	£1 250 000
Development value			
Expected rental value on completion	£200 000	£250 000	£250 000
Years purchase in perpetuity at 7%	14.28	14.28	14.28
Expected value of redeveloped property	£2 856 000	£3 570 000	£3 570 000
Development cost	£2 000 000	£2 000 000	£2 500 000
Development value of site	£856 000	£1 570 000	£1 070 000
Development viability	**Non-viable**	**Viable**	**Non-viable**

enabling development to take place. Whereas the value of the existing property has risen by 25%, the development value has risen by over 83%. Conversely, if in a subsequent recession development cost (construction, finance and fees) rises by 25% while existing use value remains stable, the development value would fall below existing use value, making redevelopment unviable once again.

The cyclical trend in development activity is illustrated in Figure 17.6. The central graph shows the growth rate of rental values relative to that of building costs (plotted from the bottom graph where the two are shown separately). This illustrates a significant correlation with the volume of new orders for offices, shops and industrial property (top figure), suggesting that the volume of new development being initiated at any point in time varies according to rental value growth vis-à-vis the growth in building costs. The development booms in 1972–3 and 1987–9 coincided with periods when rental growth dramatically exceeded the growth in building cost.

Although changes in rent and building cost are probably the two most important variables affecting development activity, it would be wrong to dismiss the impact of changing finance cost or the effect on property values of changing yields, both significant factors determining the viability of development.

The reader should note that whereas rental growth peaked close to the peak of the economic booms in 1973, 1979 and 1988, building-cost inflation

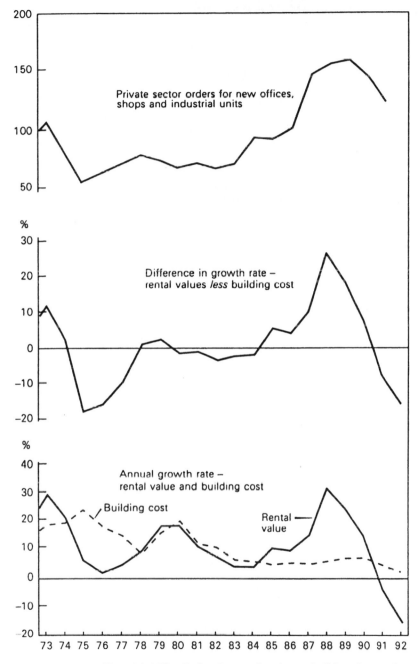

Sources: Investors Chronicle Hillier Parker Rent Index; Spons Building Cost Index; Housing & Construction Statistics.

Figure 1/.6   Cyclical variation in development activity

peaked much in line with retail-price inflation in 1975, 1980 and 1990, well after the previous booms had lapsed into recession. On the other hand, it must be acknowledged that contractors' tender prices are affected by the level of demand, and do not vary only with building-cost inflation. Thus, the illustrations given here somewhat exaggerate the impact of building costs on cyclical development activity.

Having explained cyclical influences on development starts it will be appreciated that completions must also tend to be cyclical. Assuming a development period of, say, three years for a major office project, schemes commencing during a boom phase in the economic cycle may be completed during a subsequent recession. The resultant increase in supply, exacerbated by the early marketing of uncompleted projects, can coincide with falling demand, causing a sharp decline in rental values. This, in turn, will tend to coincide with high interest rates and rising construction costs, making new development unprofitable on the basis of current figures. The consequent decline in development starts will tend to cause a shortage of supply when the next economic upturn occurs, thereby perpetuating the cyclical trend in both rents and development.

- For urban redevelopment to be viable, the existing property must be subject to substantial obsolescence, physical, functional or economic. The more obsolete a property, the greater the likelihood of its redevelopment.
- Trends in the volume of development activity depend on trends in property values and development costs, and as values and costs vary differentially over the economic cycle, the volume of development activity varies cyclically.

18 An Introduction to Development Finance

Property finance is important to a study of property values because:

(a) it is an essential input whose cost and availability can influence the viability of development and the supply of new property;
(b) its cost and availability affect the buy/sell decisions of property investors;
(c) it is a medium through which new and potentially complex investment interests in property are created.

Our aim in Chapters 18 and 19 is not to provide a detailed or comprehensive description of financing methods, but to explain the basic principles and concepts of some of the most important schemes, investigate the risks and returns to the parties involved, and explain how changing conditions have caused financing systems to change and evolve.

A company's financial structure

In this study we will concentrate on the financing of property companies, because the other principal groups involved in development – the life and pension institutions – have their own contractual inflow of funds and have no need to seek external sources. In fact, these institutions have been major *providers* of funds to property companies.

The importance of financing to the corporate developer has been highlighted by the property market slumps both in 1974–6 and 1990–2, when many property companies were forced into liquidation as much through inappropriate financing as from imprudent investment. Indeed, the selection of an optimum mix of financial liabilities is probably as important to the success of a property company as is the selection of a portfolio of property assets and development projects. Any new investment or development project should be appraised in conjunction with its financing.

The financial structure appropriate to a company will depend on many factors, e.g., its activities, assets, size, taxation liability and whether listed or unlisted. However, certain basic principles can be stated:

- A company should maintain an appropriate balance between debt and equity capital.

  Because of property's record of growth and stability, property companies have traditionally been highly geared, but excessive gearing was responsible for the downfall of many companies in 1974–6 and 1990–2.
- A company's debt should have a balance of maturity dates with the majority being long term.

  Redemptions should be spread evenly to avoid the risk of a large refinancing operation coinciding with a period of high interest rates and credit stringency. A proportion of a company's debt should have a flexible term, e.g., loans which can be repaid early without incurring a penalty.
- A company should match short-term assets with short-term liabilities and long-term assets with long-term liabilities.

  Many property companies have come to grief by financing long-term property investments with short-term borrowing, so that when loans matured the companies were unable to borrow replacement finance and were forced to liquidate assets under adverse conditions.
- A company should maintain a balance between fixed-interest and variable-interest debt.

  Whereas the former reduces a company's exposure to rising interest rates, the latter provides a hedge against a substantial fall in interest rates and inflation. An excess of long-term fixed-interest debt raised at a time of high interest rates could cripple a company in times of low inflation.
- Debt should be arranged so that interest payments are spread evenly over the year, or at times which coincide with high rental income.
- For companies involved in overseas activities, debt should aim to reduce exposure to foreign currency risk.

  Overseas assets should be matched with debt in the currency of the same country.
- Borrowing should aim at reducing taxation.

  Not all interest payments qualify for tax deduction.
- When arranging debt, the borrower should be aware of the many extra costs apart from interest payments.

  Costs include legal and valuation fees, arrangement and commitment fees, penalties for early redemption, etc.

The needs of the financier

Financing is all about incurring liabilities to create assets. But one person's liability is another person's asset – shares and debt are liabilities of a company, but assets of the providers of finance. Financiers, whether banks, insurance companies or pension funds, will strive to maximise return while minimising risk, and will maintain a balanced and diversified portfolio of assets. For financing to take place, the arrangement must fulfil both the financial needs of the borrower and the investment needs of the lender. That is the key to understanding individual financial transactions. It is also the key to understanding the evolution of property funding over the post-war period, from a relatively simple exercise to a highly sophisticated financial operation. Development finance has rarely been in short supply because changing conditions have encouraged the innovation of new methods which meet the needs of borrower and lender.

By providing capital, the financier is also making an investment in property and is sharing with the borrower its risks and returns. In the case of pure debt finance, the lender does not participate in the equity of the scheme and his concern is restricted to the risk of his investment. However in the case of equity financing the financier's risk and return are directly dependent on the success of the company's project, and he will wish to make a careful study of the proposals before committing his capital. Although the aim of both developer and financier is to maximise return for any given level of risk, traditionally, the developer will take on the bulk of development risk, for which he will look for an appropriately high return, whereas the financier will look for security and accept a correspondingly low return.

We shall now investigate methods of financing a property company's activities in general (corporate finance), and thereafter look at methods of financing specific projects (project finance). Not that there is any absolute distinction between the two. A company could make a stock-market issue for the purpose of funding a major project, but more usually such a source would be used to fund the company's activities in general, or to reduce the company's short-term debt. Conversely, a company might mortgage one or more specific properties, not necessarily to redevelop them but to raise capital to finance other activities of the company. Nonetheless, this broad distinction between corporate finance and project finance is useful.

Sources of corporate finance

Retained earnings

One feature of property investment is the relatively low level of annual income in relation to the amount of capital employed, and a further feature of property companies is their relatively high level of gearing. Consequently, a high proportion of (the relatively low) investment income is required to pay interest on debt. For many property companies, therefore, the residual equity earnings is barely sufficient to pay shareholders a reasonable dividend, never mind provide for future capital expenditure.

Two alternative methods of generating funds internally are (a) to undertake development for sale as opposed to investment, and (b) to undertake a programme of disposals of the company's property portfolio, especially low yielding and reversionary property. Both methods are employed to a greater or lesser degree, but in normal conditions the objective of most large property companies is to retain the majority of their developments as long-term investments, so disposals will be kept to a minimum.

Bank borrowing

All companies have bank accounts, and will tend to run up overdrafts from time to time as cash outflows exceed inflows over short periods. It is also justifiable (and prudent) for a company to borrow from a bank to finance such short-term requirements as interim payments to the builder of a development, provided long-term finance to repay this debt is available when needed. What is imprudent is for a company to finance long-term investments with short-term finance.

Bank borrowing, particularly from the clearing banks, is traditionally on a short-term and variable-interest basis. A company borrowing a large amount of bank finance is therefore vulnerable to rising interest rates and short-term recall of the funds by the bank. Merchant banks and finance houses are more willing to lend for specific terms of several years, sometimes at a fixed interest rate, but such sources tend to be more expensive than from clearing banks (see short-term finance).

Stock-market issues

The traditional policy of property companies has been to retain a 'narrow equity base' in order to maximise earnings and asset growth for existing shareholders. This is similar to saying that companies practise a policy of high gearing. By keeping equity capital low relative to the amount of debt capital, equity growth has been maximised. Raising new equity capital by rights issue results in 'equity dilution', i.e. an expansion in the amount of share capital without a proportional expansion in growth potential.

Traditionally, therefore, fixed-interest debt was the most popular form of long-term funding for quoted property companies, and large amounts of capital were raised by the issue of *debentures* and *unsecured loan stock* in the 1950s and 1960s. Although this led to high nominal levels of gearing, low interest rates and dramatic growth in the value of property assets kept most companies' effective gearing within reasonable bounds. However, in the late 1960s the issue of fixed-interest bonds started to decline due to a sharp rise in interest rates (and, since the early 1970s, due to the volume of gilt issues, which effectively 'crowded out' corporate bonds from the market).

The dominant place of fixed-interest bonds was taken over in 1969–70 by *convertible loan stock*, and substantial amounts of capital were raised in the 1970s by these issues. *Convertible preference shares* as well as bonds were also a popular source of corporate finance in the 1980s. The advantage of convertibles to a company is that they can be issued at relatively low interest rates. By fixing the conversion terms at an attractive level relative to the number of shares into which they can be converted, investors are tempted to accept a low interest rate in the expectation of substantial capital gain. The main disadvantage of issuing convertibles is that it leads to equity dilution when investors exercise their conversion rights. However, conversion will be delayed until the projects funded by the issue are producing returns, and if the new issue is taken up by existing shareholders they retain the full benefit.

Convertibles were also a popular form of issue in 1975 and 1991, in the wake of the two property-market crashes. In each case property companies required to raise long-term capital in order to repay short-term debt. Convertibles gave the investor the security of a fixed-interest bond, but the chance of substantial capital gain if the company made a successful recovery.

Ordinary share issues are an attractive source of new capital when share prices are high and dividend yields correspondingly low. Initially, share issues are a very cheap source because the initial cost is essentially the dividend yield, plus underwriting and administrative costs. However, in the long run the effective cost is much higher due to dividend growth over time, and the burden is not reduced by taxation relief as in the case of interest paid on debt.

With the cost of equity minimised when share prices are high, share issues by property companies have been popular during property booms, and during periods of high interest rates. This explains a series of major rights issues over 1979–81 and the large amount of equity raised during the property boom of the late 1980s. In 1987, over £1 billion of equity was raised by property companies in the UK.

Money-market issues

The London money markets (including the Eurodollar market) became an increasingly important source of property debt in the 1980s, and provide companies with a large range of possibilities. They are a source of both short-term and long-term capital, zero coupon and interest bearing, at fixed interest and floating rates, in sterling and foreign currencies. The money markets are an arcane world whose details are beyond the scope of this book.

Project finance

In the remainder of this chapter and in Chapter 19, we are principally concerned with methods of financing individual projects, in which the financier's capital is legally secured against the property being acquired or developed. Project finance is particularly important for smaller and unlisted property companies to whom the stock-market source is unavailable, whose existing assets may already be fully charged against previous loans, and whose financial status as a company provides insufficient security for the financier.

Traditionally development financing has consisted of two distinct operations: (a) short-term, interim or bridging finance, and (b) long-term funding.

(a) Short-term finance is required to pay the development costs over the development period, e.g., site purchase, payments to the building contractor, and fees.

(b) Long-term finance is required to repay the short-term finance on completion of the project. Long-term financing is not so much financing the development as financing the retention of the property as a long-term investment. If the developer sells on completion, then clearly long-term funding is unnecessary as the short-term debt can be repaid with the sale proceeds. Frequently, however, the developer will wish to retain ownership or some valuable interest in the completed development, and that requires funding.

We shall now examine these two forms of financing in more detail.

Short term

Whereas the trend in the 1970s was for insurance and pension funds to provide both short- and long-term finance (see Chapter 19), the decline in institutional interest in property in the 1980s forced developers to rely on the traditional short-term source – bank finance. This coincided with a growing interest in property lending by UK and overseas banks, and resulted in a massive expansion in bank lending to property companies, together with an increase in the complexity and sophistication of financing arrangements. The detail of these go beyond the scope of this book, but conventional arrangements and some important innovations will be explained.

The principal sources of short-term finance are the clearing banks, merchant banks, UK branches of overseas banks and certain finance houses. Clearing banks are usually developers' first choice, lending on a conservative, well-secured basis at relatively low interest rates, and frequently on a corporate rather than on a project basis. Banks would normally wish to limit their loan to, say, 67% of development cost, with the remainder being provided by the developer. However, a larger proportion may be provided (at higher cost) by a merchant bank or other bank specialising in property lending. Specialist lenders sometimes fund a higher proportion of costs by providing 'mezzanine' finance, under which the bank would receive a share of the profit of the project as well as interest on the loan. Another alternative is for the lender to provide up to 100% of costs, with the top slice of the loan covered by indemnity insurance to mitigate the risk of loss in the event of the developer's default.

Whereas bank loans are traditionally made on a short-term variable-interest basis, the recent trend has been to provide credit facilities which are designed to meet the specific needs of the project and the developer. The developer normally prefers finance which is not subject to repayment until the project's completion, i.e. 'interest only' (capital repaid in a lump sum at maturity), or 'roll-up' (compounded interest paid with capital at maturity), and which is flexible as to the exact amount and timing of the loan. The loan term would normally cover the development period, but banks will sometimes extend the period to five or seven years, occasionally to the date of the new property's first rent review.

Short-term credit can be provided on a fixed-interest basis, but variable interest is normal, being linked to the bank's base rate or to the London interbank rate (LIBOR). Agreed interest rates can vary from 0.5% (or less) to 4% above LIBOR depending on the bank's perception of the risk incurred. Exposure to changes in interest rates can be reduced by agreements for a 'cap' (maximum interest rate), 'collar' (provides upper and lower limits to the rate) or 'swap' (allows conversion from a variable to a fixed interest rate or vice versa).

In the event of the proceeds from a completed project being insufficient to repay debt and accumulated interest, a lender would normally be able to recover the remainder from the development company. However, one innovation of the 1980s was the introduction of 'non-recourse' or 'limited-recourse' finance, which would usually involve the creation of a separate company for the sole purpose of undertaking the project. As collateral security would be restricted to the assets of the company undertaking the project, the lender would have no recourse to the parent company or to its other assets in the event of the project's failure. This arrangement protects the developer from much of the project's risk (at the expense of the lender), because the developer's potential loss would be restricted to the capital that he had provided for the project. In fact, banks would rarely accept such an arrangement without some guarantee from the parent company to limit the lender's potential loss (limited recourse).

Accounting regulations require parent companies to include in their consolidated balance sheet debt borrowed by *subsidiary companies*, but allow *associated companies* to be represented in the balance sheet by their book value. The difference in status depends on the parent company's shareholding. If the parent company owns more than a 50% shareholding, the offspring is a *subsidiary*, if 50% or less the offspring is an *associate*. In the above example, the newly created company would naturally be a subsidiary, but by involving one or two 'passive' shareholders without rights to the company's profits, it could qualify as an associated company despite the fact that the parent retained full control and the right to the profit.

If the debt of the associated company is non-recourse then it is not a liability of the parent and it seems appropriate that it should not feature in the parent's balance sheet. However, in the normal case of the bank having full recourse, the creation of associated companies to carry out development projects has tended to obscure the effective debt liabilities of the parent, making it virtually impossible for investors or investment analysts to assess the parent's effective financial gearing and risk. This *'off-balance sheet'* debt was a feature of some of the largest and most active developers in the 1980s.

Another feature of the biggest development projects is *syndicated* loans. If the financial requirement is beyond that which any one bank would wish to commit to a single project, a group of banks may provide the debt collectively, thereby spreading their risk. The first phase of Broadgate in the City of London was funded by a £35 million non-recourse loan from a syndicate of seven banks for a term of 2.5 years.

A bank which is proposing to lend to a property developer will wish to be convinced about the following:

- The developer; his financial strength, his track record in previous projects and reliability.

   The lender will examine the company's audited accounts and perhaps require further information about the company's assets, liabilities and cash flow.
- The collateral to be provided as security for the loan.

   The lender will normally require the loan to be charged against the site and the development as it proceeds. He will be reluctant to lend on sites not fully assembled, or without planning permission. Frequently other collateral will also be required and, on occasion, the developer may be required to provide personal guarantees, so that if the developer's company goes bankrupt the loan can be recovered from his private wealth.
- The viability of the project and the arrangement for repayment of the loan.

The ability of the developer to repay the short-term loan on completion of the project will depend on the availability of long-term finance, or on his ability to sell the property. A banker's willingness to provide short-term credit may therefore depend on whether the developer can prearrange long-term finance or a 'forward sale', i.e. a commitment from an investor to buy the completed property. To conclude such a commitment will, in turn, require proof of the viability of the project, which frequently rests on the ability of the developer to prelet a significant part of it. Thus the whole financing operation will often depend on the ability to prelet.

Long-term mortgage finance

Long-term development finance has traditionally been raised either by mortgage or, particularly in times of credit stringency, by sale and leaseback. We shall investigate mortgage finance here, but leave sale and leaseback until Chapter 19.

In the early post-war period, long-term mortgages on commercial and industrial property were predominantly fixed-interest and provided by insurance companies. Nowadays, both fixed- and variable-interest mortgages are available for periods up to 25 years and on a variety of terms to suit the needs of the individual project and borrower. Modern arrangements can span both the development period as well as the long term.

Essentially there are three methods of repayment:

(a) Equal instalment method – equal amounts of the capital are repaid periodically over the period of the loan.

As the amount of capital outstanding declines, so the annual interest payment declines.

(b) Annuity method – the method normally adopted for building society mortgages.

Assuming no change in the level of interest rates, the combination of interest and capital paid per period remains constant over the term of the loan. Initially payments consist largely of interest, latterly largely of capital.

(c) Interest only – capital is repaid in a lump sum at maturity; a system normally used for relatively short-term loans.

Alternatively, repayment tranches may be spaced over the loan period – a 21 year loan might have one third repayable after seven years, 14 years and at maturity.

The amount lent on a mortgage has traditionally been restricted by two criteria:

(a) the sum lent would not exceed two thirds (occasionally three quarters) of the value of the property mortgaged;

(b) the net rental income from the property must exceed interest and any periodic capital repayments.

In effect, the liability must be covered in both a capital and a cash flow sense.

Example 18.1 shows how these two criteria could be met and sufficient mortgage capital raised for long-term funding in the conditions prevailing during the development boom in the 1950s and early 1960s.

Example 18.1

A prime commercial development was completed at a total cost of £700 000. The market value of the property was £1 million and it was fully let for a net rental income of £70 000 per annum. Mortgage finance amounting to 70% of market value was repayable on the annuity basis over 25 years at a fixed interest rate of 6.5%.

	(£)
Development cost (inc. short-term finance)	700 000
Mortgage debt (70% of £1 m)	700 000
Capital surplus/deficit	**Nil**
Net rental income	70 000 p.a.
Mortgage instalment	57 390 p.a.
Net income surplus	**£12 610 p.a.**

This scheme illustrates 'self-financing' in the dual sense:

(a) the long-term mortgage was sufficient to repay all short-term finance raised to pay development costs, and
(b) net rental income was more than sufficient to pay annual mortgage interest and capital repayment.

The developer gained an asset worth a net £300 000, and because he managed to retain all the equity at a 70% level of capital gearing, the rate of growth of the net asset value substantially exceeded the rate of growth in the value of the property itself.

If we assume that the property was let on 14 year rent reviews, and that rental and capital growth both averaged 8% per annum over that period, the position at the first rent review would have been:

	(£)
Value at completion	1 000 000
Compound factor, 8% over 14 years	2.937
Value at rent review	2 937 000
Less mortgage debt outstanding, say	450 000
Net value of property	**£2 487 000**
Net rental value at completion	70 000 p.a.
Compound factor, 8% over 14 years	2.937
Net rental value at rent review	205 590 p.a.
Less mortgage instalment	57 390 p.a.
Net income surplus	**£148 200 p.a**

In the space of 14 years, the net asset value would have risen from £300 000 to £2 487 000, a compound growth rate of over 16% per annum, and double the annual growth rate of the property itself. Moreover, the developer would have been able to borrow about another £1.5 million as a second mortgage secured on the increased value of the property, and pay the interest out of the surplus income. This extra borrowing would enable him to undertake further development projects with fixed-interest finance, even at a time of rising interest rates, and maintain a high level of gearing to boost asset growth.

Essentially it was by this relatively simple process that developers in the post-war boom were able to amass large fortunes. Initially, they had little need for large amounts of equity capital because their projects could be financed by borrowing, both in the short and long-term. Rental growth tended to exceed the rising rate of inflation over this period resulting in enormous returns for highly geared investors.

19 Equity Sharing and Partnership Schemes

The rise of equity sharing

As we have already seen, the traditional policy of property developers was to retain the full equity in both their development and investment activities, mainly by means of fixed-interest debt finance raised principally by mortgage or by the issue of loan stock. This process maximised equity growth and returns for shareholders and, in the early post-war conditions of rental growth and accelerating inflation, proved highly lucrative. Paradoxically, however, it was inflation and the success of developers which led to the gradual decline of a financing system based almost exclusively on debt.

In order to achieve the self-financing goal illustrated in Example 18.1 two conditions are necessary:

(a) With mortgage finance normally restricted to 67% (or at most 75%) of market value, the development's value on completion must exceed total cost by 50% (or at least 33%), otherwise the mortgage finance will be insufficient to cover cost and repay short-term finance.

(b) The interest paid on the mortgage finance must not exceed the initial rent received from the completed property.

In both these respects, conditions moved adversely for developers in the 1960s. First, competition between developers increased and profit margins fell, and second, interest rates on debt rose while yields from completed property tended to fall. In other words, the reverse yield gap appeared and gradually widened, and self-financing of a development by debt capital alone could no longer be achieved. If the developer raised the maximum loan which could be serviced by the initial rent from the completed property, a capital shortfall between this loan and the development cost would remain. Alternatively, if he managed to raise enough capital to repay the short-term loan (by providing additional collateral security on other assets), then he would suffer a cash flow shortfall.

Some developers could sustain a cash-flow deficit on one property with surplus income from other properties. Alternatively, a developer might create cash flow by selling existing property assets, especially low yielding or reversionary investments. However, the liability to pay Capital Gains Tax (CGT) on disposals is a disincentive to sell, and substantial disposals run counter to the objective of most developers of building up a property portfolio.

The widening of the reverse yield gap in the 1960s therefore imposed a substantial constraint on the growth of developers, and resulted in an increasing trend towards selling projects on completion. However, property companies were unwilling to surrender their successful formula, and modifications to the traditional mortgage were occasionally agreed which enabled pure debt financing to be maintained, e.g., schemes involving the postponement of capital repayments, and even some of the interest, until rental income rose sufficiently to cover the full annual servicing cost. Such schemes, however, were not popular with institutions because their security depended on a continuation of property growth which could not be guaranteed. In any case, from the late 1950s the insurance companies became less and less interested in providing long-term fixed-interest capital.

Concurrent with the widening of the reverse yield gap, inflation brought a major change in the investment strategy of the investing institutions, away from fixed-interest investments and towards growth investments. Furthermore, perceiving the enormous success of property companies in the development boom of 1954–64, the insurance companies (and then the pension funds) began to insist on a share of the equity in property investment. In the 1960s, the function of these institutions in property underwent a radical transition. Originally passive lenders of fixed-interest debt finance, they became active investors in the equity of property.

Initially, the most popular means of equity participation was in the field of *corporate* funding, often involving acquisition by the financial institution of a block of equity shares in the property company to whom they had lent money. Alternatively, in return for a commitment to provide mortgage finance, the developer's company sometimes granted an institution an option to purchase a certain number of equity shares at a specified price at some future date. This enabled the institution to profit from the developer's success without the risk of failure during the interim period. Another alternative was the issue of convertible stock to the financing institution. Inevitably, however, all such schemes resulted in equity dilution, making them unpopular with property companies.

After the introduction of corporation tax in 1965, such schemes also lost popularity with the institutions in comparison with financing individual *projects* by equity participation. Henceforth returns received from property through the ownership of shares became subject to double taxation (corporation tax paid by the company, and income tax paid by the insurance company), whereas income received direct from an individual project was taxed once only. For this same reason, equity sharing through the medium of *subsidiary development companies* owned jointly by the parent property company and financial institution ceased to be attractive.

Sale and leasebacks and equity sharing

Early arrangements by which financial institutions shared in the equity of development *projects* involved their provision of debt finance in return for an equity stake. However, by far the most important vehicle for equity sharing has been the sale and leaseback. In the early post-war period, sale and leaseback deals were regarded by developers as the principal alternative to mortgage finance, resorted to during periods when the government was imposing restraint on lending as part of its economic policies. Essentially, the arrangement involves the sale of the freehold (or long leasehold) interest by the developer to an institution in return for a long lease, with the developer sub-letting the property to occupying sub-tenants. Early deals had either no provision for rent review (in which case the developer/tenant effectively retained the full equity in the property), or infrequent review at, say, 33-year intervals in a 99-year lease. However, when the rent review period agreed under new leases fell to 14, then seven and five years in the late 1960s and early 1970s, such freehold interests provided the investing institutions with the equity investments they required in property.

The main benefits arising from the replacement of conventional mortgage finance by sale and leaseback clearly went to the investing institutions. The system enabled them to acquire equity investments in modern property with a reliable property company as head tenant, who would collect rents from his sub-tenants and relieve the institution of the management of the property. The developer lost the freehold interest, much of the equity and the advantages of gearing. However, self-financing by conventional mortgage was no longer an option. Sale and leaseback provided all necessary capital, and still enabled the developer to make an adequate return.

It is useful to remember that such deals were undertaken because developers needed the institutions' finance, both to undertake a project and to retain an investment interest in it thereafter, whilst the institutions wished to acquire modern equity property investments. Both parties needed each other, and the deal that was struck would depend on the cost and availability of finance, investment market and property market conditions, and the relative bargaining strength of the two parties.

Equity-sharing sale and leaseback arrangements are potentially complex and of infinite variety, and careful examination and analysis of the details is required to assess the risk and potential return to the two parties. In order to explain the essential concepts and clarify the important issues we shall employ a series of examples. First, we shall illustrate the two fundamental methods of sharing the investment income from the *completed project*.

Top/bottom-slice arrangements

Originally, sale and leaseback was used in the absence of mortgage finance as a means of funding the retention of a long-term investment in a completed development. The developer would undertake the project with the aid of short-term finance as previously explained and, on completion, would sell the property to an institution on condition that it was leased back. The developer would then sub-let to occupying tenants. If the developer sold at the full market value he would be required to pay the full rental value as head tenant. He might receive a small profit rent, but this would have no significant market value, being merely a return for rent collection, management and accepting the risk of rent voids.

However, if the developer wished to retain a substantial investment in the property he would sell the freehold interest for a figure less than the full market value, on condition that the head rent payable would be less than the property's rental value. The sale price of the freehold interest would normally be the sum required to repay the short-term finance, and the head rent payable to the freeholder would be determined by the yield appropriate to such an investment. In modern conditions the head rent would be subject to regular review, but only to that proportion of the rental value determined initially. The developer/tenant would therefore hold a substantial profit rent, and both parties would retain valuable investments with a growth potential similar to that of the property as a whole.

Note: for simplicity and clarity, the following examples are based on a completed value of £1 million, although, in reality, most developments would be worth much more.

Example 19.1 (Scheme A)

The developer of a completed prime office property, fully let at the rental value of £60 000 net and worth £1 million, has sold the freehold interest to an investing institution for £750 000, on condition that the property is leased back on a 125-year lease, subject to an initial head rent of £40 000 and reviews at five-year intervals to the same proportion (two thirds) of net rental value.

If sold for its full value, the investment yield of the freehold would have been:

$$\frac{60\,000}{1\,000\,000} \times 100 = \mathbf{6.0\%}$$

but under the above arrangement, the yield to the investing institution is:

$$\frac{40\,000}{750\,000} \times 100 = \mathbf{5.3\%}$$

and the yield to the developer/tenant is:

$$\frac{20\,000}{250\,000} \times 100 = \mathbf{8.0\%}$$

The investing institution is willing to accept a yield below the 6% investment yield available on comparable properties because in this arrangement its income is protected from the risk of rent voids by the head tenant. The institution's income is the 'bottom slice' which is more secure than the total income of £60 000 yet having the same growth potential. Conversely, because the developer is left with the risky 'top slice', he requires an initial yield higher than the yield available from the investment as a whole. If £750 000 was the price necessary to repay the short-term finance, then the investor's required yield of 5.3% determined the head rent that the developer/tenant must pay, thereby determining his initial profit rent and the split of the net rent at subsequent review.

The top/bottom-slice relationship is shown in Figure 19.1. The developer/tenant's interest is the risky top slice because, with the head rent being two thirds of rental value he must guarantee that payment to the freeholder, and any income loss occurring through the default of sub-tenants or voids in the occupation leases must be borne by the head tenant alone. The landlord's bottom-slice income is unaffected by rent voids.

Note that in the long run there is no element of gearing in this method of sharing the investment income. Over the long term, the rental income to both investors will grow (or decline) at the same rate as the rental value of the property as a whole. If at the first review the net rental value of the property has risen by 50% to £90 000, both the institution's and the developer's income will also rise by 50%, respectively, to £60 000 and £30 000.

Note also that the scheme illustrated here is concerned only with sharing investment income from the completed development. The developer alone has gained the profit or suffered the loss from the development project.

This scheme is ideal from the point of view of the institution. It has acquired a prime growth investment with a reliable head tenant paying a secure income on a long lease. Furthermore, virtually all the management functions will be undertaken by the developer/tenant. From the point of view of the developer, the scheme has enabled him to retain a valuable investment producing a significant income, something which would have been impossible with mortgage finance. It has, however, two main flaws – the insecurity of the top-slice income and the resultant difficulty in attracting a buyer should he wish to sell. In most such agreements, therefore, the contract will make provision for either party to buy out the other's interest on some prearranged formula, should either wish to sell.

Side-by-side, or vertical leaseback schemes

In modern leaseback schemes, the financial institution may be involved in the project from its inception, and provide all short-term finance as well as the long-term funding, thereby absolving the developer from the responsibility of raising any capital. The institution will purchase the site and pay for construction, fees and all development costs, and on completion of the

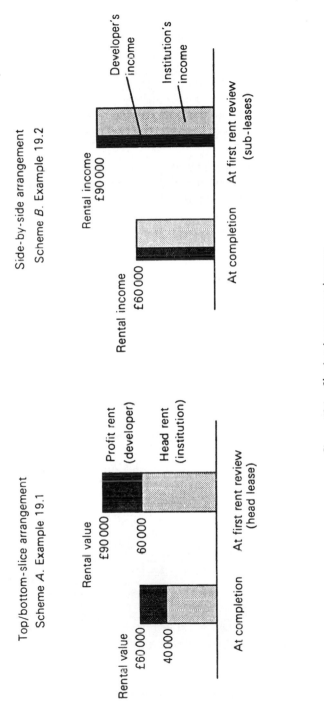

Figure 19.1   Sharing investment income

project will grant a long lease to the developer who in turn will sub-let to occupying tenants and act as manager of the property.

'Side-by-side' refers to the method of sharing the rental income from the completed project. Instead of the developer paying the institution a guaranteed head rent fixed between rent reviews as in Scheme A, all net rental income is shared in an agreed proportion, and the income to both parties will rise or fall according to changes in the net rental income received from sub-tenants. This avoids the top/bottom-slice relationship of Scheme A, and the investment risk is shared between the two parties according to the share of the income they receive.

The division of the investment income between the parties is usually based on a previously agreed return on the development cost incurred by the institution (including interest 'rolled up' over the development period). All future net rental income from the property will be shared in the proportions established by the formula.

Example 19.2 (Scheme B)

A developer and financial institution have agreed to undertake a development project on the following terms: the institution will purchase the site and pay all development costs, and on completion of the project will lease the property to the developer on a 125-year lease. The net rental value on completion is expected to be £60 000 and the developer will guarantee the institution an initial income of 6.5% of total development cost, estimated at £750 000, including interest rolled up at 6.5%. The developer's initial income will be the remainder of the initial rental achieved from the completed project. All future rental income will be shared in the same proportion as the initial rent.

On the basis of these figures, the initial income to the two parties will be:

	(£)
Expected net rental value	60 000
Expected initial income to:	
Institution 6.5% of £750 000	**48 750** (81.25%)
Developer	**£11 250** (18.75%)

If these cost and rental figures prove correct, then the institution will receive 81.25% and the developer 18.75% of all future net income, whether it rises or falls, or is subject to voids or not. In contrast to Scheme A, the two parties are sharing the risk of the investment in proportion to their income. There are no rent reviews as such in the head lease because all net income from sub-tenants is shared in this way. In effect, the relationship between landlord and head tenant is side-by-side rather than vertical as in normal leases, but the income is sliced vertically, hence the alternative description of 'vertical lease-back' (this is shown in Figure 19. 1). As investors in the completed property, the institution and developer are effectively in partnership and, in fact, the two parties to a side-by-side arrangement are sometimes joint landlords rather than landlord and tenant.

In comparison with the top/bottom-slice scheme, the side-by-side arrangement avoids the risky top-slice nature of the developer's investment income, thereby making his interest more marketable. For the institution, however, the investment risk in the completed property is significantly greater, but no greater than would be incurred by investing in a similar property let directly to the occupying tenants.

So far, we have only examined the method of sharing the investment income from the completed property and the investment risk attached to that income, but the division of income between the two parties derives from the development project which itself imposes far greater risk. It is essential when analysing schemes such as this to distinguish the risk deriving from the development project from the risk attached to the investment in the completed property.

In this example the risk attached to the completed investment is shared in proportion to the division of income, but the risk attached to the development project is almost entirely borne by the developer, in much the same way as in a traditional development. If, as in this case, the developer has to guarantee a specific rate of return on the finance, it is immaterial whether that money is actually borrowed or not. The developer essentially has a gearing ratio of 100%, just as if all the short-term finance had been borrowed on a traditional basis, although the effective gearing here is reduced by the relatively low interest rate. Although after completion the investment income is shared side-by-side, these shares – and thus the profit from the development project – are determined on a top/bottom slice basis (see Figure 19.2). The developer bears the large majority of the development's risk and his return is highly geared.

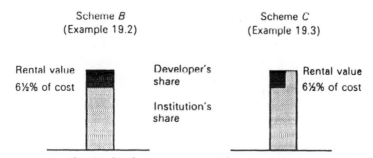

Scheme *B*
(Example 19.2)

Scheme *C*
(Example 19.3)

Rental value
6½% of cost

Developer's share

Institution's share

Rental value
6½% of cost

Figure 19.2   Sharing development returns; determination of initial income

The high potential volatility of the developer's return from this project derives from the requirement to pay the institution a fixed percentage return on development cost. If over the development period cost rises relative to rental value on completion, the developer's initial income will fall. Conversely, if rental value rises relative to the development cost, the developer's income will rise.

The potential impact on the developer's return of changes in net rental value and development cost is shown below. If net rental income on completion proves to be £65 000 instead of the projected £60 000, and if cost is restricted to £700 000 instead of £750 000, then the developer's initial income will rise by 73.3% over that previously expected, being a larger proportion of a larger sum:

	(£)
Net rental value on completion	65 000 p.a
Initial income to institution	
6.5% of £700 000	**45 500** p.a (70%)
Initial income to developer	**£19 500** p.a (30%)

Conversely, if net rental income on completion proves to be only £55 000 and cost rises to £850 000, then the initial income is insufficient to cover the guaranteed return to the institution, leaving the developer to make up this shortfall from other sources:

	(£)
Net rental value on completion	55 000 p.a
Initial income to institution	
6.5% of £850 000	**55 250** p.a
Deficit to be paid by developer	**£250** p.a.

This system has the advantage of providing full incentive for the developer to maximise rental value and minimise costs. The more attractive is the completed property to the tenants, the higher will be the rental income in which the developer will share. The lower the costs, the higher will be the developer's share of the rental income. The risk incurred by the developer in the project is high, but so is the potential reward, whilst the risk and potential return for the institution are relatively low. That, of course, reflects the traditional functions and needs of the two parties.

Geared top slice arrangement

In Schemes A and B, the proportion of the completed property's net income received by both parties remains essentially fixed (after being initially determined). In the long run, investment income is ungeared. However, in Scheme C below, the developer retains a geared investment interest such that, as the property's net income grows, the proportion receivable by the developer increases.

Example 19.3 (Scheme C)

As in Example 19.2, the financial institution will purchase the site and pay all development costs. On completion of the project it will lease the property to the developer on a 125-year lease subject to five-year rent reviews. The developer will again sub-let to occupying tenants. The expected development cost and net rental value on completion are again respectively £750 000 and £60 000. The income to the institution will be a basic 6.5% of total cost plus 50% of the amount by which the net rental value exceeds this, both at completion and at future rent review. The developer here does not guarantee the basic 6.5% to the institution, but he will receive no income until the institution's basic income is met.

The expected initial income of the two parties at completion of the development is as follows:

At completion of development	(£)	(£)
Expected net rental value:		60 000 p. a.
6.5% of £750 000	48 750	
50% of surplus	5 625	
Expected initial income to institution		54 375 p.a. (90.6%)
Expected initial income to developer		£5 625 p.a (9.4%)

Assuming a 50% increase in net rental value at the date of the first rent review, the subsequent division of income will be as follows:

At first rent review	(£)	(£)
Net rental value:		90 000 p.a.
6.5% of £750 000	48 750	
50% of surplus	20 625	
Income to institution		69 375 p.a. (77.1%)
Income to developer		20 625 p.a. (22.9%)

Although the developer's initial return is minimal, the high level of gearing built into Scheme C provides him with a far superior percentage growth rate than that of the institution. The 50% rise in net rental value assumed over the five years until the first review implies an annual rental value growth rate of just under 8.5%, but whereas the institution's income over the five years grows by approximately 5% per annum, that of the developer grows by just under 30% per annum.

Note, however, that as the developer's income increases relative to that of the institution, the effective gearing falls. Assuming the same rate of rental growth between Years 15 and 20, the growth rate of the institution's income is 7% whilst that of the developer is just under 11%. Although the developer's income can never catch up with that of the institution (they must always differ by £48 750), proportionally they become closer and thus the gearing gradually becomes less and less significant. So long as the percentage of the future growth received by the developer is higher than his percentage share of the property's initial income, then some element of gearing exists.

It is unlikely that a financial institution would agree to part with such a high proportion of the equity, in fact institutions are reluctant to agree to any element of gearing in the division of investment income.

Note that the *investment* income is being shared on a top/bottom-slice basis. The developer's income is the risky top slice because, with the head rent linked to rental value rather than rental income, he will suffer the full loss from rent voids or occupiers' default.

Now let us turn to the division of the risk and return deriving from the development *project*. In contrast with Scheme B, the financial institution is sharing in the risk and return from the project to a significant extent and thereby reducing the risk to the developer. In this scheme there is no possibility of the developer making a loss, except in the sense that he may get no return for his work and effort. He provides no capital for the project and in the absence of the guarantee (or 'yield protection clause') included in Scheme B, he is not liable to pay any minimum return to the investor. The worst that can transpire is that net rental income fails to reach the institution's 6.5% basic return. On the other hand, he must share on a 50/50 basis all initial income in excess of the 6.5% basic return, consequently this scheme does not possess the potential profitability of a pure top/bottom-slice arrangement of the kind illustrated in Example 19.2. Both the upside potential and the downside risk are reduced. In fact, the profit from the project is effectively being split on a part 'top/bottom' and a part 'side-by-side' basis, as illustrated in Figure 19.2.

Turning to the institution's view of this development scheme, there is no doubt that it is more risky than in Example 19.2, but the *expected* initial return on capital is higher, and could be higher still. Although the basic rate of return, at 6.5%, is the same as previously, the *expected* initial return (after including the share of the expected surplus) is 7.25%, probably a reasonable figure in consideration of the risk of this scheme to the institution.

Such a scheme for sharing development profit is called a 'participation' arrangement. As it is important to distinguish the risk and return from development from the risk and return attached to the subsequent invest-ment, it is therefore important to distinguish the 50/50 participation in the development profit (Figure 19.2) from the 50/50 sharing of subsequent rental growth. As institutions are happy to accept gearing in a project but not in the completed investment, a more likely arrangement would be for the development profit to be shared as illustrated in this example but for the investment income to be ungeared and shared on a side-by-side basis, as in Scheme B.

Before introducing the complication of a public authority as a third equity sharing party, it seems sensible at this stage to summarise the main points introduced so far.

- The risks borne and the returns received by both parties to an equity-sharing agreement may derive partly from the development project and partly from the subsequent property investment.

The scheme adopted should distinguish the two sources because development is risky and investment relatively secure, and the traditional function of a developer is to take risk whilst that of an institution is to undertake relatively secure investment.

- Top/bottom-slice arrangements must be distinguished from side-by-side sharing.
- Income shares determined by the property's rental value must be distinguished from shares determined by the property's rental income.

This will determine whether one or both parties bear the burden of rent voids, as well as the income division when rent reviews between landlord and head tenant are out of phase with reviews between head tenant and sub-tenant.

- Proportional sharing arrangements must be distinguished from geared arrangements.

This complex subject is often confused further by the misuse of the term 'gearing'. Some practitioners use the expression to describe investment income which varies in proportion to changes in the rental value or rental income of the property as a whole, i.e. what we have referred to here as proportional sharing.

- Another key clause determining the relative burden of risk is whether the percentage return due to the financial institution is *guaranteed* by the developer, or is merely a *priority* payment.
- It is also essential to determine if either party bears the cost of repairs, insurance and management. Are the shares based on gross rental or net rental?
- The agreement between the two parties should make provision for either party to buy out the other's interest on some prearranged basis, should either wish to sell.

Neither top-slice nor even minority side-by-side interests are easily market-able or simple to value, and without a prearranged formula the party selling his interest may be unable to realise a price which would be considered fair.

Although the developer will normally take executive control of the development project, the institution will require to be consulted on certain crucial issues, especially where there may be a conflict of interest between the parties. Such matters may include the quality of the building, selection of tenants and letting policy, indeed anything which may tend materially to affect the quality of the institution's investment. The legal document formalising the agreement is liable to be long and detailed, but it is impossible to cover all problems which may arise between the parties. That is why institutions tend to build and maintain a special relationship with developers whom they can rely on and trust.

Investment interests created by equity-sharing schemes tend to be some of the most complex in the property market. In all cases, before entering into any irrevocable agreement each party should carefully analyse and rehearse the impact that a whole range of possible scenarios could have on the risk and return from his investment.

Partnership with local authorities

Post-war trends in urban planning have emphasised the positive role that a public authority can take in the land market to promote economic welfare – such as by the development of job creating industrial property and the redevelopment of semi-derelict inner city areas. Also they have increasingly tended to take for the community a share in the profits of the land which they can control, not just by selling or leasing land for its full value, but by participation in the equity of development. Furthermore, by retaining an ownership interest a local authority can more actively control or influence the form of development than is possible by the use of its planning powers alone.

The active participation of public authorities in development projects can create problems of conflict between the parties, as their objectives are more complex than the profit-oriented considerations of the developer and financial institution. However, creating a commercially successful scheme is also important to public authorities, because their income will depend on the value of the completed property, and because of the beneficial impact that a successful development will have on the area as a whole. Trust, goodwill and cooperation between the parties is essential for the success of these schemes; mutual distrust can create endless problems.

We shall concentrate here on the place of local authorities in equity-sharing partnership schemes, but a similar place could be occupied by other public sector agencies such as new-town development corporations, special development agencies, public utilities or even private investors who, as land-owners, wish to enter into a scheme for the redevelopment of their land.

The essential factors required in the development process are land, building, finance and expertise. Any party taking on the entrepreneurial role can acquire these factors on a non-equity-sharing basis. Sites for development may be purchased outright, and building is normally provided by a contractor for a specific sum (subject to cost fluctuation). Debt finance is available on a fixed- or variable-interest basis, and expertise can be obtained for a fee from certain professional firms and development companies. Thus it is possible for local authorities, financial institutions and developers to undertake projects without sharing the equity with any other party. Indeed many of them do.

Nonetheless, many urban development projects involve equity sharing of some kind because it is advantageous for the parties involved – each party needs the other. Financial institutions are needed as providers of capital. Development companies are required because of the importance of skill, experience and entrepreneurial flair in identifying development opportunities, assembling a site and managing a project. Local authorities are needed due to their ownership of and powers over land. Their compulsory purchase powers may facilitate site assembly, and their planning powers may also be beneficial. These three parties also need a builder, but perhaps it is because of the abundance of building capacity and the lack of bargaining strength that builders are less frequently involved in equity-sharing partnerships.

It is financial institutions, local authorities and developers which are the principal groups involved in equity-sharing schemes because they possess (or control) the factors of production essential to development projects. Each party is vying with the others for a maximum share of the profit for the minimum risk, and the division will tend to rest largely on the bargaining power of each party and the skill of the individuals involved in negotiation.

Let us now examine a relatively straightforward scheme which successfully combines the specialist inputs of the three parties to the benefit of the project as a whole, and provides each party with the type of interest it requires.

Example 19.4 (Scheme D)

A local authority owns an urban site ripe for commercial redevelopment and, after inviting tenders, has agreed with a financial institution and a development company to share in the return from the completed project on the following basis. The local authority will retain the site, but the institution will finance all other development costs and, on completion of the project, the local authority will lease the property to the financial institution and developer as joint tenants on a 125-year lease subject to five-year rent review. The local authority as freeholder will be guaranteed an initial ground rent of £9000, the institution will receive an initial income of 6.5% on development costs, and the developer will receive the remainder of the rental income on completion. At future rent review, the income to the local authority will be adjusted to the proportion that £9000 bears to the net rental value established at the completion of the project, and the institution and developer will share the remaining investment income on a side-by-side basis, also in the proportions established at completion. The expected net rental value at completion is £60 000 and expected development cost (excluding the site) £600 000.

The offer of the initial ground rent of £9000 was determined as follows:

	(£)	(£)
Expected net rental value on completion		60 000
Expected initial income:		
Institution (6.5% of £600 000)	**39 000**	(65%)
Developer (2% of £600 000)	**12 000**	(20%)
	51 000	
Ground rent payable to local authority	**£9 000**	(15%)

The initial return to the local authority was calculated after deducting the target returns of the institution and developer from the expected net rental value on completion. If the outcome for development cost and rental value is as anticipated, then the shares of the initial income will be as shown above. However, if cost rises relative to rental value over the development period the developer's return will suffer first, and if cost rises sufficiently the institution's income will be at risk. Conversely, if rental value rises relative to cost only the developer's share will rise.

The risks and returns from the project are thus shared on a top/bottom-slice basis, with the developer holding the highly geared risky top-slice interest, the institution holding the medium-risk middle slice, and the local authority the safe bottom slice (see Figure 19.3). Of the subsequent invest-ment income, the local authority still holds the secure bottom slice, and the developer and institution share the remaining top slice on a side-by-side basis.

Example 19.5 (Scheme E)

As it stands, Scheme D is unlikely to be acceptable to the local authority and possibly the institution, because if the project proves to be highly profitable only the developer will gain directly. Let us therefore assume that the local authority and institution insist on a participation arrangement which divides equally between the three parties any initial rental income in excess of a return to the developer of 2% on cost. In return for this restriction on his potential profit, let us also assume that the other parties agree to guarantee the developer a minimal fee for his work as a 'safety net', but payable only in the event of the project proving so unprofitable that the developer receives no other initial return.

The chart illustrating the determination of income from the project is now revised (Figure 19.3). The pattern of investment income is unchanged, but the

271

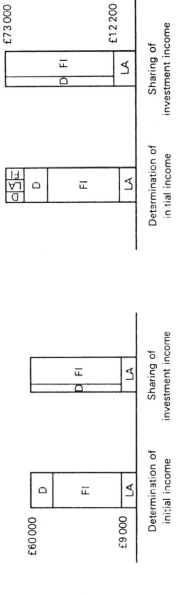

Figure 19.3 Partnership with local authority

proportions allocated to each party will be altered if the project proves to be more profitable than expected.

On the basis of this revised agreement let us see how the parties would fare if, on completion, the net rental value proves to be £73 000 and development cost totals £640 000:

	(£)	(£)
Net rental value on completion		73 000
Basic return to:		
Local authority	**9 000**	
Institution 6.5% of £640 000	**41 600**	
Developer 2% of £640 000	**12 800**	
		63 400
Surplus		9 600
One-third share		3 200
So, initial income to:		
Local authority	£12 200 p.a.	(16.7%)
Institution	£44 800 p.a.	(61.4%)
Developer	£16 000 p.a.	(21.9%)

Rather than being presented as ideal, Schemes *D* and *E* have been used to illustrate certain concepts, on which there are an infinite number of variations. Such schemes make use of the inputs that each party can offer to the project, and provide them with an investment close to their requirements. They enable the local authority to use its compulsory-purchase and planning powers, and provide it with an equity freehold interest with a ground rent which will return to the community a fair proportion of the profit of the project and subsequent investment. Such schemes make use of the equity finance available from the financial institution, and in return provide it with a long-term growth investment. They also employ the skills and experience of the developer, provide him with sufficient incentive to undertake the project efficiently, and make use of his willingness to bear the principal risk of the project, thereby shielding the other two parties. In return, he should receive a substantial long-term equity investment. He will also normally undertake the management of the completed property for an appropriate consideration.

Lease and leaseback

Local authorities have a responsibility to promote development which is likely to attract job-creating industry or to revitalise inner city areas, and they have a role to play in undertaking projects (especially the development of small industrial units) which may be marginally viable or commercially unattractive to property companies and financial institutions. Neither the major developers nor the financial institutions will wish to retain a long-term interest in a development which imposes a significant risk of rent voids. However, by interposing themselves between the occupying tenants and the institution in the tenure structure, local authorities may be able to provide the necessary security, and thereby attract institutional finance which would not otherwise be forthcoming.

One option is for the local authority itself to undertake the development and on completion to sell the freehold to the financial institution and lease it back as head tenant. The local authority would then sub-lease the property to occupying tenants and manage it thereafter. This system is similar to that illustrated in Example 19.1, except that the local authority is in the place of the developer. The sale price would normally be aimed at recovering the cost of development, and the initial head rent would be the institution's required yield on that capital. The local authority would retain a substantial but risky top-slice profit rent, being the difference between the rents received from sub-tenants and the head rent paid to the institution.

Alternatively, and more frequently, the 'lease and leaseback' system is employed. Essentially, this involves the local authority as freeholder granting a long lease of the site to a financial institution (with or without a developer in partnership), at a low or 'peppercorn' rent. The institution would sub-let the completed development to the local authority for a marginally shorter duration, who in turn would lease to the occupying tenants. The initial rent that the local authority (sub-tenant) would pay to the institution (head tenant) would be the institution's required return on the capital provided to fund the development, and the rent would be revised at future review to the proportion of rental value established initially. The local authority would receive a top-slice profit rent, being the difference between the amount received from occupiers and that paid to the institution.

On the assumption that a developer is employed to undertake the work for a prearranged fee, but retains no long-term interest in the development, the division of risk and return from both the project and subsequent investment are shown in Figure 19.4.

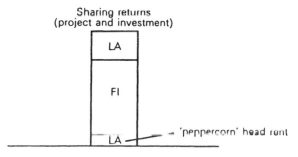

Figure 19.4   Lease and leaseback

The advantage of this scheme is that the local authority stands between the occupying tenants and the institution, whilst still retaining the freehold interest. It is able to attract institutional funds because of the greater reliability of a local authority as a rent-paying tenant in comparison with occupiers of industrial property. As well as bearing the risk of voids and default, the local authority will undertake the letting and management of the property, thereby enabling it to control tenancies and letting terms on a basis which will promote industrial activity, rather than on purely profit-maximising criteria.

V Property Investors and Property Pricing

20   The Property Companies

In Chapters 20 and 21, we investigate the activities of the two principal groups of operators in the investment and development sectors of the commercial and industrial property market. In this chapter we look at the property companies and in Chapter 21 the property-investing institutions. Not that these are the only groups taking part – major building contractors, other industrial and commercial companies and public authorities are also involved, but the property companies and financial institutions have dominated the market in the post-war period, and it is chiefly by a study of their functions and activities that an understanding of the market can be gained.

Post-war growth of property companies

Property companies in the UK, as they operate nowadays, are essentially a post-war phenomenon. In the 1920s there were around two dozen quoted companies but few were active developers, many being involved in the ownership and management of housing, which originated from the urban estates of Victorian industrialists. The effective origin of the majority of companies now quoted in the London Stock Exchange is in the first post-war property boom. According to Marriott[1] the 20-year period from 1945 created at least 110 property millionaires, a remarkable number in comparison with other industries. The large number of fortunes reflects not only the huge profitability and low taxation of property development during that period, but also the relative ease of entry and simplicity of the operation. The list of millionaires is made up largely of people who were involved in the property market, particularly estate agents, solicitors and builders, few of whom owned significant wealth before embarking on their property careers. A number of proprietors in the clothing trade also became involved through their ownership of shops and other property, including bomb-damaged sites in London at the end of the Second World War.

The reasons for the post-war boom are explained more fully in Part VII; here it is sufficient to appreciate that an imbalance between supply and demand for office space arose in London primarily through massive devastation during the war, coupled with a surge in demand in the post-war economy. In such conditions the value of existing offices rose dramatically and the proliferation of bomb-damaged and slum housing in central areas provided cheap and abundant development sites.

Although restricted by a variety of controls in the early post-war years, development proved highly profitable, helped by the combination of rising rental values, low interest rates, ease of letting and virtually nil taxation. Developers did not necessarily expect or budget for enormous profit – it was inflation and the rental spiral which was largely responsible. The price of a building contract was fixed whereas the rental value rose over the development period. Marriott[2] quotes the example of one office development of 60 000 ft² in which the developer predicted a rent of 12/6d (62 ½p) per ft² at completion to provide a profit of £340 000. However, such was the rise in rental values over the development period that it let for £3 per ft² to give a capital value of £2.7 million and a profit of £2.2 million. Even more incredible was the profit of £2.9 million made on a joint development with the Church Commissioners in which the developer contributed only £1000.

Such profits were effectively tax free following the abolition in 1953 of the 100% development charge imposed under the Town & Country Planning Act 1947. Provided the completed development was not sold but retained by the developer as a long-term investment, no tax was payable on the development profit, only on the subsequent rental income. Development was taxed on much the same basis as manufacturing activity; tax became payable only when the goods were sold and the profit was realised. In fact, despite retaining their completed properties, developers could effectively realise much of their profit, both by raising long-term mortgages on the property or by 'going public' and selling shares and debentures on the stock market.

So the explanation for the early post-war growth in the number of property companies is twofold. First, the profitability and availability of development projects, and second, the taxation system, growth in property values, and the availability of cheap fixed-interest debt, which provided the incentive and opportunity for developers to retain their completed properties as long-term investments. Logically, developers would then 'go public' (a) to realise a proportion of their profit by the sale of part of their equity, (b) to gain access to further sources of long-term finance, and (c) to satisfy the insurance companies, who in the later 1950s were starting to acquire portions of developers' equity in return for the provision of long-term finance. They required such shares to be marketable, partly to improve their liquidity and partly to reflect a true market value, qualities not provided by shares in private companies.

The number of public property companies rose from 35 in 1939 to 185 in 1964, with their market capitalisation surging from £30 million in 1939 to £800 million at the height of the property company shares boom in 1962. An outstanding example of the growth of an individual company is the case of Land Securities Investment Trust (now substantially the largest property company in the UK). At the time of its acquisition by Harold Samuel in spring 1944, it owned three houses in Kensington and some gilts worth £19 351.[3] By March 1952, assets totalled over £11 million, by March 1967 £193 million, and in its 1990 accounts the portfolio was valued at £5.6 billion.

Trends since 1964

The period of declining development activity after 1964 (like other dull periods in the 1970s and 1980s) was used by property companies to improve and rationalise their portfolios and reorganise their finances. Any remaining residential property was frequently sold off to sitting tenants or to other companies which specialised in housing. Sales often included commercial property with limited growth potential, including reversionary investments and property with infrequent rent review. Portfolio rationalisation would include the acquisition of interests in properties in which the purchaser already held an interest, e.g., the purchase of the freehold interest in a property in which the head leasehold was already held, or vice versa, thereby benefiting from the 'marriage' value which would tend to result. A portfolio might also be improved by renegotiating leases with existing tenants and by the refurbishment of existing investments. Financial reorganisation would include refinancing short-term debt with long-term, or reducing a company's gearing by asset sales or by issuing new equity shares. Such financial and portfolio management activities would be the policy of any well-run property company.

After the end of the first post-war development boom, the number of listed property companies substantially declined. A few companies went into liquidation but the majority met their demise as a result of takeover deals, mainly involving other property companies or financial institutions such as insurance companies. Certain companies, notably Land Securities and MEPC, continued to grow by means of takeover bids. Rather than by cash offer, these deals were usually effected by the exchange of 'paper'. The company making the bid would offer shareholders in the victim company a certain number of shares (and/or loan stock) in exchange for existing stock. In order for the bid to be acceptable, the value of the shares offered would have to exceed the existing value of the shares in the victim company. Companies subject to bids tended to be those with shares undervalued relative to their assets, which were inactive or poorly managed, or which owned development sites, an increasingly scarce commodity in the 1960s.

In the takeover game, success tends to breed success. Shrewd acquisitions can result in a high rate of equity growth, causing the shares of 'predator' companies to be priced on a high price/earnings multiple, in turn enabling further acquisitions to be made. Defences against takeover are good management, large size or (best of all) for a controlling proportion of shares to be retained by the directors themselves. This is frequently the case with property companies where the original founder or his family often holds a dominant shareholding.

New listed property companies emerging since the mid-1960s have rarely been created by means of a private company 'going public' with a full listing. A quoted property company may emerge from an existing industrial company whose manufacturing or trading activities have declined or been sold off, but which has built up development and investment activity based on the company's property assets. Alternatively, a listed trading company in decline may be acquired by a private property company as a 'shell' into which its property assets are subsequently transferred. A frequent method is the 'reverse takeover', by which a private property company will arrange to be taken over by a quoted company in decline, on condition that the directors of the private company will subsequently take charge of the merged company and probably sell off its original trading activities. Another alternative which proved popular in the early 1980s was to obtain a quotation on the newly established Unlisted Securities Market (USM).

The early 1980s saw an upsurge in the number of quoted property companies through such names as Rosehaugh, London & Edinburgh Trust, Speyhawk, Mountleigh and Stanhope. Rosehaugh was transformed by its chairman, Godfrey Bradman, from a tea-trading company with a market capitalisation of under £200 000. Mountleigh was originally a small wool manufacturer, but Stanhope was a private property company which joined the USM just before the stock-market crash in 1987.

Property-company functions

Essentially property companies undertake three types of activity, namely property investment, development and other dealing activity. The term 'dealing' covers a variety of activities, but implies relatively quick sale of the property after adding value in some way. It would include the acquisition of a block of flats for improvement and sale to sitting tenants, or the assembly of a development site for sale with planning permission to a developer.

Property companies can mostly be placed in one of two categories. Companies which develop and acquire property for retention in an investment portfolio (investor/developers), and those which sell their projects on completion (developer/traders). In terms of their size, investment companies dominate the property sector of the stock market (see Table 20.1), and typically grew up in the early post-war period through their ability to finance the retention of their developments with debt. On the other hand, developer/traders are mostly of more recent origin and have been forced to sell completed projects by the high cost of finance. The reverse yield gap has prevented them from building up a portfolio of property investments, and the lack of a portfolio generating rental income to pay interest on debt has forced such companies to sell completed projects. The profit of developer/traders depends on the success of their development and dealing activities, which are innately risky and vulnerable to economic trends. But the profit of investor/developers is essentially the difference between rental income and interest on debt, which is relatively stable.

The functions of development and investment are complementary. The retention of completed developments not only reduces taxation, but provides the further advantages of secure asset backing and regular income as a diversification from the risky and irregular returns from development. The greater security of investor/developers in comparison with developer/traders also facilitates and reduces the cost of raising new finance to fund new projects. The property assets can be used as collateral to raise debt, and the rental income to service interest payments. The ownership of an investment portfolio also provides the company's management team with a greater continuity of work. At times when they might be idle due to a lack of development opportunities, work can proceed on renovation, refurbishment and other portfolio-management activity.

The specialisation and emphasis of British property companies can vary significantly from one company to another. Like most of the largest companies, Land Securities' portfolio is dominated by offices and shops in central London but (unlike most others) it holds no overseas property. That contrasts with Hammerson which has 60% of its portfolio in North America, Australia and Europe. Slough Estates has about 70% of its portfolio invested in industrial property, while Bradford and Daejan specialise in housing and Wates City of London Properties is exclusively invested in City offices.

All the companies listed in Table 20.1 are primarily investment companies.

Table 20.1   Top 10 quoted property companies by market capitalisation (September 1992)

Company	Capitalisation (£m)
Land Securities	1807
MEPC	718
British Land	330
Slough Estates	278
Hammerson 'A'	235
Great Portland Estates	225
Brixton Estates	207
Bradford Property Trust	168
Daejan	131
Percy Bilton	123

Source: Financial Times.

Property-company shares

Property-company shares provide a medium for indirect investment in the property market, however shares in developer/traders are likely to display very different characteristics from shares in investor/developers and are priced by the stock market in a different way. We saw in Chapter 4 that shares of industrial or trading companies are priced at some multiple of current earnings (net profits), and this multiple (the P/E ratio) will depend principally on investors' perception of a company's risk and growth potential. A developer/trader is somewhat similar to a manufacturing or trading company. Its survival depends on making profits from its development and dealing activities, and the price of its shares will be some multiple of its current earnings, the multiple depending on investors' expectations for future profits and their perception of risk.

On the other hand, the shares of a property investment company are backed by substantial property assets. Each share represents a fractional entitlement to the investment portfolio, so the share price reflects its *net asset value*. In fact, shares tend to trade at a discount of 20–30% to net asset value per share, depending upon expectations for property values. Share prices of investment companies tend to move on changes in net asset value. If a company reports unexpectedly good profits and a portfolio revaluation in line with expectations, its share price is unlikely to move significantly. But if its profits are in line with expectations and its portfolio revaluation unexpectedly high, its share price will tend to rise sharply. Whereas the earnings volatility of property traders makes their shares risky, the stability of property values make the shares of investment companies relatively secure.

However, it would be misleading to imply that shares in investor/developers behave like a property portfolio in microcosm. First, there is the impact of a company's gearing, which increases the volatility and growth potential of net asset value in comparison with direct investment in property. Second, there is the impact of a company's management. The history of property share prices provides ample proof of the importance to investors' returns of company management. For inactive investment companies the quality of portfolio and financial management are important, but for companies actively involved in development, dealing and acquisitions, the judgement and skill of those in charge is crucial. Apparently small mistakes on such matters as financing, timing of purchase and sale, and selection of development projects can lead to enormous losses. Property companies led by 'whiz kids' can earn a dramatic return for investors in the right conditions. However, as the experience of the mid-1970s and early 1990s has shown, such leadership can involve enormous risks, exacerbated by the tendency of such people towards an autocratic style of leadership and control.

The third major reason why the performance of property shares will vary from that of direct property investment derives from differences in the markets in which they are traded. Share prices tend to be more volatile than direct property because of the greater volatility of the stock market in comparison with the property market. In fact, while reflecting trends in rental growth, property share prices are very cyclical, tending either to substantially outperform or underperform other shares.[4]

- Property companies can be categorised according to whether (a) their acquisitions and developments are undertaken primarily for retention in a property portfolio (investor/developers), or (b) they sell most projects after completion and hold an insignificant investment portfolio (developer/traders).
- Because of the availability and low cost of long-term debt in the early post-war period, developers were able to retain their completed projects, and companies from that period comprise the majority of investor/developers currently listed on the Stock Exchange.
- Companies originating since the 1960s have had to rely principally on trading due to the high cost of capital. The innate risk and cyclical volatility of developer/trading, coupled with the lack of the income and asset stability provided by a property portfolio makes them fundamentally risky.
- The price of shares in developer/traders is determined by the stock market by reference to their equity earnings, but share prices of investor/developer companies reflect companies' net asset values.
- Shares in investor/developers tend to be more risky than direct investment in property due, e.g., to the impact of gearing, corporate management and stock market volatility, but shares of developer/traders tend to be even more risky.

21 The Financial Institutions

Non-bank financial institutions in Britain are dominated by the insurance companies and pension funds, two groups which invest actively in property alongside their larger holdings in equity shares and bonds. Nowadays portfolios are managed by professional fund managers, some of which are branches of these institutions (managing their own funds as well as those of other institutions) whereas others are branches of banking conglomerates. For example, the two largest fund managers in the UK are Prudential Portfolio Managers, an arm of the Prudential which is primarily a life assurance company, and Mercury Asset Management, a subsidiary of S.G. Warburg, the merchant banking group. Other major fund managers are Barclays de Zoete Wedd, part of the Barclays Bank group, Standard Life which is primarily a mutual life assurance fund, and Postel the fund management arm of the Post Office and British Telecom pension funds.

Through their control of over 60% of shares quoted on the London Stock Exchange together with much of the best urban property in Britain, these groups potentially wield enormous power and influence over the economy. However, their essential function is to invest funds for the benefit of policy holders and pensioners, and strategic decisions to allocate funds to gilts, equities or property reflect the specific needs and liabilities of the institutions for whom the funds are managed. Therefore, to understand the allocation of investment funds we need to know something about the functions and activities of the institutions themselves.

Insurance companies

Insurance business is categorised as either 'general' or 'long term'. General insurance is essentially fire, accident, motor, marine and aviation insurance, whereas long term business is principally life assurance (although it also includes health insurance and annuities). Certain large insurance companies in the UK known as 'composites', undertake both types of business (e.g., Commercial Union, General Accident, Royal Insurance, Sun Alliance), whereas others concentrate on life assurance, e.g., Prudential, Lloyds Abbey Life, Legal & General.

There are several hundred groups authorised to undertake insurance business in the UK, but activity is dominated by large companies. These will normally either have a Stock Exchange listing, or be a subsidiary of a major conglomerate, or be a 'mutual' fund. Mutual insurance companies have no shareholders in the conventional sense, but are owned by policyholders in much the same way as most building societies are owned by borrowers and lenders.

General insurance

The contract for general insurance business is normally for one year only, and although a contract is likely to be renewed each year, the business is essentially short term. The annual income of insurance companies consists of 'premiums' and investment income. Annual premiums charged for providing insurance cover are based on the sum insured and the risk of loss, and tend to be set at a level sufficient to meet probable claims, agents' commission, administration cost and profit. In fact, general funds habitually make large losses on their 'underwriting' activities (i.e. the cost of claims usually exceeds premiums), but they hope to make a profit overall through the income earned on investments.

A feature of general insurance is uncertainty in the amount and timing of claims, partly explained by the fact that natural catastrophes are a major cause of loss. The amount of claims faced by an individual company is very unpredictable, and in any year may substantially exceed the expected liability. For example, all of the top ten British general insurers made huge losses in 1991, with the underwriting losses of the top six averaging £500 million each. These awful results derived from extraordinary weather-related claims and losses on domestic mortgage indemnity policies which arose from a fall in house prices.

In order to avoid the risk of being unable to meet all claims, an insurance company's assets must substantially exceed the expected liability. Typically, the assets of a general fund exceed their estimated liabilities to policyholders by a margin of about 50%, such a margin being determined both by prudence and by the necessity to observe a minimum statutory solvency margin. Being the difference between the company's assets and liabilities, this margin also represents shareholders' capital. So if claims exceed expectations or if the value of the company's investments fall, then it is the shareholders who suffer the loss, not policyholders.

Like banks, insurance companies must be secure, and be seen to be secure. They can go bankrupt, therefore they are subject to strict regulation and supervision, and are required to provide detailed information to enable a true assessment of their financial security.

As security is important to an insurance company's operation, it is also an important feature of its investments. This introduces one of the most important principles determining insurance companies' investments – the 'matching' principle. As in the case of banking and certain other financial institutions, prudential management requires that liabilities should be matched by assets of a similar nature. The application of this principle can be seen in various facets of general funds' investment policy.

First, the liability of a general insurance company to pay out on claims is essentially short term and unpredictable in amount. Therefore a large proportion of those assets held in respect of claims are kept in a liquid form or in securities which can be quickly liquidated. But the regularity of a company's incoming cash flow is also an important determinant of its required liquidity. For instance, if all insurance premiums were payable on one date, say 1 January, the large majority of this money would have to be kept liquid to meet claims arising throughout the year. However, because premiums and investment income are spread throughout the year, most claims can be met by incoming funds and thus a larger proportion of assets can be invested in the long term without an expectation of their having to be liquidated.

Second, the liabilities of general insurance companies are fixed in money terms. A company is not liable to pay out a sum higher than that insured for. Therefore liabilities tend to be matched by fixed-sum investments such as interest-bearing bonds and preference shares, as distinct from equities.

Third, the matching principle extends to liabilities overseas. The majority of the business of British general funds has traditionally come from overseas, and to reduce the risk which derives from currency fluctuations (see Chapter 22), liabilities in a foreign country should be matched by appropriate investments in that country's currency. General insurance companies have traditionally held large amounts of overseas government and corporate fixed-interest bonds.

The matching principle not only influences the choice of investments held in respect of underwriting liabilities, but also investments selected to back shareholders' capital. We have already explained that shareholders' capital amounts to about 50% of estimated liabilities, so if this ratio is considered to be the prudential minimum, then underwriting liabilities will be restricted to a multiple of twice shareholders' capital. The amount of shareholders' capital determines the amount of business a company can underwrite, and in order for a company to maintain the volume of its business in real terms in times of inflation, it is therefore necessary for shareholders' capital to grow at the same rate as inflation. Thus, and fourth, the appropriate investments with which to match a company's liability to its shareholders are equity investments such as ordinary shares and property.

In the mid-1970s, levels of inflation dramatically higher than the growth in the value of investments caused a dangerous decline in the equity capital base of UK insurance companies in comparison with the value of business undertaken. The problem was partly caused by a decline in the value of the pound sterling which resulted in a rise in the sterling value of overseas liabilities, and partly by the rising cost of claims in the UK. In order to regain a prudent relationship between equity capital and liabilities, the eight largest UK general insurance companies had to raise £385 million by rights issues in the four-year period 1974–7. The losses of the early 1990s are likely to necessitate a similar fund-raising exercise.

Property's security and its qualities as a hedge against inflation make it a highly appropriate medium in which to invest a general insurance company's equity base. Its lack of liquidity is relatively unimportant because circumstances would have to be dire indeed to require a general fund to liquidate its property in a hurry.

Table 21.1   Insurance companies – holdings of investments[a] (end 1990)

	Long-term funds (£m)	(%)	Other funds (£m)	(%)
Gilts				
Short dated	1822	0.8	2851	6.4
Medium dated	18 481	8.0	2 506	5.7
Long and undated	7 070	3.0	51	0.1
Corporate and other bonds	13 214	5.7	1975	4.5
Overseas fixed-interest securities	5 847	2.5	3 806	8.6
Loans and mortgages	6 883	3.0	1854	4.2
Total fixed-interest assets	**53 317**	**23.0**	**13 043**	**29.5**
Index-linked gilts	3 764	1.6	56	0.1
UK equities	80 975	34.9	8 112	18.4
Overseas equities	19 155	8.2	2 139	4.8
Unit trust units	21 113	9.1	b	b
Property	34 828	15.0	3 288	7.4
Total growth assets	**159 835**	**68.8**	**13 595**	**30.7**
Cash, short term and other assets	19 162	8.2	17 578	39.8
Total assets	**232 314**	**100.0**	**44 216**	**100.0**

(a)   Figures are market values except in the case of loans and mortgages, which are
        book values
(b)   Included with UK equities
Source: Financial Statistics.

The importance of the matching principle in explaining investment strategy is supported by the analysis of the investment portfolios of general funds (other funds) shown in Table 21.1. Interest-bearing and liquid investments amount to over two thirds of total assets, roughly the proportion representing companies' underwriting liabilities, whereas equity investments amount to just under one third, reflecting the companies' equity base.

As in the case of other investors, the portfolio policy of insurance companies will be determined by other precepts apart from the matching principle. They will strive to reduce risk by diversification and maximise returns, i.e. select those investments which are expected to perform best. In doing so, they will also have regard to their taxation liability. Insurance companies pay capital gains tax (CGT) as well as corporation tax.

Long-term insurance

Long-term insurance involves over five times the amount of capital invested by general insurance business, and is far more significant in the investment market generally and the property market in particular. Long-term business is dominated by life assurance, with 80% of UK households being involved in some way, usually by the payment of regular premiums over many years until the policy matures and benefits are received.

The majority of life assurance policies provide a combination of life insurance cover and a long-term savings scheme. 'Term insurance' is life cover under which the sum insured is paid only if death occurs within the specified term, whereas under 'whole life' policies payment of the benefits is made on the death whenever it occurs. 'Endowment' policies place the emphasis on saving, with benefits payable on a specific maturity date or on death, whichever is the earlier.

Policies can be 'without profits', in which case the benefits to be received are fixed by contract, whereas under a 'with profits' endowment policy benefits will depend on the performance of the investments made by the insurance company in respect of the policy. Under 'unit linked' policies, benefits are linked to the performance of specific investment units which, in turn, are mostly invested in equities, gilts or property. As a result of inflation, the large majority of life assurance policies are now on some form of 'with profits' or 'unit-linked' basis. Such endowment policies effectively provide long-term equity investments for policy holders, coupled with life cover and certain tax concessions.

Long-term business is a fundamentally different activity from general insurance. The contracts are long-term, sometimes for 40 years, in contrast to the normal annual contract in general insurance. There is also a far greater certainty in the amount and timing of liabilities, partly because most policies have specific maturity dates and partly because of the statistical predictability of death. Although some policies involve the payment of a single lump-sum premium, the majority of premiums flowing into life assurance companies are on a regular periodic basis, such as monthly or quarterly. Thus, both incoming and outgoing cash flows are stable and predictable. There is little need for liquidity, especially as the volume of business is frequently expanding, and liabilities may be met entirely from inflowing funds and investment income. Investments can therefore be made in the long term to match the long-term liabilities.

Like general funds, long-term funds also observe the matching principle in selecting their investments. 'Without profits' and other fixed-sum liabilities will be backed by fixed-income investments of similar duration. Fixed-sum liabilities arising in 2005, for example, will tend to be matched by gilts, corporate bonds or mortgages maturing in that year. On the other hand, the real liability of 'with profits' policies will tend to be matched by equity investments such as ordinary shares, property and unit trust units, although fixed-interest investments will also be held against such policies to provide security and stability. Due to the liabilities of long-term funds being predominantly inflation-related, the proportion of assets held in equity investments is much greater than for general funds.

The aggregate portfolios shown in Table 21.1 reflect the difference in the functions of long-term funds in comparison with general funds. Although there is only a small difference in the overall proportions held in gilt-edged securities, the longer-term funds predictably hold mainly medium- and long-term stock, whereas general insurance funds hold predominantly short- and medium-dated stock. The relative needs of the two groups for liquidity is reflected in dramatically different proportions in cash and liquid assets. In fact, the liquidity of long-term funds was unusually high at the end of 1990, due to the investment uncertainties brought on by the Gulf War. General funds' relatively high holdings of overseas fixed-interest stock reflects their overseas liabilities, whereas the larger overseas equity investments of long-term funds is probably more to do with portfolio diversification and the quest to maximise returns.

Pension (or superannuation) funds

A pension scheme is similar in concept to an endowment scheme followed by an annuity. During his working life, the employee and employer pay regular contributions into the scheme, like premiums on an endowment policy, so that on retirement this has accumulated to a capital sum sufficient to pay an annuity for the rest of the employee's life. The size of the regular contributions would be the amount estimated by an actuary to be sufficient to pay the desired pension on retirement, perhaps two thirds of final salary.

Pension schemes can be 'funded' or 'unfunded'. In funded schemes, the pensions are paid out of the returns earned from investing the periodic contributions of employer and employee. In the case of unfunded schemes (such as the civil service scheme), contributions are not invested but treated by the government as part of its total revenue, and pensions paid out are merely a part of the government's current expenditure. Pension funds can exist only for funded schemes.

In the case of most funded pension schemes, the pensions ultimately paid depend on the success or otherwise of the fund's investment portfolio. The fund bears the actuarial risk. However, in the case of 'insured' schemes, a life assurance company manages the funds and bears the actuarial risk, and in the case of 'pooled' schemes, a number of funds combine their resources by

Table 21.2   Top 10 UK pension funds (by value of assets – 1990)

	(£m)
British Coal	12 789
British Telecommunications plc	12 403
Electricity Supply	9 492
Post Office	8 000
British Railways Board	7 562
Universities Superannuation Scheme	6 230
British Gas plc	5 982
Barclays Bank plc	5 369
The British Petroleum Company plc	4 881
National Westminster Bank	4 726

Source: Pension funds and their advisers.

purchasing units in a 'unitised' fund. Pooled schemes enable cost effective diversification across different investment types for funds too small to justify a segregated portfolio. Pensions ultimately depend on the performance of the units which, in turn, depend on the performance of the underlying investments.

The growth of pension funds in the post-war period has been dramatic. Apart from the growth in the number of workers entering schemes, the system has enjoyed an enormous in-built growth from rising salary levels (contributions by both employee and employer are linked to salaries) and the rising return from investments. The combined assets of pension funds now substantially exceed those of insurance funds, and for most funds the annual inflow of contributions and investment income more than covers benefits paid to pension holders, resulting in a net annual increase in resources for which new investments have to be made.

Pension fund investments

The liability of pension funds is to pay pensions which are linked to employees' final salaries, and thereafter to strive to keep pensions in line with inflation. Their liabilities are therefore essentially in real as distinct from money terms, and consequently pension funds invest the majority of their assets in growth investments (see Table 21.3). In comparison with life assurance funds, pension funds are prepared to sacrifice some security for growth potential and higher return. At the end of 1990, over three quarters of assets were invested in growth investments, with particularly large holdings of UK and overseas equities. With pension funds' liabilities being essentially UK-related, overseas investments are held for the purposes of maximising returns and diversifying portfolios, rather than for matching purposes.

Table 21.3   Pension funds – holdings of investments (end of 1990)

	(£m)	(%)
Gilts		
Short dated	1218	0.4
Medium dated	12673	4.2
Long dated	4269	1.4
Corporate and other bonds	6245	2.1
Overseas fixed-interest securities	6977	2.3
Loans and mortgages	258	0.1
Total fixed-interest assets	**31640**	**10.5**
Index-linked gilts	9780	3.2
UK equities	142147	47.0
Overseas equities	47460	15.7
Unit trust units	4139	1.4
Property (inc. property unit trusts)	28019	9.3
Total growth assets	**231545**	**76.5**
Cash and short-term assets (net)	20927	6.9
Other investments	18558	6.1
Total assets	**302670**	**100.0**

Source: Financial Statistics.

Three other determinants of pension funds' investment strategy are the long-term nature of their liabilities, the predictability of their payments to pensioners and their tax-exempt status. They pay neither income tax nor CGT and therefore gain the full benefit from high-yielding investments. The incentive that this provides for investment in bonds and other fixed-income investments is outweighed by the need for growth investments. At just over 10% of portfolios, the fixed-interest content is much less then for life assurance funds, but the maturity profile of their gilts is similarly biased towards medium- and long-dated stock. The relatively low liquidity of pension fund portfolios reflects not only the predictability of their payouts, but also the fact that for most funds, incoming cash flow substantially exceeds outflow. Payments will be met from the inflow of funds.

Property's qualities as a secure long-term growth investment make it an attractive investment for most pension funds, indeed in the early 1980s, seven out of the ten largest pension funds held over 30% of their portfolios in property. However, the principal factor explaining the relatively low average property content (in comparison with long-term insurance funds) is *fund size*. Most pension funds are relatively small whereas property investments are individually large and indivisible. The purchase of even one property can take up a disproportionately large part of annual investment, and it can be difficult to build up a balanced property portfolio, adequately diversified by type and location. Generally speaking, the larger the pension fund, the greater the proportion of assets invested in property direct.

Allocation of new investment

We have examined the functions of the two main institutional groups and attempted to reconcile their liabilities with the content of their portfolios. However, portfolio structures are not static but constantly changing, and a further understanding of institutional investment and market trends will be gained by an examination of annual changes in the allocation of *new investment* to the various investment types. In any year new investment is unlikely to be made in the same proportion as the existing portfolio. In deciding where to invest new funds, the institutions will be influenced by three main (sometimes conflicting) objectives:

(a) to reduce functional risk by matching assets with liabilities;
(b) to reduce portfolio risk by diversification;
(c) to maximise returns.

Although a fund may envisage an ideal portfolio mix towards which it is aiming, that ideal is a moving target – changing in response to changes in economic and market conditions. But even if the ideal mix remains stable, it does not follow that in every year the fund's portfolio will move closer towards it. Changes in relative values of assets held may cause the weighting of any investment type to move adversely, or the fund may consider its price too high to buy or too cheap to sell. It can be particularly difficult to buy or sell substantial portfolios of property in the short term, due not only to the amount of work and time involved, but also on occasion due to market conditions of excess demand or over-supply.

One objective which has a particular influence on annual net investment is the maximisation of returns. In any year, a fund will allocate the bulk of its new investment to the assets considered likely to perform best. The success of UK equities over the 1980s helps to explain their relentless rise in the portfolios of both insurance and pension funds over the last ten years. Conversely, property's modest performance was one reason for it falling out of favour. Another important trend in the 1980s was the growth of overseas equities in institutional portfolios. In part this was a response to the removal of restrictions on overseas investment in 1979, but the trend also reflects the internationalisation of investment, the benefit of diversifying out of the UK economy, and the high potential returns from investing in the dynamic economies of North America, Europe and the Far East.

However, changing portfolio distributions not only reflect changing demand but also supply. Arguably the most dramatic change in institutional portfolios over the last ten years was not the rise of UK and overseas equities, but the decline of gilts. Their share of institutional portfolios has fallen by almost two thirds over the ten year period from 1982. This is not so much a response to modest performance, as a relative decline in the amount of gilts available, particularly in view of the negative PSBR in the late 1980s and the redemption of existing stock. In view of the return of a large borrowing requirement in the early 1990s, gilts are likely to feature as a more important portfolio constituent in the coming years.

Of all investment categories, the one which tends to receive the most volatile allocations from year to year is liquid investments. Primarily this is money deposited with banks and in the money markets. Institutions tend to build up their liquidity in times of economic or political uncertainty, particularly early in a recession when interest rates are high and the value of long-term investments is tending to fall. Liquid investments are safe, because they are not liable to capital loss like marketable investments.

Figure 21.1 shows changes in the institutions' annual net investment (difference between acquisitions and disposals) for six categories over the three years, 1989–91. It illustrates the build-up of liquidity in 1989–90, at the onset of recession when interest rates were high, and then a run-down of liquidity in 1991 after the resolution of the Gulf war and on the (false) hope of economic recovery. Figure 21.1 also shows funds' disinvestment from gilts in

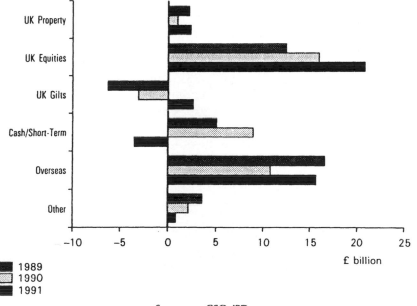

Sources: CSO; IPD.

Figure 21.1   Annual net investment by financial institutions

1989–90, a period of net redemptions by the government, and positive investment in 1991 when new gilt issues resumed after the PSBR again became positive. The figure also illustrates the emphasis towards UK and overseas equities which featured for most of the 1980s.

Although the nature of the institutions' liabilities has not changed substantially over the last ten years, the content of their portfolios certainly has. Understanding institutional investment involves more than understanding the application of the matching principle.

- The investment portfolios of financial institutions are determined by the combination of the following three main objectives:
  (1) to reduce functional risk by liability matching;
  (2) to reduce portfolio risk by diversification;
  (3) to maximise returns.
- In order to minimise functional risk, institutions match their liabilities with assets of a similar nature, e.g., unpredictable or short-term liabilities tend to be matched by liquid or short-term assets, and long-term liabilities linked to inflation tend to be matched by growth investments such as equity shares and property.
- In order to reduce portfolio risk, the institutions diversify their investments principally across fixed-interest bonds, UK and overseas equities, property, index-linked gilts and cash deposits.
- In order to maximise returns, institutions tend to allocate the majority of their annual net investment to those investment categories which are expected to provide the highest returns, net of tax. Liquid investments will tend to be built up or reduced according to the outlook for long-term investments.
- Property can serve all three objectives above. As a proven inflation hedge, it is particularly suitable for matching the long-term inflation-linked liabilities of life and pension funds. Due to its stability and the low correlation of its returns with equities and gilts, it is a particularly good diversification for portfolios dominated by equities and bonds and, on occasion, it has outperformed the other investment categories.

Before examining the property content of institutional portfolios, we shall investigate a variety of other property investing funds.

Property unit trusts

A brief explanation of the unit trust concept is necessary before examining the specialised functions and activities of property unit trusts. The purchase of units in a unit trust enables smaller investors to obtain the benefits of full portfolio diversification and specialist management, without requiring the expertise and financial resources which would be necessary for such investment direct. The units issued by unit trusts are legal claims to a fractional part of the trust's total portfolio, enabling the investor to benefit from the performance of the trust's portfolio as a whole. A unit is the trust's portfolio in microcosm.

So far, it might seem that an investment in a property unit trust would provide identical benefits to an investment in property company shares. This is not so, and an explanation of the principal differences is a convenient means of explaining the unit trust concept. In doing so, we shall also explain the differences between a conventional unit trust and an investment trust, both investing in stock-market securities. Essentially, an investment trust is to stock-market securities as a property investment company is to property – indeed, certain property companies are called investment trusts, e.g., Land Securities Investment Trust.

The principal differences between unit trusts, on the one hand, and investment trusts and property companies on the other, are as follows:

- Legally, investment trusts and property companies are not trusts, but companies owned by their shareholders. A unit trust is constituted by a trust deed which gives legal ownership to the trustee, and responsibility to the trustee and manager.
- Investment trusts and property companies are 'closed ended', i.e. in the short run their equity capital is fixed (although eventually they can expand by the issue of new shares). Unit trusts are 'open ended', i.e. they can expand or contract according to demand and supply.

In times of rising demand, the trust can issue new units, but when more investors wish to sell than buy, units will be redeemed and their number will decline. The trust manager will buy or sell the trust's investments to match the number of units issued.

- The ordinary shares of an investment trust or property company are marketable, and their prices are determined in the stock market. Units are not marketable, and are acquired and redeemed only through the unit trust. Unit prices are set by an official formula which results in their price closely reflecting the value of the assets held by the trust.
- Investment trusts and property companies can raise long-term debt capital and become highly geared. Thus their share prices are relatively volatile and can deviate substantially from the value of the underlying assets. On the other hand, the borrowings of unit trusts are usually small, so the unit price directly represents the value of the trust's investments.

We shall now investigate the functions of property unit trusts. These are of two distinct categories, first 'authorised property unit trusts' (APUTS) which are a means whereby the private investor can invest indirectly in commercial, industrial, agricultural or residential property, as well as in other property-related assets including property company shares. Second, 'unauthorised (or unregulated) property unit trusts' (UPUTS) which serve the investment needs of *tax exempt institutions*. Both types of trust provide an indirect way of investing in property and both follow the unit trust concept of being low-geared open-ended funds, where the value of the units will closely reflect the value of the property assets held by the trust.

If, for example, a property unit trust owns £100 million worth of assets and has issued 100m units, then the value of each unit will approximate to £1, and if the value of the assets rises by 50%, the value of the units will tend towards £1.50. However, the price quoted by the trust when issuing units (offer price) will be higher than the price quoted for encashing units (bid price). The margin covers administrative costs, and discourages investors from frequent switching in and out of units. In times when encashments exceed unit sales, a trust may be forced to sell off some of its property assets in order to maintain a prudential level of liquidity sufficient to meet further sales of units.

APUTs

Authorised property unit trusts (APUTs) are a recent innovation, being introduced in 1991 following a change in regulations and tax concessions which placed APUTs in a similar position as conventional unit trusts investing in stocks and shares. Being intended for private investors, APUTs are subject to a variety of restrictions designed to protect investors, e.g., a minimum level of liquidity, a maximum level of gearing and a limit on the proportion of funds which can be devoted to development schemes.

UPUTs

Unauthorised property unit trusts (UPUTs) have been in existence since the 1960s, to provide a property-investing medium enabling pension funds and charitable trusts to retain the full benefit of their tax-exempt status. UPUTs are attractive to funds which are too small to enable them to build up an adequately diversified portfolio of property, but specialist trusts (e.g., in farmland and overseas property) would help even large pension funds to become fully diversified.

The unit price of UPUTs will tend to be much higher than for APUTs, reflecting the larger resources of the investors, and portfolios will be similar to those of large pension funds investing in property direct. A general UPUT will invest in quality growth investments in shops, offices, industrial and perhaps agricultural property, and may also undertake development projects.

Property bonds

Property bonds provide another 'unit trust' method by which the general public can invest in commercial and industrial property. Property bonds are mostly administered by life assurance companies, and life assurance cover is part and parcel of the investment.

In the earlier discussion on long-term insurance, 'unit-linked' policies were briefly mentioned. In the late 1960s and early 1970s these became popular with policyholders who were seeking greater protection from inflation than was provided by the more traditional 'with profits' policies, where benefits depended on the performance of a range of investments, including fixed-interest securities. The concept of unit-linked endowment policies is that premiums paid by the policyholder can be separated into two parts, one part representing the premium required for life cover, and the other part representing a contribution towards a savings scheme which invests in equity assets by means of a fund run on unit trust principles – hence the term 'unit-linked' policies. Benefits received at the maturity of the policy depend on the value of the units acquired by the savings element of the policy. Although originally based on equity shares, such units may also be based on property, gilts, liquid assets or a combination of these. The units based on property are called property bonds.

Investment schemes are either 'single premium' or 'regular premium'. Single-premium schemes involve one initial lump-sum payment, a system which appears to be an investment in property bonds with life cover thrown in as an extra. Regular premium schemes involve monthly, quarterly or other periodic payments, a system which seems like a life assurance policy with benefits linked to property bonds. The purpose of these schemes is primarily to gain a growth investment, and income due from the bonds is not normally paid out but retained and credited to the investor. Life assurance cover under regular premium schemes attracts income tax relief, and capital gains on property bonds are tax free to investors.

Managed bonds

A managed bond is another insurance-linked unit, but instead of investing exclusively in property, the managers are given the flexibility to invest in all of the principal investment types – property, equity shares, fixed-interest securities and liquid investments. The concept on which the managed bond was first introduced in 1971 was that managers would switch funds between these types according to their expectation for future performance. The flexibility of the system provides both higher potential gain and greater potential stability in a falling market than could be achieved by investing in any one investment type individually. In times when property appears overvalued, or likely to fall in value, funds can be switched to one of the alternatives, and vice versa.

In practice, managed bonds have not performed notably better or worse than property bonds or other insurance-linked equity funds. As a fund grows, it becomes increasingly difficult speedily to switch out of one investment type into another (especially in and out of property, due to its lack of liquidity).

Undertaking a fundamental change in the portfolio of a large property fund is said to be like trying to steer a supertanker to avoid an obstacle — nothing happens until the obstacle is past, or the collision has taken place. So rather than 100% switching, managers will tend to alter the balance between the investment types by placing all new money into the favoured sector, and perhaps selling a proportion of existing investments in the other sectors.

Charitable trusts

Charitable trusts provide certain social benefits on a non-profit-making basis, and are exempt from taxation. They include educational trusts, hospitals and the churches. Only a few of such organisations have sufficient capital to justify direct investment in the property market, but certain Oxford and Cambridge colleges hold extensive property, and the Church of England owns a large portfolio of commercial, industrial and residential property (including a significant quantity of leasehold investments), and takes an active part in development projects.

Institutional property investment

We shall now investigate the property-investment activities of the main categories of investing institution. No official statistics are available to show the constituent details of the institutions' property portfolios, and the principal authoritative source of this information is the Investment Property Databank (IPD). The annual IPD Property Investors Digest provides a statistical analysis and commentary on the content of institutional property portfolios and the investment performance of property. The IPD analysis is based on properties having valuations at the end of December each year, which in 1991 covered 8700 properties with a value of £31 billion. That is equivalent to over half of the value of institutional property holdings and about one third of all investment property in Britain.

The IPD analysis is restricted to UK commercial and industrial property, which constitutes by far the largest proportion of property portfolios. However, it is also interesting to investigate the *overseas* and *agricultural* content as well as the *tenure* of UK property. Information on overseas property investment by UK institutions is sparse, however it appears to be significant. According to the WM Company, who provide an analysis of over 75% of pension fund assets (including those of the largest funds), overseas property constitutes about 1% of total assets, which is about 12% of property assets.

The size of the individual pension or insurance fund is critical to understanding the relative weighting given to property vis-à-vis stocks and shares. Only funds with assets in excess of £100 million tend to invest significantly in property direct, and, according to WM's data, only the largest category of pension funds (assets exceeding £1000 million) invest in overseas property. The size of a fund also affects the average value of properties held in a portfolio and whether the fund undertakes property development or restricts its involvement to standing investments. The reason why fund size is important is (a) the large size of property investments and the number needed for adequate diversification, and (b) the need for specialist expertise. Small funds would not have the specialists 'in-house' who are needed to undertake development or overseas investment and, rather than rely on external consultants, would tend to avoid these activities.

According to IPD, the tenure of institutional property in the UK is primarily freehold (71.6%) or long leasehold (28.0%). The remainder (0.4%) is made up by short-leasehold investments in which a small handful of pension funds specialise in order to benefit from tax-free high returns.

IPD also estimated that in 1992 farmland and woodland constituted just under 1% of institutional property portfolios. After reaching a peak in 1984, institutions have sold more than half of their farmland, and with its value falling relative to that of commercial and industrial property throughout most of the 1980s it has ceased to be a substantial part of portfolios.

It follows from the above that the property portfolios of UK institutional funds are primarily composed of freehold and long-leasehold properties in commercial and industrial property located in the UK. The following analysis relates to such property alone. Table 21.4 shows the basic structure of property portfolios according to the different categories of fund. Insurance funds on average have a higher weighting in offices and less in industrial and retail compared with both pension and short-term funds. They also have a higher weighting in London and a larger proportion invested in high value properties.

These figures are interrelated and can largely be explained by the value distribution of property around the country, and the functions and histories of the different funds. The majority of offices (by value) in Britain are in London, in fact City and West End offices account for over half of all offices in the IPD database, and London and South England account for 87% (1991). Retail and industrial property are more dispersed around the country, yet 80% of industrial property and 60% of retail property on the IPD database are in London and the South of England.

The larger average size of insurance funds and their earlier involvement in property help to explain their property portfolios. The early entry explains why insurance funds hold a higher percentage of pre-1979 buildings and, in view of the popularity of offices before the mid-1970s, also helps to explain the high office content of their portfolios. In turn, the high office content helps to explain the high London weighting and the bias towards high-value properties.

In contrast, the late growth of many pension funds to a size whereby direct property investment became practicable, accounts for the fact that about 97% of their assets have been acquired since 1970. The relatively high proportions in retail and industrial property may reflect a preference for smaller properties to facilitate diversification for smaller funds, and the higher

Table 21.4   Structure of portfolios by fund type; UK commercial and industrial property, % of portfolio value (end of 1991)

	Insurance funds (%)	Pension funds (%)	Short-term[1] funds (%)
By property type			
Retail	36.8	39.9	38.2
Office	51.9	39.4	40.1
Industrial	11.3	20.7	21.7
	100.0	100.0	100.0
By broad region			
London	48.7	34.9	25.4
South of England[2]	30.4	38.9	47.3
Rest of UK	20.9	26.2	27.3
	100.0	100.0	100.0
By value of properties			
< £1m	4.6	3.4	13.2
£1m–£10m	39.2	48.0	72.6
> £10m	56.2	48.6	14.1
	100.0	100.0	100.0

1.   Property unit trusts, unit-linked funds/bonds, pooled pension funds.
2.   South East (excluding Greater London), plus South West, East Anglia.
Source: IPD.

proportion in industrial property may also reflect the attractions of high-yielding investments for 'gross' (tax exempt) funds.

A feature of short-term funds (particularly property unit trusts) is their liability to short-term disinvestment as their investors encash their units. Another feature is their small size which enables them to change their portfolio structure relatively quickly. Like pension funds, about 97% of their portfolios have been acquired since 1970, but the average value of their properties is much smaller and their portfolios are much less biased towards London.

All institutional portfolios are dominated by good-quality investments but not necessarily prime. They mainly comprise traditional investments, eg., shop units in the best shopping streets, offices in the central business district of town centres, and modern industrial estates in good locations. However, Table 21.5 indicates a significant proportion in modern property types, e.g., business parks, warehouse centres, retail warehouses and shopping centres. In fact, although shopping centres comprise only 4% of retail properties by number, they constitute almost 40% of the value of the IPD retail database.

Table 21.5   Distribution by 10 property types – all IPD funds[1]; UK commercial and industrial property, % of portfolio value (end 1991)

Retail units, parades and arcades	18.0
Shopping centres	14.6
Retail warehouses	3.3
Department stores and supermarkets	2.4
Other retails	0.1
Offices	45.2
Office parks[2]	1.7
Warehouse centres[3]	1.1
Industrial parks[4]	3.3
Other industrial	10.3
	100.0

1. Includes property companies and traditional investors (constituting < 10% of total).
2. Office buildings on APR Business Parks register.
3. Post-1975 buildings over 30 000 ft[2] with single distribution tenant.
4. Industrial buildings on APR Business Parks register, research parks, high-quality industrial etc.

Source: IPD.

Although not regarded as part of their property investments, insurance companies also hold a significant amount of mortgages (see Table 21.1) and shares in property companies. The majority of loans and mortgages have been provided for house purchase, frequently linked with an endowment policy issued by the same company, but much of the remainder will be mortgages on commercial property. Insurance companies are major shareholders in the leading property companies, with individual shareholdings sometimes exceeding 10% of a company's equity. Pension funds tend not to invest in property shares as corporation tax paid by property companies cannot be reclaimed, and the funds will obtain the full benefit of their tax exempt status by investing in property direct.

● The high price and indivisible nature of property makes direct investment only suitable for larger funds, say with assets exceeding £100m. This, together with the need for specialist knowledge, provides the case for unitised property funds.
● Apart from significant overseas property holdings and very small investments in farmland and short leaseholds, the property investments of British institutions are dominated by freehold or long leaseholds in UK commercial and industrial property.
● The property portfolio of any fund is primarily dependant upon the fund's size, history and function. The large size of most life funds and their early involvement in property mean that they tend to have a high office

content, a high London weighting, a bias to high-value properties and a significant proportion of older buildings.
● In contrast, the smaller size of most pension and short-term funds, and their more recent involvement in property help to explain a lower weighting in offices, more in industrial, a more diversified regional spread and lower-valued property more recently required.

Property investment trends 1981–91

Although the absolute value of the institutions' property holdings increased by about 2.5 times over 1981–91, that period saw a relative decline in the importance of property to the institutions, both in terms of property's weighting in portfolios and in terms of annual net investment (see Figures 21.2 and 21.3). After peaking in 1981, property's weighting declined steadily before recovering in the boom years of the late 1980s and thereafter resuming its decline. The reasons for this decline were property's poor capital growth relative to equity shares in the periods before and after the property boom, together with property's falling share of annual net investment.

Institutions' annual allocation of funds to the different asset categories varies principally according to expectations for relative returns. Thus the bullish outlook for equities throughout most of the 1980s resulted in the bulk of new funds being allocated to shares (UK and overseas) to the detriment of property. However, the property boom induced an upturn in property investment in 1988–9, helped by the stock-market crash in late 1987 which reminded the institutions of the dangers of being overweight in equities. Net investment in property tends to vary cyclically. This is particularly true in the case of pension and short-term funds, whereas to a greater extent insurance funds have adopted counter-cyclical policies, e.g., by maintaining active property investment in the early 1980s and after the property-market collapse in 1990.

The relative decline of *net* investment into property in the 1980s, obscures not only a massive increase in both sales and acquisitions, but also a substantial rise in expenditure on property development and improvement. In fact, as illustrated in Figure 21.4, spending on development and improvement exceeded purchases of standing investments over the period 1989–91, and since 1986 sales of standing investments have significantly exceeded purchases (see Net Trading). The raw statistics for annual net investment mask an enormous increase in property transactions and fundamental changes to the institutions' portfolios.

Prior to the 1980s, the institutions had managed their property in a relatively passive way, regarding it as a long-term investment and disposing of less than 2% of their portfolios annually. However, in the 1980s management became much more active, with the rationalisation of portfolios to fit with explicit portfolio strategies. A growing perception of the depreciation of

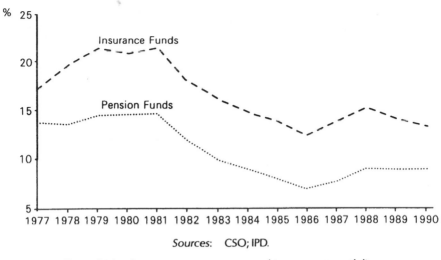

Sources: CSO; IPD.

Figure 21.2 Property as a percentage of investment portfolios

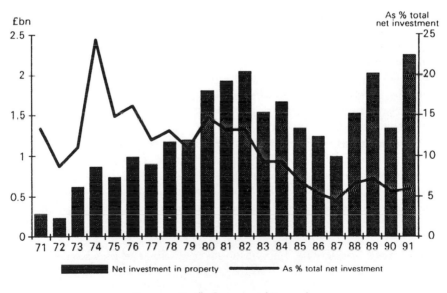

Source: Savills Commercial Research.

Figure 21.3 Annual net property investment by financial institutions

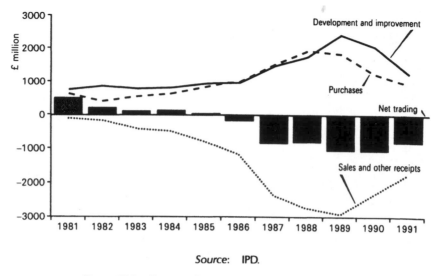

Source: IPD.

Figure 21.4   Property investments: expenditure and sales

offices thorough obsolescence brought about a substantial increase in improvement and redevelopment and a sharp rise in sales. Perhaps the single most important trend over the 1980s and early 1990s was a shift in emphasis from offices to retail property. In fact, the institutions appear to have predicted the over-supply of central London offices by substantial net sales of offices in the capital from 1988 to 1991. The trend from offices to retail is illustrated by the portfolios of pension funds where retail property rose from as little as one third of offices in 1981, to overtake the office content in 1991.

Other trends in the 1980s were to sell old buildings to buy new, to sell small properties to buy large and, prompted by the north/south economic divide, to sell provincial industrials in favour of the South of England. In fact, to quote IPD, 'the allocation of investment across sectors and regions has tended to follow their relative returns'. The institutions were particularly avid buyers of shopping centres, spending three times more on these than on retail units over the five-year period 1987–91. Active investment in modern property types such as retail warehouses, high-tech industrials, business parks and large warehouse centres was also a feature of the 1980s.

● Property's weighting in institutional portfolios and its allocation of net investment has tended to move cyclically but on a declining trend since 1981. However, this trend in net investment has obscured enormous changes in portfolio content through sales, acquisitions, development and improvement.

● Although property investment across sectors and regions tends to follow relative returns, the principal trends since the early 1980s have been to increase retail investments (particularly shopping centres) at the expense of a reduction in London offices, and to acquire modern large properties including, e.g., business parks and warehouse centres.

22 International Property Investment

The case for investment overseas

The opportunity to invest overseas opens up an enormous extra market in which the investor can seek out investments to increase his return. But overseas markets do not just offer a wider choice of investments of the same kind and characteristics as those in the UK, they offer more positive advantages. We have already noted one justification for investment abroad, namely the ability to negate the risk of currency movements by 'matching' liabilities overseas with assets in the same country. However, another advantage is that overseas markets provide the opportunity to diversify a portfolio into investments which have a low correlation with those in the UK, thereby enabling the investor to reduce his portfolio's risk.

UK equity shares (particularly those of multinational companies and investment trusts) provide a substantial element of international diversification because much of their earnings derive from trading activities or assets in other countries. Such advantages are not provided by UK property – its immobility means that investors' returns are dependent on the health of the economy in which it is located. Regional diversification within a country can reduce the risk of localised recession, but international diversification is necessary to reduce the risk of national economic decline.

One major advantage of investing in both property and financial securities overseas is therefore to diversify out of a dependence on the UK economy, both on a long-term and a cyclical basis. The post-war record of the UK economy is one of almost unrelenting decline relative to the world as a whole, and to Europe and the Far East in particular. The ability to invest in European, Japanese and other stocks therefore enables the British investor to hedge against the risks of a continuation of such a decline. Overseas investments can help to stabilise a portfolio against cyclical trends, because UK trade cycles do not necessarily coincide with booms and slumps in overseas countries. However, the rise in international trade and the facility with which capital now moves between countries has led to a greater interdependence between the major world economies which, together with the two oil price shocks of 1973–4 and 1979–80, caused them to move more into phase. Being substantially the most powerful market economy in the world, the health of the US economy tends to influence the UK and other OECD economies, and the London, Tokyo, and other stock markets frequently 'dance to the tune' of Wall Street.

Overseas stocks and property also provide investment opportunities which are either unavailable, in short supply, or relatively overpriced in the UK. Few UK companies are active in gold and precious metals, yet gold-mining shares are particularly valuable to a portfolio as they tend to be uncorrelated with other shares. The price of gold tends to rise in times of international tension and uncertainty when other investments will normally be falling. American, Japanese and Australian stocks also provide investment opportunities in high technology, airlines and mining, sectors which are under-represented in the UK.

· In property, the limited supply of certain prime investments in the UK can be overcome by the vastly greater availability in the USA and elsewhere. Overseas property markets are frequently less sophisticated and less competitive than the UK, some countries offer greater choice and opportunity for both investment and development, yields are often higher and growth prospects sometimes more attractive.

Criteria for selecting a country

Probably the two most important considerations in selecting a country for overseas investment are political stability and economic strength. Political stability implies a stable democratic system of government. The risk arising from unstable or undemocratic regimes is partly the risk of the nationalisation of assets without compensation, and the destruction of assets by civil war or riot. More important, however, is that political instability and social strife lead to economic stagnation and decline. Consequently, much of Africa and South America is considered unsuitable (particularly for property investment which, being physical and immobile, may be more vulnerable than financial securities).

Traditionally, the most popular countries for UK investors have been the USA, Canada, the EC, Australia, New Zealand (and formerly South Africa), for historical and cultural as well as political and economic reasons, but the postwar success of the Japanese, Hong Kong and other Far East economies has also attracted substantial investment capital. Certain countries may be selected due to a unique availability there of the investments required – for example, gold-mining shares in South Africa.

The return from an investment depends on both the performance of the investment itself and the value of the currency in which the return is received. As the success of a country's economy tends to influence both variables, the strength and future prospects for a country's economy must be a dominant criterion in the choice of overseas investments. British investors will measure returns in sterling, and therefore the success of an investment in Nippon Steel will depend partly upon the success of the company and partly upon changes in the exchange rate between the pound and the yen over the period of the investment. Likewise, the success of an investment in New York offices depends on changes in their value in the USA, as well as on changes in the price of the US dollar vis-à-vis the pound sterling. Thus in investing overseas, UK investors must 'take a view' on future currency movements. When the return is considered in terms of sterling, currency movements add an extra layer of risk (and potential return). Admittedly, if one takes a global perspective of investment, the value of the return from a UK investment depends on the value of sterling vis-à-vis world currencies as a whole, and in that sense currency risk of some kind is unavoidable. However. as the liabilities of UK investors are primarily in sterling, risk and return will normally be considered in terms of sterling.

The risk arising from currency movements is nicely illustrated by the following deal arranged by Courtaulds, the UK textile giant. In 1967 Courtaulds borrowed 50 million Swiss francs (equivalent to about £4 million) because the interest rate of 5.5% was more than 2% less than what it would have to pay on an equivalent sterling loan.[1] It could expect to save £90 000 per annum in interest payments. However, due to the fall in the value of sterling vis-à-vis the Swiss franc, the cost in sterling of paying the interest had risen to 18.9% per annum by the time the loan was repaid in 1978. Total interest payments over the period of the loan amounted to £4.8 million, compared with the £3.5 million the firm would have had to pay if it had borrowed by issuing debentures in the UK. Moreover, £14.3 million was required to repay the original SwF 50 million in 1978, and the exchange loss of £10 million was not an allowable expense to offset corporation tax. So, after grossing up the £10 million loss for corporation tax, the £4 million loan effectively cost Courtaulds £25.6 million over the 11-year period, equivalent to an interest rate of over 50% per annum.

This loss was incurred because over the period of the loan the pound fell from a parity of over SwF 12 to about SwF 3.50. Courtaulds then compounded their loss by electing to repay their debt early, just when the value of sterling was starting to recover. Although extreme, this example illustrates the dangers of borrowing in foreign currency to finance activity in another country (a problem faced by several UK property companies over the same period).

Conversely, this example also highlights the potential rewards of investing overseas. If instead of borrowing, Courtaulds had invested the same amount of money at 5.5% in an investment in Switzerland by converting sterling to Swiss francs at the 1967 parity, then the company would have made gains equivalent to the losses they in fact suffered (excluding the tax adjustment). On the other hand, if the company had borrowed Swiss francs to make such an investment in Switzerland, the currency risk would have been neutralised. The currency loss on the debt would have equalled the currency gain on the asset. When an investor wishes to minimise currency risk he should match overseas assets with liabilities in the same currency. If a property company requires to borrow money to undertake a development project overseas, it is advisable to borrow the finance in the same overseas country. On the other hand, one of the principal reasons for investors purchasing overseas assets is to transfer a part of their wealth abroad in order to maintain their portfolios' value in global terms, and to hedge against the possibility of a fall in sterling. To match a foreign investment with debt in the same country defeats that purpose.

An analysis of the determinants of the value of a nation's currency is beyond the scope of this book, but taking a long-term view the most important variables will tend to be the country's trade balance and its inflation rate relative to other countries. A nation's currency can fluctuate sharply and unpredictably in response to changes in capital flows, relative interest rates, and speculative views taken on future trends. Ultimately, however, it is the relative economic success of a country which will determine its exchange rate, and thus the selection of a strong economy in which to invest is crucially important.

The trend towards international investment

UK investors have traditionally had a strongly international outlook to investment, an attitude deriving from the British empire, commonwealth and strong historical and cultural links with the USA. However, from a UK perspective, the recent trend towards international investment starts with the abolition of exchange controls in October 1979, after 40 years of restriction. Rather than making overseas investment illegal, exchange controls had made it relatively expensive. By preventing a *net* outflow of investment capital from the UK, the regulations effectively created a limited pool of special investment currency. An investor wishing to invest abroad had to acquire this special currency from an investor selling an overseas investment, and as demand exceeded supply, the cost of the currency substantially increased the cost of investing abroad.

The effect of deregulation in 1979 was to unleash a pent-up demand for portfolio investment overseas (see Figure 22.1), reinforced by the high value of sterling in the early 1980s due to the production of North Sea oil in the context of rising world oil prices. During the 1980s British investors effectively invested the proceeds of North Sea oil, creating an overseas 'nest egg' to sustain the economy when the oil runs out. British investing institutions now hold over 15% of their portfolios in overseas investments and British investors are the largest holders of foreign equities in the world. In fact, according to the WM sample, UK pension funds held 26% of their portfolios in overseas equities, bonds and property at the end of 1991, suggesting that the official figures (Table 21.3) understate the true extent of overseas investment. Pension fund investment in overseas equities is evenly split between Europe, North America and the Far East.

Britain's lead in deregulating overseas investment has been followed by other countries, particularly in Europe where barriers have now largely been removed, helping to fuel an enormous expansion in international portfolio investment. Although a large part of this is in short-term money and bonds,

£ billions

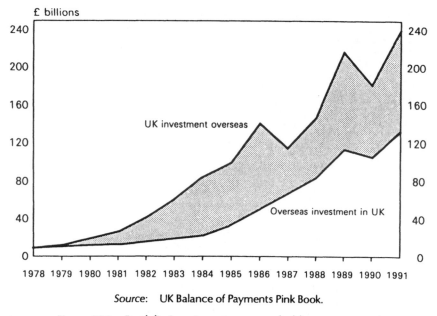

Source: UK Balance of Payments Pink Book.

Figure 22.1   Portfolio investment overseas: holdings at year end

cross-border trading in equities increased 20–fold in the 1980s, and the international flow of funds for investment now dwarfs that deriving from trade. This 'globalisation' of investment reflects the rising trend of other cross-border activities including trade and business (particularly banking and financial services), travel and information exchange, personnel and expertise.

With the growth of the Japanese and Far East economies, and the merging of Europe into a single market, the world economy is now largely focused on three economic zones, viz., North America, the Pacific Rim and Europe, as represented by the emergence of New York, Tokyo and London as the three main world stock markets. The convergence of Europe into a single market has created an economy of comparable strength to the other two, and has increased cross-border investment, both within Europe and with the other zones. Portfolio investment has tended to follow expansion in business and trade, and a continued trend towards cross-border company mergers within Europe is likely to lead to further intraEuropean cross-border investment.

So the globalisation of investment means inward as well as outward overseas investment, and property investment as well as in equities and bonds. Overseas property investment in Britain rose dramatically in the late 1980s (see Figure 22.2), primarily from Japan, Sweden, the EC and the USA, rising from less than £100 million in the mid-1980s to over £3 billion in 1989. The involvement of Swedish investors was primarily a pent-up response to that country's abolition of exchange controls. However, the inflow of Japanese money

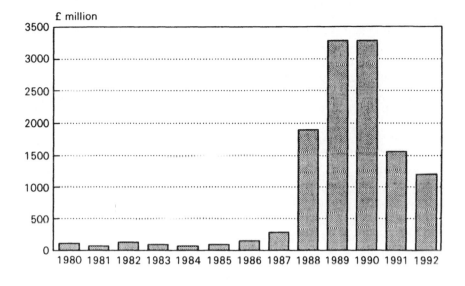

£ million

Source: DTZ Debenham Thorpe.

Figure 22.2   Overseas direct investment in UK property

reflected their huge expansion in overseas investment worldwide, but it also followed from the entry of their banks and securities trading houses into London, particularly with Big Bang in 1986. Like the lending of Japanese banks for property development, the bulk of their investment was in City and West End offices, locations with which Japanese financiers were familiar and which reflected London's position as the financial capital of Europe.

Overseas property investment in Britain declined sharply in 1991 and the trend towards globalisation in property went into reverse, largely due to simultaneous problems in the property markets and economies of the leading countries worldwide. The decline in UK property values was a disincentive to overseas investors, and the domestic problems of Japan, America and Sweden sharply reduced the funds available. Although the Japanese were still the largest overseas property investors in Britain in 1991, there was an increase in purchases from the EC, with the Dutch, French and Germans accounting for almost half of overseas acquisitions.[2]

Problems of property investment overseas

Apart from the constraints imposed by exchange controls, one of the traditional problems faced by property investors contemplating overseas acquisitions were restrictions imposed by foreign governments. Some countries imposed special taxation measures, or prevented borrowing for investment or development purposes, or effectively prohibited foreign property ownership. Even in the USA, certain states imposed major restrictions, and in Australia and Canada approval of an investment or development was frequently dependent on the involvement of local partners in the project.

Although many of these controls have now been abolished there are many other practical problems to overcome in appraising, acquiring, developing and managing overseas property. These include language problems (particularly in the continent of Europe), difficulties of decision making, control and management from a distance and, in some countries, an unfamiliar system of professional and financial back-up. Probably even more important are the systems of land transfer, tenure, planning and taxation, which are unfamiliar to the foreigner and unique to each country.

In the continent of Europe indexation of rent is common, and in France commercial leases are normally for nine years, with the tenant having the right to terminate the lease at three-year intervals, a system creating greater risk of rent voids than in the UK. Many European cities (notably Paris and Amsterdam) are subject to strict development controls, reducing development opportunities in the city centres but protecting investment values. In contrast, fundamental characteristics of the US market are the availability of land and the liberal system of planning and development control, which create a greater risk of oversupply than in the UK. An extreme example is provided by the 12 million ft^2 of space in the World Trade Center in New York, a single project which provided almost 50% more space than aggregated in the largest 20 office developments in the City of London between 1961 and 1981.[3]

Such differences in property law, planning and practice can have implications for the investor which are not immediately obvious. Prime office and shop yields in the USA have been double those of comparable properties in the UK, but there are many dangers in comparing them. Apart from the risk of oversupply, tenants in the USA are more mobile than in the UK, leases are traditionally short and until recently rent-review provision and full repairing and insuring covenants were exceptional. On the other hand, one advantage of US property is the ability to charge depreciation against income for tax purposes. Taxation of property overseas is something of a minefield, institutions exempt in the UK can be liable to tax overseas, but some investors may escape liability by means of tax havens such as the British Virgin Islands and the Dutch Antilles.

The problems of property investment overseas have been well illustrated by the experiences of British investors worldwide in the late 1950s and early 1960s, and more particularly in Europe in the early 1970s. On both occasions, UK investors were attracted overseas by the greater development and investment opportunities in comparison with the competitive and restricted home market. Europe was popular in the early 1970s because of the success of the European economy and the UK's imminent entry to the EEC. Yields were higher, and the market less sophisticated than in the UK, being still based largely on owner occupation (particularly in Germany) and relatively unexploited by institutional investors. In the event, many UK developers and investors suffered heavy losses when the European and world markets, like the UK market, turned sour at the end of 1973.

Perhaps the fundamental lesson to be learnt from the European failures is that there is no substitute for detailed knowledge of a local market. That knowledge, together with a command of a country's system of land tenure, planning, finance and taxation is essential before any prudent investment or development decision can be made. The European adventure also featured mismanagement and inadequate control of development projects, with problems arising from inadequate understanding of foreign construction contracts.

A developer who is undertaking a project in a foreign country can reduce the risks deriving from inadequate knowledge by undertaking the scheme on a joint venture basis with a developer, contractor or investor familiar with local conditions. Most investors, however, prefer to avoid such an arrangement because they lose overall control of the project and can get 'locked in' to the completed property, being unable to sell at a price reflecting their full share of the market value. In the absence of such an arrangement, the best local professional advice is essential.

The future of international property investment

Except for the activities of British and Dutch investors, and the entry of the Swedes in the late 1980s, the amount of pan-European property investment has been relatively small. But the activities of Dutch, French and German investors in 1991 could be a precursor to sharply increased cross-border investment in the future. Financial institutions in Europe are being released from restrictions which have tied them to investing in domestic markets, leading to the creation of pooled property investment funds, like British property unit trusts, which could become a major force in the European property market. After the UK market has bottomed out there could be a substantial upturn in European property investment in Britain, including take-over bids for British property companies. Similarly, British activity in the EC and eastern Europe is likely to grow, helped by a widespread branch network of chartered surveyors.

Property investment and development in Europe will become less problematic as taxation, law and practice become standardised, as intended by the Single European Act. Currency risk will depend on Britain's membership of the Exchange Rate Mechanism and would be removed entirely if the proposal for a common European currency comes to fruition.

The globalisation of the world's property market seems likely to be resumed when the problems of the early 1990s have been resolved. Despite the synchronisation of world economies, there are indications that returns from property in the main cities of the world show low correlations,[4] indicating that global diversification provides the opportunity to improve the risk/return profile of property portfolios. As the globalisation of banking and financial services, business and trade continue to develop, property investment is likely to follow.

Rightly or wrongly, the British property investor tends to believe that the UK market is the most sophisticated in the world, and too often has concluded that he can 'teach the foreigner a thing or two' about development, financing and leasing. It remains to be seen whether the lessons of earlier experience have been learnt or forgotten.

23 Property Pricing – A Reappraisal

In Chapter 11, we formulated a provisional theory of property pricing based on the principles of the pricing of stock-market securities identified in Part I. Since then, we have investigated the three main sectors of the market – the letting, development and investment sectors – and have identified the principal forces affecting price in each. It now remains to review and complete our pricing theory in the light of that information.

The pricing model

In Chapter 11, we introduced a model of the pricing of equity-type freehold interests which spanned both the DCF and YP concepts of price determination (Equation (11.8)):

$$P_0 = \frac{R_0}{r - r\left(\dfrac{(1+g)^n - 1}{(1+r)^n - 1}\right)}$$

where P_0 = market price (value) of a rack rented freehold, R_0 = current rental value (at start of lease or at rent review), g = investors' expected rental growth rate p.a., r = investors' target return (IRR) p.a. and n = period between rent reviews (years).

Alternatively, the denominator in this equation can be replaced by y (representing investors' required yield), see Equation (11.9). As y is a decimal (less than 1), a property's value can be considered as a multiple of the rent, that multiple being the reciprocal of the yield. So if $y = 0.05$ (a yield of 5%) the property's value must be twenty times the rent.

What is true for the individual property is essentially true for property in general, so the general level of property values can be considered as a function of current rents and yields. Generally speaking, yields oscillate within limited bands, and in the long run it is changing rent which is the more significant of these two components of price. But in the short run yields are variable, creating significant changes in property values. The yield is the component of price which reflects investors' expectations, being sensitive to changes in economic conditions and market sentiment.

Assuming that the rent review period is constant, Equation (11.9) shows that property yields vary in response to changes in investors' expected rental growth rate and their target return. The rental growth rate can be sub-divided into two components, viz., growth on (hypothetical) new property and the impact of depreciation through obsolescence. Investors' target return also has two components, viz., the opportunity cost of long-term investment capital and a yield premium to compensate investors for the *relative* risk, illiquidity and other characteristics of property. Thus, in explaining property yields, we should be principally concerned with these four variables – investors' expected rate of rental growth and depreciation, yields on alternative investments (particularly long-dated gilts) and investors' perception of property's relative risk, liquidity, etc. However, due to the cost and time involved in market transactions and other imperfections of the property market, yields and prices are relatively insensitive to minor or short-term changes in these variables.

The model is hypothetical rather than empirical. Its validity can never be entirely proven because there can be no recorded measures of, e.g., the risk *perceived* by property investors, nor of their rental growth *expectations*. Deriving from the concept of price as the present value of expected income flow, the model is merely a statement of how yield and price *should* be determined if market operators are rational. Although useful, it is nonetheless insufficient for a full understanding of price movements. Price is determined by the forces of demand and supply, so we will now analyse the components of demand and supply in order to obtain a fuller understanding of property values, and at the same time reappraise the validity of the pricing model.

A demand and supply analysis

The market price and yield of property investments are determined by the interaction of the demand for, and supply of, property *investments*, considered as standing properties let to occupying tenants. Thus, investment demand which determines price and yield is quite separate from occupation demand which determines rental value. Likewise, the supply of investments is distinct from the supply of property to let, except that a component of both is the supply of newly developed properties.

The property investment market is unusual in the sense that the principal demanders – the financial institutions and property companies – are also the principal suppliers. Although other groups such as overseas and traditional investors are also involved in the market, it is these two groups which dominate both sides of the equation, and to understand their activities and functions is to understand the main forces at work in the investment sector of the market. More particularly, because property investment involves large amounts of money, it is important to understand the availability of funds to each group. The heyday of property companies has occurred when borrowed capital was relatively cheap and freely available, and the influence of the financial institutions has grown with their inflow of funds and their quest for a hedge against inflation.

Investment demand for standing investments

When deciding whether to buy or sell property, the investor will take account of the yield, rent review period and his cost of capital, and make judgements about growth, depreciation, and the return required to reflect property's risk and other special characteristics. If the expected return exceeds his target return he will tend to buy. If not, he will tend to sell properties that he currently owns. That is rational, and illustrates the essential concept on which our pricing model is based.

The decisions of property companies and financial institutions to invest in property will differ as a result of differences in their functions, and differences in the availability and cost of capital to them. The cost of capital to the individual company will depend on whether it is listed or unlisted, its credit status and whether it raises money from the stock market or from a bank. In general, decisions by property companies to add to or reduce their property portfolios will depend on the availability of capital and its cost *relative* to property's expected returns. However, we must acknowledge development as an alternative and potentially cheaper (but riskier) means of acquisition for both groups. The demand for standing investments will depend on the cost and risk involved in development.

Life and pension funds receive contractual inflows of cash, and their cost of capital is best considered in opportunity cost terms, i.e, their target return from property will be based on returns expected from alternative investments. That concept is implicit in our pricing model by considering property's target return as being at a premium (or discount) to gilt yields. The demand for property from life and pension funds will vary according to how expected returns from property vary with expected returns from bonds, equities, overseas equities and cash.

Our investigation of the investment activities of the financial institutions in Chapter 22 supports the above analysis. The funds allocate their money to the various investment types partly with a view to maximising returns, but also with a view to risk reduction. Funds invest in property, not only when they believe it will outperform other investments, but when they judge that its future returns are commensurate with its risk; risk considered here both in terms of portfolio variability and in terms of funds' ability to meet their liabilities. If, as was suggested in Chapter 12, the institutions bought property in 1979–81 on a target return below redemption yields on long gilts, that was both rational and consistent with the pricing model.

Market evidence of property acquisitions by property companies and the institutions supports the above analysis. Demand from institutions has varied with expectations for property's returns relative to those of alternative investments, and with their perception of property's risk-reducing qualities. The period over which financial institutions most actively built up their property portfolios, 1967–82, was generally a period of high cost-push inflation. The institutions' property acquisitions must be explained largely by a perception that property was the investment category which performed best in these conditions and which was most able to hedge against the risks inherent in 'stagflation'.

The supply of property investments

The market supply of property investments has three main sources:

(1) standing investments being resold;
(2) newly developed property being sold for the first time;
(3) transfers from owner occupation.

The conditions under which investors would tend to sell standing investments have already been considered when investigating investment demand above, i.e. when investors' target return exceeds their expected return. Typically, this would occur at the start of a recession when interest rates rise and rental growth expectations fall. Property companies would normally be under greater pressure to sell than the institutions, due to their gearing and the impact of high interest rates on their cash flow. The pressure to sell and the fall in demand in these conditions tend to exacerbate the cyclical nature of property values.

The determinants of the supply of newly developed investments have been fully examined in Part IV, and the comment here is restricted to the impact of development cost on market price. The effect of development completions on price is implicitly reflected in our pricing model (Equation (11.8), above), through R_0 (current rental value) and g (rental growth expectation). However, in explaining market price, it is important to reiterate the principle that price will tend towards production cost for a product with an elastic supply (see Chapter 15).

On the assumption that demand is not satisfied by existing stock, the price of a good with an elastic supply will tend towards its production cost, however great is the level of demand. Of course, the supply of property investments is not perfectly elastic, obviously in the cases of prime High Street shops and farmland, but also in certain specific locations and for any property type in the short run. However, for office and industrial property in the long run over the country as a whole, supply probably is relatively elastic, and one would expect to see a close relationship between market price and development cost. That would provide the main origin for property being a hedge against inflation; through the dominance of construction cost in total development cost, and the relationship between construction cost and inflation.

The link between market price, development cost and inflation requires floorspace demand to exceed existing stock. However, due to property's durability, that link may be broken in the short run due to recession or, conceivably, over a longer period for a specific property type in a specific location. Nonetheless, the impact of development cost is an important elaboration to our pricing theory, not explicitly represented in the model.

Sale and leasebacks

Transfers from owner occupation to the investment sector of the property market include (a) the sale of vacant possession property and (b) sale and leasebacks. In the case of (a), a pure investment interest will be created only if the property is acquired by an investor who then leases it to an occupying tenant. The acquisition of vacant property is not attractive to institutional investors, but it is common for a property company to acquire such property, improve it, lease it to a reliable tenant, and then either retain it as a long-term investment or sell it to an institution.

A sale and leaseback occurs when an owner-occupier remains in occupation but sells his freehold (or long leasehold) interest on the condition of being granted a lease in return. If the property is prime this will instantly create an attractive investment, usually with a reliable tenant on a long lease. Let us examine the circumstances under which sale and leasebacks take place.

The essential purpose of undertaking a sale and leaseback transaction from the point of view of the owner-occupier is to raise capital — or, more accurately, to release the capital tied up in the property so that it can be employed for other purposes, e.g. to expand trading activities, restructure company finances, acquire new property or improve existing premises as needed for trading activities. The sale and leaseback provides the occupying firm with an alternative source of capital to borrowing or issuing new shares. Consequently, sale and leasebacks tend to proliferate when companies need to raise capital, when interest rates are high and share prices relatively low.

The start of the recessions in 1979–80 and 1989–90 both provided classic scenarios for sale and leaseback activity, predominantly in good-quality retail property. In 1979–80, major retailers such as Tesco, Woolworth, Burtons and House of Fraser sold (mainly) to life institutions, whereas in 1989–90 the food retailers Tesco and Sainsbury were prominent in striking deals with property companies. Both periods saw a sharp decline in disposable incomes, and therefore the prospect of a fall in retail turnover and profit, conditions in which a retailer with high borrowings would be wise to degear. However, the principal reason for the food retailers selling in 1989–90 was to raise capital to develop new superstores.

The 1979–80 scenario nicely illustrates the merits of such deals to both parties. In the context of rising cost-push inflation, the institutions were keen to increase the property content of their portfolios. Retail property was particularly popular, with prime yields being pushed as low as 4%. With interest rates close to 20%, a sale and leaseback looked highly attractive to a retailer with a bank overdraft and a cash-flow problem. If the subject of the deal was a prime shop, then immediately after the transaction, capital which had previously been costing 20% in interest payments would cost a mere 4% in rent. Of course, the rent would be expected to rise at the first review, and after allowing for rental growth, the long-term cost of the leaseback capital would be much higher than 4%. However, in 1980 rental growth prospects were poor and the need to repay bank debt was paramount.

Alternative methods of raising capital in 1980 were very expensive. Long-term fixed-interest debt was not a realistic option because of the high interest rates payable and the expectation of a decline in inflation and the level of interest rates. Funding by rights issue was also expensive and unattractive as retailers' share prices were subdued and dividend yields relatively high due to the prospect of declining profits. On the other hand, the value of retail property had risen strongly over the previous two years, shop yields were near an all-time low, and the high level of investment demand from the institutions meant that retailers had no difficulty in finding a buyer for a prime retail investment. Conditions pointed clearly to leaseback as the optimal financing method.

In considering the sale and leaseback option, the owner-occupier will take account of the prospects for future rental growth as well as the long-term cost of capital. In that respect the supply of leaseback investments is covered by the pricing model; but firms will also arrive at such decisions according to trading conditions and the circumstances of their individual business.

Property pricing – a summary

The price of property is determined by activity in the three main sub-sectors of the market – the development sector, the letting sector and the investment sector.

Capital value is determined in the investment sector by the interaction of investment demand with investment supply, but investment demand depends on current rents and expectations for rental growth, which are determined in the letting sector by occupation demand and supply. In turn, both the supply of new investments and the supply of new property to let are affected by activity in the development sector. Investment price depends on rental values and development activity, but development activity and site values depend on rental and investment values. So the three sectors are interdependent but, unlike chickens and eggs, we *can* say what comes first. Ultimately the main determinant of both investment demand and development activity is the level of occupation or tenant demand. The attractions of property investment – security and growth – depend on a stable or rising level of occupation demand. In the absence of that, investment demand will fall, property prices will fall, and development activity will cease.

Property prices are primarily demand led. The demand for property is a derived demand – occupation demand is derived from the demand for the goods or services that a property is suited to provide, and investment demand is largely derived from occupation demand. So ultimately the demand for property depends on the profitability of using it, because profitability determines the rent that a tenant is able to pay and therefore the price that the investor will pay. It is the rising demand interacting with a relatively inelastic supply which induces development activity, but both property values and development activity tend to vary cyclically because of the economic cycle and the time lag involved in development.

The ability of supply to respond to demand varies from one property type to another, one location to another and from one time period to another. But generally speaking, the supply of farmland and prime High Street shops is inelastic, values will be primarily demand determined and will reflect the profitability of the business for which the property is best suited. In the cases of offices and industrial property, supply is normally more elastic in the medium/long run, and values will tend to reflect development cost.

In each of the three sectors of the market, our pricing theory has employed both a pricing model and a demand and supply analysis. Essentially, the model used in each sector is the same – price in terms of site value, rental value or investment value is a residual (or surplus) after deducting target returns from expected returns. In the development sector, the development value of a site tends towards the residual after deducting developers' target return on capital employed from the return expected from the completed project. In the letting sector, rental value tends towards the residual after deducting tenants' target return on their productive factors from the returns expected from carrying on business activity. In the investment sector, investment value tends towards the residual after deducting investors' target return on capital invested from the expected return in the form of future rental income and capital growth. In each case, price tends towards the residual because in each case competition forces those acquiring the interests to pay over the residual.

In the case of investment value, the comparison of target and expected return must be expressed in DCF terms, because the interest is a long-term one and price must reflect the time value of money. In the case of site value, a DCF approach is less critical as the development period is relatively brief. Strictly speaking, a DCF view is also appropriate to the concept of rental value because (in considering the rent that he can afford to pay) the tenant will take a view on expected costs and returns over the period until the first rent review, not simply over a single year. In each case, the residual price is dependent on expectations which may not be met – in fact, virtually the only certainty is that the outcome will either fall short of, or exceed, the expectation. The costs and revenues of developers, tenants and investors are uncertain, and risk is a feature of each sector of the market.

The surplus or residual model is primarily a demand-side model. It does not take *explicit* account of factors affecting supply, e.g., the impact of existing use value on the market value of development sites, and the impact of new development and development cost on the price of investments. The model is a useful indicator of market price and helps to explain buy and sell decisions, but it is frequently a better indicator of a ceiling price than market price. Ultimately it is the interaction of demand and supply which is the mechanism causing price movements to take place, and a full analysis of both sides of the equation is necessary to explain price movements.

Finally, our pricing theory has been based on the assumption that financial risk and return are virtually the only considerations determining the actions of tenants, developers and investors. Clearly this is simplistic; some tenants will pay higher rent for a building which reflects prestige, many developers will be concerned with the architectural merit of their products, and some investors may take account of the impact of their actions on the national economy or society at large. However, maximising return while minimising risk must be the dominant motivation in the determination of the value of business property.

We will conclude this chapter with the following points:

- The market price and yield of property investments are determined by the interaction of the demand for, and supply of, investments. It is critical to distinguish these forces from the occupation demand and supply (of property to let) which determines rental value.
- The property pricing model is a useful simplification of price determination, but a full analysis of supply and demand forces is necessary to explain price change.
- The demand for standing investments depends on the availability of capital and its cost relative to expected returns. The cost of capital to property companies is its direct cost in the capital markets, but the cost of capital to institutions is best regarded in opportunity-cost terms, so that the institutions' demand for property will depend on expected returns from other investments.
- Development provides an alternative means of acquiring property investments, and the demand for standing investments will depend on the relative cost and risk of development.
- The supply elasticity of a particular property type in a particular location, together with its price elasticity of demand, will determine whether price is principally a function of development cost or of the profitability of the business use for which the property is best suited.

VI Government Intervention in the Property Market

24 Aspects of Government Intervention in the Property Market

Introduction

Until now, the public sector has featured only briefly in our analysis, and the pricing theories have been developed on the assumption of a free market. We must now examine how government action influences property values, but the objective of this chapter cannot be to provide a comprehensive coverage of the subject, nor can we analyse the full ramifications of public-sector intervention. Rather, the aim is to illustrate how the general theory of property pricing developed in this book can explain the impact on market price of government intervention as well as private-sector activity. This is done by illustrating the effect of a few of the more important aspects of government intervention – planning control, rent control, and property taxation.

If we include local government and public corporations with central government, then there are perhaps three broad facets of public-sector intervention in the property market. First, the public sector operates as an integral part of the market, e.g., as an occupier of office space, as a developer of industrial estates, and as an investor in land and buildings. Second, the government affects the market indirectly through its ability to influence the actions of market operators by its management of the economy, e.g., by monetary and fiscal measures, and by regional policies. Third, the government acts directly on the market by imposing a framework of legislative constraint within which market forces must operate, e.g., by planning control, rent control and property taxation. In none of these areas does intervention invalidate our theory of pricing, the effect is merely to influence the variables in our pricing model and to affect the forces of demand and supply.

Planning control

Property values are influenced by any factor which has consequences for the economy of the site, town, region or country in which the property is located. That includes physical, geographical and technological factors, as well as social or institutional considerations, of which legislation is one aspect. Such factors may affect (a) the value of individual properties, (b) the pattern or spatial distribution of values, and (c) the aggregate of property values in any location.

Such a three-dimensional view is particularly important when analysing the impact of planning controls on property values. The ban on redevelopment which results when an obsolete building is 'listed' as being of architectural or historical merit will primarily affect the value of the site on which the building stands, but by improving the amenity and restricting the supply of new floorspace, it may increase the value of property nearby, and possibly also have an influence on the aggregate value of property in the town. Similarly, the effect of density and land-use controls is to affect the value of the individual property, the spatial pattern of land values, and probably also the aggregate value of property, assuming that the controls have a net overall effect on business profitability and utility.

This is no place in which to undertake a detailed investigation into the justification for planning, but the reader will have noted that our pricing theory has been based on the assumption that tenants, investors and developers act solely on the basis of expected returns, costs and risks *faced by themselves*, whereas their actions must tend to impose other costs and bring other benefits to the rest of the community. In deciding on the optimum height for a building, a developer will not voluntarily take account of the losses suffered by neighbouring property as a result of reduced daylight, increased traffic congestion, or the blocking of a view. Thus, in a free market, the allocation of land to its various uses may not be optimal because such 'externalities' are excluded from the costs and returns on which land-use decisions are made.

Planning should create a more satisfactory blend of uses, both within the private sector and between private and public-sector uses. The provision of new roads, car parks and open space will tend to create a higher value for property nearby, and the amalgamation of factories into industrial estates conveniently close to good transport links and employees' housing can minimise the cost of services, time and pollution. Planning can act as a catalyst to speed up desirable land-use changes, or as a suppressant to slow down or stop undesirable trends. It should serve to increase the efficiency and profitability of business activity as well as to improve amenity, thereby resulting in an increase in aggregate property values.

However, a more obvious and immediate effect of planning controls is to cause a shift in value from one location to another, affecting both the value of individual property and the spatial distribution of value. This can be illustrated by examining the impact of land-use and density controls.

Impact of land-use control

One objective of land-use control is to contain development and limit urban sprawl. By its very nature, 'containment' implies restricting the supply of development land relative to demand, causing a rise in price. Scarcity value created by the planning system is particularly evident at the periphery of a town or city. Land with planning permission for development for housing or industrial purposes might have a value of £250 000 per hectare whereas similar land restricted to agricultural use might be valued at £5000 per hectare. Such a large discrepancy can be explained only by planning controls. In the absence of control, the market value of all such land with development potential might have tended towards, say £10 000 per hectare, or whatever would be sufficient to persuade farmers to sell after allowing for all taxes and costs. Thus the effect of the control is to cause a spatial shift in land value – higher value for some land and lower value for other.

Land-use control will also tend to increase the density to which land is developed for higher-order uses. Taking an example of office property in a city centre, if the area allocated for office use is restricted in conditions of rising occupation demand, then ultimately (when all gap sites have been developed and lower-order uses squeezed out), supply will be unable to respond to the rising demand without an increase in the density of development. The occupation demand/supply imbalance will result in a rise in the rental and capital value of existing office space to whatever level is necessary to cover the cost of redeveloping existing property to the density required to satisfy demand. If the supply of office space cannot expand by spatial changes in land use, it will tend to do so by greater intensity of development. The value of development sites will tend to rise to reflect the higher surplus available from development, and so within the restricted area, rental, capital and site values will tend to rise to levels higher than would have existed in the absence of control. On the other hand, property outside the restricted area, being relegated to a lower-order use, will tend to have a lower value and to be less intensively developed than would have been the case in the absence of control.

Impact of density control

Whereas the tendency of land-use control is to concentrate land value spatially, the tendency of density control is to spread value over a wider area. Strict density control will ultimately prevent supply being able to respond to a rise in occupation demand in that location, so rental values will tend to rise to a level higher than that which would have existed in the absence of control. Capital values may rise even more, because restriction on density reduces the risk of oversupply in that location and increases investors' growth expectations. The rise in rental values would tend to cause tenants to use space more intensively.

Despite the higher value of floorspace, site values in prime locations will tend to be lower than in the absence of density control (because of the reduced surplus available from development, see Figure 17.4) and with site values restricted relative to existing use values, redevelopment activity would be inhibited.

Again adopting city centre office property as an illustration, unsatisfied occupation demand for office space in the best locations would be diverted to close substitute locations just outside the prime area, causing rental, capital and site values there to rise. Lower-order uses such as housing would be squeezed out by redevelopment for office use. Paradoxically, in these locations development density might be higher than would have been the case in the absence of density control. Thus the tendency of density control is to cause an outward spatial dispersion of land value and high-order land uses.

Impact of density and land-use control combined

If density control is imposed in conjunction with land-use control the tendency will be to cause the rental and capital values of property to rise to a greater extent than with either density or land-use control in isolation. If there is a sufficient amount of underdeveloped property in the controlled area, supply will be able to respond to a rise in demand, and value will be little affected. However, if an area is more or less fully developed to its highest-order use then controls mean that the stock of such property is virtually fixed, and property values will vary only according to changing floorspace demand.

Occupation demand from firms unable to justify the high level of rents in the controlled area will be diverted to close substitute locations. Such locations would not necessarily be the closest physically, but locations which provide benefits closest to those of the restricted area, which may be another town or city. Strict controls on office development in the centre of Paris have had the effect of diverting demand to a specially planned office development area, La Défense, as well as to other suburban areas and satellite new towns around Paris.

Timing of value changes

An analysis of the timing of value changes is simplified by imagining the extreme case in which a total prohibition on new development is suddenly imposed in conditions under which gently rising demand is inducing a similar volume of new development. Again, we shall assume that the subject of our analysis is office property in a city centre.

When analysing the impact of planning controls, or indeed any other influence on property values, it is best to examine the letting sector first. So how would the sudden imposition of a total ban on development affect rental values? There is little in our pricing theory to suggest that a development ban would affect occupation demand or the supply of *existing* property for relet. Nor in the short run could the ban affect *new* supply because, with a development period of, say, two to three years, property already in the course of development would continue to be completed over the succeeding few years. Thus the development ban may affect rental values only when new supply started to fall after a time lag of about two years. After, say, three years, new supply would virtually cease, office stock would be fixed, and rental values would vary only according to changes in occupation demand and the supply of existing property for relet, both deriving principally from expectations about the profitability of tenants' business activities.

Thus there tends to be a significant time lag before the impact of office development controls is reflected in rental values. New supply would take longer to dry up if the controls merely involved a moratorium on the granting of new planning permissions, because permissions granted in the past could continue to be acted upon within the statutory period of five years. It is possible that some tenants would anticipate the future dearth of accommodation and seek more space before a shortage occurred. It is also probable that developers would postpone the marketing of their developments in order to gain from any rise in rental value over the development period. Thus to a certain extent occupation demand might rise and supply of new space to let might fall within the development period to shorten the time lag from that indicated.

The 'Brown Ban' on new office development which was introduced in 1964 and rigorously applied to the City of London up to 1968 had an effect on City office rents which seems to conform to our analysis. The effective development period for City offices appears to have been about four-five years, and evidence from Richard Ellis[1] shows City office rental growth outperforming office rental growth in other centres over the period 1968–72, that is a period lagged approximately four years from the period during which large development projects were prohibited. Although the effect of the development controls is difficult to quantify in isolation from other rental determinants, there is no doubt that their rigorous application in the latter 1960s was a major contributory factor in the office rental boom in central London from 1968–73. Conversely, the relaxation of such controls in 1970, and the ensuing development boom was clearly a major factor contributing to the dramatic decline in office rents in London which took place between 1974 and 1976.

The 'Brown Ban' also had the effect of stimulating office development outside the areas in which the office development permit (ODP) system was rigorously applied. Our theory would suggest that tenants who were unable to obtain accommodation in London at a rent which they could afford would direct their demand to favoured provincial locations. The consequent rise in rental values would enable profitable redevelopment to take place there, thus achieving one of the objectives of the ODP system, namely the deployment of office-related job opportunities away from London and South East England. The controls would have had the effect of forcing developers to turn their attention to provincial locations and, as we have already noted, to Europe and other countries overseas.

Investors' decisions to buy or sell property are largely determined by expectations for rental growth. Immediately after an announcement of strict development controls, investment demand would tend to rise in anticipation of higher growth and a reduced risk of oversupply. Yields would therefore tend to fall marginally and capital values rise before any change in rental growth became evident.

Although small yield changes resulting from the imposition of such controls might not be discernible in practice, it was interesting to note that property share prices rose sharply when the Labour-controlled GLC announced a new ban on office development in 1981. Because the stock market is much more sensitive than the property market, property company share prices often reflect short term changes in property-market sentiment which are not identifiable in the property market itself.

A freeze on new development approvals would also have an immediate impact on the development value of sites. The value of property with development potential but without planning permission would tend to fall to a level somewhat above existing-use value, reflecting the hope that the ban might be withdrawn at some future date. The value of sites with planning permission (assuming development was still allowed to go ahead) would tend to rise somewhat, reflecting the higher expected value of the project on completion.

There can be little doubt that relatively strict planning control, particularly with respect to office property in central locations, contributed to the post-war success of property investment in the UK until the late 1980s. By restricting supply in the face of generally rising demand, rental growth in excess of inflation was created and the risk of oversupply was reduced. Conversely, however, relaxation of controls throughout much of Britain in the 1980s released a development boom which was largely responsible for the decline in rental values in the early 1990s.

Influence of structure plans

The policies laid down by a planning authority in its structure plan will potentially have major implications for commercial property values and investment returns. The structure plan provides a framework for both private- and public-sector economic development, and may identify depressed areas in which economic development is to be encouraged and other areas in which further development will be restricted.

Structure plans frequently include policies restricting office development in cities in favour of housing or industrial development, or for such reasons as conservation or the limitation of traffic congestion. Planning authorities also commonly pursue policies of restricting development liable to prove harmful to town centres. In particular, the security and growth potential of an investment in traditional town-centre shopping and established shopping centres may be dependent on restricting the development of out-of-town shopping centres and regional centres.

- By containing development, land-use control tends to concentrate land value spatially, whereas density restriction tends to disperse land values. The combination of land-use and density controls tends to increase the rental and capital value of development property, and the imposition of controls and their relaxation has had a substantial effect on property values in Britain.

Rent control

As in the case of planning control, an analysis of the impact of rent control requires an investigation of all three sectors of the market – the investment and development sectors as well as the rental sector. Rent control could take a variety of forms, e.g., a rigid rent freeze, restriction on the amount of (or the increase in) rent, control of the rent payable by sitting tenants only, or new tenants as well. In each case, the effect on the market will depend on the precise legislative measures, and here it is possible only to outline certain general principles.

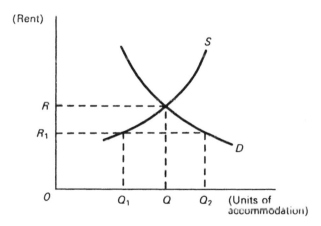

Figure 24.1   The impact of rent control on accommodation for rent

The objective of rent control is to restrict rental payments below a market level in order to relieve tenants of some of their rental burden. In an otherwise free market, this must have the effect of creating an imbalance between occupation demand and the supply of property to let. According to Figure 24.1, rental value as determined by a free market would be OR, but because rental payments are restricted to OR_1, OQ_2 units of accommodation will be demanded whereas the market will supply only OQ_1 units. Unless the public sector supplies the difference, some form of rationing will be required.

There are a variety of sound practical reasons for this demand/supply imbalance. Occupation demand will tend to be higher than in the absence of controls because tenants will seek more space due to its lower cost. The supply of accommodation to let will tend to be lower, for the following reasons:

(a) Fewer tenants will voluntarily vacate property at breaks in, or at the end of, their leases, and as rent-control legislation normally provides tenants with security of tenure, many tenants will stay on indefinitely.
   With rent being restricted below rental value, tenants benefit from an effective profit rent which they will be reluctant to surrender.
(b) Landlords will be reluctant to relet any accommodation which becomes vacant – they will tend to sell for owner occupation or possibly retain the property unlet
(c) Under long term rent control little or no new development will take place for letting purposes.

Thus rent control will tend to affect all three elements of supply – the supply of existing rented property for relet, the supply of existing property through transfers into (or out of) owner-occupation, and the supply of newly developed property. In order to explain (b) and (c), the impact of rent control on the actions of investors and developers will be investigated.

Whatever the form that rent control takes, it must tend to lower the value of the investor's interest, if only because his income is restricted. But normally rent control restricts a landlord's ability to adjust rents in line with market trends, and may take the form of a rent freeze. In the extreme case where a rigid rent freeze is imposed for a long and indefinite period, the effect of the legislation would be to convert an equity property investment into a fixed-income one. If prior to the imposition of such a freeze the yield on an investment was 6%, then immediately afterwards it would have to rise to the level appropriate to a fixed-income investment, say, 12%. This implies a 50% fall in market value because, with income fixed, price must vary in inverse proportion to the change in yield.

Even if rent controls allow some upward adjustment in times of inflation, the value of let property is liable to fall below the value of similar property subject to vacant possession. Consequently, if a property becomes vacant the landlord is unlikely to relet, but instead will sell for owner occupation. For similar reasons, owners will sell newly developed property at completion, and little or no new development will be initiated for letting purposes. After letting, the value of a new development subject to rigid long term controls would tend to fall below the cost of development.

All three elements of supply will tend to decline to a greater or lesser extent, depending on the amount by which rents are restricted and the expected duration of the controls. If the controls are expected to operate only briefly, then the actions of investors and developers may be little affected, although the risk of a continuation or reimposition would have some restricting effect on supply. The business-rents freeze introduced by the Conservative government under Edward Heath in 1972 was stated to be temporary, partly in order to avoid the problems of reduced supply, but to the surprise of few people the controls were extended until abolished by the subsequent Labour administration in 1975.

The market's response to the introduction of rent controls is, therefore, to reduce supply. So unless the public sector intervenes to provide the accommodation shortfall, firms which are unable to purchase property as owner-occupiers will be unable to satisfy their space needs. This frustrated demand is then diverted to the closest alternative accommodation not subject to rent control, leading to a rise in its rental value and illustrating the paradox that one effect of rent control is to cause rental values and the cost of accommodation to rise.

In the days when unfurnished housing was subject to control, the supply of such property fell, and demand was diverted to the furnished sector, causing rents to rise and forcing the government to extend control to furnished housing. Even during the relatively brief business rent freeze in the 1970s, a reduction in supply was reputed to have contributed towards a rise in rental values. Under the legislation in force at that time, property newly developed or previously unlet could be let at its rental value. It seems that the rent freeze discouraged tenants from vacating existing property, and occupation demand focused on the relatively small supply of property being let for the first time, causing rental values to rise to a level higher than would otherwise have been reached.

The problem of rising rents in times of rent control can be exacerbated by the tendency of some owners to retain property unlet. This phenomenon has been observed in both housing and commercial property. During the 1972–5 business rent freeze a number of newly developed office buildings owned by Oldham Estates remained unlet, notably the renowned multistorey block in the West End of London called Centre Point. Oldham Estates was a property company led by Harry Hyams, branded by the press as the arch villain amongst property developers. Although no financial benefit could accrue from keeping a property unlet in the long run, nonetheless it would maximise short term capital gain in times of a rent freeze and sharply rising rental values.

A further consequence of rigid long term rent control is a decline in the quality of the stock of property which is subject to control. Landlords tend to neglect their properties, repairs and necessary improvements are left undone, leading ultimately to dereliction, as in the case of much tenement housing in the UK this century.

Traditionally, the case for rent controls on business property is based on the argument that, because rising rents impose increased costs on firms, this leads to higher prices for goods and services. This argument is economically flimsy, but (at least in the short run) there may be a political or equitable case for control. The rent freeze introduced in 1972 was part of a package of measures designed to curb inflation, and as legislation at the time prevented firms from raising prices unless justified by increased costs, then in that context, frozen rents may have helped to restrict prices. Moreover with wages, dividends and profits subject to control in 1972, it seemed inequitable not to control rents also.

Even if some short term benefits may result from rent control, inefficiencies in the use of property will inevitably result. The function of the price mechanism in allocating land and property is unable to operate. Firms which can justify a prime location are prevented from gaining occupation there by the presence of other firms whose occupation is being subsidised by their landlords. Indeed, one effect of rent control is to reallocate income and wealth from landlords to tenants without consideration of their needs. As many tenants are wealthy companies and many landlords are institutions effectively owned by the working man as policyholder or pensioner, this seems inequitable. Additionally, in the long run (unless the public sector intervenes), space will be available only for firms which can afford to purchase as owner occupiers, a situation unlikely to promote economic efficiency.

- The imposition of rent control reduces the value of controlled property and results in a fall in market supply. Unless the shortfall is fully met by the public sector, frustrated demand is diverted to alternative uncontrolled property forcing up rents and prices.

Land taxation

The impact of taxation on the property market is all pervasive. The occupation, ownership and development of property in the UK gives rise to a range of taxes, including business rates, CGT, corporation tax and stamp duty. Occupiers, investors and developers are ultimately concerned with net-of-tax returns, and the incidence of taxation must tend to affect all land use and property values through the price mechanism. Here we shall investigate the impact of a tax which is specific to business property – the uniform business rate (UBR), which was introduced in England and Wales in 1990 to replace the local rates, levied by local authorities.

In examining the impact of land taxation, it should not be forgotten that the market will be influenced by the expenditure of tax revenues as well as by the raising of taxes. However, because the imposition of a tax on property does not necessarily give rise to any consequential benefit from increased expenditure, the impact of taxation is considered in isolation.

Uniform business rate

The UBR is an annual tax levied on the occupier of business property in England and Wales, the amount payable being determined by the rateable value of the property and the 'multiplier' set by the government. The rateable value represents the rental value of the property at a specific date (initially 1 April 1988), on the assumption of an FRI lease with regular rent review. Unlike the rating system previously in force whereby the tax rate was set by the local authority and varied from one authority to another, a uniform 'multiplier' is set for the whole of England (initially 34.8p per £ of rateable value), with a somewhat higher figure for Wales.

From the point of view of the occupier, rates are part of the total cost of occupation along with rent and service charges. Thus changes in the amount of the tax must tend to affect occupation demand and, therefore, rental and capital values. However, a more detailed insight into the tax's impact on rental values may be gained from the surplus model, particularly in the case of prime shop property. As part of the unavoidable cost of his business, a prospective tenant may deduct the anticipated tax along with other costs from his expected sales revenue in order to determine the surplus available to pay in rent. That does not mean that any rise in the rates would cause an equal fall in rental value, because some of the increased burden may be borne by the tenant in reduced profit, or shifted forward to consumers in increased prices for goods, or shifted backwards in reduced wages or other savings. The ability to shift the burden forward in higher prices will depend primarily on the price elasticity of demand for the goods, which will vary from product to product, place to place and from time to time; for example, it will be easier to increase prices in times of boom than in recession.

It is unlikely that in the short term the retailer will be able to shift all of the burden of an unexpected increase in the rates, and as rent is fixed within the rent review period, the retailer may bear the brunt in the short term. However, the reduced profitability of business will tend to be reflected in a fall in rental value so that after the subsequent rent review, the tenant will have shifted the remaining burden on to the landlord through a reduction in rent (in real terms).

Insofar as the incidence of rates is reflected in rental value, it might seem that in the medium run (after rent review) the landlord will bear the burden of the tax through a reduction in both rental income and capital value. In the case of property with an inelastic supply, such as prime High Street shops this may well be so. Ultimately, prime shop values reflect the profitability of retailing. However, in the case of property with an elastic supply such as industrial property, the ultimate burden is likely to be borne by consumers. This is because any reduction in property values relative to development costs will tend to cause a reduction in the supply of new property. Therefore in the long run, the reduction in supply may equate with the reduced tenant demand, leaving rental values little affected. Ultimately the value of industrial property is likely to reflect development cost, not the profitability of tenants' businesses. Insofar as landlords of industrial property may have faced a rent reduction in the short/medium term, they will be able to shift the burden back again to tenants who, in turn, will shift it on to consumers in increased prices.

The replacement of local rates by the UBR together with the first revaluation for rating purposes since 1973 caused a substantial redistribution of the tax burden when introduced in 1990. In view of the relatively high growth of property values in London and South East England over the period 1973–88, and of retail property in particular, the rates burden shifted markedly from industrial property in the Midlands and the North of England to retail property in the South East. In fact, some prime shops in central London faced rates increases of 400%, although the worst effects of this were mitigated by phasing the rise over five years. In view of the fact that rates are a higher percentage of business costs for retailers than for other businesses, the burden of the UBR in London and South East England seems likely to have had a significant effect on shop rents.

● The impact of a change in the rates on business property is likely to vary according to the property type, location and time dimension. In the short run, particularly in recessionary conditions, the effect of an unexpected rise in the rates may be to cause some reduction in rental value, and in the case of prime High Street shops this reduction could remain. However, in the case of industrial or other property with an elastic supply, value is unlikely to be affected in the long run.

VII A Post-War History of the Property Market

25 The Early Post-War Boom and its Aftermath

Traditional land ownership in the UK

Prior to the Second World War, much urban as well as rural property was owned by a relatively small number of aristocratic families who in most cases had owned the land for centuries. Indeed, despite the impact that the payment of death duties has had in splitting up the old estates, the aristocracy nowadays still hold large amounts of both urban and rural property, with four large estates – Grosvenor, Howard de Walden, Cadogan and Portman – owning some of the most valuable property in central London. Large tracts of urban and rural property are also owned by the Crown and by institutions such as the Oxford and Cambridge colleges, trade guilds and the churches. The Church of England is one of the largest landowners in the UK, with property comprising over half of its investment portfolio.

In comparison with the present day, public authorities held an insignificant proportion of urban property before the Second World War, although since the mid-nineteenth century local authorities have had the power to acquire land for slum clearance, road and other improvement schemes, and in the interwar period the programme for improving the housing stock brought much housing into public ownership. A sharp increase in public ownership of land took place in the early post-war period following the Town and County Planning Act 1947, which granted local planning authorities powers of compulsory purchase, and by the nationalisation of major industries and public utilities. In particular, the nationalisation of the railways in 1947 brought into public ownership some of the most valuable urban land in the country.

Relatively few listed property companies were in existence in the interwar period, and they owned little commercial and industrial property. They acted mainly as corporate landlords of housing, collecting rent which was then redistributed as dividends to shareholders.

Prior to the Second World War, property investment by insurance companies was confined largely to mortgages and ground rents, direct investment being mainly restricted to the ownership of property occupied in whole or part by the company itself. However, with the mildly inflationary trends of the latter 1930s, a small number of insurance companies, including Legal and General, became aware of the long-term advantages of property, and began cautiously to increase their equity involvement through direct purchases of freeholds, as well as by investment in property shares. However, the management problems and risk in times of economic slump (as evidenced by the huge rent voids suffered by American insurance companies holding property

339

after the 1929 Wall Street crash) deterred UK insurance companies from becoming more actively involved in direct property investment.

Thus, partly due to a lack of investment interest and partly because industrialists were generally unenthusiastic about leasehold tenure, most commercial and industrial property was owner occupied in the pre-war period and the property market was not considered as a significant part of the investment market.

Economic basis for the post-war boom

The Second World War introduced economic, political and social changes which collectively brought about a radical alteration to the property market. In order to examine the causes of the first post-war property boom, it seems appropriate to base the study on the London office market, because it was central London offices which formed the principal subject of the initial post-war boom, and which formed the most popular subject for subsequent institutional property investment. It has been estimated that up to the mid-1960s about 80% of new post-war office building was in the London region,[1] approximately half being developed by owner occupiers and half by development companies.

Little office development, either for owner occupation or for investment purposes, took place in the interwar period, largely due to a substantial Victorian legacy of office property, coupled with the economic depression which caused long rent voids and falls in rental value in the period 1925–34. On the other hand, massive destruction of property took place during the war: 9.5 million ft^2 of office space in central London, and about one third of the City was destroyed by bombing.[2]

In contrast to this reduction in office stock, occupation demand increased dramatically after the war. A rise in real incomes led to rising demand for goods and services, particularly for commercial and financial services, and demand for office space also rose as a result of the post-war trend in the UK away from industrial activity in favour of office-based service activity. London was particularly affected as the country's capital and as the centre for the expanding financial services and markets. Trends towards amalgamation by UK firms led to a need for a headquarters in London, and there was a substantial influx of US firms who tended to seek accommodation in the capital. Equally significant was the rise in occupation demand from the public sector deriving from the Labour government's expansion of the social services.

The inevitable effect of this increased demand and reduced stock of offices was to cause rental and capital values to escalate. Offices which could not be let in 1939 readily found a tenant, and bombed sites in prime locations were eagerly bought up by speculators and developers during and immediately after the war. However, several factors prevented wholesale redevelopment immediately after the war. First, the construction industry could not cope with the demand – there was inadequate plant, skilled labour and building materials, and many firms had gone out of business during the war. A system of building licensing was therefore imposed, which gave priority to repair work, work in aid of exporting industry, and work in providing accommodation for public authorities. In order to obtain permission to develop, developers therefore sought to prelet property to such authorities, and many developments were built and leased to government departments on this basis.

Second, in order to encourage reinvestment by industries vital to the economy, the Labour government maintained a policy of artificially cheap money and capital rationing which militated against property development. Developers who were unable to raise capital by bank borrowing or other means were forced into partnership arrangements with insurance companies, or the major building contractors who were not subject to such restriction. Third, the Town & Country Planning Act 1947 imposed a 100% tax on the development value of land, thereby drastically reducing the supply of land, and the incentive for developers.

Due to these three main areas of restriction, redevelopment was slow to respond to the rapidly rising demand, and it was not until 1954 that the intense phase of redevelopment started. This resulted from the abolition of the development charge under the Town & Country Planning Act 1953 by the Conservative government, and the ending of the system of building licences in November 1954. The effect of these measures was dramatically to increase the potential for (and profitability of) development, causing a huge increase in site values, and to set a scenario for 10 years of intense redevelopment activity.

The development boom 1954–64

In comparison with current circumstances, the development operation in the early post-war period was relatively simple, secure and profitable. Not only were bomb sites readily available, but much Victorian housing had deteriorated through neglect during the war (a problem made worse by rent control) and could be acquired cheaply for office development. High occupation demand for offices meant low risk of rent voids at completion, and developers were little exposed to rising construction cost as contractors normally tendered on a fixed-price basis. Short-term finance for site purchase and construction was normally available from clearing banks, and long-term fixed-interest mortgage finance from insurance companies, both at relatively low interest rates. The retention of completed developments was mainly self-financing (see Example 18.1).

In the early post-war years, the developer could contract out of most of the disadvantages of inflation, while gaining all the benefits. By means of fixed price contracts, the main risk of rising construction costs was passed to the builder; by raising fixed-interest mortgages, the risk of rising interest rates was passed to the financier. On the other hand, all the gains from rising rental and capital values in this period of inflation and economic growth went to the developer. Risk was low and returns were high, particularly as development profit was untaxed, provided the completed property was retained as an investment (see Chapter 20).

The developer's business was also relatively simple. He had no need to own large amounts of capital, nor did he require large numbers of staff. In fact, some of the most successful developers employed only a small office and a secretary. This ease of entry eventually resulted in stiffening competition for the available prime sites, forcing many established developers to operate in partnership with landowners such as the private estates, the Church Commissioners and local authorities.

In the early 1960s, developers increasingly diversified out of London offices into provincial shops and town-centre redevelopment. A trend towards decentralisation due to the high rents payable in central London was fostered by the LOB making office development viable in certain suburban locations, particularly Croydon. Increased competition in the UK encouraged other developers to diversify overseas, particularly Canada, the USA, South Africa and Australia.

Conditions in the early 1960s gradually moved adversely for the UK developer. Competition increased, successive credit squeezes made short-term financing difficult, and insurance companies invariably insisted on an equity share. As the stock of office space in London increased, the letting of new developments became more difficult, and the 1962–3 recession severely affected demand.

The office development boom in London was eventually brought to an end in November 1964 by the new Labour government under Harold Wilson. By effectively banning further office development within the greater London area, the 'Brown Ban' reduced the risk of rent voids on developments subsequently completed, and caused rental values to spiral again in the latter 1960s, thereby sowing the seeds of the next major property boom in the 1970s.

Trends in the late 1960s

Under the Control of Office and Industrial Development Act 1965, the office development ban in London was subsequently extended to apply (less rigidly) to industrial property and the rest of South East England. It was a major aspect of the government's regional policies, and was intended to counter the population and economic drift to the south and east in favour of the north and west of Britain. In view of the overwhelming dominance (in terms of value) of London and South East England in the UK property market, the development controls had a significant effect in restricting the supply of investments, despite the fact that new investments were being created by sale and lease-back deals and the trend away from owner occupation towards tenancy.

Elsewhere in the country development opportunities were being created. Development area grants, the creation and growth of new towns, the development of expanding towns and the long-term trend away from heavy to light industry with its less critical locational needs, provided scope for the development of industrial estates. The trend from manufacturing activity towards wholesaling and importing, together with the continuing development of the motorway system which required firms to reorganise their distribution facilities previously geared to the railway network, all induced a major expansion in warehouse development. The increased mobility of shoppers and the revolution in retail trading likewise created opportunities for retail development, notably shopping centres, often redeveloped in partnership with local authorities.

Of particular significance in the late 1960s was the upsurge in direct property investment by the non-bank financial institutions and a relative decline in the influence of property companies. Property companies were hampered by the rising cost of debt and the scarcity of development opportunities in London and the South East. However, the institutions switched from their mainly passive role as providers of development finance to become major direct investors in property, with annual net acquisitions almost quadrupling in the latter half of the 1960s.

This trend by the financial institutions can be explained first by the declining opportunities for financing development due to the introduction of development controls in 1964, the recession of 1965–7 and the Land Commission Act 1967; second, by the trend towards full repairing and insuring leases with more frequent rent review, and third by a growing appreciation of the innate qualities of property as an investment, and its suitability to the financial institutions in times of accelerating inflation and relative economic decline.

The strategic diversification into property derived largely from the need of the institutions to back their 'with-profits' and pension liabilities with equity-type investments, coupled with a wish to diversify from the dominance of ordinary shares as virtually their only other equity investment asset. The need for equity investments would be confirmed by the sharp acceleration of inflation in 1968, but the rising power of the trade unions and the inability of the government to control wages and industrial militancy in the late 1960s would have alerted investors to the vulnerability of shares. The gradual erosion of shareholder power to worker power was seen as a long term threat to industrial health and equity earnings, and the devaluation of sterling in 1967 induced a realisation of the long term relative decline in UK industry and its vulnerability to foreign competition. The 'bear' market of 1968–71, in which share values fell by over 40% while prime property values seem to have faltered only briefly, convinced many investors that property was not only a more secure investment, but provided a superior long-term inflation hedge.

A further factor underlying the rising demand for property investments in the late 1960s was the rapid growth in the flow of funds into life assurance companies and pension funds, together with the latters' tax exempt status which, since the introduction of corporation tax in 1965, made direct investment in property more attractive than investment in the shares of property companies. The introduction of property unit trusts facilitated investment in commercial property for the smaller pension funds, and the expansion of property bonds satisfied the private investor's demand for a stake in commercial property.

26   The 1970s Cycle

Market conditions 1970–3

The decade dawned with property values apparently on a mild decline from their high market level of summer 1969, due to a tightening of the credit squeeze introduced by the Labour government in 1968. Commentators at the time noted the increasing sensitivity of the property market to changes in the stock market, this trend being attributed to the rising influence of institutional investors who were regarding property as an alternative to stock-market investments.

In June 1970, the Conservative party under Edward Heath came into power on the election pledge to 'cut prices at a stroke'. The new government adopted a determined stance against trade union wage demands and maintained tight monetary and fiscal policies in an attempt to curb inflation. Consequently, the gloomy economic conditions continued into 1971, unemployment rose to its then highest level since the 1930s, and a series of major bankruptcies culminated with the collapse of Rolls Royce. Yet despite these conditions, wages and inflation continued to rise. It seemed that the ability of the trade unions to win substantial wage awards was defeating the government's attempts to curb inflation.

Although an improving trend in inflation in the second quarter of 1971 probably justified some relaxation of the strict deflationary policies, it was probably a feeling that the problem of inflation could not be defeated by such means without unemployment rising to politically unacceptable levels that persuaded the government to reverse its policies. From an attempt to curb inflation by restrictive monetary and fiscal measures, the government switched to a policy of all-out expansion in an attempt to combat inflation and the chronic balance of payments problem by increased production. The measures were initially bound to be inflationary, and the Conservatives had renounced wage controls, but they hoped that a voluntary agreement with the CBI (employers' organisation) would curb prices until production rose to a sufficient level to meet the rising demand. It was argued that rising production would lead to an expansion of exports and a reduction in imports, thereby curing the balance of payments problem. Industry was therefore encouraged to reinvest and expand in the belief that long-term economic growth could be sustained without recourse to deflationary measures, and the availability of cheap credit in a climate of domestic expansion was the method by which this would be achieved.

This, then, was the scenario for the commencement of the property boom whose starting date can best be identified as early in the second quarter of 1971, when yields on prime commercial property started to fall, probably triggered off by the sharp rise in share values earlier in the year, the mildly reflationary budget, the fall in bank rate on 1 April and the relaxation of bank-lending ceilings.

The budget of March 1971 was followed by further expansionary measures in July and November, but even more significant were the implications of the Competition and Credit Control (CCC) agreement, which was introduced in September 1971 in order to eradicate the anomalies and problems resulting from existing methods of monetary control, and to foster competition between banking institutions. Bank rate was reduced to 5% and restrictions on bank lending were abolished. The inevitable effect was to cause bank lending and money supply to accelerate sharply from the fourth quarter of 1971, further boosted by inflows of foreign capital to London as the trend in inflation and the balance of payments moved favourably.

The expansionary measures created great activity and confidence in the stock market, the property market and in the commercial sector of the economy. The boom in financial activity boosted demand for City offices, but the measures also caused rising shop and office rentals throughout the country leading to an upsurge in investment demand. The certainty of EEC membership further inflated demand for property and provided optimism for long-term economic recovery.

The economy was again boosted in 1972 by increased public expenditure and income-tax allowances, and although share prices peaked in May, the property market experienced boom conditions with increases in values which 'far exceeded any year within living memory'. Escalating rental values and a sharp fall in yields, particularly in the first six months of the year (see Figure 12.2), caused a rise in capital values in 1972 averaging about 60%, although the value of some secondary property doubled.

Both the economy and the property market continued to boom in 1973. Surging office rents in London were partly attributed to the 'Brown Ban' and the rent freeze and, in provincial locations, to demand from central and local government. But in 1973 the boom was at last felt in the industrial sector of the economy, causing the largest annual increase in industrial property rents since the war, amounting to as much as 100% in some locations in South East England. This growth induced renewed development activity but, as in the commercial sector, delays in obtaining development approval, rising building costs and the scarcity of building materials all complicated the development process. The inadequate supply of prime investments prompted a number of successful institutional bids for property companies and increased the activity of UK companies and institutions abroad, particularly the EC. Agents noted the reluctance of institutions to buy commercial property north of Birmingham.

Analysis of property market trends 1971–3

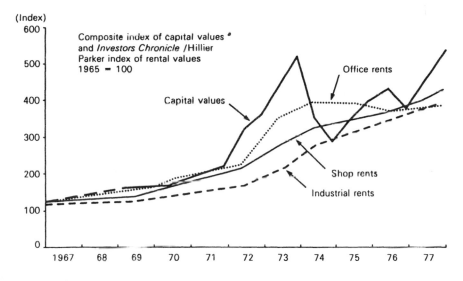

(a) The index of capital values was constructed from a variety of sources to indicate general trends in the vacant possession value of property. In compiling the index, allowance was made for diversification in location and property type (shops, offices and industrial). The indices estimate values twice annually at May and November, the latter date coinciding closely with crucial turnround dates at end 1971, 1973, 1974 and 1976

Figure 26.1   Trends in commercial property values

Despite office-development controls and the rise in property investment by insurance companies and pension funds, Figure 26.1 indicates an average increase in commercial property values of only 11% per annum over the five-year period to May 1970. Yet over the next three and a half years to November 1973 values multiplied three times. What, then, were the forces that caused this formidable explosion in values? In analysing the investment sector of the market we must examine the activities of the two main categories of investors – the financial institutions and the property companies.

Table 26.1 (line 6) shows that whereas financial institutions substantially increased their acquisition of existing property in 1968 and 1969, this fell in 1970, 1971 and 1972. On the other hand, after deducting property companies' development expenditure (line 2) from their estimated total annual property expenditure (line 1), their flow of funds into existing property is seen to increase dramatically in 1971, 1972 and 1973. Thus it was principally the property companies which were responsible for the boom in property investment.

The lack of fixed-interest mortgage finance since the early 1960s had imposed a check on the growth of property companies, particularly unlisted companies without the alternative source of a stock-market issue. However, as a result of the innate suitability of property as collateral to a lender, banks were keen to lend for property development or investment. A massive expansion in bank lending, particularly from banks outside the clearing-bank sector, provided the means by which property companies could retain the full equity in their activities. In the context of economic growth and relaxed office-development controls, they could hope to emulate the achievements of their predecessors in the early post-war period.

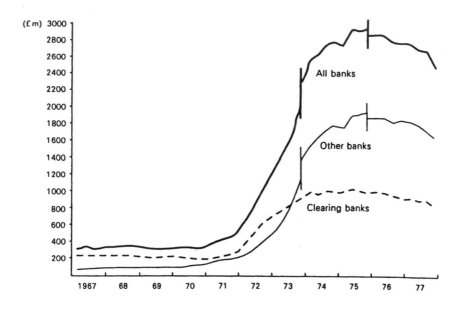

Lending by six finance houses reclassified as banks included from November 1973. One institution gave up banking status, and is excluded from November 1975.

Source: Financial Statistics.

Figure 26.2   Bank advances to property companies (amounts outstanding)

Figure 26.2 illustrates that, after remaining stable from 1967–70, bank advances to property companies increased dramatically in 1971–3. As by far the largest source of new capital to the property investment market, this explosion in bank lending was outstandingly the main destabilising influence on the property market over this period.

Although the London and Scottish clearing banks multiplied their lending to property companies in Great Britain by five times between November 1970 and November 1974, over the same period lending to property companies by 'other banks' multiplied by over 11 times. Merchant banks and finance houses appear to have been proportionally the most heavily committed to property lending, although US and other overseas banks were also significantly involved.

Excluded from Figure 26.2 is lending by other institutions such as finance houses without full banking status which were also heavily involved in property lending. One feature of 'secondary' or 'fringe' banks (with or without banking status) was that deposits from the public accounted for a relatively small proportion of total deposits, the bulk being obtained through the London money markets. One unforeseen result of the introduction of CCC was a major expansion of these markets which, by enlarging the availability of deposits, enabled these banks to expand their lending and in many cases achieve phenomenal growth over the succeeding two years. Thus the expansion of property lending derived from CCC, excessive monetary expansion and also the relatively low borrowing demand from industry, which resulted in the clearing banks holding surplus funds which they on-lent through the money markets.

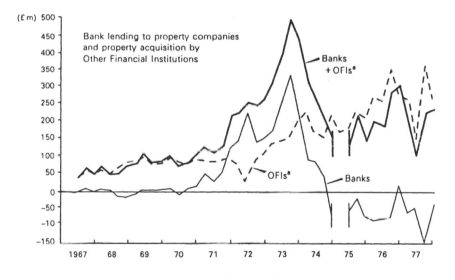

(a) The statistical category Other Financial Institutions (OFIs) excludes recognised banks. Over the period 1970–7, property acquisition by insurance companies and pension funds amounted to over 94% of the property acquisition of OFIs.

Source: *Financial Statistics.*

Figure 26.3   Quarterly flow of funds into property

Table 26.1 Estimated flow of funds into property (£m)[1]

	1967	1968	1969	1970	1971	1972	1973	1974	1975	1976	1977
Property companies											
Acquisition of property	130	149	393	316	729	1146	1904	3	−102	−247	−285(1)[2]
Less new building and works	103	97	111	126	143	168	197	313	213	235	205(2)[3]
Acquisition of existing property	27	52	282	190	586	978	1707	−310	−315	−482	−490(3)[4]
Financial institutions											
Acquisition of property (OFIs)[5]	199	269	359	346	333	323	664	788	820	1194	1065(4)[6]
Less new building and works (financial companies and institutions)	88	102	109	125	153	161	281	401	442	519	511(5)[7]
Acquisition of existing property	111	167	250	221	180	162	383	387	378	675	554(6)[8]

1. Although it is considered that this table gives a reasonable indication of the direction and timing of trends, the figures should be considered as indicative rather than precise.
2. Author's research.
3. CSO.
4. = (1)–(2).
5. Other financial institutions.
6. Financial Statistics.
7. National Income and Expenditure 'Blue Book'.
8. = (4)–(5).

The speculative nature of the boom

The significance of bank lending in the total flow of funds into property over this period, and the high proportion of this money (almost three quarters) that was lent to small and unlisted companies, confirms that a large proportion of purchases were essentially speculative. Even in late 1971 to early 1972 when bank rate was 5%, any prime commercial property purchased purely with bank finance would necessarily result in a cash flow deficit, thus tending to impose a limit on new borrowing. However, as the availability of finance increased, some bankers became increasingly willing to lend on a 'roll-up' basis, or if a property company found itself with a cash flow problem it had little difficulty in raising further finance to pay interest on previous debt. So long as capital values were expected to increase at a rate substantially higher than the rate of interest, rising interest rates were little deterrent to further borrowing. After the dramatic rises in minimum lending rate (MLR) in 1973, some borrowers were paying over 20% for their debt.

Without the discipline of having to maintain a cash-flow surplus, the only limit on property companies' bank borrowing was the amount of collateral security that they could offer. The boom was therefore self-feeding in the respect that rising property values enabled companies to borrow more finance, which when used to purchase more property caused further value increases. The boom was also self-feeding in the 'bandwagon' sense that the fortunes being made attracted more and more speculators into the market, many of whom had little or no previous experience or knowledge of property.

It has frequently been said that the property boom was based on the view that property was the ultimate inflation hedge, due to its almost flawless record of security and growth in the post-war period. Certainly that view seems to have been held by the bankers lending on property. With funds freely available from the money market and profit margins high, banks competed to expand their property lending, offering in many cases up to 100% of cost. Some secondary banks, attracted by the profits made by their clients, increasingly sought to share in the equity of development, or built up substantial portfolios of property investments themselves.

It is interesting to note from Table 26.1 that for property companies – the traditional developers – expenditure on development became a relatively small proportion of total annual expenditure during the boom years, whereas the difficulty in acquiring standing-property investments appears to have spurred the financial institutions into a substantial increase in development expenditure.

The financial crisis 1973–4

The Conservative government's economic strategy to promote a revitalisation of the industrial base of the economy soon started to go wrong. Money supply expanded dramatically and, despite a creditable export performance, reflation caused imports of foreign manufactures to escalate and the balance of payments to deteriorate from the summer of 1971 onwards. This trend precipitated sterling crises and spectacular increases in MLR in the latter halves of 1972 and 1973. By mid-1973, the economy was grossly overheated and, despite prices and incomes controls imposed in the autumn of 1972, inflation again rose alarmingly.

It was against this economic background as well as growing industrial unrest that quadrupling crude-oil prices finally forced the government to deflate in November 1973. Even apart from the oil crisis, the government's economic strategy had failed. Industry had not undergone fundamental reconstruction and had not made use of the available finance to the extent expected. Instead, the alarming propensity to import in the context of rising consumer expenditure had exposed the long-term decline of British industry, and temporary prosperity had increased rather than subdued the militancy of the trade unions. The finance which was supposed to provide for industrial regeneration had been seen to go into the pockets of a few property speculators, invoking the wrath of the press, politicians and public.

The property industry became subject to increasingly adverse publicity which led to demands for swingeing new taxation of property ownership and development. The disruption of communities by planners and developers, and the ugliness of many modern buildings antagonised the public. Centre Point and other prominent empty office blocks were cited as examples of the property industry's irresponsible attitude. Adverse publicity subjected both speculators and responsible investors to widespread political attack, exemplified by Denis Healey's famous promise to 'squeeze the property developers until the pips squeak'.

The calls for taxation resulted in development gains tax (DGT) being introduced by the Conservative government, the imposition of rates charges on unoccupied property, and in 1974 the Labour government proposed and subsequently introduced development land tax (DLT) and the Community Land Act which, it was intended, would ultimately lead to the complete nationalisation of development land.

It seems strange, with the benefit of hindsight, that the ominous trends in the economy even before 1973 were ignored or misinterpreted by the government, the financial community and the property market. Yet the dominant events which precipitated the crisis – the quadrupling of oil prices following from the Arab-Israeli conflict of Yom Kippur 1973 and the collapse of London & County Securities – could hardly have been foreseen, nor the speed and severity of the crisis which followed these events.

Despite the overheated state of the economy little deflationary action was taken until the oil crisis developed. Following cuts in Arab oil production, industrial action by the electricity power workers and an overtime ban by coal miners, the government on 13 November declared a state of emergency, raised MLR to 13% and took steps to control money supply. This was followed on 17 December by the introduction of hire-purchase controls, restrictions on personal loans, public-expenditure cuts, a 10% surtax charge and DGT.

This, then, was the context in which the 'secondary banking' crisis erupted. On 30 November, London & County Securities (a fringe bank known to be heavily involved in property) announced a liquidity problem. This problem resulted from the inability of the bank to renew money-market deposits after the resignation of one of its directors, a respected City banker. Whereas it is now clear that the problems of London & County Securities derived from a unique blend of irresponsible and fraudulent management, a number of major depositors in the money markets — aware of the potential problems facing property companies — started to withdraw deposits with other secondary banks similarly exposed to property.

The inadequate liquidity and imprudent lending policies of many secondary banks had rendered them particularly vulnerable, and a crisis of confidence grew into a full-scale 'run' on the secondary banks. After liquidity problems were announced by a series of other banks, the Bank of England announced a support operation to prop up the secondary banks in order to avoid the crisis of confidence spreading into the primary banking system, and perhaps causing a 'domino' series of failures throughout the UK financial system. Deposits withdrawn from secondary banks had largely been redeposited with the clearing banks, so essentially this 'lifeboat' operation consisted of an agreement by the London and Scottish clearing banks to recycle these deposits back into banks faced with a liquidity problem. A total of 26 companies eventually received support.

The property market crash

Despite the rent freeze introduced in 1972, the enormous rise in MLR in July 1973, and various calls by the Bank of England to restrict property lending, it was not until December 1973 that the property market faced its crisis. Following the announcement of the 17 December measures, investment demand disappeared 'virtually overnight'. These measures signalled an end to the consumer boom which had provided the fundamental support of rising rental values. Without the expectation of further capital gain, borrowing at the current level of interest rates could no longer be justified.

Faced with rising interest payments on their bank debt and with rental income frozen, liquidation of assets was essential for highly geared property companies. Not only were they unable to borrow further, but they were faced with the repayment of short-term debt to the imperilled secondary banks. Even companies without an immediate cash flow problem became exposed to falling values, the introduction of DGT and the threat of further taxation on the return of a Labour government. Thus from a situation of high investment demand and great scarcity, conditions in the property market were reversed as companies were forced to liquidate to remain solvent.

As 1974 progressed and economic conditions deteriorated, more and more property was put on the market by the property companies. But the main potential purchasers, the institutions, appeared reluctant to buy. With high interest rates obtainable on the short-term money markets, expectations of further falls in the value of property investments and the deteriorating economic climate, there was little incentive for the financial institutions to buy property. Substantial funds were committed to development schemes already under way, and some institutions were involved in providing assistance to property companies in which they had a significant or dominant share holding. The indefinite continuation of the rent freeze made the purchase of investments unattractive, and their valuation virtually impossible.

Whilst reversionary and secondary property became virtually unsaleable on the general investment market, many deals were made by special purchasers (such as occupying tenants buying their landlord's interest, or mortgagees taking the opportunity to extinguish their highly unprofitable fixed-interest investments).

Despite the deteriorating economic climate, the *rental* value of commercial and industrial property generally held up well – that is, with the notable exception of City of London offices, where the problem of the financial community caused a reduction in occupation demand to coincide with a sharp rise in completions of new property. Provincial office rents were partly protected by the expansion in space needs arising from local authority reorganisation.

Virtually no new commercial development schemes were initiated after December 1973 due to the fall in the value of property, building costs rising at 25–30% per annum, high interest rates, and the liquidity problems of many development companies. Even at a nil site cost, most development would have been unprofitable.

Although a large number of smaller property companies went into liquidation only three listed property companies failed. Excessive financial gearing was the basic problem, coupled with an overdependence on short-term borrowing. A few companies had embarked on excessively ambitious development programmes, which often proved to be highly unprofitable due to escalating construction costs and an inability to let at completion, as well as through rising interest rates and the fall in values. Amalgamated Investment & Property eventually failed in 1976 largely through holding a high proportion of 'top-slice' leaseholds and development sites whose values fell by a higher proportion than freehold interests in standing property. Other companies were caught with excessive foreign borrowings when sterling fell, and the worldwide problems of the property industry hit companies such as MEPC, who had large development commitments in Australia, Europe and North America.

Just as the problems of the secondary banks were partly responsible for the problems of the property market, the problems of the property market now rebounded on the banks. The inability of property companies to liquidate assets prevented payment of interest as well as repayment of debt, and the falling value of property uncovered bank loans, sometimes as high as 100% of (often overoptimistic) valuations. So banks which had originally appeared merely to be suffering from a liquidity problem fell into bankruptcy. Banks were 'locked into' property, partly by being unable to insist on loan repayment without forcing a company into liquidation, and partly because of commitments previously entered into to provide finance for continuing development projects.

The fall in values continued throughout 1974 under the influence of the huge supply of investments overhanging the market and the rising yields required by the institutions as the main purchasers. The high yields reflected the rent freeze, the fear of further property taxation, rising yields on long-dated gilts, high short-term interest rates, the expectation of falling rental values as the country headed for a recession, and the general lack of appeal of long-term investments in the context of falling markets and increasing economic uncertainty.

Recovery 1975–7

Following industrial unrest which resulted in a three-day working week for industry and culminated in a coalminers' strike, a general election was called in February 1974 which brought the Labour Party back into power. The Labour administration tightened controls on prices and profit margins, and although serious industrial disputes virtually ceased, this was at the cost of huge public-sector wage increases, frequently in the range 20–30% per annum, causing the inflation rate to accelerate to a peak of over 26% in mid-1975.

The problems of industry in 1974 were critical. It was faced on the one hand with massively rising labour, fuel, raw material and finance costs, as well as an increased tax liability, and on the other hand by strict price controls and a declining demand, together with the prospect of a long and severe international recession. The decline in share prices accelerated so that early in January 1975 the *Financial Times* index fell to 146.0, a 73% decline since the high point of May 1972.

The stock-market recovery in January 1975 (said to have been set off by the concerted buying activity of a small group of financial institutions) was probably due more to a feeling that share prices discounted virtually all possible disasters than to any short-term improvement in economic prospects. However, the stock-market revival proved to be soundly based as the trade figures moved into an improving trend, sterling strengthened and interest rates fell. A further boost to investment confidence was provided by a deflationary budget and the introduction of a strict wages policy, causing the inflation rate to fall steeply over the next 12 months.

Signs of recovery appeared in the property investment market at the end of 1974 in response to the assurance that the rent freeze would be phased out from February 1975, coupled with a statement from the Secretary of State for the Environment, who spoke of 'the need to maintain a healthy market in commercial property in the interests of the country and the economy as a whole'. This appeared to mark a turning point in the government's attitude, and with no further property taxation measures proposed after the introduction of DLT and the Community Land Act, it was appreciated that, by tending to restrict future development, the net effect of the government's measures would be to enhance the future growth and security of an investment in commercial property.

The market was also revived by property purchases by Arab interests, but of dominant importance were the actions of the British financial institutions. Property companies in 1975 desperately needed to reduce their gearing, and huge sales were required to enable the market to regain stability. Fortunately, the insurance companies and pension funds, encouraged by the abolition of the rent freeze and flush with liquid cash, took the opportunity of the low prices to build up the property element in their portfolios. Over the period 1974–7, the market was dominated by property purchases by the institutions from degearing property companies. Even companies which had been prudently managed and were in no risk of bankruptcy, such as Land Securities, felt a need to make substantial sales.

The recovery was interrupted in October 1976 by another sterling crisis, which caused a sharp rise in interest rates and a temporary fall in property values. However, the decline in inflation resumed in 1977 and interest rates fell sharply. With the balance of trade on a healthier trend and North Sea oil about to flow, the UK economy seemed set for a more stable period when interest rates would not have to be used to protect sterling, and the independence provided by oil would enable the government to turn its attention to the problem of unemployment and the 'real' economy.

From the point of view of institutional investors, the fall in interest rates provided an incentive to run down liquidity, and increase their property acquisitions. With rental growth in a recovering economy almost guaranteed by the virtual absence of new development, the case for substantial property acquisition seemed watertight. From the point of view of most property companies, the year provided the opportunity to complete their degearing operations, but with interest rates falling, the pressure to degear subsided. With rising investment demand from the institutions and reduced sales, property values in 1977 generally regained (or even surpassed) the levels of 1973.

The 1970s crash proved advantageous to the life assurance and pension funds in the sense that they were able to acquire large amounts of property very cheaply. The institutions emerged from the crisis as the dominant operators in the property market, and property emerged as one of their three principal long-term investments, alongside gilts and equity shares.

27   The Thatcher Cycle

Thatcher and Thatcherism

Just as the 1970s boom and bust was a product of economic mismanagement by the government of Edward Heath, the latest boom/bust cycle has been a consequence of the economic excesses of Margaret Thatcher's premiership. The roots of both property cycles were intimately interwoven with the economic and political trends of their periods. In order to understand the causes of the 1980s boom, it is important to understand the philosophy and aims of the Thatcher government.

First and foremost Thatcherism stood for a reliance upon free and deregulated markets, a reduction in state subsidies and government intervention in the economy, and an end to monopoly power, particularly that of the trade unions. At a personal level, Thatcherism implied individual responsibility, personal choice, self-improvement and patriotism. It was a creed for the hard working, fit and successful, for these owning their own homes, with jobs and marketable skills, not for the weak, poor or unemployed. It looked forward to universal home ownership and widespread ownership of shares; a society in which the working man or woman shared in the nation's prosperity through his or her abilities and effort.

Thatcher espoused the political philosophy and economic liberalism of the 'New Right' as championed by von Hayek and Milton Friedman. Particularly in its early years, the Thatcher government adopted Friedman's 'monetarist' philosophy for macroeconomic management which viewed inflation as essentially the product of excess money supply. Rather than attempting to generate prosperity by the discredited Keynesian demand-management policies of the 1960s and 1970s, the government saw its essential macroeconomic function as being to create stable inflation-free conditions in which people and firms could create wealth. Thus in the early 1980s, monetary policy consisted primarily of attempts to squeeze inflation by phased reductions in the growth of the money supply, while fiscal policy concentrated on the reduction of public expenditure with a view to reducing the PSBR and taxation, the latter as a supply-side incentive to promote economic activity and efficiency.

The recession of 1980–1

The Thatcher government came to power in May 1979 at a buoyant phase in the economic cycle, after growing trade-union militancy had culminated in a series of public-sector strikes in late 1978 and early 1979. By influencing public opinion against the labour movement and the Labour Party, this so-called 'Winter of Discontent' was partly responsible for the Conservative Party's victory in the 1979 general election.

The most urgent economic objective of the Thatcher government was to reduce inflation, so interest rates were raised to record levels to control money supply, major cuts in public expenditure were introduced, and the rate of VAT was doubled to 15%. These measures, together with a second dramatic surge in world oil prices, plunged the economy into a new recession which was to prove the deepest since the 1930s. The severity of the 1980–1 recession was exacerbated by a strong rise in the value of the pound sterling due to the combined effects of high interest rates, sterling's status as a petro-currency (due to North Sea oil development) and the 'Thatcher factor', i.e. international confidence in Thatcher's policies for the UK economy. The high level of sterling in the context of a world recession caused a sharp reduction in overseas demand for UK exports and simultaneously increased the exposure of UK industry to competition from imported goods. Taking account of the high cost of money, fuel and ever-rising wages, UK industry went through a torrid period. The impact was greatest in manufacturing and traditional industry and, consequently, it was the Midlands and North of Britain which suffered most. Many firms went into liquidation, others closed branches or reduced operations and unemployment rose to levels reminiscent of the 1930s.

The breakthrough came in 1982 with a steep fall in inflation to around 5%, down from its peak of 22% in 1980. This enabled a crucial reduction in banks' base rates which, together with a successful outcome to the Falklands War, created the conditions necessary for an economic upturn and the re-election of the Thatcher government in the following year.

The decline of institutional property investment

Despite the severity of the 1980–1 recession, rental values of good-quality property remained positive and, in contrast to previous recessions, yields kept low as institutions continued to build up the property content of their portfolios. In fact, property proved to be the outstanding investment sector during the recession, as gilts were affected by high interest rates and inflationary pressures and equities were subdued by the squeeze on corporate profits. The institutions were well rewarded for their huge property acquisitions of the mid-1970s.

However, 1982 proved to be a watershed in the long post-war rise of property investment. Property indices indicated declining rental growth and investors started to question whether the historically low level of yields could be justified. For the first time since 1976 prime yields rose and capital values fell.

In order to explain why 1982 marked the high point for property in the portfolios of the major financial institutions, we need to examine property's merits *relative* to the alternatives. The case for the institutions purchasing any investment is threefold:

(1) to increase returns;
(2) to reduce portfolio risk;
(3) to reduce functional risk (by matching liabilities).

On these grounds, property's performance throughout the post-war period had justified a substantial place in institutional portfolios. Conventional gilts and corporate bonds had proved a dismal failure in the context of high inflation and rising interest rates. Equity shares had failed to perform in the cost-push inflationary environment of the 1970s, and the value of liquid cash had been eroded by negative real interest rates.

However, 1982 introduced a turn of the economic tide. With the dramatic fall in inflation and disinflationary trends worldwide, the markets perceived a fundamental change in the economic scenario, namely from high inflation and negative real interest rates to low inflation and positive real interest rates. This change crucially boosted the investment prospects of gilts, equities and liquid cash. Just as rising inflation is disastrous for fixed-interest securities, the reverse is ideal. In 1982 conventional gilts provided returns to investors of around 50%. Equity shares were boosted by the decline in cost-push inflationary pressures and the prospects for corporate profits arising from the fall in interest rates and an upturn in demand. In fact, equity shares embarked upon a five-year period of spectacular growth ending in October 1987 with the stock-market crash. Even at lower interest rates, liquid cash offered positive real returns for the first time for many years.

On the other hand, the changed economic context crucially undermined the relative merits of property. Who needs a hedge against inflation if inflation is no longer a threat? The new economic trend was a reversal of that which had brought property to prominence in the 1960s and 1970s. However, there were other sound reasons for the institutions to turn away from the sector. The introduction of index-linked gilts in 1981 provided similar diversification and matching functions as property, at lower risk and without the disadvantages of high management costs, poor liquidity and indivisibility. The case for UK property was further undermined by the removal of exchange controls in 1979, which opened up a huge overseas market in equities and bonds and provided endless scope for portfolio diversification outside the UK economy. Overseas investments could provide the low correlation with UK gilts and equities which was one of the attractions of property, and the availability of limitless amounts of overseas property further reduced the attractions of UK property.

The decline in institutional demand for property also resulted from the achievement by certain institutional funds of their long term target for property investment. Several large pension funds had been frequently quoted as pursuing a strategy to raise the property content of their portfolios to some 30–35% of assets. But by 1982, seven out of the top ten UK pension funds had exceeded the 30% mark. Demand from pension funds in the 1980s must also have been affected by the declining membership and cash inflow of several of the largest funds due to privatisation or large-scale redundancies. The steel, electricity and coalmining industries are obvious examples.

The case for property in the early 1980s was also weakened by doubts about its true historic performance, and scepticism as to whether a competitive performance could be maintained in the future. The question of historic performance largely revolved around depreciation through obsolescence; whether it had been adequately allowed for in performance indices and whether it was adequately reflected in current values. The market's growing awareness of depreciation had arisen largely through the need to refurbish or completely redevelop offices less than thirty years old to make them fit for the age of the computer. There was a general view that depreciation was likely to impact on returns to a greater extent in the future.

Additionally, property's performance over the late 1970s had derived not just from rental growth but from falling yields. This fall in yields was due to high demand from the institutions meeting a limited stock of good quality investments. Up to a point, the excellent performance of property in the late 1970s had been a case of self-realising expectations, a situation which could not be sustained.

These are the principal reasons why the institutions' annual net investment in property started a *relative* decline in the early 1980s. Consequently property as a proportion of the institutions' portfolios also declined, exacerbated by property's poor performance relative to equity shares in the period up to the stock-market crash in 1987 (see Figures 21.2 and 21.3).

The economic background to the boom

Despite a downturn in the rate of economic growth in 1984, the five-year period from 1982 was generally a time of rising confidence, low inflation and steady growth for the UK economy. The recovery started in London and thereafter spread outwards and northwards like a ripple, only reaching northern regions and Scotland in the later years of the decade. Thus for much of this period there was a north/south divide in Britain, with buoyant conditions in the more service-orientated economies of southern England and sluggish conditions in the industrial and manufacturing based economies of the north.

The outlook in 1987 when Margaret Thatcher won her third general election was optimistic. After five years of growth and low inflation there seemed a real prospect of an economic miracle. The defeat of the coalminers in 1985 and successful legislation to limit the power of the trade unions had subdued wage-push inflation. The government's policy of privatising nationalised industries and utilities was proving a success and the country seemed to be imbued with a new spirit of enterprise. It seemed that the dream of long term non-inflationary growth was becoming a reality. But no; the seeds of excessive demand, renewed inflation and economic downturn had already been sown.

One of the early policy areas which had epitomised the creed of Thatcherism was financial deregulation. Apart from the abolition of exchange controls, a series of measures were taken to deregulate the financial markets, particularly banking. This resulted in the breakdown of the building societies' cartel, the involvement of banks in lending for house purchase and fierce competition among banks and building societies to lend to consumers.

These measures were to be the fundamental cause of the excessive expansion of consumer credit in the late 1980s. The abolition of exchange controls allowed the free flow of capital in and out of the UK and led to the abolition of all quantitative restrictions on bank lending. The government viewed such restrictions as impracticable, as any limits imposed on banks in Britain could be made up by lending 'offshore', i.e. by banks resident overseas and outside UK government control. The government therefore relied upon the manipulation of interest rates (the price of credit) and banking prudence to limit the expansion of lending; indeed the manipulation of interest rates became essentially the sole implement of macroeconomic management.

Of particular importance in the 1980s was the relationship of house prices to the national economy. Hitherto, cyclical fluctuations in house prices were largely a function of wage levels and the cost and availability of mortgage finance, together with confidence and 'bandwagon' factors which encourage people to buy houses in times of boom. Previously a rise in house prices would have been restrained by the effective rationing of mortgages by the building societies, but in the 1980s mortgages were freely available from competing banks and building societies. However, a novel feature of the 1980s was the extent to which rising house prices were a cause of the boom rather than merely an *effect*. Houses provided the collateral security for borrowing, not merely for house purchase or improvement, but for consumption. A rising house price made the owner feel wealthier and gave him the ability to raise debt on its inflated value, perhaps to spend on a new car or an overseas holiday.

Thus, through the medium of the house market as well as by the expansion of plastic credit, financial deregulation brought about a massive expansion in consumption. The latent inflationary impact was increased by reductions in the standard rate of income tax in the budgets of 1987 and 1988, by the depreciation of sterling after a collapse in world oil prices in 1986, and by the reduction of interest rates following the stock-market crash in October 1987. The fall in base rates was the Chancellor's reaction to the expected deflationary impact of the stock-market crash which, being redolent of the Wall Street crash of 1929, invoked fears of a repeat of the worldwide depression of the 1930s. Base rates were allowed to fall further in 1988 as part of the Chancellor's policy of keeping sterling in parity with the German Deutschmark.

After unsuccessful attempts to control money supply in the early years of the Thatcher government, Nigel Lawson effectively rejected strict monetary control, aiming to maintain price stability by 'shadowing' the Deutschmark. Money supply was allowed to expand much too fast (M3 doubled in the five years to October 1987) resulting in excessive demand and an overheated economy. Economic statistics failed to detect the extent of the overheating until the summer of 1988, when a dramatic deterioration in the balance of payments and an upturn in inflation forced a belated rise in interest rates.

The property boom

Rental trends

Rental growth tends to lag the economic cycle, and it was the latter half of 1983 before the rate of rental growth started to rise. With consumer expenditure leading the recovery, shops proved the best performing sector in the period up to 1987. In particular, central London shops outperformed other locations in the three years 1984–6, but subsequently were overtaken by suburban London shops and then by other South-East locations as the boom spread like a ripple outward from London.

The first experience of boom conditions in the office sector was felt in the City of London. City office rents had maintained positive growth rates throughout the recession, but with the prospect of Big Bang, growth moved

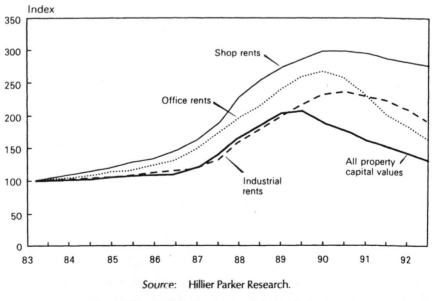

Source: Hillier Parker Research.

Figure 27.1   Trends in commercial property values

into double figures and then surged in 1986–7, reaching a peak of 45% in the core of the City before the impact of the stock-market crash subdued demand. Well before City rents peaked, the office boom had spread to the West End and other areas of central London. The Hillier Parker Rent Index indicated rental growth peaks of 68% p.a. in the West End and 87% p.a. in Holborn/Marylebone. With top rents approaching £70 per ft^2 at their height, Mayfair rents exceeded those in the best City locations, helped by more rigid planning restrictions, a more attractive environment and by the boom spreading from finance to other service activities.

The office-rental boom also spread like a ripple from central London. Whereas London outperformed in 1987, in 1988 it was overtaken by East Anglia, South West and South East England. In 1989 the highest rental growth (about 80% p.a.) was achieved in the Midlands, Wales, the North West and Yorkshire and Humberside, whereas in 1991 Scotland was the top-performing office location, providing rental growth of around 13% at a time when central London rents were falling by over 30%.

Typically, industrial property lagged the property cycle, it being 1987 before rental values really took off. Again, regional performance demonstrated a ripple effect, with London outperforming in 1986 followed by East Anglia, the South East, the South West and the Midlands. Northern England performed best in 1990 and Scotland in 1991. In fact at the trough of the recession in 1991, Scotland was the only region to show positive rental growth for all three property types.

Investment sector

As pointed out in Chapter 21, the declining net investment in property by the insurance companies and pension funds which continued until the stock-market crash of October 1987, hides a large increase in both acquisitions and sales. The institutions concentrated on restructuring their portfolios, weeding out or redeveloping obsolete offices (particularly in London) and building up their retail content.

The combined effect of rising investment in shares and their escalating value as the economy recovered meant that before the 1987 stock-market crash the institutions' portfolios were heavily weighted towards equities. Therefore the crash provided the institutions with a timely reminder of the risk of shares and the diversification merits of property. This, together with accelerating rental growth, was responsible for an upturn in the demand for property and a recovery in market sentiment in the wake of the stock-market crash.

These trends in property investment are reflected in yield movements (see Figure 12.3). In particular, office yields rose relentlessly over the 1982–7 period, then fell in the wake of the stock-market crash. To an extent, shop yields bucked the rising trend in the early and mid-1980s, as rental growth out-stripped the other types and institutional investment concentrated on the

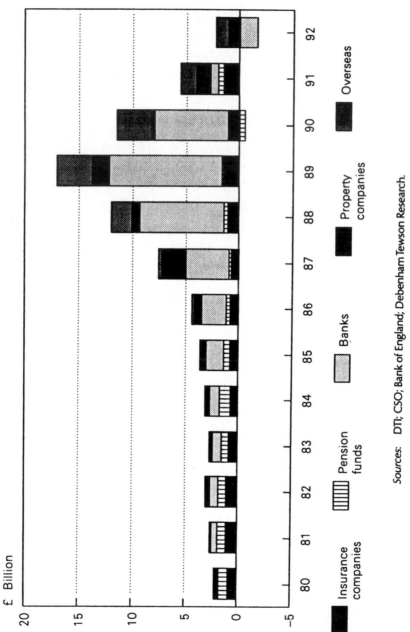

£ Billion

Sources: DTI; CSO; Bank of England; Debenham Tewson Research.

Figure 27.2   New money into commercial property

sector. Then, when office and industrial yields turned down in 1987, shop yields remained static until the 1988 hike in interest rates started to affect consumer spending. Due partly to this late rise in shop yields, the ICHP Average Yield (all property) fell by only 0.5% over the boom period, i.e. from 7.7% in May 1987 to 7.2% in November 1988. Clearly the principal source of property's capital growth over the boom period was tenant demand, not investment demand. The 1980s property boom was a boom in rental values and development activity, not in property investment.

Development sector

Understanding trends in property investment and development is largely a matter of understanding the involvement of the two groups, investing institutions and property companies. The involvement of financial institutions depends primarily upon the expected performance of property relative to gilts and equities, whereas the activity of property companies is largely dependent on market opportunities and the availability of capital, particularly bank finance.

The 1980s provided developers with an unusual variety of opportunities. In particular, the retailing revolution created the need for new shopping centres, superstores and retail warehouses, while expansion in air travel, car ownership, the motorway system and the microcomputer influenced business location and brought about opportunities for new industrial estates, business parks and mixed office and industrial developments. Of particular relevance to city-centre offices was the acceleration of obsolescence and disposals of obsolete property by the financial institutions. Accelerating obsolescence, represented by a widening gap between a property's value and that of its potential replacement, is analogous to increasing development viability, which was boosted in turn by the rise in property values relative to development costs. Thus, there was an abundance of development opportunities, helped by a general liberalisation of planning controls throughout the country.

One aspect of the institutions' declining interest in property in the 1980s was a drop in their provision of development finance, forcing property companies to rely heavily on bank finance. Also, it is interesting to note a correlation between the rise in property disposals by the financial institutions in 1981 and a rise in bank lending to property companies as the latter bought obsolete property from the institutions. In the five years 1982–6, bank lending to property companies grew at over 25% p.a., then accelerated in 1987 as the development boom gathered pace, despite a warning to the banks by the Governor of the Bank of England. Although the *rate* of growth of bank lending to property companies peaked in 1989, the total continued to rise to over £40 billion in 1991, in real terms a figure approaching two and a half times the peak of 1975.

The principal contributors to this enormous expansion of bank lending to property companies in the 1980s were the UK clearing banks and overseas

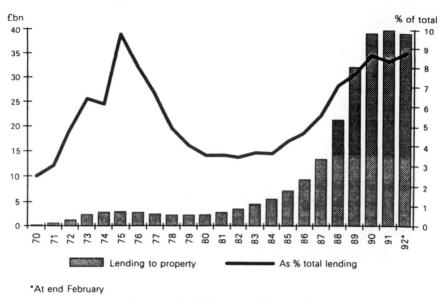

Source: Savills Commercial Research.

Figure 27.3   Bank advances to property companies

banks. In the first half of the decade clearing banks provided over half of new loans, but in the latter half their contribution was matched by loans from overseas banks, a particular feature being active lending by Japanese and European banks. At November 1991, overseas banks accounted for 40% of loans to property companies and UK clearing banks 46%. The remainder were provided by merchant banks and other British banks, two groups whose property lending declined relatively over the decade.

The expansion of lending by overseas banks, reflected:

(a)   the globalisation of the world's financial markets, arising partly from the removal of exchange controls and deregulation in the UK, Europe and elsewhere;

(b)   major overseas banks seeking to establish a diversified portfolio of loans worldwide, and European banks seeking to diversify within the EC;

(c)   the continued influx of foreign banks into London, reflecting its position in the world's financial markets;

(d)   the dramatic growth of Japanese banks, based on the success of the Japanese economy.

Banks were attracted to property lending in the 1980s due partly to its relative profitability and apparent security, but also as a result of the decline of alternative lending outlets. In particular, lending to developing countries which had formed a substantial part of their business in the 1970s was dramatically reduced following the eruption of the third-world debt crisis in 1982.

The attractions of property lending drew many banks into this area for the first time, the competition leading to falling profit margins (particularly for central London projects), forcing banks to lend a higher proportion of the collateral and to concede attractive terms to the borrowers (e.g., limited recourse). Inexperience of property lending led some banks to make mistakes, and anecdotes redolent of the early 1970s abounded concerning the unreliability of valuations. Too often, developers were able to dictate the valuation of properties offered as security for a loan. A valuer who was not prepared to value at the required figure would lose the commission and another found who would be less scrupulous. The lack of in-house property expertise meant that many banks failed to identify the risk of projects being financed and little attempt was made to analyse the market.

Concern about the growth of bank debt was voiced as early as 1987. Comparisons were made with the early 1970s and commentators frequently predicted a collapse similar to that of 1974. However, the market was reassured in the knowledge that this time the lenders were predominantly large and well-capitalised banks whose property loans as a percentage of total loans were generally below the levels of the 1970s boom. Property company gearing also appeared to be lower than in the 1970s.

One particular concern revolved around the ability of property companies to repay debt, given the lack of 'end-buyers' since the decline in institutional investment demand. However, debt was frequently on a 5–7-year term, i.e. not repayable at project completion but at a subsequent date. This seemed to provide a reasonable timescale to find buyers, specially after the revival of institutional demand late in 1987, and in view of the demand expected from the proposed unitisation of property.

In the early years of the boom most banks preferred to lend on City office developments, which therefore offered the best terms for borrowers. But the stock-market crash in 1987 alerted banks to the risk of City offices and encouraged them to lend on provincial property, including major new retail developments as well as offices. With the economic recovery and surge of rental growth moving north, bank finance and development activity followed. It is not possible to identify the proportion of bank lending which was devoted to development as distinct from investment in existing property, but indications suggest that the large majority was for development projects or to buy sites for future development.

The property-market slump

Stock markets have an uncanny instinct for sensing economic turning points although they are not always reliable, hence the quip, 'Wall Street has predicted five out of the last three recessions'. Certainly the stock-market crash of October 1987 was well ahead of events, but it represented a belief that there were fundamental problems in the national and international economies and that share prices were much too high.

The end of the 1980s property boom began where it had started, in the City of London, and the 1987 stock-market crash was an important contributory factor. The buoyancy of the stock market and the volume of transactions in the year after Big Bang had resulted in the establishment of far more dealerships than the market could sustain when activity slumped in the wake of the crash. Many market operators and 'back-room' staff were made redundant and estimated floorspace needs were substantially reduced. Nonetheless, frustrated demand meant that City rents continued to grow (but at a slower rate) for another couple of years until supply caught up with demand and rents began to fall.

Outside of the City the UK economy continued to boom, until the sharp deterioration in inflation and the balance of payments in the summer of 1988 forced a doubling of the banks' base rate to 13%, followed by a further increase to 15% in 1989. With mortgage interest rates rising in parallel, these measures signalled an end to both the housing and consumer booms, and thus, to the forces which had fuelled rental growth and the property boom.

The manipulation of interest rates as a tool of macroeconomic management is a blunt instrument and is slow to affect demand, particularly if asset values continue to rise. Having had its crash the year before, the stock market reacted calmly to the hike in interest rates. The economy remained buoyant and the consensus view was that there would be a 'soft landing' rather that a recession. The deflationary effect was greatest in London and South East England where the high level of house prices and high mortgage debt meant that the average family's spending was affected to a greater extent than in northern regions.

The first shock for the property market was the bankruptcy in August 1989 of Kentish Properties, a house builder active in London's docklands. Kentish was forced into liquidation by its inability to sell completed houses in view of high mortgage rates and the market downturn. Kentish's demise had little significance for the commercial property market, but the rise in interest rates was now perceived as affecting shop rental growth throughout the country as well as offices and industrial property in London and the South East. In response to declining rental growth, office yields rose to follow the lead of shop yields, although a more substantial rise may have been prevented by the surge in overseas investment (see Chapter 22) into prime London offices.

The hope that the UK economy might escape recession was finally dispelled by Iraq's invasion of Kuwait in July 1990. The threat of war caused a sharp rise in oil prices and loss of business confidence for which the brevity of the subsequent conflict and its successful outcome failed to compensate. A number of prominent deals in the property market, including a takeover of Speyhawk by a Swedish group, were abandoned as a result of this crisis, and the slump in property values accelerated. Yields rose sharply in 1990 and, for the first time since its origin in 1965, the Hillier Parker Rent Index (all property) registered a fall. Despite relatively buoyant conditions in the north and Scotland, national rent indices were falling for all three sectors by the end of the year, with particularly dramatic falls for central London offices.

Property companies

The first real indication of problems in the corporate sector of the commercial property market came in February 1990 with the announcement of a major rights issue by Rosehaugh to raise £125 million. As a developer/trader of only ten years standing, Rosehaugh had hoped to build up a substantial portfolio by retaining many of its own developments, but the need for capital to finance its large development programme had resulted in enormous bank debt, mainly off-balance sheet. Apart from Broadgate in the City, the company was involved in over fifty other projects throughout the country including retail, industrial, housing and leisure property. With rental income a small fraction of interest payments, Rosehaugh was badly overgeared and needed to raise equity capital to avoid forced sales of completed developments on to the falling market.

As property values started to slide, the highly volatile nature of development profit and site values had a particularly savage effect on the net asset value of developer/traders. Over the two years to June 1991, Rosehaugh reported losses close to £400 million, mainly due to the falling value of sites and developments. With these properties pledged as security for bank loans, the company breached covenants made to its banks and was required to negotiate and reschedule its loans. In early 1992 Rosehaugh's share price fell to 4p, and by the end of the year the company was in receivership, its market value having declined to nothing from a peak of £746 million in the heady days of 1987.

Initially it was assumed that Rosehaugh's problems were unique due to the cash demands of its large development programme, but subsequently it emerged that its circumstances were quite typical of developer/traders. In contrast to investor/developers, the essential problem of these companies was that they lacked a substantial portfolio of property investments providing a stable net asset value and generating rental income with which to pay interest on debt. Instead, they relied upon selling completed developments to create liquid capital. However, with the decline of institutional investment, there were few buyers. Additionally, the increasing glut of office property made lettings difficult, and if a property was unlet there was no prospect of a successful sale.

A further inherent problem of developer/traders is that their assets primarily comprise developments in progress and sites held for future development. Site values and development profit are geared residuals and highly vulnerable to a decline in the market. In the context of 1990–2, developers were frequently having to write down the value of sites by as much as 80% of their purchase price.

These problems were typified by the experience of Speyhawk, another 1980s developer/trader. This company was particularly exposed to the City office market with a large number of developments under construction and half of its portfolio unlet. Of pre-tax losses of £217 million in the year to September 1991, almost £205 million arose from provisions against losses on developments and site values. Speyhawk was reported as being technically insolvent with liabilities exceeding assets by some £70 million, but the company's bankers initially agreed to keep the company afloat by rescheduling £300 million of debt. The chairman's warning that shareholders 'should not expect a dividend for some time' was described by the *Financial Times* as an understatement comparable to that of Captain Oates before he strode to his death in an Antarctic blizzard in 1912.

The acid test of a property company's survival in 1991–2 was whether it was generating enough rental income to pay interest on debt. Even in the case of investor/developers, share prices and financial analysis focused on cash flow rather than net asset value. After the rise of property yields in 1990–1, asset sales frequently did little to improve cash flow. Indeed, in the context of plummeting rental values, in which rental income often exceeded rental value, a property's current yield could exceed interest on debt, and its sale could exacerbate a cash-flow problem rather than relieve it. So property companies concentrated on cutting costs and cutting dividends to shareholders.

Many companies went into liquidation, apart from Rosehaugh the best known listed companies being Sheraton Securities, Mountleigh and Speyhawk. Others might have been forced into liquidation but were kept afloat by their banks, on the basis that 'if you owe the bank £100 that is your problem, but if you owe the bank £100 million, the problem is the bank's'. It is frequently in a bank's best interest not to force a company into liquidation, partly because of the costs entailed through professional fees and claims for damages from building contractors or joint-venture partners in development projects, and partly because the forced sale of properties exacerbates the decline in values. In many cases banks felt that they would recover more of their loans by supporting the companies until a market recovery allowed an orderly sale of property assets. On the other hand, in cases which might involve 'throwing good money after bad', or where company directors refused to follow a strategy favoured by the banks, then the banks would tend to 'pull the plug'.

One feature of property companies in trouble has been the large number of banks involved in each case, thereby complicating the negotiations. Speyhawk was reported as having 46 banks, Sheraton Securities 33, and over 50 banks are understood to have taken part in the financing of Broadgate.

The most dramatic corporate collapse of the 1990s property slump must be that of Olympia and York, together with its development at Canary Wharf in London's docklands. Here it is difficult to avoid superlatives. A Canadian private company, Olympia and York was owned by the three Reichmann brothers, reputed to be the world's seventh richest family. It was the largest property company in the world and its project at Canary Wharf was the largest property development in Europe. The company owned some 50 million ft² of property, principally in Canada and the USA, including the World Financial Centre in New York and, with loans of $12 billion (£6.7 billion) raised from about 100 banks, its debt was equivalent to that of many small countries.

In March 1992, Olympia and York announced that it was experiencing a liquidity crisis arising principally from difficulties in raising enough debt to complete the first phase of Canary Wharf. The problem had arisen largely as a result of fears about the company's solvency due to dramatic falls in the value of its North American property where a property slump had left values about 40% below their 1987 peak.

Apart from its completion (first phase) coinciding with the oversupply of office space in the City of London, the essential problem of Canary Wharf was its peripheral location and inadequate transport communications with central London. This meant that over 40% of floorspace was unlet at completion despite generous incentives being offered to tenants. Canary Wharf had been initiated in 1987 without prearranged finance, venture partners or prelets. Effectively it was financed by mortgaging the company's American property. Its cost was estimated by the administrators at £1.5 billion, but in June 1992 its value seemed unlikely to exceed £500 million.

A tale of two cycles

We will conclude our investigation of the 1970s and Thatcher cycles by a brief comparative analysis. The two cycles featured some uncanny similarities but in other respects were radically different. We will identify both of these and then highlight a few lessons to be learnt.

The similarities

(1) The two booms were created under Conservative Party administrations espousing policies of market deregulation.

(2) Both cycles were concentrated on commercial property in London and South East England, but particularly focused on central London offices.

(3) In each case a surge in office redevelopment resulted from a strong rise in values and a relaxation of development controls. The peak of completions coincided with a downturn in tenant demand as the economy moved into recession, causing a substantial fall in values, exacerbated

by a trend towards tenant decentralisation due to the growth of rents in the previous boom.

(4)   Both booms were fed by enormous increases in bank lending to property companies in the wake of financial deregulation which had the effect of increasing competition between banks, resulting in excessive and reckless lending, sometimes without adequate project analysis or on inflated valuations of the property provided as collateral security.

(5)   The property cycles were led by national economic cycles featuring excessive monetary expansion and consumer expenditure followed by high interest rates, a Middle-East war, rising oil prices (relatively brief in 1990–1), a deep recession and the downfall of both prime ministers responsible.

(6)   Both market slumps featured many property company failures due partly to imprudent corporate financing but also to huge development losses and the inability to let or sell completed projects after the market collapse had begun.

The differences

(7)   The 1970s boom and bust was relatively brief and dramatic with greater changes in value over shorter periods than in the recent cycle. It had clear turning points in December 1973 and December 1974 'triggered' by events, whereas the recent cycle 'evolved' with different property types in different locations sometimes following different trends.

(8)   In the recent cycle changing values resulted primarily from changing *rents* responding to the growth in *tenant demand* during the boom years and the rise in *development supply* in the slump. To a much greater extent, the 1970s boom/bust reflected changes in *yields* resulting from dramatic changes in speculative demand for (and supply of) property *investments*.

(9)   In the 1980s boom the bulk of bank lending financed property development, whereas in the 1970s it was principally used for speculative investment.

(10)   Bank lending to property in the 1970s featured many speculative 'secondary' banks, inadequately capitalised and imprudently run. Their own collapse was both a cause and an effect of the property collapse and rendered them incapable of supporting property companies. In the latest cycle, the banks involved were mostly large and well capitalised international banks. Their property lending was a reasonable proportion of their total lending and, although suffering major losses, their financial strength has enabled them to maintain support to property companies.

(11)   The 1990s context has been more favourable to property companies than after the 1970s collapse in respect to the political climate and the lack of a rent freeze or threat of new property taxation. However,

in many ways the economic climate in the 1990s is more difficult and the recovery will be more long drawn out.

(12)   The very high inflation rates of the mid-1970s were largely responsible for the speed of the recovery. Real interest rates were emphatically negative and the real value of debt was speedily eroded. As property is an inflation hedge inflation supports property values, but more specifically, in the 1970s the high levels of inflation made property an attractive investment for the financial institutions who were primarily responsible for unwinding the crisis. The low level of inflation and high real interest rates of the 1990s make recovery more difficult.

(13)   Compared with the 1970s the financial institutions played a minor role in the recent cycle, and their reluctance to invest heavily in property is one reason why the 1990s recovery may be long drawn out. To some extent their 1970s role of buying property after the collapse has been taken by overseas investors, and those two groups seem the most likely source of property investment in the 1990s.

Lessons to be learnt

The two boom/bust cycles provide many lessons about the management of the economy and the banking system, in particular about the dangers and unforeseeable consequences of financial regulation and deregulation. However, the experience of both cycles also provides lessons specific to the property market, a few of which are worth emphasising here.

● The property market is inherently cyclical.
    This arises from the cyclical nature of both tenant demand and development activity (due to differential movement in property values and development cost), property's short-run supply inelasticity and the time lags involved in property development. The central London office market is particularly prone to cycles due to the large size and duration of development projects; a surge in development activity induced by an upturn in demand has resulted in a glut of completions coinciding with a downturn in demand a few years later. The stability of London offices in the 1980–1 recession illustrated that a property collapse need not follow a boom, but in both the 1970s and the recent cycle, market instability was exacerbated by the relaxation of development control and the trend towards decentralisation due to the high level of rents in central London.
● Relaxation of planning controls in the context of rising demand is inherently destabilising.
    Given the relatively strict planning controls in the UK, any significant relaxation releases pent-up pressure to develop. Market prices are based on previous supply constraints and give a false indication of future values and development profitability in the context of decontrol.

- Property developer/trading companies are uniquely vulnerable to market slump.

  Despite the need for large amounts of capital, this is not a major barrier to entry into the business of property development because property is ideal collateral security for borrowing, enabling the developer to become highly geared. High gearing is one aspect of the instability of developer/traders, another is their reliance upon selling projects on completion, because property development does not generate a regular cash flow with which to pay interest on debt. Thus the lack of property's marketability (combined with its illiquidity) in the slumps of the 1970s and 1990s prevented companies from liquidating assets to repay debt. Another aspect of the innate risk of developer/traders is the volatility of development profit and site values in times of changing property values. Even relatively small changes in values and development costs can wipe out profit and decimate site values. Developer/traders need to be conservatively financed and prudently run.

- Aspects of the cycles illustrate the globalisation of finance and property.

  The active part played by overseas banks in both cycles is a function of Britain's open financial system and London's position as the financial capital of Europe. Not only does this attract overseas banks to Britain, providing a base for lending, but it also caused property investors from the same countries to follow in 1988–91.

  Another aspect of the globalisation of the British property market was the demise of Olympia and York. It is debateable how far the failure of Canary Wharf was an *effect* of the property slump in North America (where falling values precluded the raising of sufficient capital to fund Canary Wharf) or how far Canary Wharf *caused* the company's collapse (through its need for cash and huge loss). However the example illustrates the interdependence of property markets in different countries.

  It is interesting and hardly a coincidence that the three main financial centres of the world, New York, Tokyo and London suffered simultaneous property slumps in the early 1990s.

- Regional diversification of property investment within the UK reduces portfolio risk.

  The concentration of both boom/bust cycles on London and South East England, and the divergence of value trends with Scotland and the North of England illustrates a low correlation of returns as between the north and south.

- The national economy and the banking system is dependent on a healthy and stable property market.

  Wealth is created by the ability to borrow, and much of the nation's corporate debt is secured on property. Additionally, property is a medium for holding the wealth of all sections of the community through insurance and pension funds. Sharp fluctuations in the value of property are destabilising for the national economy.

Prospects for recovery

The stabilisation of property yields in 1991–2 brought some hope that the worst was over and that the demise of Olympia and York might mark the trough of the property slump. However, the continuing decline of office rents and the failure of the UK economy to recover after the Conservative election victory indicated that the property recovery will be long and slow.

The two main imponderables are:

(a) How long will it be before the oversupply of office space in central London is taken up?
(b) How long will it take for property companies to repay their excessive debt and reduce their gearing to a sustainable level?

In each case it is likely to take longer than in the 1970s. The appetite of institutions for property is much less and the oversupply of office space in London is much greater. At its peak in 1991, the supply of office floorspace to let in the City was almost three times its peak in 1976, and some observers suggest that surplus space in peripheral locations in and around London will not be occupied until the end of the century. The questions above are interrelated, the institutions are unlikely to become avid investors until there is a prospect of rental growth, but office rental growth in central London seems unlikely to resume until the mid-1990s.

One of the problems in the wake of the 1990s collapse is 'over-renting', i.e. tenants paying rents above rental value, due to the infrequency of rent reviews, the standard 'upward only' review clause and the length of the standard lease in the UK. By preventing tenants from moving to modern cheaper accommodation, the inflexible conditions of existing leases are an obstacle to the letting of completed developments and, to some extent, to a market recovery. IPD estimated in May 1992 that over 70% of central London offices were over-rented by an average of 35%. One effect of the 1990s slump is increased bargaining power for the tenant and a move to more flexible leases.

The period 1981–92 saw property fall from an all-time high rating relative to gilts and equities to an all-time low. Property's yield has risen from below that of equity shares to exceed that of long dated gilts.[1] Yet despite this extra-ordinary downrating, property still outperformed inflation. According to IPD,[2] property provided a real return of 3.2% p.a. over the eleven-year period 1981–91. Rental growth averaged 7.5% p.a., 1.2% p.a. above the rate of inflation.

Thus, arguably, property emerges from the turmoil of the recent cycle with its long term performance record intact, and historically high yields make it attractive to institutions and overseas investors. The market's recovery could be faster than expected, as the sterling devaluation and fall in interest rates in the autumn of 1992 lead to an economic upturn in 1993. The supply of City offices started to decline in 1992 and revived confidence in the financial markets could lead to a sharp increase in take-up. Even at a vacancy rate of 18%, prime City rents are likely to stabilise at their 1985 levels of over £30/ft². A major benefit of the recent cycle is that City offices are now cheaper, more plentiful and of better quality than before, thereby enhancing the attraction of London as a world financial centre. Indeed, property investments have never been cheaper in modern times and, despite the lack of short term growth, seem likely to provide the investor with excellent long term returns.

Questions for Discussion

Part I

1. Explain the significance for the housing market of a change from negative to positive real interest rates.

2. Explain:

   (a) the functions of the stock market;
   (b) how the system for settling transactions in the London Stock Exchange enables purely speculative transactions to take place.

3. Suggest reasons for the different price/earnings ratios and dividend yields shown by shares in the following sectors (*Financial Times*, 5 December 1992):

	P/E ratio	Dividend yield
Engineering – Aerospace	9.6	8.8%
Food Retailing	16.0	3.0%.

4. Argue the relative merits of conventional and index-linked gilts in the current economic circumstances from the point of view of both:

   (a) a pension fund seeking a long-term investment;
   (b) the government seeking to finance its budget deficit.

5. The value of an investment can be considered as the present value of expected future income flows. Use this principle to explain:

   (a) the pull to redemption;
   (b) the conventional term structure of gilt yields;
   (c) the inverted term yield structure in the recessions of 1980–1 and 1990–1.

6. Explain why the price of most stock-market securities tends to be more volatile than their interest or dividend payments.

7. Explain the 'reverse yield gap' and the reasons for its emergence in 1959. Discuss the conditions which could lead to a reappearance of the 'yield gap'.

8. Identify the current 'reverse yield gap', explain it by reference to economic and market conditions and predict whether the gap will widen or narrow over the next twelve months.

9. The value of an investment can be considered as the present value of expected future income flows. Use this principle to explain:

   (a) how the yield on convertible debentures would tend to move as the date for conversion draws near;
   (b) why the dividend yield of shares in highly geared (but reasonably secure) companies tends to be relatively low (compared with shares of comparable low-geared companies) in times when rising profits are confidently expected.

377

10. The conversion rights of the 10% convertible debentures in Urban Promotions PLC lapse in six months' time, after which the stock is irredeemable. Briefly explain the circumstances which could be responsible for the interest yield now being:

    (a) 5%
    (b) 10%
    (c) 20%.

11. Explain or suggest the principal reasons for the differences in the redemption yields provided by the following stocks (as at December 1992):

Treasury 2% (index-linked) 2006	3.6%
Exchequer 12% 2013–17	9.1%
Exchequer 3% 1990–5	5.5%

12. 'The reverse yield gap varies only in accordance with changes in investors' inflationary expectations.' Discuss.

13. Explain recent share-price trends by reference to national and international economic events.

14. Identify and explain which macroeconomic variables are particularly important to the profitability of investing in (a) gilts, and (b) equities.

15. 'Investment prices are a function of time, investors' income expectations and their target returns.'
    'Investment prices are fixed by the flows of demand and supply.'
    Explain the link between these two statements and illustrate it by explaining the probable reaction of share prices to a substantial fall in the level of interest rates.

Part II

16. Explain the characteristics of property which justify its inclusion as a substantial part of the portfolios of major institutional investors.

17. Yields on investment property failed to rise on the advent of the recession in 1980–1, yet rose substantially over the 1982–7 period of economic recovery. Reconcile these trends with yield trends in the 1970s.

18. Contrast the relative 'perfection' of the stock market in comparison with the property market.

19. Discuss fully the relative risks involved in investing in conventional gilts and property. Is it possible that property is the more secure of the two?

20. Consider the following investments and estimate:

    (a) the current income yield;
    (b) (where appropriate) the equivalent yield;
    (c) investors' target IRR

    which would be appropriate in current market conditions. Make and state any necessary assumptions and briefly justify your estimated yields.

(1) A freehold interest in a prime city centre shop recently let for 25 years on a five-year review basis to a well-known multiple trader.

(2) A freehold interest in a prime city centre site let for 999 years in 1950 at a fixed rent of £10 000 per annum.

(3) A freehold interest in a city centre office property let 40 years ago on a 42-year lease at a fixed rent; the current rent is £2000 per annum and the rental value is £50 000 per annum.

(4) A freehold interest in a prime 200 hectare arable farm let for five years in 1960; the rent has recently been reviewed.

(5) A leasehold interest with eight years to run in a shop in a secondary location, sub-let to an independent local trader for the remainder of the head lease; a rent review is due in three years.

21. Estimate and explain what you believe may currently be the market's target return on good quality office investments in (a) central London, and (b) in your home town.

22. Explain the existence of the 'in-hand' premium on the value of agricultural land.

23. Explain the differences in the income yields provided by the following invest-ments (as at summer 1992):

	(%)
Prime shops	5.0
Average shops	7.4
Average offices	9.3
Average industrials	10.4
FT-A All Share Index	4.6
Long dated gilts	9.2

Sources: Healey & Baker; Hillier Parker.

24. If offices (let on five-year rent reviews) yielded 7% when the yield on long-dated gilts was stable at 10%, discuss what change in office yield you might expect if the gilt yield rose to 12% in each of the following circumstances:

(a) the rise in gilt yield resulted from a rise in interest rates imposed by the government to protect sterling, but was expected to be temporary;

(b) the rise in gilt yield resulted from investors' fears of accelerating inflation following large wage increases;

(c) the rise in gilt yield resulted from monetary measures to severely deflate the economy.

25. Can the stability of property values compared with share prices be explained by the innate characteristics of the two investments or by the nature of the markets in which they are traded?

26. In 1992, for the first time since the 1960s, yields on long dated gilts fell below yields on good-quality commercial property investments. Explain this by refer-ence to macro-economic conditions.

·Part III

27. Explain the tendency of shop rental growth to lead the property market cycle and industrial rental growth to lag.

28. Explain the growth in the value of arable farmland until the late 1970s and its decline in the 1980s.

29. Taking account of economic prospects and government policy, explain whether you expect the rental growth of prime retail (or office or industrial) property to rise or fall over the coming year.

30. Explain by reference to land rent theory why the rental value per hectare of a 200-hectare arable farm tends to be higher than the rent per hectare of an equivalent 100-hectare farm.

31. Have building costs any relevance to the rental value of offices in the City of London?

32. Explain the significance of a distinction between (a) farms and prime shops, and (b) offices and most industrial property, in predicting long-term investment returns.

33. Explain why the real rental growth of prime UK office property has tended to follow a cyclical trend.

34. Reconcile the following statements:
    'The value of property reflects the cost of its development';
    'The value of property reflects the profitability of using it'.

35. 'In 1991, over the UK as a whole, the rental value of prime offices exceeded the rental value of prime industrial property by a multiple of about three. Yet the rental value of some prime industrial property in West London matched the rent of prime offices in some locations in the Midlands of England.'
    Explain these rental value relationships, with particular reference to the concept of supply elasticity.

36. Examine the reasons why, for significant periods in the 1970s, 1980s and 1990s, the rental growth trend of prime offices in the City of London was moving in the opposite direction to that in Scottish cities.

37. Select a property type and location, and analyse the rental growth prospects for that sub-market over the next few years, contrasting its prospects with those of the UK property market as a whole.

Part IV

38. Explain the relationship between changing interest rates in the economy and changing values of sites ripe for commercial redevelopment.

39. 'High site values cannot be said to be caused by high building density, nor can high building density be said to be caused by high site values' (Newell, 1977). However, the two tend to be associated; discuss the causes of this relationship in the context of a city-centre commercial site.

40. Discuss the relative price volatility of:
    (a) a freehold interest in a prime office property
    (b) a head leasehold interest over a similar property
    (c) a freehold interest in a cleared development site suitable for office development and similarly located to (a) and (b).

41. 'Almost all the risk involved in development derives from fluctuations in the national and local economy.' Discuss.

42. Discuss the principles which should be applied in formulating an agreement between a developer and a financial institution to share the profits of a development project.

43. Explain the reasons for the growth of sale and leaseback transactions as a means of financing development projects in the 1960s and 1970s.

44. Discuss the various factors which a property developer should take into account in selecting a scheme for financing a major commercial development project, including factors relating to the developer's company, the project and the national economy.

45. From the point of view of both developer and financier, discuss the advantages and disadvantages of 'top/bottom' and 'side-by-side' equity sharing schemes as means of financing major development projects.

Part V

46. Explain why property companies are traditionally more highly geared than companies in most other sectors of industry and commerce. Do you believe that this high gearing is still justified?

47. Assume that you are the investment manager of a large pension fund. Taking into account the current economic situation and future prospects, discuss and explain what proportions of your net new annual investment you would allocate to property, gilts, equities and liquid assets.

48. Discuss the relative merits of APUTs and property shares as investments for the small saver.

49. Identify and explain the principal differences in the content of the investment portfolios of general insurance companies, life assurance companies, and large self administered pension funds.

50. Discuss the present case for property investment overseas by UK life and pension funds, and explain the problems and risks involved.

51. Do you consider that the property market is an 'efficient market'? Has Efficient Market Theory (EMT) any relevance to the pricing of property investments?

52. Discuss the extent to which the concepts of portfolio theory are relevant in explaining the pricing of property investments.

53. In the light of current market conditions and economic prospects, discuss the attractions of property for institutional investment vis-à-vis gilts, equities and liquid assets.

54. Explain whether you expect the number of sale and leaseback deals in prime retail property to increase or decline over the coming year.

55. 'Property investment values, rental values and site values are all residuals.' Discuss.

56. Predict the effect on commercial property values of this year's budget, taking account of:

    (a) any provisions specifically relevant to property and
    (b) the government's general economic policies.

57. Explain the increase in property transactions in the 1980s by major institutional investors, despite the fact that property investment by these groups was in a period of relative decline.

58. Over the three-year period 1990–2, the capital value of offices in Britain halved (ICHP) whereas the cost of building materials and labour continued to rise. Does that prove that there is no relationship between building costs and property values?

59. You have been retained by a major life assurance fund as property investment advisor. Taking account of market conditions and economic prospects, explain what types of property investments you would advise the fund to make over the coming year.

60. Discuss the relative attractions of equity shares and property as an inflation hedge.

61. By reference to (for example) the advent of the single European market and the trend towards globalisation of business and investment, forecast the future for international property investment.

Part VI

62. Explain how changes in business rates may affect the volume of development activity and the density to which sites are developed.

63. Assume that an immediate ban has just been imposed on the commencement of major office development projects in the central London area. Discuss the effect that this would tend to have on the rental and capital value of office property, both within and outside the restricted area, giving some indication of the timing of the changes.

64. Discuss the case for long-term rent controls as a means of protecting industry and commerce from some of the ravages of inflation.

65. 'Every change in business rates must have an equal and opposite effect on rental values.' Discuss.

66. Discuss the possible impact on property values (in terms of property type, location and time dimension) of the introduction of the Uniform Business Rate in England.

Part VII

67. Discuss the reasons for the office development boom in London between 1954 and 1964, explaining why the boom commenced and ended in these years.

68. Explain the reasons for the growth of quoted property companies in the early post-war period.

69. Explain why the main excesses of the commercial property 'boom/bust' cycles have primarily been located in London and South East England.

70. The commercial property 'boom/bust' cycles of the 1970s and 1980s/1990s were:

    (a) an inevitable consequence of the unbridled forces of capitalism, or
    (b) the inevitable result of excessive and inept interference in the price mechanism

    Argue the merits of these opposing viewpoints.

71. Explain how far the secondary banking crisis was the cause of the property-market collapse in 1974, and how far the effect.

72. The virtual collapse of the commercial property investment market in 1974 was fundamentally the fault of:

    Property companies
    Banks
    The Bank of England
    The Conservative government under Edward Heath
    The Labour government under Harold Wilson

    Select a scapegoat from this list, and by reference to the 'guilt' of the other parties, explain why it should bear the greatest blame.

73. In 1981, interest rates were much higher and the recession much deeper than in 1974 but no property collapse took place. Explain the relative strength of property values in the recession of 1981–2.

74. 'Property values ultimately depend on the state of the country's economy.' Discuss with reference to shop, office and industrial property.

75. Compare and contrast the principal features of the commercial property boom/bust of 1986–93 with that of 1971–5.

76. By reference to the attractions of stock-market securities, examine the current case for a substantial increase in property investment by UK financial institutions.

77. Explain the relative decline in property investment by institutional investors over the period 1982–92.

78. Why is it that developer/trading property companies are more vulnerable to a property-market slump than investor/developers?

79. Identify the various sources of the property market's propensity to lurch periodically into a 'boom/bust' cycle.

80.   The property market collapse of the early 1990s was fundamentally the fault of:

Property companies
Banks
The Bank of England
The Conservative government under Margaret Thatcher
The Conservative government under John Major
The planning authorities.

Select a scapegoat from this list and, by reference to the guilt of the other parties, explain why it should bear the greatest blame.

References

1 Introduction

1. Investment Property Databank (1991) *IPD Property Investors Digest* (April).

8 Modern Theories of Investment Pricing

1. London Business School (1992) *Risk Measurement Service* (April–June).

10 Property Investments and the Property Market

1. G. R. Brown (1991) *Property Investment and the Capital Markets* (E. & F. N. Spon).

11 Property's Yield and a Pricing Model

1. W. D. Fraser (1977) 'The Valuation and Analysis of Leasehold Investments in Times of Inflation', *Estates Gazette*, 15 October.

12 Property's Risk and the Level of Yields

1. W. D. Fraser (1985) 'The Risk of Property to the Institutional Investor', *Journal of Valuation*, vol. 4, no. 1.
2. Barclays de Zoete Wedd (1988) *BZW Equity – Gilt Study* (January).
3. Wilson (1980) *Report of the Committee to Review the Functioning of Financial Institutions*, Cmnd 7937 (London: HMSO).
4. J. J. Rose (1975) *Rose's Property Valuation Tables* (Freeland Press).
5. W. D. Fraser (1986) 'Property Yield Trends in a Fluctuating Economy', *Journal of Valuation*, vol. 4, no. 3.

13 The Spectrum of Property Yields

1. Savills-IPD (1991) *Agricultural Performance Analysis* (May).

15 Rental Value – a Demand and Supply Analysis

1. Healey & Baker Research (1989) *Food Stores*.
2. Hillier Parker Research, *Specialised Property*, nos 1, 2, 3 (February 1991; July 1991; January 1992).
3. Hillier Parker Research, *A Forecast of Industrial Rents*, nos 1, 2 (April 1982; April 1983).
4. Richard Ellis (1981) *City of London Office Accommodation Review* (January).

16 Rental Value and the Sub-Market

1. *Investors Chronicle* Hillier Parker (1979) *The Effect of Town Centre Size on Shop Rental Growth*, research report no. 3 (May).
2. Hillier Parker Research (1987) *A Forecast of Shop Rents No.10* (January).
3. Healey & Baker (1986) *Retail Property Spotlight No.1*.
4. *Investors Chronicle* Hillier Parker (1985) *The Effect of Tourism on Central London Shop Rents*, research report no. 8 (November).
5. Healey & Baker (1987) *Retail Property Spotlight No.4*.
6. *Investors Chronicle* Hillier Parker (1984) *Secondary Shop Rent Index*, research report no. 6 (August).
7. Richard Ellis (1980) *The Prime Office Market* (May).
8. Institute of British Geographers (1991) Annual Conference (January).

17 Site Values and Development Activity

1. Royal Institution of Chartered Surveyors, *Building Cost Information Service* (BCIS).

20 The Property Companies

1. O. Marriott (1962) *The Property Boom* (Hamish Hamilton).
2. Ibid.
3. Ibid.
4. UBS Phillips & Drew (1991) *UK Equities, Property Perspectives* (March).

22 International Property Investment

1. *Investors Chronicle*, 8 September 1978.
2. Debenham, Tewson & Chinnooks (1992) *Money into Property* (August).
3. Hillier Parker Research (1982) *City of London Office Map* (March).
4. A. Baum and A. Schofield (1991) *Property as a Global Asset*, University of Reading (March).

24 Aspects of Government Intervention in the Property Market

1. Richard Ellis (1980) *The Prime Office Market* (May).

25 The Early Post-War Boom and its Aftermath

1. Pilkington Research Unit, Liverpool University.
2. O. Marriott (1962) *The Property Boom* (Hamish Hamilton).

27 The Thatcher Cycle

1. Hillier Parker (1992) *Average Yields* (November).
2. Investment Property Databank (1992) *Property Investors Digest*.

Further Reading

The stock market and general investment

M. Brett (1991) *How to Read the Financial Pages* (Business Books Ltd).
B. Gray (1991) *Beginners' Guide to Investment* (Century Business).

Investment analysis and financial theory

T. E. Copeland and J. F. Weston (1983) *Financial Theory and Corporate Policy* (Addison Wesley).
R. Brealey and S. Myers (1992) *Principles of Corporate Finance* (McGraw-Hill).
London Business School, *Risk Measurement Service*, LBS Financial Services, quarterly.
S. Lumby (1991) *Investment Appraisal and Financing Decisions* (Chapman & Hall).
J. Rutterford (1983) *Introduction to Stock Exchange Investment* (Macmillan).

The economics of property

P. N. Balchin, J. L. Kieve and G. H. Bull (1988) *Urban Land Economics and Public Policy*, 4th edn (Macmillan).
R. Barlowe, *Land Resource Economics* (Prentice Hall).
J. Harvey (1992) *Urban Land Economics* (Macmillan).

Property investment and finance

A. Baum and A. Schofield (1991) *Property as a Global Asset* (University of Reading).
A. Baum and N. Crosby (1988) *Property Investment Appraisal* (Routledge).
M. Brett (1990) *Property and Money* (Estates Gazette).
G. R. Brown (1991) *Property Investment and the Capital Markets* (E. & F.N. Spon).
N. Dubben and S. Sayce (1992) *Property Portfolio Management* (Routledge).
S. E. Hargitay and S.-M. Yu (1993) *Property Investment Decisions* (E. & F.N. Spon).
A. R. MacLeary and N. Nanthakumaran (eds.) (1988) *Property Investment Theory* (E. & F.N. Spon).
A. McIntosh and S. Sykes (1985) *A Guide to Institutional Property Investment* (Macmillan).
J. Plender (1982) *That's the Way the Money Goes* (Andre Deutsch).
A. Ross Goobey (1992) *Bricks and Mortals* (Century Business).
P. Venmore-Rowland et al. (eds) (1991) *Investment, Procurement and Performance in Construction* (E. & F. N. Spon).

Property valuation

A. Baum and D. Mackmin (1989) *The Income Approach to Property Valuation* (Routledge).
D. Butler and D. Richmond (1990) *Advanced Valuation* (Macmillan).

N. Enever (1989) *The Valuation of Property Investments* (Estates Gazette).
D. Isaac and T. Steley (1991) *Property Valuation Techniques* (Macmillan).
A. F. Millington (1988) *An Introduction to Property Valuation* (Estates Gazette).
W. H. Rees (ed.) (1992) *Valuation: Principles into Practice* (Estates Gazette).
D. Richmond (1985) *Introduction to Valuation* (Macmillan).

Property development

D. Cadman and L. Austin-Crowe (1990) *Property Development* (E. & F.N. Spon).
C. Darlow (ed.) (1988) *Valuation and Development Appraisal* (Estates Gazette).
O. Marriott (1967) *The Property Boom* (Hamish Hamilton).
S. Morley *et al.* (1989) *Industrial and Business Space Developments* (E. & F.N. Spon).

Property indices

Investors Chronicle/Hillier Parker: *Property Market Values; Average Yields; Rent Index.*
Investment Property Databank: *IPD Monthly Index; IPD Quarterly Review; IPD Annual Review; IPD Property Investors Digest* (annually).
Jones Lang Wootton, *JLW Property Index.*
Richard Ellis *Monthly Index.*
Savills – IPD, *Agricultural Performance Analysis* (annually).

Periodicals

Chartered Surveyor Weekly.
Estates Gazette.
Estates Times.
The Farmland Market.
Financial Times.
Investors Chronicle.

Academic journals

Journal of Property Finance.
Journal of Property Research.
Journal of Valuation and Investment.

Index